500
NATIONS

ALVIN M. JOSEPHY, JR.

500 NATIONS

AN ILLUSTRATED HISTORY OF NORTH AMERICAN INDIANS

BASED ON A DOCUMENTARY FILMSCRIPT BY
JACK LEUSTIG, ROBERTA GROSSMAN, LEE MILLER, AND WILLIAM MORGAN
WITH CONTRIBUTIONS BY JOHN M. D. POHL

ALFRED A. KNOPF • NEW YORK • 1994

This Is a Borzoi Book
Published by Alfred A. Knopf, Inc.
Copyright © 1994 by Pathways Productions, Inc.

Library of Congress Cataloging-in-Publication Data

Josephy, Alvin M., [date]
   500 nations : an illustrated history of North American Indians /
by Alvin M. Josephy, Jr. — 1st ed.
     p.   cm.
   "Based on a documentary filmscript by Jack Leustig, Roberta
Grossman, Lee Miller, and William Morgan with contributions by
John M.D. Pohl."
   Includes bibliographical references.

ISBN 0-679-42930-1
ISBN 0-375-70320-9 (paperback)
   1. Indians of North America—History.   I. Title.   II. Title: Five
hundred nations.
E77.J787   1994
970.004'97—dc20   94-29695
                                                          CIP

Manufactured in the United States of America
Hardcover Edition Published October 20, 1994
First Paperback Edition

CONTENTS

500
NATIONS

CHAPTER 1

A CONTINENT

AWAKES

In this moving photograph by Father Don Doll, more than three hundred riders follow the trail of Big Foot and the Miniconjous through the Badlands to Wounded Knee Creek, a hundred years after the fateful events of December 1890. The fourteen-day ride was part of a ceremony of remembrance and healing attended by over a thousand people.

OVERLEAF: Indian Camp at Dawn, *by Jules Tavernier.*

To Chankpe Opi Wakpala

On an unusually mild December day in 1890, a small band of hungry, desperate Miniconjou Sioux—120 men and 230 women and children, led by their ailing chief, Big Foot—hurried across the hills of South Dakota's Pine Ridge Indian reservation. The Miniconjous, some on ponies, others in aged wagons or trudging beside their travois, were tired from their long flight.

Fear drove them on. American armies were searching for them, intent on arresting Indians who continued to practice the banned Ghost Dance religion, which the whites believed was whipping them up for war. Long since defeated militarily and penned on reservations, many of the demoralized and helpless Plains tribes had turned to this new religion, which had reached them from Wovoka, a Paiute Indian holy man in far-off Nevada. Wovoka's message was peaceful: with certain dances, songs, and prayers, the tribes could bring back their dead ancestors, the vanished hosts of buffalo, and the old ways of life that had existed before the coming of the white

man. To government agents and the army, the dancing Indians seemed, instead, to be preparing for an uprising. Two weeks before, Indian police, working for a fearful reservation agent, had murdered the great Hunkpapa Sioux chief Sitting Bull, whom the government regarded mistakenly as one of the leaders of the new religion. Then the army had sought to arrest Big Foot, whose Miniconjou band included many of the most devout Ghost Dancers.

In alarm, Big Foot and his people had abandoned their village on the Cheyenne River Sioux reservation and fled for 150 miles across the plains and the silent, wintry Badlands, through snow and icy windstorms. Evading pursuing armies, they hoped to find safety on the Pine Ridge reservation among Oglala Sioux followers of the aging chief Red Cloud, who had invited them to come. During the journey, Big Foot, whom the Sioux knew as a quiet, generous man of peace and wisdom, often called on to settle quarrels among the bands, was stricken with pneumonia. His people put him in one of the lurching horse-drawn wagons, wrapped like a mummy in an old overcoat, a scarf, and a blanket. Blood dripped from his nose and froze on the floor of the open wagon bed, and the fugitive Miniconjous knew he was dying in the cold.

Now, having reached Pine Ridge, they were close to where they expected to reach Red Cloud's Oglalas. On this day, December 28, fate ran against them. Early in the afternoon, they topped a ridge. Spread across the lower ground, barring their way about two miles distant, was a long skirmish line of dismounted cavalrymen of the late Lieutenant Colonel George Armstrong Custer's old regiment, the 7th U.S. Cavalry, reconstituted after its disastrous defeat by Northern Cheyennes and Sioux— including the Miniconjous—fourteen years earlier at the battle of the Little Bighorn. Army-employed Oglala scouts had given notice to the military of the arrival of Big Foot's band on the Pine Ridge reservation.

The Miniconjous debated what to do. They did not want to fight but decided

ALEX WHITE PLUME/LAKOTA
"So with the killing of our relatives in 1890 at Wounded Knee, here we are in 1993, 103 years after that happened. The U.S. 7th Cavalry today want to come down here and apologize for what they did. As Lakota people, we've only had contact with the white world for 163 years, that's all. And it takes centuries and centuries to develop forms of government, to develop a way to live. And we have not yet developed a ritual to forgive the white man for what he did. We have a ceremony to forgive enemy tribes, Tokaklah ceremony, but that was developed after millions of years of living here. But like I said 163 years is just a blink of the eye, it's just been a short time. And we have not yet adjusted to this way of life. And we have not yet come up with a ritual to forgive the white man for what he did. He can't just come out here and apologize. First he has to 'wipe the tears of our nation.'"

CELANE AND MARIE NOT HELP HIM/MINICONJOU

Marie: "And when Grandpa Beard used to tell it, he would say that the Wounded Knee Massacre was very, very tragic. And he would say, if only they had just killed us men and left the women and the children, he said it would be good. And as he would speak, he would call out the names of the men, the first six men that were killed. It was like a roll call. The first six men that were killed under the white flag of truce were Big Foot, Spotted Thunder, Horn Cloud, Ghost Horse, Iron Eyes, Wounded Hand. It was like a roll call. And it's sad, and yet it's very beautiful. And that's how we learned it. And I think that's how it should be told. It was sad, and yet it's beautiful because it's bringing back history and in a way telling about what happened. And if we don't tell it now, then it'll be lost. And if we don't teach our children, then that too will be lost, because most of the history of the Lakota people is oral. But I think it's important for history to be brought out."

that there was nowhere to go but straight ahead toward where they would find Red Cloud's people. Hoping they could parley peacefully with the soldiers, they attached a white cloth to a pole and raised it on the wagon that was carrying the sick chief. The women and children were fearful, and the men were tense but determined to defend the families. As the little band moved down the slope toward the waiting soldiers, the young warriors spread out to right and left, forming a protective battle line opposite the troops.

At the bottom of the ridge, the Indians halted, and several went forward to ask the troops' commander, Major Samuel M. Whitside, for a parley. Whitside refused, demanding, instead, to see Big Foot. The chief's wagon was driven forward, and Whitside, leaning over from his horse, saw that the Indian was sick. The officer reached down and shook the chief's hand, then through an interpreter reassured him that if he surrendered, there would be no fighting. According to Whitside's account, Big Foot agreed to surrender and with his people to accompany the troops across the hills to where the cavalrymen had their camp—to Chankpe Opi Wakpala, said the Sioux interpreter, Wounded Knee Creek. That was all right, Big Foot nodded. It was in the direction where his people were going anyway.

So they set off together, troops and Indians, both of them watchful and on edge, and that night they camped together sleeplessly at Wounded Knee Creek. The next morning, a random shot started a panic. By noon, it was over. The mild-mannered chief, Big Foot, and almost 250 members of his band were dead, some of them lying in heaps where the soldiers had first surrounded them and where Hotchkiss guns had mowed them down. Others were strewn across the frozen campgrounds and in the ravines where screaming survivors had tried to flee from the frenzied hatred of the troops. More than 50 additional Miniconjous, some of whom would not survive, were wounded, and still others who had got away were thought to have died or been wounded. The frightened cavalrymen had also suffered, many by their own cross fire. The army counted 25 dead of its own and 37 soldiers and 2 civilians (an interpreter and a priest) wounded.

In the smoke and agony of the massacre at Wounded Knee on that morning of De-

A camp of Sicangu (Brulé) Sioux on the South Dakota plains near Wounded Knee three months after the massacre of Big Foot's band.

cember 29, 1890, there died the last tortured hope of freedom among the Indian nations of North America. That night it turned suddenly cold, and the snow began to fall gently and covered the fallen bodies. It was the end of a long story of dreams and drama and courage, one that had involved many different peoples of hundreds of Indian nations and had begun in myths and shadows when humans were new-made and still young, fifteen thousand or more years ago. . . .

Creation

In the nineteenth century, most of the Sioux people like the Miniconjous lived on the Great Plains, and it was there that the last of the great battles and confrontations took place between the expanding whites and the resisting Indians whom they were dispossessing. Largely because of the romance and color of the mounted Plains tribes and the skills and fierce determination of their chiefs and warriors, which dime novels, Wild West shows, and movies publicized far and wide, the Great Plains came to be associated in the minds of non-Indian peoples throughout the world as the land of the North American Indians.

A Sioux of the Great Plains: Hollow Horn Bear, a member of a Sicangu (Brulé) Lakota Akicita, or band police society, photographed by Edward S. Curtis. As a young man, Hollow Horn Bear distinguished himself in battle against the Pawnees, traditional enemies of the Lakotas, and rode with Crazy Horse during the wars for the Bozeman Trail. A Sioux leader, and head of the Rosebud Reservation Indian Police, he negotiated for the Brulé during the Ghost Dance movement of 1890. He lived to ride in Theodore Roosevelt's inaugural parade in Washington, D.C., and was buried there when he died.

Samuel American Horse, an Oglala Sioux, was a member of William F. "Buffalo Bill" Cody's Wild West Show performing in New York City when Gertrude Käsebier photographed him in her studio in 1900. Cody's immensely popular shows were forerunners of hundreds of Hollywood films that stereotyped the Plains Indians as violent and bloodthirsty people.

What is little understood even today, however, is that almost every community in Canada, the United States, and Mexico was once an Indian community, and those communities before the arrival of the whites were part of hundreds of unique Indian nations that blanketed the entire continent. They stretched from the Atlantic to the Pacific and from Central America to the Arctic, with borders between many of them that dated back to far before the time of the Roman Empire. Including Mexico and the Caribbean, it was a continent of perhaps as many as forty million people, some nomadic, but most of them permanently settled in communities that ranged in size up to cities as large and sophisticated as any in the world at that time. Every part of the land and all of the natural world within it was sacred to one Indian nation or another.

Not unlike today, the most dense populations were along the coasts and the major rivers, around the Great Lakes, and in Mexico, Florida, and the Caribbean islands and California. Six hundred distinct languages were spoken by the different communities, bands, and chiefdoms that made up the nations. There were Indian kings and prophets, artisans and architects, sculptors and poets, mathematicians and doctors. Land and water trade networks interconnected the continent, spreading commodities and ideas. In medicine, sports, military service, dance, religion, diplomacy, art, and a dozen other fields, Indian children could dream of personal accomplishments. And not unlike today, also, all of these possibilities existed in a different way in each nation. Traditions, environment, and form of government all played a role in giving each nation an individual identity and directing it along an individual path. Some were committed by thousands of years of tradition to perfecting an unchanging way of life. Others built massive armies and military empires.

From the very first arrival of Europeans in the Western Hemisphere, the whites marveled at what they saw and wondered where it had all come from. Who were the peoples of these Indian nations, they asked, and where did they originate? The question tantalized generations of non-Indian scholars and scientists, some of whom spent lifetimes trying to prove that the Indians were descendants of seafaring Phoenicians or Chinese, pyramid-building Egyptians, one of the Lost Tribes of Israel, Welshmen, or even survivors of Plato's legendary lost continent of Atlantis.

The question of their origin has never puzzled most Indian nations. All human societies have possessed versions of their own beginnings, and the Indians of North America have been no different. Stories of natural or supernatural creation on their own land or of emergence from another, lower world or of migration from elsewhere have existed among all Indian tribes and, like the white man's biblical narrative of Genesis, have been clung to as matters of faith and spiritual truth.

Among the Nez Perce and other Indian peoples of the mountainous Northwest, generations of grandparents told children stories of a time when the world was inhabited only by animals, all of whom spoke like humans and had humanlike characteristics. Living by one of the waterways was a fierce monster who kept all the animals in fear by devouring them. Finally, the bold and courageous Coyote, the tribe's culture hero, jumped down the monster's throat and killed him by sawing up his heart with a flint. When the monster was dead, Coyote

Grace Jajola stands outside her home at Isleta Pueblo in the Rio Grande Valley of New Mexico in 1902. During almost five centuries of determined resistance to Spanish, Mexican, and American invasions, the Pueblo peoples were largely successful in keeping their lands and maintaining their traditional values and customs.

OPPOSITE: *This stately Nez Perce man, photographed by Edward Curtis in the Northwest near the turn of the century, wears the hairstyle of the traditionalist, non-Christian members of Chief Joseph's band who had been exiled to a Washington State reservation after their 1877 war with the United States.*

A Yakima woman in tribal dress early in the twentieth century. Related to the Nez Perces, the Yakimas of what is now Washington State fought valiantly for their lands in the 1850s and now occupy an extensive reservation in their original homeland on the eastern side of the Cascade Range.

cut its body into small pieces, creating from each part a different tribe. In each case, the group telling the story related that it had sprung from the monster's heart or blood, which had made it the bravest and wisest of all the tribes.

In the desert Southwest, Hopi, Zuñi, and Pueblo descendants of the Anasazis and other radiant pre-Columbian societies possess a large body of sacred-origin stories. Some of them tell of the emergence of their people through a hole, known as *sipapu,* from an underground lake. Others relate in great detail the climb of their ancestors toward perfection through three underworlds and their final emergence through *sipapu* into the present, or fourth, world. All of them then tell of migrations to the sites that became their homes in this world.

The most common origin stories, however, illustrate a close spiritual bond between the Indians and all of creation within their universe. The Creator, the Master of Life, the Great Spirit, Wakan Tanka—whatever terms the various native American groups used—breathed life into humans and bound their spirits to those of all else in their universe. "My strength, my blood is from the fish, from the roots and berries . . . and game," said a Yakima man. "I . . . did not come here. I was put here by the Creator." At the same time, Taos Pueblo elders told their young, "When Earth was still young and giants still roamed the land, a great sickness came upon them. All of them died except for a small boy. One day while he was playing, a snake bit him. The boy cried and cried. The blood came out, and finally he died. With his tears our

lakes became. With his blood the red clay became. With his body our mountains became, and that was how Earth became." Most tribes believed that the people of their nation were created on their land, and their land, where they were created, was the center of the world. But there was a symbiosis between the land and the people. Because of their spiritual attachment, one gave life to the other, and it behooved humans to keep that attachment in balance and harmony by proper conduct and thoughts, lest it harm the people's well-being.

As might be expected, tradi-

This young Hopi woman of Oraibi displays an exquisitely woven basketry plaque, an example of tribal artistry that began among her Anasazi ancestors of two thousand years ago. The mesa-top village of Old Oraibi itself was founded about A.D. 1150 and is one of the oldest continuously inhabited towns in the United States.

OPPOSITE: *An early twentieth-century Curtis photograph of an artisan of San Felipe Pueblo—who also held the office of governor of the town—drilling turquoise beads to be strung on a necklace. His Anasazi forebears mined turquoise from the Cerrillos Hills near present-day Santa Fe, sending it by trade from the Chaco Canyon region to the Toltecs in the Valley of Mexico.*

An older woman from the Pueblo town of Acoma, or Sky City, photographed by Laura Gilpin, is adorned by her necklaces of silver, turquoise, and beads.

tional tribal versions of the Indians' origins differ greatly from the beliefs of modern-day science. In contrast to the certainties of the Indians' stories, however, the scientists themselves are still far from possessing all the answers. Since no remains of a pre–Homo sapiens type of man have ever been discovered in the Americas, it is assumed that humans did not evolve there, as they did on other continents, but arrived in the Western Hemisphere after the development of modern man. Most of the scientists and scholars also agree—from archaeological findings in Siberia, Mongolia, and North America, and studies in linguistics, physical anthropology, and other disciplines—that the Indians came in one or more migrations from eastern Asia, crossing a land bridge to Alaska that appeared from time to time during the Ice Age when the formation of huge glaciers caused the sea levels to fall by as much as three hundred feet.

So far, scientists do not agree on much more, including the date of the arrival of the first migrants from Asia. It is thought that the land bridge across what is now the Bering Strait existed sometime between seventy thousand and thirty thousand years ago; again from twenty-five thousand to fifteen thousand years ago; and once or twice more between approximately fourteen thousand and ten thousand years ago. During any of these periods, small bands of Asian hunters and their families, following herds of mastodons and other large Ice Age game animals across the land bridge or along its coasts, could have reached Alaska. From archaeological discoveries, all that is known definitely is that people were living in all parts of North and South America by at least twelve thousand years ago—long before the time of Egypt, Phoenicia, China, Israel, or any other nation known to history. Indeed, gaining increasing acceptance, but still controversial, are finds from Alaska to Chile and from Pennsylvania to California suggesting the presence of people in the Americas even earlier—perhaps as long as thirty-five thousand, or even fifty thousand, years ago.

Whether the ancestors of the Indian nations came in one wave or in separate movements at different times during the Ice Age, once they entered Alaska, they and

This Yupik-speaking Eskimo woman, photographed at the end of the nineteenth century by Curtis on the infrequently visited island of Nunivak in the Bering Sea off the western coast of Alaska, wears facial ornaments of the time, including a beaded nose ring and labrets with beaded pendants.

their descendants continued to hunt the mastodons and other big-game animals, killing them in group attacks with spears, clubs, and ingenious spear-throwing shafts called atlatls, but living also by fishing and gathering wild foods. Gradually, they moved with the animals along ice-free routes on the Alaskan coasts, up the Yukon and other river valleys, and south along the chains of the Rocky Mountains, through natural corridors that existed from time to time between the massive glaciers. Eventually, reaching the vast tundra and forest environments south of the ice sheets, the bands spread toward the Atlantic coast and to Central and South America.

In their movements, the people often sheltered themselves in caves or beneath overhanging rocks. But it would be wrong to think of them as stereotypical "cave-

The Inuit (Eskimos) were well adapted to the demanding life of the Arctic, supplementing their fishing with seasonal hunts of sea mammals and caribou. This 1899 Curtis photograph was taken in a summer seal-hunting camp of Inuit. The wood used to erect the frames of their skin-covered tents was a scarce and valued commodity.

men," with stooped shoulders, heavy brows, and dull, brutish features. Physically, they were fully developed modern people, intelligent, sensitive, and already endowed with spiritual impulses that bound them as relatives under a common creator to their natural surroundings and to the various plant and animal sources of their food. In a material way, they were also more advanced than is generally thought. Their chipped stone tools, weapons, and utensils were among the most efficient in the world at that time; in addition, they were adept at fashioning trim hide clothing and basketry sandals, painting various possessions, and making personal adornments and religious objects from stone, horns, bones, walrus-tusk ivory, shells, and other natural materials.

Although their population at first was sparse, here and there the bands came in contact with one another, combined, divided into new groups, or drove one another into less hospitable and accessible areas. Until about ten thousand years ago, these bands shared North America with the great mammoths, mastodons, outsized bison and bears, giant sloths, small prehistoric horses, and other animals of the Ice Age. Then the Ice Age came to an end, the great glaciers receded, and the earth was re-formed. The tundra and evergreen forests at the southern edge of the ice sheets moved north, following the retreating glaciers, and were replaced by great grassland prairies, hardwood forests, and arid plains and plateaus. Jungles grew in Mexico, and virgin woodlands covered North America from the Atlantic coast to the center of the continent. And in two thousand years, all the mastodons, giant sloths, miniature horses, saber-toothed tigers, and many other animals of the Ice Age became extinct.

A Curtis photograph shows Maricopa women gathering the fruit of saguaro cacti in the desert of southern Arizona. Working from the end of the nineteenth century until the 1920s, Curtis, who feared that Native Americans were vanishing peoples, carefully staged his photographs to convey idealistic images of Indians and their daily lives as he thought they might have appeared before the whites disrupted their cultures.

In most parts of the continent, the humans studied the smaller creatures that had survived with them and, changing their hunting methods and the size of their spear points, hunted deer, antelope, and other small animals, at the same time relying more on fish and shellfish and the gathering of nuts, berries, grass, seeds, and wild vegetables and fruits. With the passage of time, different groups came to identify themselves with special parts of the land, understanding in some cases that it was the place of their ancestors' origin or in others that the Creator or other supernatural beings meant them to live there. Century after century, they established spiritual harmony with their particular territory, learning to understand and take care of its resources so that the resources, in turn, would take care of them.

In time, as population increased and the ancient Indians adapted to the different environments, cultural and physical variations began to appear among them. Those along the coasts developed maritime-oriented cultures with economies based largely on their ability to harvest fish and collect shellfish. In the eastern forests and California, woodland peoples learned to use fire to clear the land for new growth that would increase the yield of deer and other animals. In the Canadian North, caribou hunters traveled on snowshoes and employed mannequins to herd frightened animals into corrals. In the Great Basin of the West, one of the harshest and poorest regions on the continent, nomadic bands, living on anything that was edible, including pine nuts and desert reptiles, estab-

The Crow country is exactly in the right place. Everything good is to be found there. There is no place like Crow country. —ARAPOOISH

The Detroit souvenir company that sold this 1899 hand-colored photograph of Ute Indians titled it simply "Chief Severa and Family." The many bands of the Utes lived in the deserts and forested mountains of present-day eastern Utah (which was named for them), western Colorado, and parts of Wyoming, Nevada, and New Mexico. They were mainly hunters of small game and gatherers of seeds, berries, nuts, and other wild foods, but when they acquired horses, some of them adopted the traits of the buffalo-hunting Plains tribes.

This Cheyenne boy, obliging a turn-of-the-century photographer to help create a surefire souvenir sales item of the day, poses for his snapshot with a gun and wearing a bone breastplate and the eagle-feathered headdress of one of his elders. For centuries the Cheyenne people lived as part-time farmers in Minnesota until they moved west, adopted the horse, and specialized in buffalo hunting on the plains.

lished a satisfactory and stable way of life that lasted for thousands of years, into the nineteenth century. And in Mexico and river valleys in the East, hunters and gatherers began to turn into part-time farmers, learning below the Rio Grande how to grow corn, beans, and squash and in the eastern woodlands cultivating such edible plants as sunflowers, sumpweed, and goosefoot. In every part of the continent the ancient Indian peoples continued to build relationships with their land, harmonizing their needs with what their natural worlds could provide them, and their spiritual life with the spirits of all of the universe about them.

The Buffalo

Most Indian nations of North America lived in the equivalent of what Christianity would call the Garden of Eden—the place of creation—the place of plenty, the single place on earth most perfect for them. For every nation that place was unique.

"The Crow country is a good country," said Arapooish, a leader of the Crow Indians of Montana, to white men in the nineteenth century. "The Great Spirit put it exactly in the right place; while you are in it you fare well; whenever you are out of

Cheyenne hide moccasins decorated with elaborate beadwork.

A Plains Indian depiction of a duel between buffalo who are competing for rank in the herd. Illustrations like this one, made in the 1870s, are generally known as ledger drawings because they were done on paper from ledger books given by the government to Indians who had been defeated and imprisoned. The creator of this drawing was Frank Henderson, an Arapaho orphan who was in the first class at the Carlisle Indian School in 1879.

it, whichever way you travel, you fare worse. . . . The Crow country is exactly in the right place. Everything good is to be found there. There is no place like Crow country."

On the northern Great Plains, long before Arapooish's time, the ancient peoples lived on a vast homeland of grass cut by occasional rivers and streams lined by trees and underbrush. Small extended families of fewer than twenty-five people moved in seasonal rounds of hunting game and gathering berries, nuts, seeds, and roots. They had no horses; they were people on foot, depending on experience and intelligence to guide them. But among the many foods and natural resources available to them, one animal above all others—the bison—truly provided for them.

"The great Father of Life who made us and gave us this land to live upon, made the buffalo . . . to afford us sustenance," said a warrior of the northern plains. "Their meat is our only food; with their skins we clothe ourselves and build our lodges. They are our only means of life—food, fuel, and clothing." He, like Arapooish, was talking to whites in the nineteenth century, but he might have been speaking as well for his ancestors of thousands of years before. The ancient Indians of the northern plains studied, revered, and established strong spiritual relationships between themselves and the buffalo, associating it directly with the Creator and centering most of their religious life around the great shaggy animal. And no wonder. No animal, the Indians said, ever gave so much of itself to people. There was almost no part of the buffalo that Plains Indian nations did not use: the tongue and flesh for food; the rawhide for shields, buckets, moccasins, rattles, drums, bullboats, ropes, splints, thongs, and con-

Plains Indian families often painted their tipis with geometric or realistic designs, which had a personal meaning to their owners, who were given special places within the camp circle. For an 1897 exposition in Tennessee, Kiowa artists from the southern plains constructed a circle of miniature tipis with twenty-eight-inch-tall painted buckskin covers. This extended tipi cover from the exposition, featuring buffalo pictures, was copied from a heraldic design of a Kiowa named Never Got Shot.

tainers; the hair for headdresses, ornaments, and ropes; the tail for brushes; the horns for cups, fire carriers, and ladles; the hooves for glue and rattles; the skull for ceremonies and rituals; the beard for ornamentation; the bladder for sinews, pouches, and bags; the muscles for thread, glue, and sinews; the paunch for the lining of cups, basins, and buckets; the scrotum for rattles; the stomach for medicines and the lining of containers; the bones for clubs, sleds, game dice, knives, scrapers, awls, digging sticks, and other implements and utensils; the chips for fuel; and the hide for clothing, robes, cradles, bags, lodge covers, dolls, and a hundred other products.

For people in small bands who had to move on foot, hunting the large aggressive buffalo that traveled in huge herds and stampeded easily could be especially dangerous and not always successful. There were more effective ways to hunt, and for that many Plains bands would come together in tribal gatherings near a herd. Cooperatively, they would lay out drive lanes, like avenues across the plains, lining them with piles of rocks and brush behind which their hunters could hide. The drive lanes were funnel shaped, with their wide mouths near the herd and the narrow ends leading into a stout-walled corral or pound, or to the abrupt edge of a steep cliff or bluff over which the stampeding animals could be driven to their death. The killing site was known to the Indians as a *piskun,* meaning a deep-blood-kettle, and later-coming whites called the cliff-type hunting sites buffalo jumps.

In southern Alberta is a famous one, used by the people of the northern plains for more than five thousand years. It is called the Head-Smashed-In Buffalo Jump for an unfortunate Indian of long ago who, legend says, became trapped against the base of the cliff and was crushed under the weight of the falling animals. Today, Head-Smashed-In is a vivid example of what the many buffalo jumps on the northern plains were like and how they were used.

First, the peoples' shamans, or spiritual leaders, went out on the plains and, employing *iniskims,* small, buffalo-shaped stones that were believed to have the power to attract the bison herds, called to the buffalo to come toward the drive lanes. As the herd moved slowly toward the lanes, the hunters who were hiding emerged suddenly from behind the rocks and brush and, shouting and waving robes, panicked the animals into a thundering rush down the funnel and over the cliff or into the corral or pound. Indians lining the kill areas at the foot of the cliff easily dispatched the stunned and injured animals that had not died in the fall, and Indian women hurried to skin and butcher the slaughtered bison, making use of virtually everything. At one time, the cliff at Head-Smashed-In was a sheer drop of more than sixty feet, but talus from the crumbling cliff edge and

The great Father of Life who made us and gave us this land to live upon, made the buffalo . . . to afford us sustenance.

—A WARRIOR OF THE NORTHERN PLAINS

Plains Indian children played with realistic toys like this model of a buffalo made of the animal's hide and conveying its strength, power, and special bond and importance to the people.

A painting by Alfred Jacob Miller, an American artist who accompanied a British sportsman, Sir William Drummond Stewart, across the plains to the Rocky Mountains in 1837, depicts mounted Indian hunters stampeding columns of panicked buffalo over a "jump" to their death. Miller never saw this scene himself, but made his painting from descriptions given him by Shoshoni Indians.

the bones of hundreds of thousands of animals who had plunged blindly to their death had piled up century after century until the fall was less than thirty-five feet.

The mass hunts were hard work and often dangerous, but they were also a spiritual communion between the people and the bounty who were giving their lives to sustain the Indians. While the skillful method that drove the bison into pounds or over the cliffs was impressive and could mean the difference between the people's well-being and starvation, an equally notable accomplishment was the Indians' ability to coordinate the gatherings for the cooperative hunt. Small bands, scattered over thousands of square miles of High Plains country, had to be brought together—had to know where and when to meet. How it was achieved is still debated. Some believe that an answer may lie in remarkable creations in stone found in various parts of the northern plains and known as medicine wheels.

Formed by piles of rocks laid out on the ground in a pattern of concentric circles or ovals intersected by spokes radiating out from a central cairn, they were un-

doubtedly sacred sites, used by northern Plains peoples for vision quests, prayers, and other spiritual purposes. But they may also have allowed the users to create an annual calendar based on the relation of the spokes to the positions of the sun or certain stars. It would have been easy to keep track of the time for traveling to communal hunts, as well as for other things, such as when berries would ripen in a particular valley or when waterfowl would return to a certain lake.

In addition, some archaeologists have speculated that the reckoning of time by the northern Plains bands may not have been the only unique use of the wheels. Hunting and gathering peoples traveling in small groups needed an intimate knowledge of their territory. The medicine wheels, most of which were located on high points that provided expansive views, may have offered people the ability to familiarize themselves with the land the Creator had given them. Spokes pointed out toward major landmarks and toward other medicine wheels on far-off peaks. Year after year and from one generation to another through the course of centuries, hunters could have used the wheels to learn the shape of their world and, by studying several wheels, construct a mental picture of thousands of square miles of territory. When traveling great distances, for example, to the tribal hunts, they would have been able to read the landscape and know where they were and where they were going.

In that sense, the wheels could have been pathfinders and maps, as well as calendars. Whatever roles they actually played in the lives of the ancient peoples, however, Indian nations of the northern plains still

I love the land and the buffalo, and will not part with it. . . . I love to roam over the prairies. There I feel free and happy.

—WHITE BEAR (SATANTA)

The Majorville medicine wheel, near Calgary in Alberta, Canada, was constructed by aligning rocks and boulders to form a central circle about a hundred feet in diameter. The spokes radiating from this central hub point to sacred sites in the surrounding hills and mountains, while the mound within the central circle contained iniskims, *the stones used by Blackfeet buffalo-calling societies.*

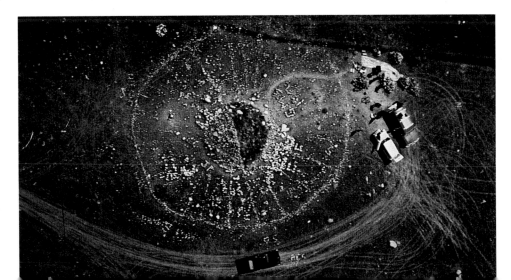

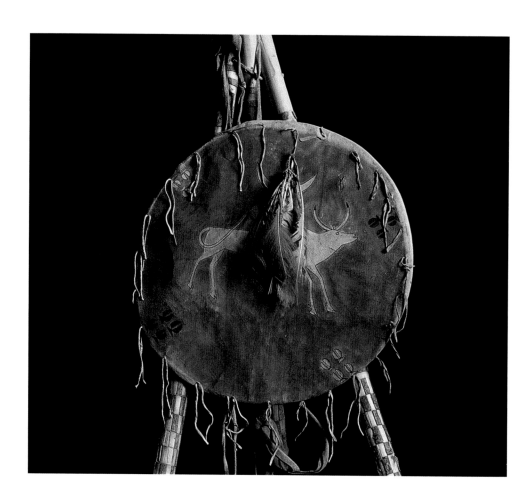

A Cheyenne shield of painted buffalo hide stretched across a wooden frame.

hold them sacred. It is hard to imagine otherwise. In their silence and timelessness, the medicine wheels have connected people with the supernatural, the land, and with one another through uncounted generations.

Agriculture and Expansion

Thousands of miles away in southern Mexico, Guatemala, and Honduras, the connections between Indian nations and their land were, meanwhile, providing a very different bounty. There, in a region of extreme diversity of environments and wild plants, an important development had taken place. People who had depended largely on gathering wild-growing foods had learned how to domesticate certain crops and become farmers. In settled agricultural villages, they were raising an increasing number and variety of products that would not be known outside of the Americas until the time of Columbus. These included tomatoes, peanuts, avocados, cacao, tobacco, pumpkins, and many kinds of chili peppers, beans, and squashes. And what had been a wild grass, the Indians had developed into maize, their word for corn, from which great Indian civilizations would rise and which would eventually become a staple in the diets of peoples throughout the world.

So important had maize become to them that some people traced their own origin to the plant. In the highlands of Guatemala, the *Popol Vuh,* the sacred epic narrative of the Quiché Mayan Indians, recounted from generation to generation

Of all these wonders that I then beheld today all is overthrown and lost, nothing left standing.

—BERNAL DÍAZ

how their creator gods, Tepeu and Gukumatz, had formed the earth, the animals, and the plants, and then had tried to make people. First, they used mud, but the figures oozed back into mud. Then they tried wood, but the people had no minds, and the other gods destroyed them. A third attempt created people of flesh, but they proved wicked, and a great flood caused by black rains wiped them out. Finally, the creator gods used maize dough, and from it successfully fashioned true men, the ancestors of the Quiché.

The Indians' development of agriculture, like the start of farming in the Near East or in other parts of the world, did not happen all at once. Beginning perhaps eight thousand years ago, after the close of the Ice Age, the intensified interactions between gathering peoples in sections of Mexico and particular wild plants that they favored stimulated the study, protection, and special care of those plants. In addition, over the course of centuries, as people focused on plants that bore the largest or most desirable fruits and seeds, the gathering process itself may have caused genetic changes to the plants. Learning to cultivate, protect, and disperse the food-bearing plants took millennia; it was more millennia before the hunting and gathering peoples could rely on agriculture to provide a significant part of their diet. Maize, for example, which eventually became the most important food among numerous Indian nations of

Between three and five thousand years ago, Indian people began to domesticate corn from a basic wild seed crop, possibly a hybrid of the Tripsacum grass, shown here, which still grows abundantly in Mexico. The first cobs were tiny and may have been used only to make mild fermented beverages, being adopted later as a staple food when developments increased the size of the ears.

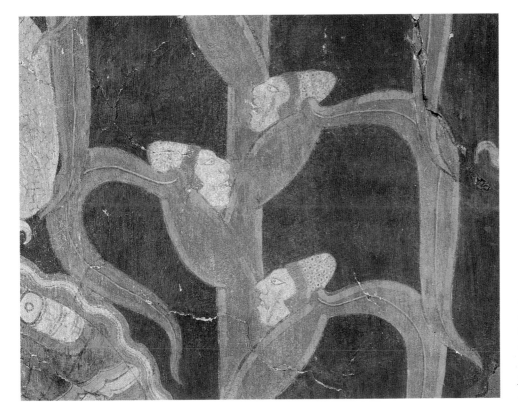

This detail from a mural in the ancient Tlaxcalan ceremonial center of Cacaxtla in Mexico portrays ears of corn in the form of human heads. Religious parables emphasized the theme of self-sacrifice, describing heroes who lived in a desolate, half-formed world and bargained with gods to provide corn to feed mankind in return for the sacrifice of their own lives.

North America, took thousands of years for Indians in different regions of Mexico to develop from the original, tiny cobs of the wild grass teosinte into many varieties of large ears—similar to those of today— that could sustain huge populations.

As cultivation grew more important, various Indian groups in southern Mexico and Guatemala began to settle down in permanent villages near their fields and gardens. By about 1700 B.C., improved agricultural technologies were producing surpluses of food which, in turn, allowed the farming populations to expand. A plentiful food supply in the proliferating villages also gave many people more time for activities other than food gathering. With a heightened aesthetic sense, they fashioned all kinds of religious and utilitarian objects, as well as articles of adornment and ornamentation. In different areas, some of the villagers began to accumulate objects of wealth; specialists and stratified societies of differently ranked people appeared; and religious and political systems, needed to organize and lead the growing concentrations of population, became widespread and more complex.

Along the Mexican Gulf coast there arose about 1500 B.C. (some three hundred years before the time of Moses and the Egyptian pharaoh Ramses II) the first, and in some respects the "mother," civilization of all of what archaeologists call Mesoamerica, that is, Mexico, Belize, Guatemala, and part of Honduras. Evolving from simple lowland agricultural villagers, Indians known today as Olmecs created a highly sophisticated society with great ceremonial centers, a single authoritarian ruler, and a strong, influential, religious-based culture that traders, missionaries, and perhaps warriors spread across most of Mesoamerica and into parts of Central America. The somewhat-urbanized Olmec centers included huge earthen temple

A ceramic effigy vessel representation of the Mayan creator god, Gukumatz, found at Kaminaljuyú in Guatemala. According to the Popol Vuh sacred text of the Quiché Mayas, the gods Gukumatz and Tepeu formed the world, raised the sky, and populated the earth with animals. Only when they saw that the animals could not speak and praise their makers did they set about trying to create mankind.

mounds, monumental stone carvings, sacrificial altars, and vertical stone slabs, known as stelae, with images and symbols incised on their surfaces.

The principal Olmec deity was Rain God, represented in architectural carvings and Olmec sculptures and art by what was long thought to have been the face of a snarling half-jaguar, half-human figure, but what many now believe, instead, was the stylized image of the convergence of the bodies of two serpents. The Olmecs' Rain God, in various outward forms and associated with serpents, floods, ice, lightning, hail, mountains, and droughts, was adopted and worshiped universally by later Mesoamerican civilizations. The Olmecs also developed a numbering system and a complex calendar and produced exquisite sculptures, terra-cotta figurines, decorated pottery, and magnificent jade statuettes, masks, and other objects. There are some scientists who believe that the Olmecs were in addition the first Indians to invent writing in an early form of glyphs.

Among the most striking works of the Olmecs were huge heads, sculpted in the round from basalt, eight feet high and weighing up to twenty tons. Their head-dresses, looking like tight-fitting, old-fashioned football helmets, suggest that the sculptures were those of religious or secular rulers. Found resting in the jungle growth covering an Olmec site, they raised the question of how they got there, for the nearest source for the basalt is forty miles away, and the Olmecs, like all Indian peoples until the time of Columbus, had neither wheeled vehicles nor large domesticated draft animals like horses or oxen. Today, it seems clear that the Olmecs themselves contrived to pull the huge blocks on rollers through the jungle and then floated them down the rivers to the site where they were found.

Lasting until about 300 B.C., the Olmec civilization influenced and contributed to many new local and regional Indian cultures and urbanized civilizations that arose

This small jade bust may once have been part of the royal jewelry of the Olmec chieftain whose image it bears. To ancient Mesoamerican peoples, jade was more precious than gold. Later, the Aztecs thought that it could even cure certain diseases. The light blue-green varieties, emblematic of plants, water, and the sky, were preferred by Olmec carvers and were probably imported from present-day Costa Rica.

Olmec artisans commemorated their gods on jade ornaments exquisitely carved with images of their deities and hieroglyphic writing. This jade plaque was suspended from a necklace or belt.

and flourished in the central Mexico Valley, Oaxaca, the Yucatán, Guatemala, and other sections of Mesoamerica. By the time of Christ, the different nations encompassed millions of people, divided into classes of warriors, artisans, traders, and other specialists, as well as the common people, the farmers and laborers. A powerful elite was emerging. Some individuals were taking charge of agricultural technology and becoming members of authoritarian religious hierarchies and spiritual intermediaries between the people and the powers of nature: fertility, the weather, the animals of the forests, and the signs of the heav-

The colossal carved stone heads of the Olmecs like this one at La Venta in Tabasco, Mexico, reflect the transformation of spiritual leaders into powerful chiefs and warlords. Although the actual function of these monuments is unknown, they document an emerging cult of the royal authority of people who were thought to have possessed the powers of gods.

ens. Other men were becoming kings, with retinues of counselors, warriors, nobles, and the power of life and death over their subjects.

The greatest and most awesome of the new Indian civilizations in Mesoamerica was that of the Mayas, whose culture flourished after about A.D. 200 in numerous large and small centers in both the highlands and lowlands of southern Mexico, Belize, Guatemala, Honduras, and El Salvador.

Among the Mayas, the kings no longer divined the wishes of the gods; they, like the Egyptian pharaohs and Chinese emperors, were worshiped as gods themselves. By A.D. 650, the height of what is called the Mayan Classic Period, the population had soared to well over ten million. At least sixty capital centers with monumental stone structures had been erected in the lush, steamy jungles of a homeland which the many different groups of Mayas had claimed since their hunting and gathering ancestors had first arrived there at least ten thousand years earlier.

The Mayas portrayed scenes at the courts of their kings on the sides of magnificent painted cylindrical pots, vases, plates, and drinking vessels. In this rollout of the design on a Late Classic vase of about A.D. 800, two seated dignitaries bow in submission to a lord named Morning Star, while two other attendants hold burning cigars. The scene commemorates the payment of tribute in the form of woven cloth and other valuables, which is contained in the tied bags to the left. The text around the rim of the vase identifies its owner as Morning Star himself, and states that it was created for drinking a beverage made from chocolate beans.

By A.D. 850 many of the once-great Mayan cities lay in abandoned ruins, overgrown by jungle growth. Forgotten even by the descendants of their builders, they began to be rediscovered in the nineteenth century by explorers like John Lloyd Stephens and the artist Frederick Catherwood, whose watercolors, like this one of Palenque, provided the rest of the world with romantic portrayals of the "lost" civilization.

These Classic Period seats of power—Tikal, Uxmal, Becan, Seibal, Uaxactún, Copán, Dzibilchaltún, Bonampak, and dozens of others—were the religious and cultural centers of independent kingdom-states. Many of the capitals had large urban populations, while others were ceremonial centers served by outlying towns and villages. Among the centers was Palenque, a powerful capital in the foothills of southern Mexico's Chiapas Mountains and one of the jewels of the Mayan world.

In the nineteenth century, European and American explorers, writers, and scientists speculated wildly about the origins and life of the mysterious "lost" civilization of the Mayas, whose great centers had become abandoned and overgrown by jungle long before the time of Columbus. Only in the twentieth century did the Western world begin to understand the background and the culture and history of the Indians who had created and lived among these architectural wonders.

In June 1952, the Mexican archaeologist Alberto Ruz, examining the Temple of Inscriptions atop a sixty-five-foot-high stepped pyramid at Palenque, noticed a large stone slab in the floor with a double row of holes filled with removable stone stoppers. Lifting the slab, Ruz and his helpers discovered a vaulted stairway leading down into the interior of the pyramid. The stairway was filled with rubble that took the archaeologists four field sessions to clear, after which they reached a chamber containing the skeletons of five or six men, probably sacrificial victims, and a corridor blocked at its far end by another huge slab.

Removing that slab, Ruz looked into a great funerary crypt that had been sealed for more than twelve hundred years, containing a monolithic limestone sarcophagus with a five-ton stone lid covered with relief carvings. Inside the sarcophagus, surrounded and covered with a wealth of jade objects, were the remains of an obviously important ruler, over whose face had been placed a magnificent life-sized mask of jade. Archaeological study, particularly of the carved figures and inscriptions on the lid of the sarcophagus and in the temple above, revealed the tomb as that of Palenque's greatest ruler, Lord Pacal, or Great Shield in the English language, who had died in A.D. 683 at the age of eighty. It appeared that Pacal had had the crypt and the pyramid and temple built for himself during his lifetime, which suggested that most of the Classic Period temple-pyramids in the Mayan world were funerary monuments, where the people could worship dead kings, a function of the structures not dissimilar from that of the pyramids in Egypt.

The exciting discovery of Pacal's burial site came on the eve of another dramatic event in the study of the Mayas. After years of intense work, scholars gained the ability to decipher most of the Mayan glyphs, unlocking the Mayas' history and disclosing much about their culture that had not been known before or had been misunderstood. Previously, the Mayas had been regarded generally as peaceful, unwarlike peoples ruled by religious leaders who were devoted largely to intellectual pursuits. Now the glyphs portrayed just the opposite, revealing aggressive, military-oriented societies, the conquests of states and kings, and the practice of cruel and

The five-ton carved stone lid, unseen for more than twelve hundred years, that covered Pacal's sarcophagus in the Temple of Inscriptions at Palenque. The relief carvings and hieroglyphic texts commemorate the start of the ruler's descent as a god into the Mayan underworld, symbolized by the massive jaws of a monster. From Pacal's loins grows the sacred World Tree that marked the center of the Mayan universe.

The monumental structures at Palenque, built of cut limestone blocks, finished with stucco plaster, and painted in brilliant hues of red, were erected between A.D. 600 and 750 by Pacal and his sons. The Temple of the Count at the top of the stepped pyramid was one of Pacal's earliest buildings. In the background are ruins of three sections of the Great Palace, built later and incorporating a number of innovative construction techniques.

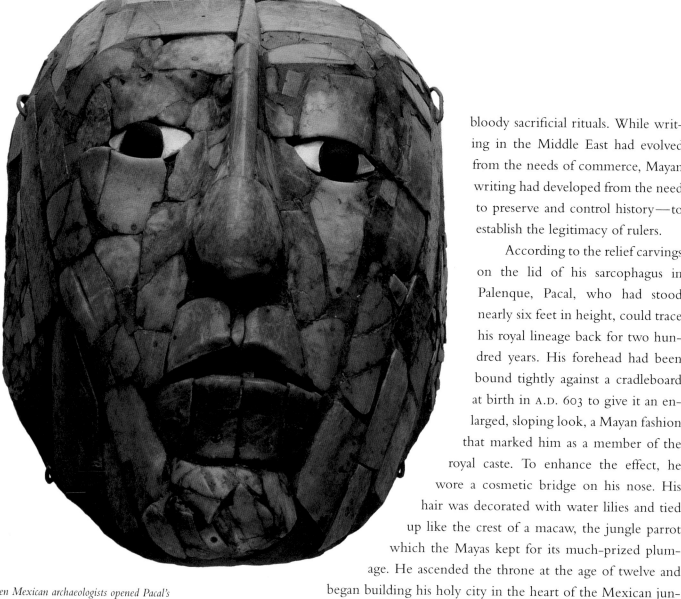

bloody sacrificial rituals. While writing in the Middle East had evolved from the needs of commerce, Mayan writing had developed from the need to preserve and control history—to establish the legitimacy of rulers.

According to the relief carvings on the lid of his sarcophagus in Palenque, Pacal, who had stood nearly six feet in height, could trace his royal lineage back for two hundred years. His forehead had been bound tightly against a cradleboard at birth in A.D. 603 to give it an enlarged, sloping look, a Mayan fashion that marked him as a member of the royal caste. To enhance the effect, he wore a cosmetic bridge on his nose. His hair was decorated with water lilies and tied up like the crest of a macaw, the jungle parrot which the Mayas kept for its much-prized plumage. He ascended the throne at the age of twelve and began building his holy city in the heart of the Mexican jungle. After ruling for almost seventy years and acquiring the status of a descendant of the gods, he was buried in his most spectacular creation, the Temple of Inscriptions. On his sarcophagus lid, he is depicted as a god who, at the moment of death, is beginning his descent toward the Underworld, down the sacred World Tree at the center of the universe.

After his death, his sons established an ancestor cult dedicated to the memory of Pacal and expanded Palenque, adding a ball court and erecting other magnificent structures, but being careful never to overshadow the temple-pyramid of their exalted father. Each new temple contained a carved monument showing Pacal confirming the succession of his sons. From Palenque they ruled as living gods over some two hundred thousand Mayan people dwelling in regional communities of farmers, weavers, stonemasons, feather workers, and other specialists. A principal complex in Palenque, known today as the Great Palace, dominated by a four-story square tower that may have been an observatory or a watchtower, included a maze of in-

When Mexican archaeologists opened Pacal's sarcophagus, they found his body covered richly with jewelry. On his face was this life-sized mask of jade plaques, conveying an awesome sense of Mayan mystery and beauty.

terconnecting halls and plazas where the great lords of the realm gathered for sumptuous feasts and to discuss the affairs of state. Painted scenes on ancient Palenque

drinking vessels reveal that the palace walls were hung with exquisite tapestries that could be drawn aside or closed to transform the courts and chambers into private areas for the lord, his wives, concubines, and servants.

By A.D. 720, Palenque had reached its highest glory. For reasons long lost in the past, the Mayan world would soon be changing. Warfare broke out among the

Scenes like this on painted drinking vessels reveal much about Mayan customs and living arrangements.

Mayan hieroglyphic writing graduated from full-figured glyphs like this one, found on a tablet at Palenque, to simple cartouches that contained purely phonetically based symbols like a standard writing system. The Mayas were the only pre-Columbian Indian peoples to develop such a system. The glyph here represents the patron god of an important date in the Sacred Maya Calendar. Elements of the headdress, mask, jewelry, and clothing, together with other signs, provided the phonetic pronunciation of his name.

This fragmentary stucco mask on a façade of the Palace at Palenque may be a portrait of Pacal's second son, Lord Kan Xul. Eventually this prince was defeated by a rival kingdom, and his capture foreshadowed the fall of Palenque.

states, and farmers became soldiers. Carved monuments in Palenque's Palace bear testimony to a world transformed by widespread violence. One by one, the enemies of Palenque appear as bound captives brought before the warlord for judgment. But the days of Palenque's triumphs and greatness were ending. Finally, the lord of Palenque, Kan Xul, the second of Pacal's sons to rule, was defeated, his captivity commemorated on a monument preserved by a rival kingdom.

For decades, others would try to hold the once-powerful center of the western Mayan country together, but by A.D. 800 the beautiful legacy of the god-king Pacal was abandoned and left to be reclaimed by the jungle. But Palenque did not fall alone. Regional upheavals spread well beyond the boundaries of the Mayan world, and throughout the Indian nations of Mexico great cities collapsed. In time, they would be replaced by others.

Meanwhile, the building of mounds and the development of Indian city-states had not been confined to Mesoamerica. Farther north, in parts of the present-day

United States, some Indian peoples had also been building mounds and were evolving toward urbanization.

The City of the North: Cahokia

The heart of the continent is bisected by the Mississippi, one of the world's great rivers. With its hundreds of tributaries, some as major as the Ohio, the Missouri, the Tennessee, the Arkansas, and the Red, the Mississippi's network links a third of North America by water. Along these rivers and across much of the center of the continent there developed, beginning about A.D. 700, one of the most spectacular and least known of the great North American Indian civilizations, that of the Mississippians, given that name by archaeologists because their culture appears to have originated along the bottomlands of the middle Mississippi and the lower Ohio, Illinois, and Tennessee rivers. Known also as Temple Mound Builders for the religious structures that surmounted their huge, flattopped earthen mounds, they had evolved over many centuries and were the stunning climax of other mound-building societies that had preceded them.

As early as 1500 B.C., Indians in some parts of the northeastern woodlands had adopted the practice of burying their dead, along with personal ornaments, tools, and other grave goods, on ridges, knolls, and other elevated sites. Later, some groups began raising dome-shaped mounds of earth above the burials. By about 1000 B.C., this simple burial-mound practice, reflecting spiritual motives, developed into the

A rollout of a painting on a ceramic vase depicts victorious Mayan warriors escorting a captive prince who stands stripped of his clothing, with his arms tied behind his back.

more sophisticated Adena culture, spreading among peoples in the Ohio Valley, New York, and New England who, though they still hunted and gathered wild foods, had domesticated local plants like sumpweed, marsh elder, squash, and sunflowers and had settled down in permanent or semipermanent villages. Without maize, the population was still small, but the Adena Indians built circular earthworks and large mounds and turned out as well many utilitarian and artistic objects, often of mica and copper.

About A.D. 200, maize finally reached some of the mound-building peoples, diffusing north to them probably from the Southwest or Mexico. Population increased, and a new, vital mound-building culture, the Hopewell (named for the owner of one of its principal sites in the Ohio Valley), replaced the Adena and spread among proliferating Indian farming villages along the rivers of the Midwest and East. Flourishing until about A.D. 500, the Hopewellian civilization was far more complex than the Adena. Large ceremonial centers, with elaborately constructed earthen walls, contained conical or dome-shaped burial mounds up to thirty feet or more in height and two hundred feet in circumference. Religious leaders and the elite dwelled in the centers, surrounded by the nearby farming settlements and the round or oval-shaped wigwams of the general population.

One of the most distinctive achievements of the Hopewellians was the creation of an amazing trade network that was almost continent-wide and brought to the Hopewellian centers objects and materials from the Atlantic coast to the Rocky Mountains and from the Great Lakes to the Gulf of Mexico. Hopewellian artists and artisans flourished, using the materials received from the trade to turn out a

A steatite pipe, carved in the image of a beaver and inlaid with bone and pearl by a Hopewellian artist more than fifteen hundred years ago. Tobacco was placed in the bowl in the beaver's back, and the smoke was drawn through the hole in the base. Personal possessions like this were buried with their deceased owners in graves in earthen mounds.

A bird claw cut from mica by a Hopewellian artisan.

wealth of articles, including sacred and ceremonial objects, pendants, necklaces, armbands, and other decorative items, panpipes and rattles, tools, spoons and other utensils, and stone pipe bowls sculptured beautifully in the form of humans and animals. Fashioned from copper, bone, antler, stone, and shell, many of the objects were buried in the mounds with their deceased owners.

The mounds and other evidence suggest that Hopewellians had a highly developed social system that included a class structure, with rulers of hereditary rank and privileges; a strong religious system; specialists like artists, traders, and metalworkers; and organized direction over cooperative labor. After A.D. 500, the Hopewell star faded. It is not known what happened, or why. Perhaps the trade network on which so much had depended collapsed. At any rate, artistic abilities declined, fewer large burial mounds were constructed, and in various places people took to building,

The human hand was a predominant symbol in the art of the Temple Mound Builders. This example, a little larger than life size, was created from a single sheet of mica and was found in the grave of a high-ranking Hopewell chief in present-day Ohio.

OVERLEAF: *The Great Serpent Mound, a quarter-mile-long religious effigy rather than a burial mound, was built by Hopewellian people in southern Ohio and represents an uncoiling snake.*

Between A.D. 1000 and 1200, Mississippian artisans of the Southeast produced distinctive black pottery like this beaker engraved with pictographs of a skull and forearm bones found at Moundville in Alabama. Although the Mississippian people never developed a true phonetic writing system, the skull, along with other signs representing bones, human eyes, axes, shields, and crosses, probably inspired recitations of sacred songs dedicated to ancestors or deceased warriors, who were celebrated during feasts.

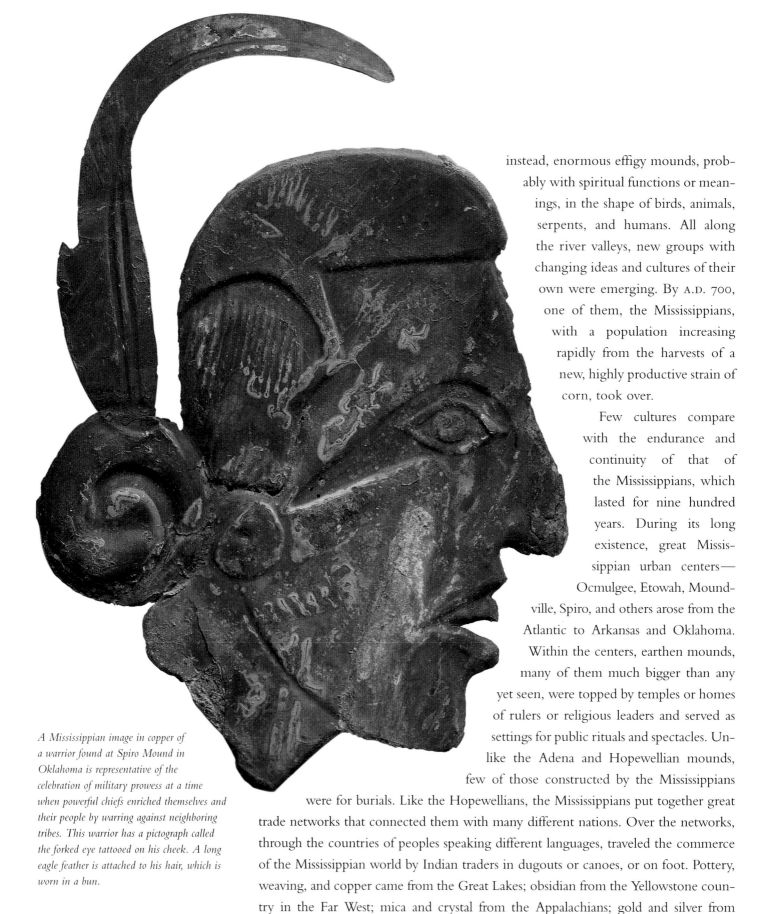

instead, enormous effigy mounds, probably with spiritual functions or meanings, in the shape of birds, animals, serpents, and humans. All along the river valleys, new groups with changing ideas and cultures of their own were emerging. By A.D. 700, one of them, the Mississippians, with a population increasing rapidly from the harvests of a new, highly productive strain of corn, took over.

Few cultures compare with the endurance and continuity of that of the Mississippians, which lasted for nine hundred years. During its long existence, great Mississippian urban centers— Ocmulgee, Etowah, Moundville, Spiro, and others arose from the Atlantic to Arkansas and Oklahoma. Within the centers, earthen mounds, many of them much bigger than any yet seen, were topped by temples or homes of rulers or religious leaders and served as settings for public rituals and spectacles. Unlike the Adena and Hopewellian mounds, few of those constructed by the Mississippians were for burials. Like the Hopewellians, the Mississippians put together great trade networks that connected them with many different nations. Over the networks, through the countries of peoples speaking different languages, traveled the commerce of the Mississippian world by Indian traders in dugouts or canoes, or on foot. Pottery, weaving, and copper came from the Great Lakes; obsidian from the Yellowstone country in the Far West; mica and crystal from the Appalachians; gold and silver from Canada; and conch shells from the Gulf of Mexico.

A Mississippian image in copper of a warrior found at Spiro Mound in Oklahoma is representative of the celebration of military prowess at a time when powerful chiefs enriched themselves and their people by warring against neighboring tribes. This warrior has a pictograph called the forked eye tattooed on his cheek. A long eagle feather is attached to his hair, which is worn in a bun.

Relatively few Mississippian artifacts have been found at the Cahokia site. A rare example is this ceramic vase or urn, portraying a woman holding a tiny child in her arms. The figurine's broad head is typical of those of the elite class, who practiced skull deformation and cut and formed their hair into exotic shapes as marks of beauty and nobility.

This Mississippian conch shell is engraved with the image of a dancer dressed as an eagle. Indian nations had very different perceptions of value and wealth that led them to trade their goods over great distances. The varieties of shell that were commonplace to coastal peoples were rare and highly valued by woodland tribes, who applied their skills as artisans to enhance the beauty and craftsmanship of an object, giving it greater value as a gift for exchanges during feasts. Hundreds of similar carved shell offerings have been found deposited as far from the sea as the mounds of Spiro, Oklahoma.

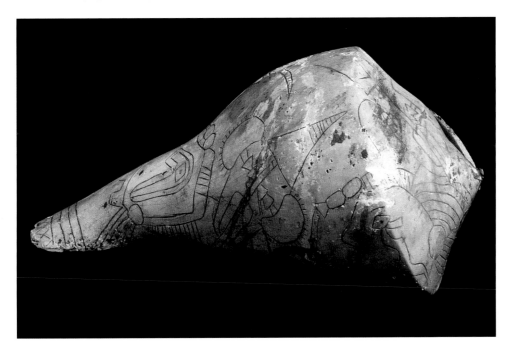

By the year 1000, much of the continent was again interconnected by trade. At its center, and at the center of the Mississippian world, three miles from the Mississippi River, across from the site of present-day St. Louis, one powerful city, Cahokia, stood alone. It was the largest urban community in the history of what would be the United States prior to the nineteenth century. Only in 1800 did the population of Philadelphia finally surpass the historic size of the Indian Cahokia. For almost seven hundred years, it was inhabited, and for three hundred years, from A.D. 850 to A.D. 1150, it was the heart of the Mississippian civilization.

The elite walled city of five square miles, containing more than a hundred large and small truncated pyramids and earthen mounds, was renowned over tens of thousands of square miles. At its peak, perhaps, more than ten thousand people lived within the city in homes of wattle and daub, with thousands more dwelling in outlying villages along the Mississippi River's bottomlands. Farmers, fishermen, hunters, artisans, builders, traders, and other specialists supplied the needs of an elite class of war chiefs and political and religious officials and their families and retainers who inhabited the city. At the top of the social system was Cahokia's absolute ruler, a revered chieftain known as the Great Sun, who dwelled with his relatives on the flattened top of Cahokia's biggest mound. Now called Monks Mound, it was ten stories high and had an earthen base far larger than that of any pyramid in Egypt or Mexico. From this forbidden holy estate, elevated toward the sky above the bustling urban center, Cahokia's hereditary monarch, the head of both state and religion, ruled like a god over all aspects of Mississippian life.

At the height of its power some ten thousand people lived at this Mississippian Temple Mound Building center, Cahokia, across the Mississippi River from the site of present-day St. Louis. Its main plaza and temple built upon an enormous truncated earthen pyramid also served as a religious center for thousands more in outlying settlements and farmsteads along miles of the Mississippi and its tributaries.

While centuries passed and other nations and civilizations around the world rose and fell, Cahokia lived on, and the Mississippian civilization spread its influences among scores of Indian societies, sometimes peacefully and sometimes by violence. Large, opulent centers of the Temple Mound Builders appeared from Florida to Texas, bound together loosely by common rituals, art motifs, symbols, and practices like the purification rites involving the use of a powerful emetic known as the Black Drink.

In time, Cahokia came to an end. By the sixteenth century, when invading Spanish conquistadors marched through the Mississippians' country, this once-great Indian urban center on the Mississippi River had become a ghost city of overgrown mounds. Perhaps it had outgrown its ability to feed itself, forcing its population to disperse and migrate elsewhere. But across the South, the Europeans found many Temple Mound Building nations still flourishing—Timucuas, Cherokees, Coosas, Muskokees, Mobiles, Choctaws, Chickasaws, Quapaws, and others—and in the country of the lower Mississippi as late as the eighteenth century, they encountered a regal Indian atop a grand mound who was carried on a litter and was venerated as a god—the Great Sun of the Natchez nation. He was the last major mound builder.

The influence of the Mississippians was felt most strongly across the southeastern part of what is now the United States. In the Northeast and in the area of the Great Lakes, meanwhile, the demise of the preceding Hopewellian civilization about A.D. 500–700 had been followed by the ascendance of a number of different regional and local groups. Among them were the ancestors of the Iroquois, a family of Indian nations destined for greatness.

Lesser-ranking chiefs and councillors at Cahokia lived in homes like this one built on smaller mounds surrounding the estate of the paramount chief, or Great Sun. Some elite families constituted craft guilds specializing in the production of pottery, shell or copper jewelry, or special tools or weapons. The re-created images on these two pages and throughout were made especially for 500 Nations on the computer, incorporating the latest scholarly research.

The Hodenosaunee: Dawn of Democracy

Whenever the statesmen of the League shall assemble for the purpose of holding a council, the Onondaga statesmen shall open it by expressing their gratitude to their cousin statesmen, and greeting them, and they shall make an address and offer thanks to the earth where men dwell, to the streams of water, the pools and the lakes, to the maize and the fruits, to the medicinal herbs and trees, to the forest trees for their usefulness, and to the animals that serve as food and give their pelts for clothing, to the great winds and the lesser winds, to the Thunderers; to the Sun, the mighty warrior; to the moon, to the messengers of the Creator who reveal his wishes, and to the Great Creator who dwells in the heavens above who gives all the things useful to men, and who is the source and the ruler of health and life.

Then shall the Onondaga statesmen declare the Council open. . . . All the business . . . shall be conducted by the two combined bodies of Confederate statesmen. First the question shall be passed upon by the Mohawk and Seneca statesmen, then it shall be discussed and passed by the Oneida and Cayuga statesmen. Their decision shall then be referred to the Onondaga statesmen, the Firekeepers, for final judgment.

FROM THE GREAT LAW OF PEACE OF THE
LEAGUE OF THE HODENOSAUNEE, OR IROQUOIS

A French engraving of 1734 depicts Hodenosaunee women cooking in the foreground while others at the rear work in the fields. Although they spent their lives toiling in the fields, preparing meals, and caring for their families, Hodenosaunee women held positions of great honor and respect. Property was inherited through the mother, and the oldest woman in every longhouse was known as "mother of the household."

Surrounded in large part by Algonquian-speaking peoples, the five nations of the Hodenosaunee, or Iroquois—the Mohawks, Oneidas, Onondagas, Cayugas, and Senecas—lived side by side in long parallel bands of territory running north–south in the valleys and along the lakes of what is now upper New York State. By A.D. 1000, they had been well established for centuries. Skillfully managing the natural bounty of the region, they hunted, fished, gath-

ered nuts, berries, and other wild foods, and cultivated increasingly productive gardens, principally of corn, beans, and squash.

The tribes were divided into clans that served as extended families, with clan membership passing from mother to child. Within the clans, the children were taught by elders, the needy and the sick were cared for, and community responsibilities were defined. When persons were ready to marry, they had to do so outside of their own clan—an injunction that tended to weave the entire tribe together into a single great family. The clans lived in large bark-covered longhouses, barrel roofed, like the Quonset huts of World War II, and extending up to two hundred feet in length and twenty-five feet in width. A single longhouse could shelter ten or a dozen families through a harsh winter, each one with its own private space and a fire that it shared with others. The family sections contained raised platforms covered with reed mats or pelts that served as seats during the day and beds at night. Articles of clothing were hung on the walls or, with food and supplies, were stored in bark bins and baskets.

Theirs was a world in which each person, man and woman, had an important

Pre-Columbian Hodenosaunee (Iroquois) people lived in villages of great longhouses, some over 150 feet in length and occupied by up to a dozen families. The members of each family slept on platforms at ground level and used the upper platforms to store tobacco, corn, baskets, wooden bowls, clothing, and skins.

Taking full advantage of his woodland environment, a Hodenosaunee craftsman carved this remarkable set of a bowl and spoons from hard maple. Such utensils undoubtedly impressed visiting delegations who would travel great distances to discuss the affairs of their confederated nations with feasts and religious celebrations.

function. Men were hunters and warriors, providers and protectors of the community. Women owned the houses, gathered wild foods, cooked, made baskets and clothing, and cared for the children. Spiritual life, strong and pervasive throughout the society, was highly organized. It included a priesthood of men and women Keepers of the Faith who supervised religious rites and various secret organizations that performed curing and other ceremonies. Like many Indians, the Iroquois believed that the spirits of all humans were joined to those of the objects and forces of nature, and, in addition, that a human's own inner spiritual power, called *orenda,* combated the powers of evil that could harm the individual as well as the rest of the people. Although an individual's *orenda* was small, it contributed to the total *orenda* possessed by a family group or clan. When a person died, the group's total *orenda* was reduced and was often replenished by the adoption of a captive or a member of another tribe to acquire his or her *orenda.*

Whenever the statesmen of the League shall assemble they shall offer thanks to the earth where men dwell, to the streams of water, the pools and the lakes, to the maize and the fruits.

—FROM THE GREAT LAW OF THE HODENOSAUNEE

Bravery and fortitude were highly respected virtues among the Iroquois. When a man died in warfare against an enemy, it was the clan, not just the parents or wife of the fighting man, that mourned the loss. In addition, the clan was held responsible for avenging the warrior's death. Generations ago, prior to the coming of the white man, an unending cycle of raid and counterraid, death and revenge, began to run out of control among the five Hodenosaunee nations. The fabric of their civilization was on the verge of being torn apart by the feuds and warfare among them.

In the engraving opposite, published in France in 1664, Hodenosaunee women are shown grinding corn or dried berries. In the rear a baby rests on a cradleboard. Lineages were traced through women, and when men married, they left their own homes and resided with the families of their wives.

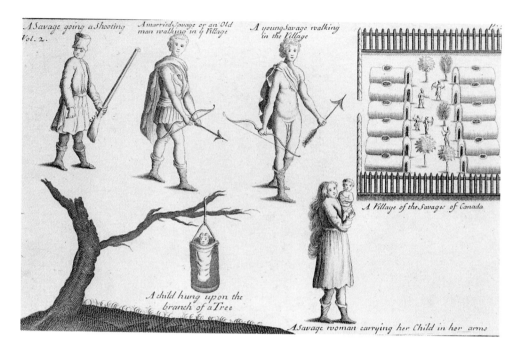

When Europeans first penetrated the Northeast, they found many Indian villages surrounded by defensive palisades. The longhouses within the walls were arranged in rows, and gardens were maintained next to the longhouses. This engraving from a French book published in 1703 depicts Hodenosaunee in Canada.

Attempts to break the cycle of violence had been thwarted repeatedly by a sinister Onondaga war priest named Thadodaho, who in Iroquois legend was a monstrous figure with snakes for hair, hands like turtle claws, and the feet of a bear. Committed to warfare and the death and destruction of his enemies, he opposed all efforts to achieve peace.

One year, a visionary Huron elder named Deganawida appeared in the Iroquois territory, preaching a powerful message of peace. In his travels, he met an Onondaga man named Hiawatha, who was himself caught in the violence of the time. Hiawatha listened to the message of Deganawida. The Peace Maker, as Deganawida was becoming known, conceived of thirteen laws by which people and nations could live in peace and unity—a democracy where the needs of all would be accommodated without violence and bloodshed. To a modern American, it would suggest a society functioning under values and laws similar to those of the Ten Commandments and the U.S. Constitution combined. Each of its laws included a moral structure.

Longfellow borrowed the Hodenosaunee name Hiawatha for the hero of his famous poem about a Chippewa Indian of the Midwest. Here, compounding the confusion, the fictitious Hiawatha of the poem is pictured romantically by the celebrated American artist Frederic Remington, dressed as an Indian of the western plains.

> In all of your . . . acts, self-interest shall be cast away. . . . Look and listen for the welfare of the whole people, and have always in view not only the present, but also the coming generations . . . the unborn of the future Nation.

Hiawatha became a supporter of the Peace Maker and his Great Law and, because of his strong oratorical skills, was its principal spokesman, constructing, according to legend, the first wampum belt, a beaded system of coded information employed in reciting the Great Law. Then, with this system for recording and expressing their beliefs, both Deganawida the Peace Maker and Hiawatha took the word to each of the most powerful leaders among the five tribes. The simple truth and justice of the new law was undeniable, and soon only one chief, Thadodaho, stood as an obstacle to regional peace. Hiawatha went to the village of the violent leader and, using all his skills of persuasion, expressed the dream of peace. So moving was the message that, as legend has it, Thadodaho was transformed from a demon into a man, and finally to a champion of the Great Law. The Hodenosaunee, or Iroquois, Confederacy had begun. The Peace Maker then planted as a symbol of peace a great white pine tree.

> Under the shade of this Tree of Great Peace . . . there shall you sit and watch the Fire of the League of Five Nations. . . . Roots have spread out from the Tree of Great Peace. . . . These are the Great White Roots, and their nature is Peace and Strength. If any man or any nation shall obey the laws of the Great Peace . . . they may trace back the roots to the Tree. . . . They shall be welcomed to take shelter beneath the Great Evergreen Tree.

To administer the law, the Hodenosaunee imposed an order and a structure on their world. They envisioned the combined territory of the five nations as a gigantic longhouse that stretched 250 miles across the present-day state of New York. The

Hodenosaunee wampum belts were made of purple and white beads cut and drilled from the shells of whelks and quahog clams by Long Island and New England coastal tribes and traded inland. Bearing symbolic images, the belts were used to commemorate important events and solemnize agreements. This belt, damaged and incomplete but still perhaps the most important of all Hodenosaunee belts, is known as the Hiawatha Belt and symbolizes the formation of the League. The pine tree in the center represents the League, and the joined rectangles symbolize four of the member nations.

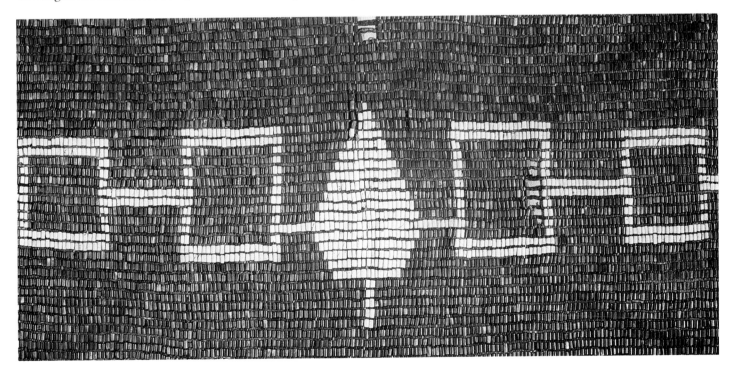

ALICE PAPINEAU/ONONDAGA

"We are known as the people of the Hodenosaunee, which means people of the longhouse. That was the type of houses that we lived in. And for each house were clans, clan houses. . . . And we all had one way of believing throughout the Hodenosaunee. Maybe a little difference in the ceremonies, maybe a little different way, but all with the same meaning. And we all basically ate the same kind of food. Our basic food is corn, beans, and squash. . . . And one of the rules to live in a community like that was to get along in harmony. And we had our teachings from our Peacemaker—we're not allowed to use his name, but we call him the Peacemaker—who is the one who originated our political structure and also the spiritual way of life."

OPPOSITE: *The Mohawk chief King Hendrick, painted in London in 1710.*

Great Longhouse's central aisle was the Hodenosaunee Trail, the principal route of communication between the different members of the League. The eastern end of the domain was guarded by the Mohawks, who were declared the Keepers of the Eastern Door. The Senecas watched over the western door, and the Onondagas, located at the center, were the Keepers of the Fire for all five member nations of the Great Longhouse.

The posts conceived as supporting the Great Longhouse symbolically represented the tribal chiefs, who among the Iroquois attained their position in a unique way. In each nation, the women of every clan selected the most respected woman among them to be the clan mother. The clan mothers, in turn, appointed the male chiefs to represent the clans at the Grand Council. In this way, the men most trusted by their people for wisdom, integrity, vision, fairness, oratorical ability, and other statesmanlike qualities were given the responsibility of the Great Law.

With endless patience, they shall carry out their duty. Their firmness shall be tempered with a tenderness for their people. Neither anger nor fury shall find lodging in their minds, and all their words and actions shall be marked by calm deliberation.

The structure of the Hodenosaunee government, allowing different states to coexist under one rule of law, was a concept in democracy. The Grand Council met at the Hodenosaunee capital of Onondaga. The Oneidas and Cayugas, the younger brothers in the League, sat to the west of the council fire, the elder brothers, the Mohawks and Senecas, sat to the east, with the Onondagas to the north. Decisions were made by the representatives of each nation, who first reached consensus among themselves; then the brothers on the east and west would confer until they reached consensus. After that was accomplished, the elder brothers passed their decision to the younger brothers. If the younger brothers could accept the decision, the permanent leader of the council, an Onondaga, would announce consensus. If, on the other hand, the younger brothers could not accept the decision of the elder brothers, the Onondaga would cast the deciding vote and break the deadlock.

The system worked. The confederacy envisioned by the Peace Maker and Hiawatha, together with the republican and democratic principles that lay at the heart of its form of self-government, influenced enlightened seventeenth- and eighteenth-century white philosophers and writers in the colonies and Europe who were seeking just ways for their own people to be governed. In 1754

To secure their friendship and assistance against the French, British colonial authorities in 1710 sent four chiefs, a Mahican and three Mohawks of the Hodenosaunee League, to England to meet Queen Anne. In London they were dressed in court costume and had their portraits painted against imaginative backdrops. The distinguished Mohawk chief on the previous page, known to the English as King Hendrick, is shown holding a wampum belt. At his side the artist has included a wolf, representing Hendrick's lineage. In 1755, Hendrick was killed fighting for the English against the French at Lake George in upper New York State. Seen above is another of the three Mohawk chiefs who visited England, listed by the artist as Ho Nee Yeath Taw No Row, was painted in strange court garb, holding a bow, and with a quiver full of arrows on the ground at his side. At near right, the third Mohawk chief, holding a musket and displaying his body paintings or tattoos, was a member of the Bear Clan and the grandfather of Joseph Brant, the pro-British Iroquois leader during the American Revolution. At far right, the fourth "Indian King," painted with a ball-headed war club and an English dress sword, was a Mahican neighbor of the Mohawks from the upper Hudson River Valley.

Benjamin Franklin's Albany Plan of Union for the British colonies drew inspiration from the example of the Iroquois League. Later, the structure of the League had an indirect influence, through the studies of the political philosophers by the Founding Fathers of the United States, not only on the union of the colonies, but on the government of the United States as it was constituted in 1789. In the method, for instance, by which Congress reaches consensus on bills through compromise meetings of House and Senate conferees, one may recognize similarities to the way in which the Iroquois League functioned.

The new United States did not go as far as the Hodenosaunees, for, unlike the Indians, it did not accord equality to all men and both genders among its people. While the United States and other nations of the world struggled during later generations to rectify such inequities, the Great Law of the Hodenosaunee remained unchanged and still guides the Grand Council of the People of the Longhouse—one of the world's oldest continuing democracies—to this day.

The Anasazis

Far off in the American Southwest, Indian peoples, in the meantime, had developed still other high cultures and civilizations totally unlike those of the Mound Builders or the politically astute Iroquois in the Northeast. Among them were the ancestors of the present-day Pueblos, Zuñis, and Hopis of New Mexico and Arizona. Still among some of the most traditional Indians in the Americas, most of them—as expressed by a modern-day Bluebird chief of one of the Hopi villages—continue to observe the spiritual beliefs and practices of their forefathers of thousands of years ago:

> Our religious teachings are based upon the proper care of our land and the people who live upon it. We must not lose the way of life of our religion. . . . We believe in that; we live it, day by day. . . . We the leaders of the traditional Hopi . . . want our way of life to continue on; for ourselves, for our children, and for their children who come after. . . .

Carved on boulders near the ruins of Wupatki, Arizona, these petroglyphs are representations of serpents, corn, and human beings. Petroglyphs often mark sacred sites that are important to the recounting of the histories and odysseys of the original clan ancestors of the Hopi, Zuñi, and Rio Grande Pueblo peoples. Tribal members still visit these sites to document the stories of their ancestors.

The boy cried and cried. The blood came out, and finally he died. With his tears our lakes became. With his blood the red clay became. With his body our mountains became, and that was how Earth became.

—TAOS ELDERS

The forefathers of the modern-day tribes were themselves descendants of some of the earliest-known peoples in the Americas—nomadic groups who had hunted mastodons and other big-game animals across much of the Southwest during the Ice Age. Later, when the glaciers retreated and those animals disappeared, the people developed a different culture, suited to the more arid conditions. Based on fishing and the hunting of small animals and birds, but most important on the gathering of all manner of edible, wild-growing foods, their lifeway is known to archaeologists as the Desert culture. Spread far and wide through the dry country of the West and into northern Mexico, it lasted in various places, particularly in the desert areas of the Great Basin, for almost ten thousand years.

In some areas, however, beginning about 1000 B.C., agricultural knowledge and skills were introduced from Mexico, and during the following two thousand years, three major civilizations of farming peoples arose in parts of the region. The first, the Mogollon, developed in the forested mountain country along the present Arizona–New Mexico border. Some of the Mogollon Indians, who lived in New Mexico's

Mimbres Valley from approximately A.D. 750 to 1250, were expert potters, whose works, painted with exquisite natural figures or geometric designs, have been acclaimed by art critics and collectors as among the most beautiful produced anywhere in the world, including ancient Greece. When the Indian owner of a pot died, holes were punched through it to "kill" the spirit of its painted figures, and the pot was buried in the owner's grave, where archaeologists and modern-day pot hunters and grave robbers have found them.

The origin of a second civilization, the Hohokams, which was centered in the hot, lower desert country of southern Arizona, is still something of a puzzle. Archaeologists are not yet decided on whether the Hohokams were a migrant group who brought their culture with them from Mexico, or whether they evolved locally from previous Desert culture Indians. Flourishing from approximately 300 B.C. to A.D. 1450, they were highly skilled farmers who seem to have introduced irrigation agriculture to the arid West, building hundreds of miles of canals to carry water from the Salt and other rivers to their fields of maize, beans, squash, and cotton around present-day Phoenix and Tucson. The Hohokams maintained trade networks with tribes in northern Mexico, including peoples who lived along the Gulf of California, produced many articles of artistic beauty, and constructed ball courts similar to those

The Mimbres people lived between A.D. 200 and 1150 in an area of some thirteen thousand square miles in the southern part of present-day New Mexico. They produced some of the finest painted pottery in the world, decorated with lively art both in geometric and figurative styles.

Shells from tribes on the Gulf of California and the Pacific coast were highly valued and exchanged in trade for turquoise, copper, and other commodities by the Hohokam people of the interior Southwest, whose craftsmen transformed the shells into personal ornaments and religious objects. The horned toad on this Hohokam shell pendant was etched with acidic cactus sap that ate away the surface around the toad's silhouette.

Covering a 140-foot-long section of vertical sandstone cliffs in Horseshoe Canyon, west of Canyonlands National Park in southern Utah, these giant figures with elongated bodies were painted with red ochre by Anasazis.

used much farther south by the Mayas and other nations of Mesoamerica. Their end is also in doubt, although it is widely believed that they were the ancestors of today's O'Odham (Pima and Papago) Indian nations of the Southwest.

By A.D. 900, a third, and greater, civilization, encompassing some influences from both the Mogollons and Hohokams, had arisen on the Colorado Plateau in the high Four Corners country of southern Utah and Colorado, northern Arizona and New Mexico. Today, their Hopi descendants refer to them as the Hisatsinom, but they are better known by the name the Navajos gave them, the Anasazis, meaning "Ancient Enemies."

For hundreds of years, the earliest Anasazis lived in subterranean pit houses, sunken homes with stonework walls and broad, strong roofs, providing protection from the searing summer sun and the bitter winter cold of the western environment. In time, they began to adapt their aboveground storage houses into living quarters, retaining the underground pit houses as spiritual centers, known as kivas, used for religious teaching and rituals and as meeting places for clans. In the center of the circular kivas was a hole, symbolizing *sipapu,* the place of origin through which their ancestors had emerged into this world. Here in the kivas, the Anasazi clan leaders formalized a theocratic society and a faith that have guided and protected the Puebloan peoples to this day.

Gradually, the Anasazi society expanded. Indian villages joined together to harness water with earthen dams, reservoirs, and irrigation systems, turning parts of the high desert into gardens of corn and other crops. Where there was no surface water,

The social life of the early Anasazis was centered in small villages of subterranean pit houses with a roof supported by poles, a central fireplace, and a smoke hole in the roof. Eventually, as the Anasazis began to live aboveground, these single-family dwellings evolved into kivas, the secret religious centers of male members of the clans.

I have lived surrounded by the earth on six sides. It is all around me. It is above my head and beneath my feet. It is in four directions also.

—NANCY WOOD

they utilized moisture deposited deep down in the sandy soil during seasons of flood and developed plants with roots deep enough to reach these invisible pools. Well-fed, stable populations increased and experienced a flowering of culture and art.

The Anasazis' abilities at basket making, which had been evolving for more than a thousand years, were joined by another skill—that of pottery making. With every generation, the beautifully crafted and painted pots improved in durability and variety. Religion and trade unified the region, and as the movement of goods and ideas increased, the Anasazi leadership planned a new strategy.

In the very center of their world was a vast and treeless region that supported little habitation. In this harsh environment in northwestern New Mexico's Chaco Canyon, they constructed a center for their civilization—a place where traders exchanged goods and spiritual pilgrimages ended. They built more than four hundred miles of roads and broad avenues leading to the canyon from the different regions of

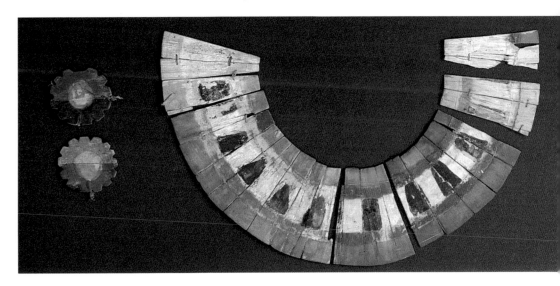

These Anasazi carved and painted wooden objects, found in a cave at Chaco Canyon, are personal decorations, or jewelry, dated at about A.D. 1100. They include a set of wooden earrings and the slats of a wooden necklace.

By A.D. 1100, many Anasazi communities in the canyons and mesas of the present-day Four Corners country of the American Southwest had developed into large settlements of multiroomed apartment buildings constructed of masonry blocks covered with adobe plaster. The biggest, Pueblo Bonito in Chaco Canyon, whose semicircular dwelling units, great circular kivas, and outlying gardens are seen here in a computer-generated re-creation, covered more than three acres and could house more than a thousand people. Built a millennium ago, it was the world's largest "apartment house" until 1882, when it was eclipsed by a bigger one in New York City.

their country. The roads were unique and distinctive, perfectly straight lanes that passed through or over obstructions rather than around them. At distant points along the roads, signal stations were erected and fires maintained to communicate across the vast stretches of the desert and guide travelers at night. On the roads the Indians hauled the timber and resources to build and maintain twelve towns having a population of five thousand or more in the canyon. Carried along also were new ideas gleaned from other peoples that would help the development of the new Chacoan civilization.

Like the Gothic cathedrals, whose construction in Europe began a hundred years later, beautifully crafted great kivas were built throughout the Anasazis' territory. Chaco's were huge and magnificent, many of them able to hold more than five hundred people. Tons of timbers, making up the vast roofs and support systems, had to be transported from far distances without the use of beasts of burden. Within the great kivas, the Anasazi clans kept alive the ancient underground heritage.

Grand as the various towns and structures in Chaco Canyon were, none compared with the largest single building the Anasazis ever constructed, Pueblo Bonito, the architectural jewel of the canyon. At the peak of its occupation, Pueblo Bonito housed over a thousand residents in more than six hundred rooms—craftsmen, merchants, and government and religious leaders and their families. The main plaza was constructed as a great amphitheater with some sections looming five stories above the canyon floor. It was the busy heart of Anasazi religion and trade. The commerce in one stone, turquoise, more valuable to traders who came up from Mexico than gold or jade, was the engine of Pueblo Bonito's wealth and power. Here, the raw stone would arrive from distant mines for the craftsmen of Pueblo Bonito to cut and shape into small tiles. Once prepared, the turquoise tiles would be shipped south to the merchant centers in the heart of Mexico. There they would be transformed into extra-ordinary jeweled creations. For a hundred years the precious North American stone flowed out of the canyon while goods and technology flowed in from throughout the Southwest, California, and Mexico.

Chaco was the center of a sophisticated and creative civilization, but its wealth and power were fleeting. We do not know exactly what made its populations move after two centuries. Turquoise began trading heavily from other locations in Arizona and Nevada. Its abundance may have devalued it. At the same time, Chaco's major turquoise consumer, Tollan, the Toltec capital in Mexico, fell to civil strife. More likely, a terrible fifty-year-long series of droughts, beginning about A.D. 1130, which dried up the water sources, was a deciding factor in the abandonment of Chaco Canyon. By the thirteenth century, it was deserted, and the great turquoise road over the Mexican High Sierra had been abandoned with it.

During the abandonment of Chaco Canyon, the Mesa Verde Anasazis farther north began to move from the tops of mesas to recesses in the walls of cliffs. This may have been for defensive reasons, but it is not yet known who might have threatened them. Shown here is the Cliff Palace, the largest of the Mesa Verde cliff-wall ruins, which contained some 220 rooms and twenty-three kivas.

Despite the demise of the powerful capital, the hush over Chaco Canyon did not mean the end of Anasazi society. In fact, it was now expanding and flourishing anew in the surrounding Four Corners region. To the north, high on the pine-studded mesas and in the fertile valleys of southern Colorado, a large population had become concentrated around Mesa Verde. As Chaco Canyon was being abandoned, the Mesa Verde Indians, many of whom migrated from Chaco itself, started to move their dwelling sites, seeking the protection of recesses in the steep cliffs that dropped from the top of the mesas. While the adjacent Montezuma Valley had a population of thirty thousand, the Cliff Dwellers of Mesa Verde numbered only three thousand but lived in some of the most stunning and enduring buildings of all time, built in the recesses of the cliff walls. The largest of them has been called the Cliff Palace.

Among the Anasazis, there were, in fact, no palaces or special buildings set aside for the powerful or wealthy. All lived alike, the religious and civil leaders, the farmers, the pottery makers, hunters, stonemasons, healers, and spinners and weavers of fine cotton. At Mesa Verde, the people farmed the mesa top, reaching their town by climbing the sheer cliff walls with finger- and toe-holds.

In time the cliff towns, too, were given up. By A.D. 1300 entire regions had been abandoned by the Anasazis. One can only speculate why scores of towns and thousands of square miles in the Southwest were suddenly emptied of people. The Anasazis' lucrative trade with Mexico had evaporated, droughts may have crippled their economies, and it is possible that peace itself had come to an end as the Navajo and Apache nations, Athapascan peoples at the end of an epic migration from northwestern Canada and Alaska, moved into the region. The question of the abandonment of the cliff towns may always be a mystery.

Once more, the Anasazi people themselves did not disappear. By the tens of thousands, they moved again—most of them to the east and the Rio Grande Valley, to Alcanfor, Taos, Piro, and many other towns, where the Spaniards came upon them two centuries later and called them Pueblo Indians. Others went to the Hopi and Zuñi towns in present-day Arizona and New Mexico and merged with the population of those nations. The Navajos eventually took over the heart of the traditional Anasazi country, while most of the Apache peoples established themselves in the more southerly areas that Mogollons and Hohokams had once dominated.

The period of the ancient ones came to an abrupt end, and the modern Southwest world began. The traditions that live today among the various Puebloan peoples and were encountered by the Spaniards in the sixteenth century are the resonance of the Anasazi heritage that reaches back through generations to places like Chaco Canyon and Mesa Verde.

JIMMY REYNA/TAOS PUEBLO

"And when I quit the city and came home, I found myself where I was supposed to be before. Everything is beautiful, the mountain changes, every, every time I look at it, it changes. The water, don't change the sound—the air is the same, flows. The spirit, when the tree is shaking then I realize that the spirit is there. . . . People live not even knowing, all they know is the top of their shoes today. They don't know the glory, the what we're living underneath. Beauty, nighttime, daytime that is what the things are that I value."

OPPOSITE: *Mesa Verde's Spruce Tree House was constructed in a recess in a cliff wall adjacent to a spring, and more than 150 people may have lived there at once. The courtyard between the apartments was constructed on the roofs of two underground kivas. By the end of the thirteenth century, the inhabitants had migrated elsewhere, and these remarkable dwellings had been abandoned. Today, many Hopi, Zuñi, and Pueblo peoples trace the origin of their clans to the Cliff Dwellers of Mesa Verde.*

CHAPTER 2

EMPIRES

This ceramic incense brazier, with the mask of a god in a quetzal-feathered headdress, was the work of an artisan at the great urban center of Teotihuacán, near present-day Mexico City, about A.D. 650.

OVERLEAF: *This twentieth-century mural by Diego Rivera, in the Presidential Palace in Mexico City, depicts incidents from the life and legends of the god-king Quetzalcoatl.*

The Mexican Hearth

Today North America is seen as three nations: Canada, the United States, and Mexico. But the political lines that separate them are relatively recent creations, drawn clearly only a hundred and fifty years ago. Similarly, a language difference now acts bluntly to separate Mexico from its neighbors to the north. In pre-Columbian days, that division had no meaning. By trade and migration, the diffusion of ideas and skills from Mexico, including the knowledge of maize agriculture, moved north across a landscape without modern political borders, affecting with varying degrees of intensity the lives and cultures of Indian nations from the present-day American Southwest to eastern Canada. Until the coming of Europeans, Indian Mexico in many ways was the vital hearth of the continent, radiating out from its center the traits and influences of its great native civilizations.

During the first millennium A.D., while Mayan rulers like Pacal at Palenque built powerful city-states in southern Mesoamerica, other Indian nations created civilizations of their own in the highlands and valleys of central Mexico and along the coasts of the Gulf of Mexico and the Pacific Ocean.

The area was a dynamic one, with a population of millions of people representing diverse tribal backgrounds and languages. During the preceding centuries, some groups had kept pace with the Mayas, adopting many elements of the widespread but receding Olmec civilization, adding to it innovations and inventions of their own and developing important new local and regional cultures based largely

The Pyramid of the Sun, 213 feet high, looms above the ruins of one of Teotihuacán's multi-roomed palaces.

on intensive agriculture. Like the Mayas, they employed slash-and-burn farming techniques, in which new fields were burned, cleared, and planted about every three years while the old ones rested or returned to forest; practiced terracing and crop rotation; constructed large-scale irrigation systems; and built artificial islands, called *chinampas,* of rich muck on rafts that took root in lakes and swamps, and on which agricultural yields increased dramatically. (One can still see *chinampas,* or "floating islands," in daily use in the Xochimilco section of Mexico City.)

By about A.D. 500, at a time when the Dark Ages were settling over western Europe, Teotihuacán, a center of population in the Valley of Mexico, had developed into North America's first large urban area and the seat of a far-reaching military and economic empire. Covering eight square miles and surrounded by suburbs and small farming communities, Teotihuacán was a true city, with a metropolitan population of almost 150,000, which dwarfed the size of Rome and all other European cities of the time. To put it into perspective, even eight hundred years later, in A.D. 1300, London had attained a population of only 60,000 and Paris 80,000.

Teotihuacán was laid out on a grid system with careful urban planning by surveyors, engineers, architects, artisans, and priests. The city's broad, central axis, the regal Avenue of the Dead, almost two miles long, was flanked by monumental temple platforms, palaces, courtyards, schools, a central marketplace, and blocks of multiroomed residential units, with

GULF OF MEXICO

Lake Texcoco •Tollan
Tenochtitlán •Teotihuacán
Valley of Mexico •Cholula

Monte Alban • •Oaxaca
•Mitla

PACIFIC OCEAN

lime-plastered walls painted, inside and out, in brilliant colors or with magnificent murals. At one end of the avenue, the city was dominated by the Pyramid of the Sun, a stepped construction 213 feet high with a base more than 730 feet long on each side, and a smaller Pyramid of the Moon. Rising in five terraces to a temple platform, the Pyramid of the Sun was built originally over a sacred cave and was one of the largest structures in Mesoamerica. At the other end of the avenue was the Citadel, the center of the city's ruling power, the home of its highest-born lords, and the site of the carved and painted Temple of Quetzalcoatl, or Feathered Serpent, a principal god inherited probably from the Olmecs and worshiped in many guises and with varying attributes by numerous Mesoamerican nations.

Teotihuacán's population was a cosmopolitan one, composed of chieftains, pilgrims, and others from many parts of Mexico who had been drawn for political or economic reasons to the metropolis. The society was highly stratified. Elite families occupied luxurious housing, while workers, artisans of all types, and traders from other towns and regions—some of which were joined with Teotihuacán in a confederacy—lived in apartment complexes within ethnic compounds specially designated for their respective groups.

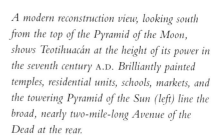

A modern reconstruction view, looking south from the top of the Pyramid of the Moon, shows Teotihuacán at the height of its power in the seventh century A.D. Brilliantly painted temples, residential units, schools, markets, and the towering Pyramid of the Sun (left) line the broad, nearly two-mile-long Avenue of the Dead at the rear.

A carved and painted image of the Feathered, or Plumed, Serpent, from a replica of the façade of Teotihuacán's Temple of Quetzalcoatl in the National Museum of Anthropology and History in Mexico City.

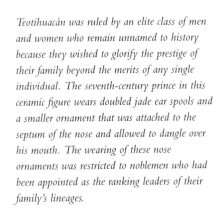

The demands and needs of the elite class for functional and luxury goods led to an outpouring of beautiful works by full-time painters, sculptors, masons, craftsmen, and other specialists. A wealth of ornamentation, jewelry, featherwork, and other decorative garb was produced by Teotihuacán artisans, as were murals, carvings, pottery, and exquisitely wrought utensils and household wares. The city's streets and plazas were paved with cement that covered underground conduits and, with the grandeur of the public buildings, reflected the presence of highly accomplished planners and builders. Calendar systems were in use, and at the end of each cycle of fifty-two years, fires were extinguished and new ones lit, temples were enlarged or reconstructed, and the world's rebirth was celebrated. At other times, frequent rituals and ceremonial processions from the Pyramids of the Sun and Moon to the shrine of the Feathered Serpent, presided over by hierarchies of priests and secular leaders, bound the people together in observance of a common heritage, mutual worship of the gods, and allegiance to the ruling kings.

By commerce, alliances, and sometimes military conquests, Teotihuacán spread its influence and many elements of its culture across much of Mesoamerica, even into the Mayan lowlands far to the south in Belize, Guatemala, Honduras, and El Salvador. And in time, Teotihuacán ideas, practices, and products were carried northward by traders and others over large parts of the Mexican plateau and up the Sierra Madre Occidental to the Indian nations in what is now New Mexico and Arizona, and possibly beyond to peoples in the Mississippi Valley and the present-day U.S. Southeast.

Not every move was a peaceful one. In some places, the Teotihuacán empire established authority over native populations by threats or force. Little is known of military expeditions that may have brought other cities under the domination of Teotihuacán agents or colonies, but recent excavations at Teotihuacán's Temple of Quetzalcoatl have unearthed the skeletal remains of nearly twenty warriors believed to have been captive enemy noblemen who were ritually killed there. Around the necks of many of them were strung trophies of human jaws.

After almost a thousand years of existence, Teotihuacán declined. The overuse and

Teotihuacán was ruled by an elite class of men and women who remain unnamed to history because they wished to glorify the prestige of their family beyond the merits of any single individual. The seventh-century prince in this ceramic figure wears doubled jade ear spools and a smaller ornament that was attached to the septum of the nose and allowed to dangle over his mouth. The wearing of these nose ornaments was restricted to noblemen who had been appointed as the ranking leaders of their family's lineages.

deforestation of the surrounding countryside may have led to economic crises and a recognition that the land and natural resources on which the city had depended could no longer support its large population. At some time in the seventh or eighth century, Teotihuacán was destroyed, burned either by rebellious factions within the city or by outside enemies. Although people continued to live in the ruins, it was never rebuilt. In time, the population drifted away. Other cities rose, attracting Teotihuacán's former residents. By A.D. 900, the origins of Teotihuacán were lost in myth; the city was abandoned and silent. The people of Teotihuacán had left architecture, but no writing or commemorative art, and the leaders had been cremated rather than entombed. To the later-arriving Aztecs, the city's mammoth pyramids, shrines, and empty Avenue of the Dead were a mystery. In awe, they called it simply "The place where men became gods."

With Teotihuacán's end and the dispersal of its population, other cities in central Mexico assumed importance. The Zapotec and Mixtec Indian cities of Monte Alban and Mitla in the hills of Oaxaca became almost as influential and architecturally grand as Teotihuacán. Elsewhere, at Cholula, near present-day Puebla, urban dwellers led by a dynasty of Olmeca-Xicalanca rulers enlarged an ancient pyramid into the biggest structure ever built by American Indians. Approximately 180 feet

As Teotihuacán rose to become North America's first military empire, soldiers were recruited through obligatory service to the state, and for the first time conventional armies of thousands of men dominated the battlefield. This ceramic figure portrays an ornately dressed Teotihuacán warrior, around A.D. 650. The tiny disks attached to his cheeks and the jade ear spools represent awards for achievement in combat and for service to his lord. His hair is decorated with a crown of short feathers, and a heraldic device is attached to the leather strap that passes over his forehead. His shield would have been made of wicker and reinforced with carved wooden ornaments.

A ceramic portrayal of a Teotihuacán nobleman in a huge headdress, about A.D. 650.

New excavations have uncovered evidence of ritual sacrifice in Teotihuacán. These ceremonial flint knives, inlaid with shell and obsidian to form faces, were used by Aztec priests to cut the living hearts from sacrificial victims. To the Aztecs, the offering of the human heart—shown below in a sixteenth-century Aztec drawing—was the supreme sacrifice to their gods, ensuring the continued strength of the deities on whom the people's life and well-being depended.

high and more than 900 feet long on each side, it covered 40 acres and exceeded the volume of Teotihuacán's Pyramid of the Sun, Cahokia's Monks Mound on the Mississippi River, or any pyramid ever erected in Egypt. Inside the pyramid, which was dedicated to Quetzalcoatl, were miles of tunnels, one of them painted with lively murals of *bebedores* (drinkers). Other notable successors to Teotihuacán were Xochicalco, a large, fortresslike city on steep, terraced hills in Morelos, and El Tajín, a Totonac Indian city on the Gulf coast in Veracruz, towered over by a seven-tiered pyramid with 365 niches, one for each day of the solar year, and including palaces, temples, and seven ball courts, one with carved panels depicting a ball game and human sacrifices.

By A.D. 900, Mesoamerica had become a world of ferment and change, ripe for new regional leadership. The vast trade network and routes of communication that interconnected the economies of the populated centers still remained, but once the region had settled into a pattern of new states smaller than Teotihuacán had been, it needed a strong, new agent to maintain peace, regulate orderly trade, and secure the states and their borders.

The Toltecs filled that void.

Calendars were important to pre-Columbian cultures. This sacred calendar from an Aztec manuscript known today as the Codex Borgia reflects the religious philosophy that recognized both good and evil attributes in the gods. The two pages depict, from the lower left corner, Tecciztecatl, the goddess of the moon who presided over the day Death, followed, at the right, by the water goddess Chalchiutlicue, who ruled the day Serpent. In the upper right corner appears Tezcatlipoca, the fierce war god, patron of the day Eagle, followed, at the left, by the ferocious demon Itzpapalotl, or "Obsidian Butterfly," who presided over the day Vulture.

The Toltecs

Rising to dominance from their city of Tollan, about fifty miles north of present-day Mexico City, Toltec priests and kings for two centuries ushered in to Mesoamerica a new age of glittering artistic and intellectual life, backed by military might. Largely because their rulers became identified with—and were worshiped as—gods, their origin and history became shrouded in myths, told and retold in many versions.

It is known that some of their ancestors were once members of Teotihuacán's elite, who fled from that city and migrated north of the Valley of Mexico, wandering for a long time in distress and suffering among less advanced agricultural and hunting and gathering peoples, some of whom joined them. According to an account of the Toltecs' history that the Aztecs later related to the Spaniards:

> They eventually went to settle at a place in the desert. At this place there were . . . seven caves. These different people made the caves serve as their temples; they went to make their offerings there for a long time. No longer is it remembered how long they resided there. Then the one whom the Tolteca worshipped [Quetzalcoatl] spoke to them; he said to them: "Turn back. You shall go from whence you came." Then they went to make offerings there in Chicomoztoc. Then they departed. First they came to arrive at a place called Tollantzinco. Then they passed over to Xicocotitlan, called Tollan.

Tradition says, indeed, that during the tenth century, the Toltecs and northern Indians who had joined them, led by a ruthless conqueror named Mixcoatl, whom some historians have called "a Mexican Attila," came back to the Valley of Mexico. In a story reminiscent of *Hamlet,* Mixcoatl was murdered by his wicked brother, the Lord of the Water Palace, who, in turn, was slain by Mixcoatl's avenging son, Ce Acatl Topiltzin, who was a priest of Quetzalcoatl and was also known by that god's name. Merging with the accomplished Nonoalcas, who were migrating from Veracruz on the Gulf coast of Mexico, Ce Acatl in the mid-900s established the Toltecs' capital at Tollan.

From there, the Toltecs seem to have extended their conquests over large parts of central Mexico and into the Mayan lands of Guatemala and northern Yucatán. Ce Acatl, meanwhile, died, and his legend dissolved into that of the benevolent god Quetzalcoatl, bringer of light, learning, and all beneficial things to the Toltec people. Led thereafter by a succession of Nahuatl-speaking high priests and kings whom the people also knew and revered as the god Quetzalcoatl, the Toltecs assimilated the cul-

Representing one of the many aspects of the ruler-god Quetzalcoatl, this fifteen-foot-tall column was built by Toltecs about A.D. 1000. Carved in sections from blocks of basalt and then fitted together, it helped to support the roof of a temple to the deity on the platform of a pyramid at Tollan, the Toltecs' imperial capital.

A Toltec plumbate effigy jar in the shape of a dog fattened for eating.

tural traits of nations they overran, absorbing much of the inheritance of Teotihuacán's days of glory. Soon they created a rich and powerful culture of their own that spread its influence across a large part of Mesoamerica and north to Indian nations of the present-day United States.

During the two hundred years of their military empire, the Toltecs became great architects and builders who constructed heavily ornamented pyramids and public buildings, palaces with pillared halls, and masonry courts for ceremonial ball games. They decorated their walls and pillars with carved and painted figures of warriors and deities. During the period of their reign, metalworking was introduced into Mesoamerica, coming presumably from Indian nations farther south in Panama or South America's Andean region. The Toltecs were among the first peoples in Mexico to do fine work in gold, silver, and copper. Although artistic, they were also stern and disciplined, and practiced human sacrifice on a much larger scale than their Olmec and Teotihuacán predecessors had done, believing that feeding the hungry gods was necessary to keep the world alive and in harmony with the deities.

Tollan was not a populous metropolis like Teotihuacán, but, with a sophisticated leadership reflecting diverse ethnic backgrounds, and a forceful and pervasive militaristic strain in its culture, it stamped its authority over many other peoples, coordinating markets and arbitrating disputes within the religious framework of their respective states. In modern-day terms, Tollan functioned like Wall Street, the Vatican, and the United States Supreme Court all in one. And it worked.

Tollan also was where turquoise from Chaco Canyon in present-day New Mexico, shells from the Pacific Ocean and the Gulf of Mexico, and the plumage of birds from the southern jungles were fashioned into magnificent creations. In addition, it was where the religious and cultural future of Indian Mexico was being shaped. Emerging from the powerful families that had guided Teotihuacán before its fall, many of the Toltec lords had an intimate understanding of trade, regional organization, and the art of leadership. Their knowledge brought them wealth and unparalleled prestige throughout central Mexico.

In Tollan, as in other parts of pre-Columbian Mexico, plumage of birds was made into wonderful creations. This royal Aztec headdress, formed by concentric bands of red and blue feathers ornamented with gold beads and surmounted by the green tail feathers of the sacred quetzal, towered more than four feet above the wearer's head.

But while Tollan was still finding its limits of power and influence, there arose an internal rift. Within its religious hierarchy, which was not separated from its political leadership, a struggle developed between the followers of Quetzalcoatl, the Feathered Serpent, and those of the god Tezcatlipoca, Smoking Mirror, the deity of blackness and night and associate of the gods of death and evil. Within years, the prophets and apostles of each god were moving along the major trade corridors to the

Tezcatlipoca, the angry rival god to Quetzalcoatl, was also known as Smoking Mirror for the dusky obsidian plate that replaced his right foot after an earth monster had bitten it off.

OVERLEAF: *Pictured in the pre-Columbian pictorial manuscript, the Codex Borgia, the widely venerated creator god, Quetzalcoatl, is seen in the aspect of Ehecatl, the wind god, wearing a conical hat with a wide brim and a red bird-beaked mask, below which hang strands of his beard.*

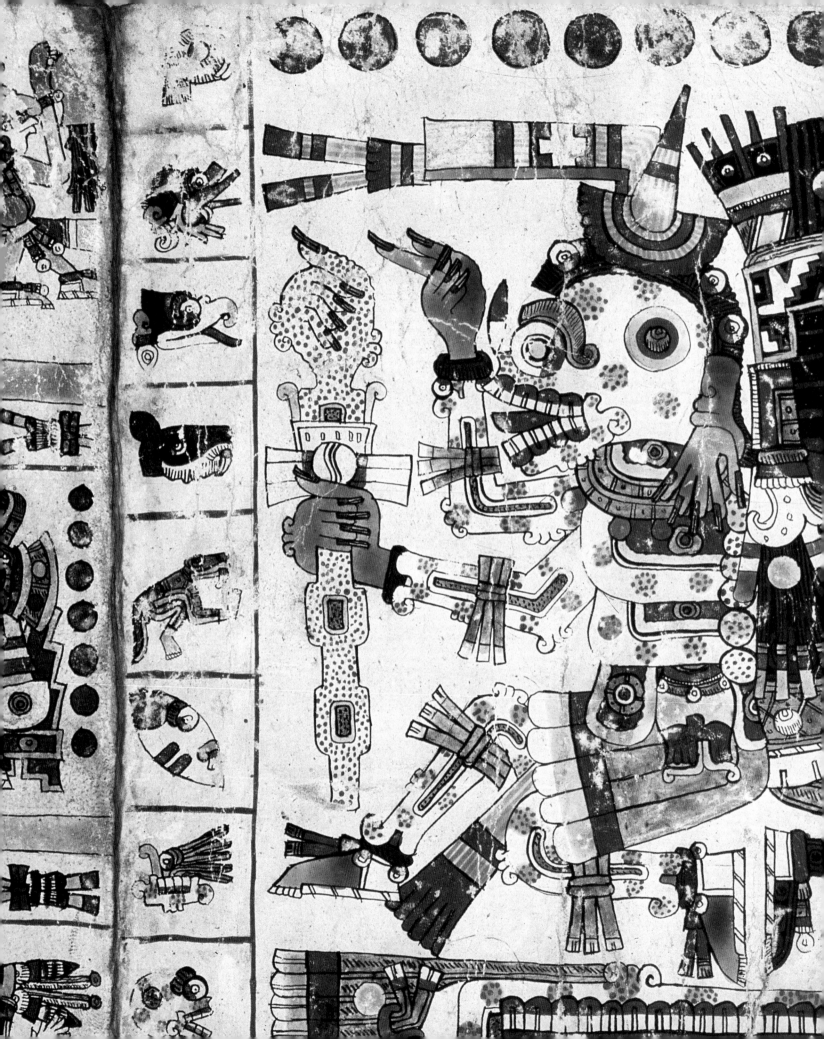

south and east, spreading two very different cults.

Tezcatlipoca was a war god who called for conquests and subjugation. He was a god for the powerful. Quetzalcoatl was the Father and Creator, the source of agriculture, science, and the arts. He was an enlightened god, the morning star and the evening star. Moreover, he was the historic founder of Tollan, Ce Acatl Topiltzin, who in myth had become the god. He could be embraced by the common people, and he offered hope.

The opposing doctrines created a major division in Toltec religion and leadership. And since the two ideological beliefs could not coexist, finally, in A.D. 987, the enlightened king-priest who carried the name Quetzalcoatl was forced out of Tollan. With his followers, he went to Cholula, the city with the mammoth pyramid, then to Yucatán, where as leader of an invasion of the Mayan center of Chichén Itzá, he became known as the god Kukulcán, the Mayan translation of Quetzalcoatl. There are numerous versions of this god-king's death: he sailed away toward the east on a raft of serpents; he parted the waters of the Gulf of Mexico and walked off between them; his heart rose into the heavens and became the shining morning star; and smoke from his funeral pyre became radiant quetzal birds. One overriding legend of his death was not forgotten: the prophecy that, as the protecting god of goodness and light, he would one day return to the Valley of Mexico. He would appear on a day named Ce Acatl, the day of his birth as Ce Acatl Topiltzin Quetzalcoatl.

In the meantime, Tollan continued to grow in influence. By A.D. 1050, it reached a peak that would last for another century. By the early part of the twelfth century, however, its geographical position in the northern part of the Valley of Mexico exposed it to attacks and harassments by bands of Chichimecs, so-called barbarian hunting and gathering peoples living in Mexico's northern regions. Much as had happened to Rome, the pressures from these less civilized, nomadic peoples on the border wore down Tollan's resistance. People began leaving the city for safer places; feuds and open warfare broke out among those who remained; and about A.D. 1180, Tollan was all but destroyed by another internal conflict. Within a few years, the city was abandoned. By then, Quetzalcoatl and the prophecy of his return had been widely embraced throughout the nations of Mexico. The prophecy would haunt the future of another great Mexican empire waiting to be born.

Eight Deer and Six Monkey

While Tollan consolidated power in central Mexico, far to the south in Oaxaca, small, independent kingdoms emerged in the period after the fall of Teotihuacán. Royal warriors, like medieval knights in Europe, fought under their kings on the field of honor, struggling for regional power and influence.

The Indians of the Oaxaca region had already had a long and glorious history of their own. Beginning about 700 B.C., an important center of Zapotec Indians, highly influenced by the civilization of the Olmecs, had risen in the hills at Monte Alban, near the present city of Oaxaca. Rivaling some of the accomplishments and stature of Teotihuacán, the urban area boasted large public structures, dramatic bas-relief sculptures of figures who seemed to be dancing, one of the earliest-known systems of glyph writing in the Western Hemisphere, and the use of calendars. By A.D. 500, the site had grown into a monumental ceremonial center on the slopes of hills surrounding major structures that the Zapotecs had built on a leveled mountaintop. Covering fifteen square miles and trading with Teotihuacán and other important centers of the time, the city of the Zapotecs, like their culture, reached great heights.

Then toward the end of the tenth century, construction of new buildings came to a halt at Monte Alban, and the old site on the mountaintop became a necropolis, or cemetery. In the following century, Mixtec Indians, led by kings, settled in the area, building the beautiful city of Mitla—a civic, rather than a ceremonial, center—

Here no one fears to die in war. . . . Keep this in mind, oh princes.

—AZTEC SCRIBE

Displayed today in the Presidential Palace in Mexico City, this mural by the great twentieth-century Mexican artist Diego Rivera envisions the lively world of the pre-Columbian Zapotec Indians in the present-day Oaxaca region.

Eight Deer's brother and sister, pictured in the Codex Zouche-Nuttall.

and establishing many small states of their own among the Zapotecs. Although the new states were bound together by royal blood and trade, there were constant intrigues and conflicts among them. Some of the dramatic stories of these wars and the individuals who were involved in them were recorded in epic terms in one of the few Mixtec books that survived destruction by the Europeans.

Among the best known—conveying a picture of the lethal feuding of the times—is the saga of Eight Deer of the Mixtec province of Tilantongo, who was born in A.D. 1063 and whose name was that of the day of his birth. Four years later, in the neighboring valley of Jaltepec, Princess Six Monkey was born. At the time, their two kingdoms were at war with each other.

As a young man, Eight Deer became a champion warrior for Tilantongo, while Princess Six Monkey lost three of her brothers in the fighting. Finally, however, her father's army prevailed; the kingdom of Tilantongo fell; and its king committed suicide, leaving no heir to the throne.

Eight Deer was not blind to this opportunity to seize power and tried to make an alliance with Jaltepec. But Six Monkey's father no longer regarded Tilantongo as a threat, so he sent his daughter to be married to the warlord of a rival kingdom called Red Bundle. The union of Jaltepec and Red Bundle, how-

ever, threatened the balance of power in the entire region. To prevent the marriage, two lords from a nearby kingdom called Hill of the Moon, allies of Tilantongo, threatened to kill Princess Six Monkey. Seeking help, Six Monkey and her betrothed traveled to the kingdom of a powerful high priestess who, promising to support their marriage as well as the new alliance, gave Six Monkey and her suitor king an army which they led to Hill of the Moon. Six Monkey then captured the two lords and sacrificed them. No longer challenged, the marriage took place, consummating the alliance between Jaltepec and Red Bundle.

Meanwhile, in Tilantongo, the great warrior Eight Deer had finally seized power. Again Tilantongo became a formidable adversary, and the old rivalry between the two valleys resurfaced. War seemed inevitable, but Eight Deer was determined to avert it, sending his brother on a diplomatic mission to Red Bundle. During the peace conference, the brother entered a ritual sweat bath unarmed and was treacherously slain by an unknown murderer with a concealed knife.

A pictorial manuscript page from the Mixtec Codex Zouche-Nuttall narrates the conquests of Eight Deer, the victorious Tilantongo warlord, who appears at the lower left, attacking a hill town, the name of which is signified by a red fire-snake. Other conquests include kingdoms whose names are symbolized by pictographs representing lakes, plains, and temples.

Now there was no stopping the war. Within days, Eight Deer avenged his brother's death by attacking Red Bundle, capturing Lady Six Monkey and her husband, and sacrificing both of them by cutting out their hearts. He also killed two heirs to the throne of Red Bundle, carrying out a ritual execution that included a gladiatorial combat in which warriors dressed in jaguar skins and armed with obsidian-tipped claws killed one of the princes.

Six Monkey's youngest son, however, escaped and plotted revenge. After several years, in A.D. 1115 when Eight Deer was fifty-two years old, the orphaned prince lured the Tilantongo warrior king to a sacred cave and murdered him. Having revenged the death of his mother, the young prince took the daughter of Eight Deer for his wife. Through their union, they brought the two royal bloodlines together and founded a dynasty that eventually ruled a powerful confederacy of Mixtec kingdoms in southern Mexico until the arrival of the Spaniards four hundred years later.

The Founding of Tenochtitlán

> Behold, a new sun is risen,
> A new god is born,
> New laws are written,
> And new men are made.

In the central Valley of Mexico, the fall of Tollan about A.D. 1180 was followed by years of turbulence. Hordes of plundering Chichimec peoples poured into the valley from the north, at first seizing and destroying what they wished, but then rapidly adopting the cultures of the civilizations they overran. Tollan was no more, but its rich legacy, including its inheritance from Teotihuacán and other earlier Mesoamerican civilizations, lived on, and the newcomers soon built or expanded a number of competing city-states around Lake Texcoco with new civilizations based largely on the old ones.

Eventually, three of the states became dominant—Azcapotzalco, ruled by Tepanec Indians; Texcoco, to whose ruling Acolhuas some seventy towns paid tribute; and Colhuacán, the seat of power of the Colhua tribe. For a time, the Colhuas employed as mercenaries a rude and landless tribe of spearmen known as Mexicas, who migrated to the valley from the northwest about the middle of the thirteenth century. Later, when the Mexicas rose to power and needed a history worthy of a great people favored by the gods, they called themselves Aztecs for Aztlán, their legendary homeland in the north from which they had started their migration.

The Mexicas had already had a difficult time in the valley. Regarded by some as

The might of our arms will be known and the courage of our brave hearts. —AZTEC SCRIBE

A mural by Diego Rivera portrays the great marketplace of Tenochtitlán, where exotic foods and other products could be purchased from throughout the Aztec empire. With a view of the temples and capital city in the background, the emperor himself is shown in a litter chair at left, wearing his turquoise crown and holding a feather fan.

upstarts without Toltec lineage and by others as violent barbarians, they had suffered attacks that had cost the lives of many of their people. The rest had been driven into a rocky, snake-infested part of the valley where their enemies thought they could not survive. But the tough Mexicas were used to adversity. They survived, flourished, and in a generation had won the grudging respect of competing states in the valley and had become mercenaries of the Colhuas.

During their migration, the Mexicas—so their legends later told them—had been guided and comforted by their god of war, Huitzilopochtli, who had said that when they saw an eagle standing on a cactus growing out of a rock, their journey would end. There they should stop and build their city, calling it Tenochtitlán (the Place of the Cactus in the Rock). Until the year 1325, the story goes, they had not seen the sign. Huitzilopochtli was a demanding god, and that year the Mexica priests declared that they needed to offer him a special sacrifice. Thinking they would be honoring the Colhuacán king, they asked him to send his daughter to become a Mexica goddess. Flattered, and not understanding the implications of the request, the lord of Colhuacán complied. Days later, when at the invitation of the Mexicas he and

A map of Tenochtitlán, published in Europe in 1524, soon after its fall. Although it is a Spanish version, with European-style houses, it shows the Aztec temples and many of the city's distinctive features, such as the causeways across Lake Texcoco.

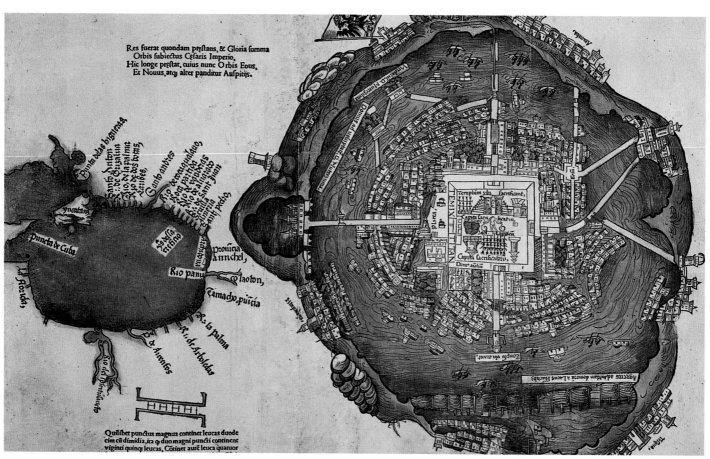

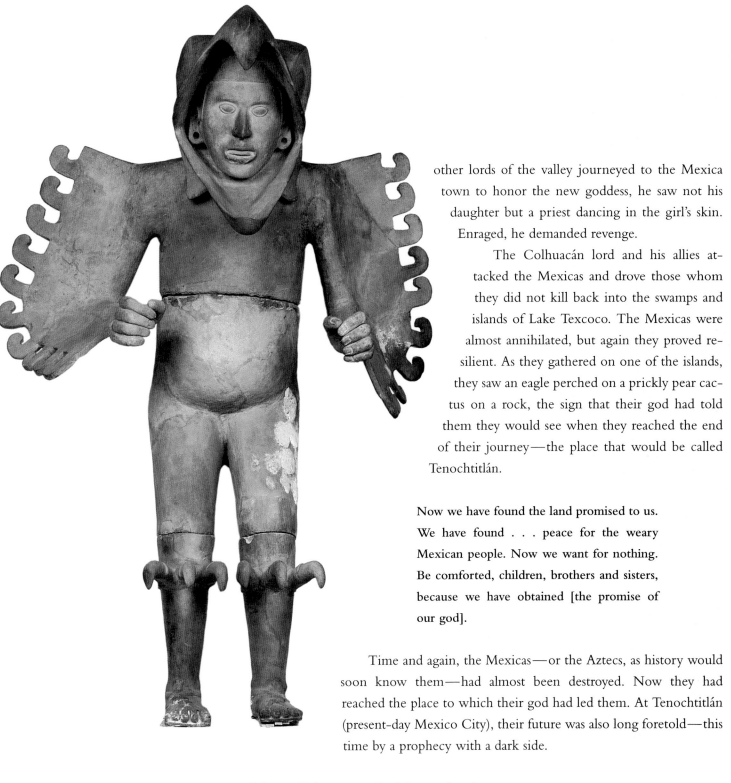

other lords of the valley journeyed to the Mexica town to honor the new goddess, he saw not his daughter but a priest dancing in the girl's skin. Enraged, he demanded revenge.

The Colhuacán lord and his allies attacked the Mexicas and drove those whom they did not kill back into the swamps and islands of Lake Texcoco. The Mexicas were almost annihilated, but again they proved resilient. As they gathered on one of the islands, they saw an eagle perched on a prickly pear cactus on a rock, the sign that their god had told them they would see when they reached the end of their journey—the place that would be called Tenochtitlán.

Now we have found the land promised to us. We have found . . . peace for the weary Mexican people. Now we want for nothing. Be comforted, children, brothers and sisters, because we have obtained [the promise of our god].

Time and again, the Mexicas—or the Aztecs, as history would soon know them—had almost been destroyed. Now they had reached the place to which their god had led them. At Tenochtitlán (present-day Mexico City), their future was also long foretold—this time by a prophecy with a dark side.

A life-sized ceramic figure from A.D. 1450–1500, wearing the wings, beaked helmet, and claws of an Aztec eagle warrior.

The Rise of the Aztecs

For a hundred years, the Aztecs improved the island and a neighboring one which they called Tlatelolco, reclaiming land and building temples and other public structures while living in rudimentary housing. They gradually acquired wealth by trade and by working as mercenary warriors for the strong city-states in the valley, and they arranged marriages that brought their families honored Toltec bloodlines. An ambitious, driven people, they built causeways of hewn stone across Lake Texcoco to the north, south, and west, connecting the islands with the mainland. Early in the

fifteenth century, they constructed an aqueduct to bring fresh water to Tenochtitlán from a mainland spring four miles away and dug canals throughout the island to serve as the city's principal arteries of transportation and commerce.

Meanwhile, they were gaining political and military strength. Becoming auxiliaries of Tezozómoc, the powerful ruler of Azcapotzalco, they helped his forces of Tepanec Indians destroy Colhuacán, one of Azcapotzalco's two rival city-states. Soon their growing prestige induced Tezozómoc to give his daughter in marriage to the Aztecs' leader, which further increased their status in the valley. With the support of Aztec armies, Tezozómoc launched expeditions of conquest that extended his power beyond the valley, unifying different peoples into the initial stage of another empire. Finally, in 1416, when Tezozómoc was in his nineties, he conquered Texcoco, the last of his rivals in the Valley of Mexico. Again, the Aztecs were among the vassals fighting for him. In the battle, the king of Texcoco was killed, but his son, a poet and philosopher named Nezahualcoyotl, escaped.

Tezozómoc finally died in 1427 at the age of 106. Because of intrigues, plots, and assassinations among those who tried to take over his empire, Azcapotzalco almost immediately lost power. Its strongest subject state, that of the Aztecs, rose in revolt and formed an alliance with Nezahualcoyotl and his followers in Texcoco. Together, they conquered Azcapotzalco and emerged as the two strongest states in the valley. Gradually, by conspiracies and conquests, Tenochtitlán gained leadership over Texcoco and, after

King Nezahualcoyotl, a poet and philosopher whose name meant "fasting coyote," was ruler of the kingdom of Texcoco before the Aztecs' rise to dominance.

The geometric design on the face of this Aztec shield was created with parrot feathers. Feathers were prized by Aztec artisans in much the same way as Europeans coveted oriental silk. The demand for feathers was so great that special gamekeepers were enlisted to trap and pluck parrots in the wild so that there would be no danger of extinction.

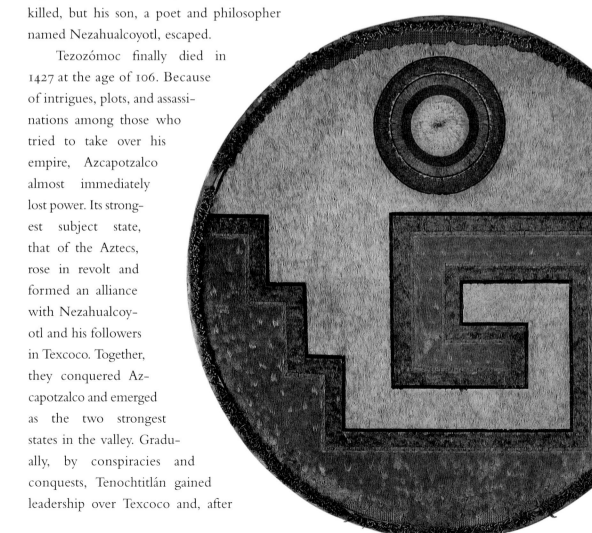

the death of Nezahualcoyotl in 1472, became the most influential state in central Mexico. By the end of the fifteenth century, the once-rude and humble Aztecs had become the successors of the Olmecs, Teotihuacáns, and the Toltecs and ruled the most powerful empire in the history of North America.

From their island city of Tenochtitlán, the Aztec rulers commanded an army of more than two hundred thousand warriors, including those of many vassal states. It was the largest army anywhere in the world at that time, and even today would be among the biggest. From Tenochtitlán, the heads of the Aztec state launched far-reaching campaigns that virtually never stopped for over ninety years. Fighting epic battles with city-states and nations, the Aztec forces conquered most of their adversaries and turned them into tributary countries, allowing them to keep their own governments, but requiring that they pay Tenochtitlán a high tribute, or taxes, in commodities or other goods.

In the Codex Mendoza, one of the pictographic records painted by scribes of the Aztec empire, the taxes of many tribute-paying states are listed: bolts of fine cotton cloth; military raiment, including feathered headdresses; disks of hammered gold; exotic plants; strings of jade beads; precious gems; and bundles of blankets. In addition, all of the vassal states maintained warehouses of food for the Aztec army so that the huge force would not be dependent on the Valley of Mexico for supplies. If a tributary rebelled and ignored or refused to pay its taxes, it faced stern punishment by Aztec warriors and then a doubling of its tax levy. Boasted the Aztecs:

The Aztecs demanded heavy tribute from the vassal kingdoms they conquered. On this tribute roll of one of the emperors, reproduced from the Codex Mendoza, are representations of the vassal states (the vertical row of glyphs at left) and the variety of exotic goods they were expected to pay, among them strings of jade beads, bundles of colored feathers, and jaguar skins. The European writing on some of the codices is that of Spaniards who were studying the ways of the Aztecs after they had toppled their empire.

Aztec officers, portrayed in the Codex Mendoza, wore tall emblems of their rank affixed to their backs to make them more visible to their followers in the confusion of battle.

The might of our powerful arms and the spirit of our . . . hearts shall be felt. With them we will conquer all nations, near and far, rule over all villages and cities from sea to sea, become lords of gold and silver, jewels and precious stones, feathers and tributes, and we shall become lords over them and their lands and over their sons and daughters, who will serve us as our subjects.

War had been refined for centuries in Mesoamerica. On the battlefield, the Aztecs, armed with spear-throwing atlatls, clubs edged with razor-sharp blades of flint or obsidian, and other weapons of their time, were as skilled as, and considerably more seasoned than, any contemporary fighting force. They had ranks equivalent to those of modern armies and wore uniforms designed for specific groups of fighters so that their commanders could identify them and direct their actions from a distance. An

elite class of warrior knights—honored for having taken captives to be sent to Tenochtitlán for sacrifice—wore uniforms of jaguar skin and eagle feathers. The common soldiers went into battle in padded cotton suits soaked in brine to make them harder and more resistant to enemy weapons and carried shields of wicker covered with painted hides or colored feathers. Not all nations and cities fell before the

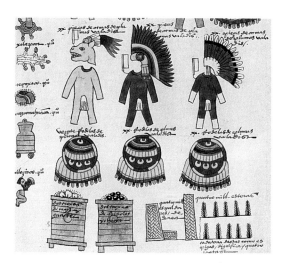

This Aztec pictorial accounting from the Codex Mendoza shows military supplies, including warriors' uniforms and richly decorated shields, as tribute paid to an emperor by one of his vassal kingdoms.

OVERLEAF: *As depicted in the Codex Tudela, Aztec noblewomen wore huipils, richly embroidered blouses that hung from the shoulders to the knees. At the same time, the Codex Tudela showed the common outergarment of Aztec noblemen, a draped cloak called a tilmatl, worn fastened over the right shoulder.*

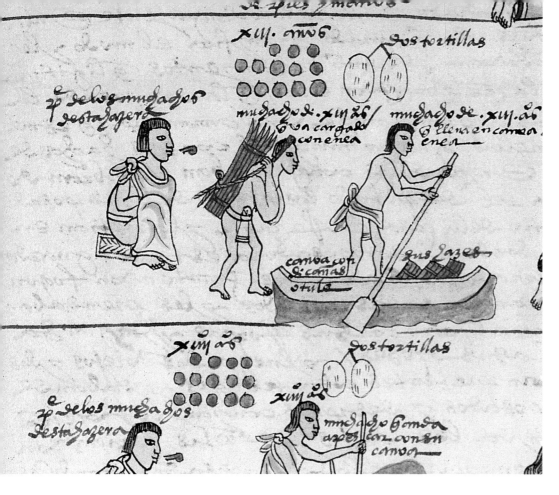

Aztec fathers commonly instructed their sons in trades they had inherited from their own fathers. Here, two youths have gathered firewood and are transporting it across Lake Texcoco in a canoe to sell in Tenochtitlán.

Aztecs. Their armies could never defeat the city-state of Tlaxcala, which was located only fifty miles to their east. The Tlaxcalans were an enemy which—like the prophecy of the return of the god Quetzalcoatl—would haunt the Aztec future.

At Tenochtitlán, laws, codes of conduct, and social position dictated almost every aspect of Aztec life. A boy born to a noble family would go to school and possibly to the university in the heart of the city. His training would be rigorous, stressing discipline and personal sacrifice. He might become a government official, a scribe, or a teacher. During his military service, he was expected to be a leader on the battlefield. If he became a government official, he could live in a palace or have a large estate.

For commoners, life was considerably less comfortable, but no less structured. Most of them were farmers, laborers, fishermen, loggers, or stonemasons. If they became traders or artisans, they might amass enough wealth to rival that of the nobles, but they could never change their class. The commoners also made up the bulk of the military forces, and serving with distinction could improve a man's status.

Women of both classes learned to weave cloth and were expected to take care of the household. But there the similarities ended. Noble persons dressed in fine, soft cotton, while commoners usually wore coarse fabrics made from yucca or maguey. The drinking of alcohol was prohibited to everyone under the age of seventy except on special ceremonial occasions. After persons reached seventy, they were allowed to drink the potent pulque whenever they pleased.

Tenochtitlán's population of about 250,000 made it the largest

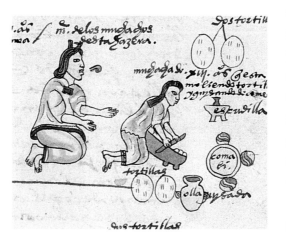

Aztec women trained their daughters in household duties from an early age. Here, a girl is taught to grind corn and make tortillas, a staple of Aztec meals.

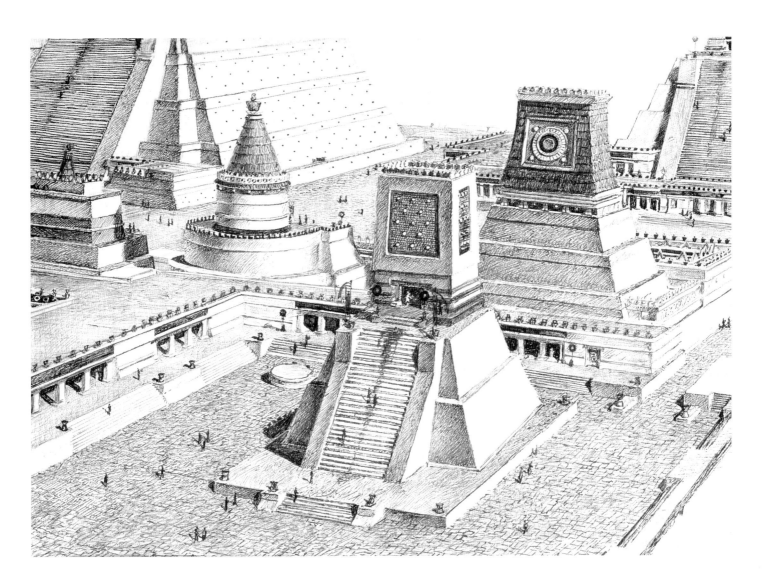

city in Mesoamerica, if not in the world, in the fifteenth century. Its ceremonial center boasted more than twenty-five major pyramids of various heights, surmounted by temples dedicated to a pantheon of deities and culture heroes. Around the plazas and gardens that lay between these shrines were numerous public buildings in which the emperor, his assistants, and a large body of nobles and civil servants administered the affairs of the empire. The city was divided into sixty residential wards, or clan districts, called *calpulli,* each one represented by a headman and containing the homes of all members of a clan and their families. In addition, each *calpulli* had its own ceremonial complex and agricultural *chinampas.*

It was a bustling metropolis with arsenals for military stores; monasteries for the priests who served in the temples; workshops for goldsmiths, feather workers, and

At the heart of Tenochtitlán were monumental public buildings, among the most important of which were temples, raised on platforms and dedicated to the major gods in the Aztec pantheon, as shown in this re-creation.

Xochipilli, shown sitting cross-legged in this stone sculpture, was the Aztec deity of youth, gaiety, feasting, and dancing.

*An elaborate painted ceramic vase depicting
Chicomecoatl, or Seven Snake, the young
goddess of the corn harvest.*

A masterpiece of monolithic Aztec stone carving from about A.D. 1500 depicts the moon goddess, Coyolxauhqui, who was decapitated by her half brother, the Aztec war god, Huitzilopochtli, for conspiring in the death of their mother.

members of other guilds; and schools for the professions. The streets and public buildings were cleaned daily by thousands of sweepers, and the city's refuse was collected and shipped away on barges. Beautiful gardens of roses and fragrant tropical flowers adorned the two-story houses of the elite; royal aviaries housed thousands of rare birds; canals laced the island; and the city's storehouses swelled with the wealth of the empire. At the start of the sixteenth century, an Aztec could truly write:

Proudly stands the city of Mexico—
Tenochtitlán.
Here no one fears to die in war . . .
Keep this in mind, oh princes . . .
Who could attack Tenochtitlán?
Who could shake the foundations of heaven?

An Empire Falls

It was the year One Reed—1519 in Christian years. Mochtezuma II, the ninth Aztec ruler, was the most powerful man in North America. From his capital at Tenochtitlán, he had reigned as emperor since 1502 over the lands of ten million Mesoamerican Indians. For ninety years his nation had strengthened the empire with its armies and become rich from the tribute of defeated states.

But Mochtezuma was troubled. He had been reading the signs.

Signs were vital to the Aztecs. They guided decisions of state. And in the year One Reed, the signs foretold disaster. For a number of years, there had been unusual omens: a huge tongue of fire burning in the night sky to the east; temples suddenly destroyed by lightning and flames; a comet blazing across the daytime sky. Then suddenly, from the coast of the Gulf of Mexico, traders and Mochtezuma's ambassadors had brought tales of houses floating on the sea, of the waters throwing up monsters—men clothed in metal, with white skin and hair on their faces. In One Reed, these aliens, indeed, were already landing on the shores.

What most troubled Mochtezuma were the prophecies. Even during their years as a wandering tribe, the Aztecs had believed that their destiny was to rule the world. But the dark side of that destiny was that the rule of their empire would be followed by its destruction. In addition, there was the prophecy of the god-hero Quetzalcoatl, the Feathered Serpent, who had promised to return to the Valley of Mexico on Ce Acatl—the Nahuatl for "One Reed"—that very year. If the prophecy were true and he returned, kings would fall, for throughout central and southern Mexico the promised kingdom of Quetzalcoatl lived in the hearts of subjugated Indian peoples. But whoever these invaders were, gods or men, Mochtezuma viewed them as a threat. A new force could crack his fragile empire of conquered city-states, which already showed signs of rebellion.

More information, all of it disquieting, continued to come to the emperor from the Veracruz coast.

They were very white. Their eyes were like chalk. Their hair, on some it was yellow and on some it was black. They wore long beards, they were yellow too.

—AZTEC DESCRIPTION OF SPANIARDS

This painting in the Codex Duran depicts the emperor Mochtezuma before the coming of the Spaniards, filled with dismay by the sight of a comet, a prophetic sign of impending death and destruction.

Hernando Cortés, the Spanish conqueror of the Aztec empire, as seen in an eighteenth-century illustration.

Aztec scribes later portrayed the strange new arrivals in pictographic manuscripts, known today as codices:

> They were very white.
> Their eyes were like
> chalk. Their hair, on
> some it was yellow and
> on some it was black.
> They wore long beards,
> they were yellow too.

Mochtezuma was greatly disturbed, for the prophecies had said that Quetzalcoatl would be the sacred color white. Deciding to try to placate the newcomers, he sent emissaries to them carrying gifts, including a costume of Quetzalcoatl for their leader to wear.

Hernando Cortés, the hot-blooded Spanish leader of the white men, met them with a rude display of force. He ordered the Aztec ambassadors shackled and then had them watch in astonishment as his men fired a lombard cannon, which, in a thunderous hail of fire and smoke, blew apart a tree on the shore. Two of the emissaries fainted, convinced that they had seen the awesome power of Quetzalcoatl in his guise as god of thunder and lightning. Released by Cortés, the emissaries raced back to Tenochtitlán, where an anxious Mochtezuma awaited word. The tale they told

A painting in the Florentine Codex shows Cortés's men frightening Mochtezuma's emissaries by a demonstration of their firearms.

terrified the emperor. Whether gods or men, whether friends or enemies, a new force in the region, sheathed in metal armor, that could muster weapons with the destructive capability of thunder and lightning, represented a serious threat to his rule. Mochtezuma decided that his subjects would eagerly embrace as a liberator someone who matched the prophecies, who arrived in houses upon the eastern sea, rode frightening, large deerlike animals (horses that Cortés had brought with him),

Quetzalcoatl, in his conical hat and bird-beaked mask, as pictured in the Codex Duran.

and possessed mastiffs, dogs larger and more vicious than any they had ever seen.

On the coast, meanwhile, Cortés was fired by tales of unimaginable wealth inside the empire of Mexico. At the same time, he faced dissension among some of his men, who wished to abandon his expedition. To prevent their sailing to Cuba, he scuttled his ships, forcing the malcontents to remain with him. Then with the invaluable assistance of a native woman of present-day Tabasco named Malintzin, whom the Spaniards called La Malinche or Marina and who had become Cortés's mistress and interpreter, he began the march inland. There would be no turning back. Over the next several months he moved his army toward Tenochtitlán, forming alliances along the way with disaffected city-states of the Aztec empire. Everywhere, he heard complaints: the Aztec tax collectors drained their wealth; Aztec soldiers took away their children to become slaves or sacrificial victims. In Cortés, rebellious city-states had found a liberator.

Cortés's most significant alliance was made with Tlaxcala, the city-state that Mochtezuma had been unable to conquer and that was still his most feared enemy. As the Spaniards advanced, the Aztec emperor held his armies in check, unwilling to leave the capital unprotected or to risk setting off a general rebellion. Paralyzed with doubt,

yliyocan.

The conqueror Cortés and Malintzin, or La Malinche, his invaluable Indian interpreter and mistress, depicted in the Codex Tlaxcala.

Mochtezuma was fast becoming merely an actor in a prophecy that was being fulfilled.

Accompanied by his Tlaxcalan allies, Cortés turned first on Cholula, the ancient city-state with the huge pyramid, whose rulers were loyal to the Aztec emperor. Later, Indian scribes recorded what happened:

Mochtezuma sent emissaries carrying the costume of Quetzalcoatl, for they wished to honor him. On the ship Mochtezuma's emissaries dressed Cortés in the costume of Quetzalcoatl. —AZTEC SCRIBE

Then there arose from the Spaniards a cry summoning all the noble-men, lords, war leaders, warriors, and common folk; and when they had crowded into the temple courtyard, then the Spaniards and their allies blocked the entrances and every exit. There followed a butchery of stabbing, beating, killing of the unsuspecting Cholulans armed with no bows and arrows, protected by no shields . . . with no warning, they were treacherously, deceitfully slain.

The Spaniards massacred more than six thousand Cholulan citizens. In the capital city of Tenochtitlán, Mochtezuma received the terrible news from Cholula in shock. It was said that the city "rose in tumult, alarmed as if by an earthquake, as if there were a constant reeling of the face of the earth."

On November 8, 1519—the year One Reed—Cortés arrived in the Valley of Mexico at the gateway to Tenochtitlán, the imperial Aztec capital. The Spanish chronicler Bernal Díaz del Castillo, who was a member of the expedition, expressed the sense of awe that came upon the Spaniards when they first gazed upon Tenochtitlán and the cities surrounding Lake Texcoco:

> When we saw so many cities and villages built in the water and other great towns on dry land and that straight and level Causeway going towards Mexico [Tenochtitlán], we were amazed and said that it was like the enchantments they tell of in the legend of Amadis, on account of the great towers and cues [pyramids] and buildings rising from the water, and all built of masonry. And some of our soldiers even asked whether the things that we saw were not a dream. . . . I do not know how to describe it, seeing things as we did that had never been heard of or seen before, not even dreamed about.

Faced by the invading army, Mochtezuma decided again to appease, rather than fight. Borne on a litter and accompanied by a large retinue of nobles and war chiefs in brilliantly colored feather headdresses and raiment glittering with gold ornamentation, the emperor went out on the great causeway to greet Cortés and welcome him with gifts. Then without opposition or hindrance, the Spanish leader and his army entered the spectacular Indian city that no European had seen before.

Crowds of stunned and curi-

The terrible slaughter by the Spanish invaders of more than six thousand unarmed and trusting allies of the Aztecs in the ancient city-state of Cholula, as recorded in the Florentine Codex.

There followed a butchery of stabbing, beating, killing of the unsuspecting Cholulans armed with no bows and arrows, protected by no shields . . . with no warning, they were treacherously, deceitfully slain.

—AZTEC SCRIBE

In Diego Rivera's mural depicting the cruelty and avarice of the Spaniards following their arrival in Mexico, Cortés is portrayed bitterly as a deformed, hunchbacked man with a green face (next page) and the look of an imbecile (left).

ous Aztecs filled the lake in dugouts and lined the causeway and streets and courtyards of Tenochtitlán to catch a glimpse of the strangers. One of them later described the Spaniards:

> The iron of their lances . . . glistened from afar; the shimmer of their swords was as of a sinuous water course. Their iron breast and back pieces, their helmets clanked. Some came completely encased in iron—as if turned to iron. . . . And ahead of them ran . . . their dogs, panting, with foam continually dripping from their muzzles.

In the following days, Mochtezuma, indecisive and riddled with fears, plied Cortés and his men with golden ornaments and other rich gifts and invited them to see the splendors of his city. They were appalled by the Aztecs' religion, which like those of the other Mesoamerican civilizations included the sacrificing of humans to keep the favor of their gods, but they were greatly impressed by the city's main market center, where the residents of the capital could find produce and goods from all parts of the empire. "Some of the soldiers among us who had been in many parts of the world, in Constantinople, and all over Italy, and in Rome, said that so large a market place and so full of people, and so well regulated and arranged, they had never beheld before," wrote Bernal Díaz.

In a letter to the king and queen of Spain, Cortés also described this heart of Mochtezuma's domain:

> Your Highnesses . . . We have discovered a land rich in gold, pearls, and other things. . . . There are in the city many large and beautiful houses . . . and many rich citizens. . . . And also very pleasant gardens. . . . Along one of the causeways to this great city run two aqueducts made of mortar. . . . Canoes paddle through all the streets. . . . The people of this city are dressed with . . . elegance and courtly . . . bearing. . . .
>
> Considering that these people are barbarous, lacking knowledge of God and communication with other civilized nations, it is remarkable to see all that they have.

Mochtezuma treated his guests royally, putting at their disposal a sumptuous palace in which to eat and rest. But the Spaniards' goal of conquering the rich empire of the Aztecs was not averted. Cortés turned upon his hosts and seized Mochtezuma himself, holding him as a hostage and forcing him to lead the Spaniards to the Aztecs' treasury.

OPPOSITE: *Another of Diego Rivera's views of Tenochtitlán's great market. The Spaniards, according to Bernal Díaz, "had never beheld before" any market that equaled its size, organization, and variety of products and goods.*

The seizure of Mochtezuma by the Spaniards, as pictured in the Florentine Codex.

"Mochtezuma's own property was then brought out," an Aztec scribe later wrote. "Precious things like necklaces with pendants, arm bands tufted with quetzal feathers, golden bracelets, golden anklets with shells, rulers' turquoise diadems, turquoise nose rods; no end of treasure. They took all, seized everything for themselves as if it were theirs."

For six months, with Mochtezuma their prisoner, the Spaniards lived in splendor and pillaged the city. In April 1520, Mochtezuma's brother, Cuitlauac, who was forming a resistance movement, gathered with his warriors for a religious observance, which the Spaniards attacked. A fierce fight resulted. One Aztec warrior saved his life by playing dead and later described the scene:

> They [the Spaniards] charged the crowd with their iron lances and hacked us with their iron swords. They slashed the backs of some. . . . They hacked at the shoulders of others, splitting their bodies open. . . . The blood of the young warriors ran like water; it gathered in pools. And the Spaniards began to hunt them out of the administrative area buildings . . . even starting to take those buildings to pieces as they searched.
>
> Great was the stench of the dead. . . . Your grandfathers died, and with them died the son of the king and his brothers and kinsmen. So it was that we became orphans, O my sons! So we became when we were young. All of us were thus. We were born to die!

The Aztec warriors finally forced the Spaniards to retreat behind the walls of the great palace. To save his army, Cortés brought Mochtezuma in chains out before the people to convince them to stop fighting. To his loyal subjects who had held their emperor in such awe that they traditionally bowed their heads so as not to look at his face, Mochtezuma was now craven. "Your ruler, the lord of men, implores you!" he cried. "We are not equal to the Spaniards! Abandon the battle! Still your arrows, hold back your shields!"

For the time being, he was able to turn back his troops and still the angry populace. But the Spaniards'

A golden figure of a serpent, worn by an Aztec nobleman as a labret through the lower lip.

An Aztec facial ornament, the golden figure of the head of a bird, was worn as a labret through the lower lip.

arrogance, misbehavior, and cruelty continued, and the Aztecs were not a people to be subjugated. Having lost faith in Mochtezuma, whom the Spaniards still held prisoner, they reformed their government, and Cuitlauac became the tenth Aztec emperor. He mobilized the army and, in the fall of 1520, led an uprising against the Spaniards. During the fighting, Mochtezuma was killed. Each side blamed the other. The Spaniards claimed that his own people stoned him to death. The Aztecs accused the Spaniards of strangling him because he was no longer useful to them. Whatever happened, one of the most powerful men on earth had become trapped in a drama of destiny. Prophecy had become reality. Following his death, Cortés's men threw Mochtezuma's corpse into one of the canals.

But the furious Aztecs were not finished. After twenty-seven days besieged in the palace, almost one year after their occupation of the city, the Spaniards attempted to escape under cover of darkness. An Aztec version of the events says:

> That night at midnight the enemy came out crowded together. The Spanish in the lead, the Tlaxcalan [Spanish allies] followed, moving undetected through a fine sprinkle of rain towards a causeway and their escape.
>
> Just as they were crossing, a woman drawing water saw them. "Mexicans! Come, all of you. They are already leaving, they are already secretly getting out!" Then a watcher at the top of a temple . . . also shouted and his cries pervaded the entire city . . . "Brave warriors, Mexicans! Your enemy already leaves. Hurry with the shield boats and along the road!"

As Cortés's men moved through the city and out onto one of the main causeways across the lake, canoe after canoe full of Aztec warriors showered the Spaniards with arrows and spears. Many of the Spaniards, weighted down by gold and other loot stolen from the palace, fell into the water and drowned, carried to the bottom by their plunder. The Aztec version says:

The canal was filled, crammed with them. Those who came along behind walked over on men, on corpses. . . . And when the Spanish thus disappeared, we thought they had gone for good, nevermore to return.

Two-thirds of the Spanish army never reached the outskirts of Tenochtitlán on this night that Cortés and his fellow survivors called the Noche Triste (Sad Night). For a moment, the city was free of the Europeans. But the occupation had cost the Aztecs the allegiance of numerous allies on the mainland surrounding the lake. Tenochtitlán stood alone. The Aztec narrative continues:

Once again the temples could be swept out . . . the dirt removed; they could be adorned, ornamented. . . . But at about the time that the Spaniards had fled from Mexico . . . there came a great sickness, a pestilence, the smallpox . . . it spread over the people with great destruction of men. It caused great misery. . . . The brave Mexican warriors were indeed weakened by it. It was after all this had happened that the Spaniards came back.

Among the victims of the smallpox was the Aztecs' new emperor, Mochtezuma's brother, Cuitlauac. He was succeeded by Mochtezuma's nephew, Cuauhtémoc, a vigorous young warrior of about twenty-five. Cortés and his men healed their wounds and rebuilt their army. New alliances were made. The Spaniards and fifty thousand Tlaxcalan and other allied Indian soldiers set siege to Tenochtitlán. The

Following Mochtezuma's death, the Spaniards threw his corpse into one of Tenochtitlán's canals, as depicted in the Florentine Codex.

OPPOSITE: *In the spring of 1520, the greed and arrogance of Cortés's men bred resistance among their Aztec hosts. As shown in the Codex Duran, the Spaniards tried to quell it by the ruthless slaughter of hundreds of Mochtezuma's unarmed followers at a religious festival in the Aztec month of Toxcatl.*

The Codex Tlaxcala pictures the Spaniards' desperate flight from Tenochtitlán, attacked on one of the main causeways by masses of Aztec warriors on the Noche Triste, or Sad Night.

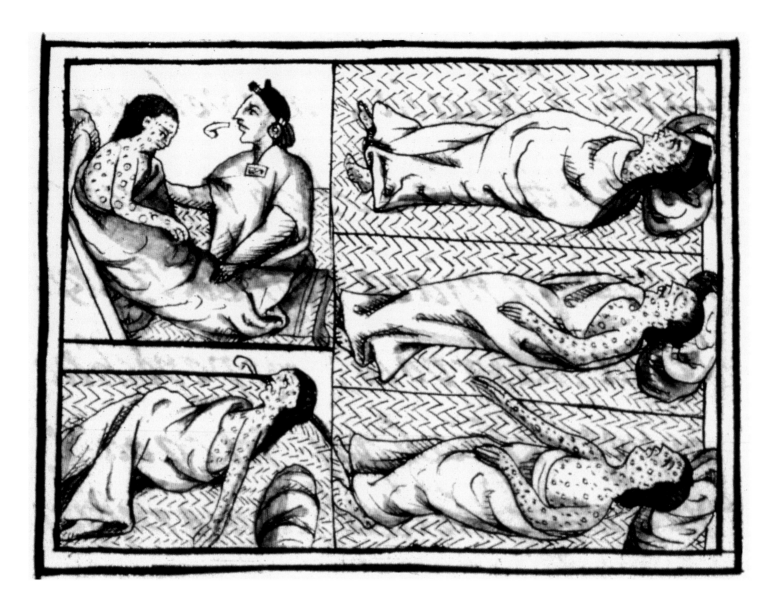

Cortés's conquistadors brought European diseases that proved far more deadly to the Indian populations than the Spanish weapons. Here, the Florentine Codex shows Aztecs dying from the dreaded smallpox, against which they had no defense.

Aztec warriors and civilian population of Tenochtitlán, now led by Cuauhtémoc, fought back, giving the Spaniards and their allies no quarter. The Aztec account says:

> Fighting continued, both sides took captives, on both sides there were deaths. Nevertheless, great became the suffering of the common folk. There was hunger. Many died of famine. There was no more good, pure water to drink. . . . Many died of it. . . . The people ate anything— lizards, barn swallows, corn leaves, saltgrass. . . . Never had such suffering been seen. . . . The enemy pressed about us like a wall . . . they herded us. . . . The brave warriors were still hopelessly resisting.

OVERLEAF: *A detail from one of Diego Rivera's murals captures the ferocity of the final fighting of the Indian warriors against the white invaders for possession of the Aztec capital.*

But after four months of one of the longest continuous battles in history, the Spaniards, with their superior weaponry and numbers of allies, ended Tenochtitlán resistance. Again, the Aztec version:

The battle just quietly ended. Silence reigned. Nothing happened. The enemy left. All was quiet, and nothing more took place. Night fell, and the next day nothing happened either. No one spoke aloud; the people were crushed. . . . So ended the war.

The Aztecs' stout, but unsuccessful, defense of Tenochtitlán against the craft and cannons of the besieging Spaniards, as pictured in the Florentine Codex.

An Aztec stone sculpture of Tepeyolohtli, god of the interior of the earth, emerging from the carapace of a tortoise.

Cuauhtémoc was taken prisoner and exiled. Tenochtitlán was leveled, and the stones of its pyramids, temples, palaces, and other public buildings were used by the European conquerors to replace the Indian structures with religious and governmental buildings in the Spanish style. The Aztec gardens, the marvel of their world, were destroyed. The rivers and canals that so amazed the Spaniards were filled in.

Then Cortés set fire to the aviaries. Thousands and thousands of birds: vermilion flycatchers, iridescent hummingbirds, scarlet tanagers, delicate egrets, green and blue macaws. . . . The beauty that was Mexico was turned to ashes.

The Aztec scribe had written:

> Proudly stands the city of Mexico,
> Tenochtitlán,
> Here no one fears to die in war . . .
> Keep this in mind, O princes . . .
> Who could attack Tenochtitlán?
> Who could shake the foundations of heaven?

Looking back to the magical days when as a young conquistador with Cortés he had first viewed Tenochtitlán, Bernal Díaz gave the Spaniards' reply: "Of all these wonders that I then beheld today all is overthrown and lost, nothing left standing."

This stone sculpture represents Coatlíque, the Aztec earth goddess. According to one story, blood rose out of Coatlíque's neck in the form of two great serpents after her children beheaded her in a war. Fearing the spiritual power of these ancient traditions, the Spaniards attempted unsuccessfully to destroy such masterpieces with iron hammers. Later they resorted to burying the monuments under Mexico City's streets.

Indian Mexico did not die. During the almost five hundred years since the fall of Tenochtitlán, Indian nations in that country have risen on many occasions for their rights. Perhaps the largest and most

protracted war of resistance waged by any Indian people was that of the Mayas in the Yucatán, who fought back all attempts to subjugate them until the twentieth century. Tens of thousands died in little-known battles against Spanish colonial and Mexican troops. At one point, British gunboats were called upon to evacuate the Yucatán capital of Mérida as the Mayas laid siege to the city.

At the same time, there is no other nation in North America where the influence of Indian cultures on the way of life, art, and values continues to be as clear as it is in Mexico. Millions of Mexican Indian peoples—Mayas, Zapotecs, Mixtecs, Aztecs, and others—hold firmly to their identities and languages to this day.

This proud stone sculpture of an eagle, the symbol of Aztec greatness, was fractured by the hammer blows of the Spanish conquerors.

Great became the suffering of the common folk. There was hunger. Many died of famine. There was no more good, pure water to drink.

—AZTEC SCRIBE

CHAPTER 3

CLASH

OF CULTURES

The landing of Columbus on one of the Bahama Islands in October 1492 opened a new era in the history of the millions of indigenous peoples of the Western Hemisphere, to whom he gave the name los indios *(the Indians). By aggression and the spreading of disease, his attempts at colonization caused the decline and disappearance of native populations, a pattern repeated throughout the Americas in the following generations.*

OVERLEAF: *A dramatic but highly imaginative seventeenth-century engraving of Arawak Indians greeting the arrival of Columbus on the island of Hispaniola.*

The Indians and Columbus

[The Spaniards] made bets as to who would slit a man in two, or cut off his head at one blow; or they opened up his bowels. They tore the babies from their mother's breast by their feet, and dashed their heads against the rocks. . . . They spitted the bodies of other babes, together with their mothers and all who were before them, on their swords. . . . [They hanged Indians], and by thirteens, in honor and reverence for our Redeemer and the twelve Apostles, they put wood underneath and, with fire, they burned the Indians alive. . . . I saw all the above things. . . . All these did my own eyes witness.

FRAY BARTOLOMÉ DE LAS CASAS
History of the Indies, 1552

Only twenty-nine years before the fall of the Aztec empire, white men in the West Indies had first shattered the isolation of the Indian world of North America.

Arriving from Spain at one of the Bahama Islands in October 1492 and then sailing along the verdant coasts of Cuba and Hispaniola (present-day Haiti and the Dominican Republic), Christopher Columbus and the bearded and heavily armored Spaniards of his fleet made frequent landings among Eden-like villages of naked Arawakan-speaking peoples. Lost and thinking he was in the East Indies of Asia, Columbus referred to the inhabitants of the islands as *los indios,* or the Indians, thus fastening that name on the populations of all the indigenous nations of the Western Hemisphere.

It was a dramatic moment of first contact between the two worlds, and both the Indians and the Europeans were filled with immense wonder about each other. To Columbus, the Arawaks (some of whose groups were known as Tainos) were "artless and generous with what they have, to such a degree as no one would believe but he who had seen it. Of anything they have, if it be asked for, they never say no, but do rather invite the person to accept it, and show as much lovingness as though they would give their hearts."

At the same time, Columbus made note of what he understood the Indians were thinking. "They believed very firmly," he wrote, "that I, with these ships and crew, came from the sky; and in such opinion they received me at every place where I landed, after they had lost their terror . . . wherever I arrived [they] went running from house to house and to the neighboring villages, with loud cries of 'Come! Come to see the people from heaven!'"

Another view of Columbus's landing. This one, by the sixteenth-century Flemish engraver Theodore De Bry, shows him being welcomed by gift-bearing Indians as he claims their country for Spain and Christianity.

OPPOSITE: *An Arawak man presenting himself to the family of his bride-to-be, from a manuscript about Arawak life believed to have been written and illustrated by a French member of one of Sir Francis Drake's sixteenth-century voyages to the West Indies.*

A fanciful illustration in a seventeenth-century European book purports to show Indians dancing on the island of Hispaniola.

The awe and innocence of the Arawaks worked to Columbus's benefit. Wherever he landed, he proclaimed possession of the Indians' lands and resources for Spain, then turned to the major objectives of his expedition: the subjugation and forced conversion of the peoples to Christianity and a search for gold and anything else that would enrich the Spanish monarchs and himself. Two days after he had made his first landing and noted how generous the Indians were, he wrote in his journal that "These people are very unskilled in arms . . . with fifty men they could all be subjected and made to do all that one wished." Action soon followed his words. "As soon as I arrived in the Indies," he wrote later, "in the first island that I found, I took some of them [Indians] by force, to the intent that they should learn and give me information of what there was in those parts."

It was a harbinger of what was to come.

In 1492, many millions of Arawaks were living on the islands of the Caribbean. Estimates vary widely, but the most recent suggest that the pre-Columbian population of Hispaniola alone may have been as high as seven or eight million. Originally the Arawaks had come from South America, migrating from island to island in large canoes about 500 B.C. and displacing earlier, more primitive hunting and gathering inhabitants known as Ciboneys. By the time of Columbus, the Ciboneys were concentrated in small areas in Cuba and Haiti, and were soon extinct.

About a century or more before the arrival of the Spaniards, the Arawaks, in turn, had come under pressure from a new wave of Indian migrants from South America—

Come l'indien aiam fait fin de son trauail po satisfaire c̃ contentu
sabun aimer se ioignent ensemble en Mariag apprea la demonstre
faicte par le pere dla fille comme orres y apprea —

L'indien aiam fait le plus grand trauail qui luy est possible po devenu
Contentans a sabun aimer s'acoustre le plus magnificquem quil puist souiens en
La maison du pere dela fille lequel luy demonstre le grand trauail qui est
en luy en labonne volon t̃ quil a dele bien nourriz. Quoy soians, le pere demonstre
a sa fille en sa presence luy disam, Il te fault auoir ce ieune homme ti ti
nourrira bien Tu bebra quil appor t̃ grand nombre de biens po nous nourrir
Il trauaille bien tans a pescher poisson, prendre bestes sauuage fait Iardinie
ba chercher fruitz bois Bref luy ce quil fault pour la nourriture dla
maison Lequel pere aiam fait laz demonstranal vierg pareillem demonstr
au ieune homme l'amit sa fille trauaille bien tans a faire du pain acoustre
l'abi, ande po mengie quelle fait cuire dedans louille au dessus dict
Le por appres auoir fait dne dte sur demonstrances Ils se ioignens ensemble
au nom de mariage en la maison du pere Es estans marie Le pere de la
mere no beullem plus viena faire es amieur Es leurs enffans les nourriss
En ny a gbne tace en chacque village en ne permetteu q̃ au dle leur tace
se demeurem. Anquel villare Ils cloisissem le plus ensien anil appelle

Pages of the Drake manuscript depict many aspects of Arawak life. The illustration above shows the way Arawaks raised crops—in meticulously kept gardens, with several types of grain growing amid the lush foliage of tall, food-bearing plants. In the next one, a skilled Arawak uses a bow and arrow to kill fish, although the most common way of harvesting the sea was with woven nets.

aggressive, warlike Caribs who terrorized the Arawaks and forced them out of the Lesser Antilles to the islands farther north. Columbus did not meet any Caribs during his first voyage, but from the Arawaks he understood that these fearsome enemies ate the flesh of their captives. On his later voyages, Columbus became familiar with the Caribs, but there is no credible evidence from any white man who witnessed the island Caribs eating human flesh. Nevertheless, from their name, which was sometimes pronounced "Caniba," Columbus's reference to them in his account of his first voyage gave the world the dreaded word "cannibal."

The Arawaks were both horticulturalists and expert boat builders and navigators, and over a two-thousand-year period, they developed a complex agricultural and trading society, living comfortably off their islands and on the waters of the surrounding sea. Their villages were governed by local leaders, known as caciques, who in turn were controlled by paramount chiefs responsible for the welfare of entire regions. In 1492, for example, in this ancient, stable world, a paramount chief named Guacanagarí—who would become well known to Columbus—ruled over a district along the northern coast of Hispaniola. He and other Arawak chiefs presided at the center of a trade network that was the lifeblood of the island peoples. Navigating in

large, oceangoing canoes, some capable of carrying 150 men, the Arawaks traveled between islands and even to distant mainland villages in Florida, Mesoamerica, and perhaps Central and South America, their craft laden with traders and their goods, including feathers, gold, wood, pottery, cotton thread and fabric, parrots, fruits, and other foods.

Important chiefs like Guacanagarí ensured their status by maintaining warehouses filled with tons of goods, while trading partners created a bond between towns, as well as individuals. Whether to express friendship or to avoid disputes, trading was ritualized as a fundamental mechanism for ensuring lasting interisland peace. At an early age, Arawak children learned the essential lesson of trade through a morality tale about their own island: There were once four brothers who went on a journey around the island. They came to the home of an old man and, greeting him as a relative although he was a stranger, one of the brothers entered his house and asked for bread to eat. But the boy failed to offer anything in return and, angered, the old man spit upon his back. The lesson was that when you ask for something, you must be prepared to give something in return.

ABOVE LEFT: *Arawak babies were born in the mother's home. During the birth, the males in the village walked around the outside of her house, playing musical instruments, dancing, singing in loud voices, and making as much noise as possible, believing that it helped drive away the mother's labor pains.*

ABOVE RIGHT: *We see Arawak hunters returning to their village with a wild hog as food for their wives who had recently given birth to their children. The Indians, according to the artist, considered the meat of pigs, introduced to the Caribbean by the Spaniards, the best and most nourishing in the islands.*

Although inaccurate in detail, these illustrations from a sixteenth-century German book show two types of craft in which the Arawaks navigated the waters of the Caribbean. The larger, raftlike vessels, with sails as well as ranks of paddlers—some "like galleys, with 15 benches," Columbus wrote—could travel long distances, plying an interisland trade that even encompassed villages on the coasts of North and South America.

From the very beginning of the contacts between the island Arawaks and the Spaniards, the monumental differences in their cultures and the ways in which they each viewed the world created mis-understandings that would have tragic consequences for the Indians. "I believe that they would become Christians very easily, for it seemed to me that they had no religion," wrote Columbus after his first encounters with the Arawaks. Actually, the Arawaks possessed a rich spiritual life inherited from centuries of ancestors. Each individual possessed a personal guardian spirit, whose powers increased according to the status of the individual. The most powerful spirits, those of the chiefs, were the gods of all the people ruled by those chiefs. In the villages, the spirits were represented by idols, called *zemis,* three-pointed stones carved with elaborate designs that symbolized humans or animals and were believed to possess the powers of the spirits. The figures of

Of anything they have, if it be asked for, they never say no, but do rather invite the person to accept it, and show as much lovingness as though they would give their hearts.

—CHRISTOPHER COLUMBUS

ABOUT THE ARAWAKS

Arawak women making unleavened flat bread, or tortillas, from cornmeal. At right, a woman grinds the meal on a metate. At rear, the tortillas are shaped and cooked, and at left they are served with stew.

the *zemis* were housed in temples, but were brought out at times of worship and ceremony, which the Arawaks observed on slab-lined ball courts, much like those of the Yucatán Mayas with whom they traded, or on dance plazas and in caves.

The Spaniards almost immediately assumed a posture of human and cultural superiority over the Indians, a Eurocentric stance that in time other European imperial powers would adopt and bequeath to generations of non-Indians throughout the Americas. Fray Bartolomé de Las Casas came to the West Indies as a Spanish colonist in 1502 but, becoming a priest and a fiery defender of the Indians, turned his voice and pen against the Spaniards' excesses. "Note here . . . ," he wrote, "the natural, simple and kind gentleness and humble conditions of the Indians, and want of arms or protection, gave the Spaniards the insolence to hold them of little account. . . . [The Spaniards] deal with them in any way they wish . . . without regard to sex, age, status, or dignity."

The Dominican missionary and historian Fray Bartolomé de Las Casas, known as the Apostle of the Indies, was the most outspoken defender of the Indians against the excesses and cruelties of his fellow Spaniards.

Arawak wood carvers worked in both wood and stone. This wood carving of a prone human figure, used as a low bench, was known as a duho. These elaborate ceremonial seats for caciques and persons of importance were among the Arawaks' most prized possessions.

Another Arawak wood carving, this unusual idol is believed to have been made either in Hispaniola or Cuba.

In December 1492, Columbus reached the heavily populated island he named Española, or, as it became known by its Latin name, Hispaniola. On Christmas Eve, while making its way along the coast, the *Santa Maria* ran aground on a coral reef. The ship was destroyed, but with the help of the friendly Arawak chief Guacanagarí and his people, the crew and most of the supplies were saved.

Guacanagarí proved a warm and trusting friend of Columbus, and the latter, in turn, was deeply impressed by the chief's noble bearing and his large village. As a token of gratitude, Columbus presented Guacanagarí with a red cape, which the Indians regarded as an object of prestige. Interpreting the gesture as the opening of trade between leaders of equal importance, Guacanagarí gave Columbus a mask, plates, a belt, and other objects of gold, revealing to him also that the source of the gold lay nearby. To Guacanagarí, the exchange of objects was a fair trade—a symbol of mutual respect and recognition. To Columbus, one of the gifts, a golden head ornament, was a crown. It represented authority, and the giving of it meant submission. He believed that Guacanagarí was delivering his land and people to Spain.

The golden gifts marked a turning point for Columbus and his attitude toward the island Arawaks. His plans had called for an immediate return to Spain, but before departing in his two remaining ships, he ordered some of his men, who would stay on the island until he came back with supplies and reinforcements, to build a tower and a fort at a site which he named La Navidad in honor of the Day of Nativity on which he had lost the *Santa Maria*. At the same time, he instructed those who would remain on the island to trade for gold with the Indians. As for Guacanagarí and the Arawaks, he noted that, "It is right that this tower be made . . . so that with love and fear they will obey."

Columbus's heart had hardened. On the coast of Hispaniola, east of Guacanagarí's domain, the ships made a brief stop, and some of the Spaniards, going ashore, had their first violent skirmish with Indians, wounding two of them. "Columbus was pleased," wrote Las Casas, paraphrasing Columbus's journal entry, "because now the Indians would fear the Christians."

On the way home, Columbus prepared a letter to the Spanish monarchs, conveying the news of a "New World," of gold, and of docile island natives—some two

This powerful stone carving of a human face shows the attention to detail, symmetry, and integration of symbolic elements common in the sculptural art of the Arawaks before the Spaniards destroyed their culture.

dozen of whom he had captured and was taking back to show off in Spain. "They are fit to be ordered about and made to work, to sow and do aught else that may be needed," he noted in his letter, adding darkly that among the sources of wealth that he could ship from the new lands for the profit of the sovereigns were Indian "slaves, as many as they shall order." (For a while, the court hesitated to approve the enslavement of Indians. But that did not stop Columbus, who, on his return to the islands, soon began shipping Indians in chains to the slave markets of Cádiz and Seville. In 1503, Queen Isabella finally granted permission "to capture" idolatrous and cannibalistic Indians, "paying us the share that belongs to us, and to sell them and utilize their services.")

With a fleet of seventeen ships, some twelve hundred colonists, and thirty-four horses—the first in the Western Hemisphere since the disappearance of small Ice Age horses—Columbus returned to La Navidad in November 1493. On his way to Hispaniola, he stopped briefly at the island now known as St. Croix, where without provocation members of his expedition attacked four Indian men and two women in a canoe, cutting off the head of one of the men with an ax and taking the other Indians aboard ship as captives to send back to Spain as slaves. It was the first recorded instance of the killing of an Indian by Spaniards and reflected the arrogance and cruelty with which the Europeans, led by Columbus himself, would now deal with the natives. While still at St. Croix, one of the colonists, a nobleman and friend of Columbus, wrote boastingly of an episode revealing another aspect of the master-slave relationship that lay in wait for the native population:

> I took a most beautiful Carib woman, whom the lord Admiral made a gift of to me; and having her in my berth, with her being nude according to her customs, the desire to enjoy myself with her came over me; and wishing to put my desire to work, she resisting, she scratched me with her fingernails to such a degree that I would not have wished then that I had begun; but with that seen . . . I grabbed a leather strap and gave her a good chastisement of lashes, so that she hurled such unheard of shouts that you could not believe. Finally, we reached an agreement in such a manner that I can tell you that in fact she seemed to have been taught in the school for whores.

In the first island that I found, I took some of them [Indians] by force, to the intent that they should learn and give me information of what there was in those parts.

—CHRISTOPHER COLUMBUS

A De Bry engraving depicts the Spanish
conquerors seizing and hanging Indians aboard
their ships. Those who jumped overboard and
escaped were later rounded up and hanged on
gallows the Spaniards erected on land.

The Indian woman was actually an Arawak. There were no Caribs on St. Croix,
but the Spaniards were already getting in the habit of terming any resisting Indian a
Carib, as if justifying the notion that one could do anything one wished to an alleged
cannibal.

Columbus finally reached Hispaniola and was stunned to discover that in his absence, La Navidad had been wiped out, the fort and settlement burned, and all of his
men killed. Wounded, in tears, and professing loyalty and friendship, Guacanagarí,
supported by his anguished people, told a convincing story of cruel and unprincipled
behavior by the Spaniards as soon as Columbus had left, of the whites' quarreling
among themselves, and of their finally having invaded the country of another powerful cacique named Caonabó, who, becoming provoked, slew them and destroyed
the town. Guacanagarí had tried in vain to defend the Spaniards and showed Colum-

bus the wounds he had received for his pains. Some of Columbus's men wanted to kill Guacanagarí, but the explorer chose to accept his story and, more interested in the pursuit of gold, left the unhappy chief and sailed farther east along the Hispaniola coast to establish a new colony which he called La Isabela and which he believed was closer to the source of the gold. As for Guacanagarí, despite his trust and sincere friendship for the whites, in the end, according to Las Casas, he suffered a bitter fate. Forced to flee "from the massacres and cruelty of the Christians, he died a wanderer in the mountains, ruined and deprived of his state."

The Spanish conquest of the Caribbean had now begun. Finding the gold he sought, Columbus put Indians to work, panning flakes from the rivers or slaving in mines in the mountains. The hard work, coupled with the brutality of the Spaniards, brought about Indian revolts, which the Spaniards crushed with unrestrained savagery. Cavalry and fierce dogs were set on Indian villages; whole populations were rounded up and either killed or shipped to the slave markets in Spain; individuals had their noses or ears cut off or were burned alive or hanged on one of the 340 gallows that the Spaniards erected across the countryside. The cacique Caonabó was seized in his village, taken in shackles to La Isabela, and shipped to Spain to be sold as a slave. En route he died—of "anguish of mind." On one occasion, Columbus ordered the decapitation of a number of Indians who were innocent of any wrongdoing. On another, he ordered every Arawak Indian over the age of fourteen to pay a tribute to him of a hawk's bell full of gold every three months. The order was "impossible and intolerable," said Las Casas, although those who failed to comply faced the threat of having their hands cut off and being left to bleed to death.

Between 1495 and 1496, famine, as well as epidemics of European diseases against which the island Indians had no defense, swept off great numbers of them. Still, the Spaniards continued to demand that they work and supply the whites with food. The Indians' suffering grew so intense that people by the thousands took their own lives. "Many went to the woods," wrote Girolamo Benzoni, another critic of Spanish cruelties, "and there hanged themselves, after having killed their children, saying it was far better to die than to live so miserably. . . . Some threw themselves from high cliffs down precipices; others jumped into the sea."

By 1502, only a few pockets of resisting Indians remained. In the mountainous region of Xaragua, the Arawaks, ruled by Queen Anacaona, the widow of Caonabó, evaded Spanish demands for labor. The new Spanish governor, Nicolás de Ovando, who had succeeded Columbus, requested a diplomatic meeting with Anacaona. She agreed to the talks and summoned her eighty regional subchiefs for the meeting. When all were assembled in the statehouse, the Spanish governor gave a signal and

the thatched roof and sides were set afire. Ovando's soldiers, with swords and bayonets, ringed the outside of the building, and the Arawak leaders who were not burned to death inside were slain as they tried to escape from the blaze. The Spaniards spared Anacaona, only to "honor" her in a public execution by hanging.

In the aftermath of the carnage, a little boy stood amid the ashes and smoke over the charred remains of his father. His name was Guarocuya, and he was the son of a noted cacique and a grandnephew of Anacaona. The young Indian heir was taken by a Spanish priest, raised by missionaries, and baptized Enrique—a name the Spaniards would know well once he grew to manhood. He became, according to Las Casas, tall and graceful, with a well-proportioned body. His face was neither handsome nor ugly, but that of a stern and serious man. He married a native woman "of excellent and noble lineage" named Dona Lucia.

By this time, Columbus had introduced to the islands an institution known as *encomienda*, by which he could give individual Spanish colonists the Indians' lands and the labor of the Indians who lived upon them— in effect, rewarding favored colonists with both lands and slaves. The region of Bahoruco to which Enrique was the rightful heir, along with the right to the Indian labor on it, had been given to a debauched young Spaniard named Valenzuela. Enrique, his wife, and his people were at Valenzuela's mercy.

According to Las Casas, the Spaniards burned thousands of Arawaks at the stake for various acts of defiance. Samuel de Champlain, later to become well known for his explorations in Canada, included this watercolor of Spaniards burning Indians in the narrative of his voyage to the West Indies from 1599 to 1601.

Valenzuela treated Enrique "as though he were dung of the market square," wrote Las Casas, "but [Enrique] is truly more suited to be his lord than his servant." Enrique did his best to comply with Valenzuela's tyrannical demands, suffering beatings and other abuse, including having one of his last remaining possessions, his horse, taken from him. But when Valenzuela raped his wife, Enrique reached the breaking point. He challenged his master, but was badly beaten. He appealed to the Spanish

In this De Bry engraving, Arawak Indian forces like those of the rebel leader Enrique are shown defending a hill in the mountains of Hispaniola against a Spanish attack.

authorities, who simply turned him back to his enemy Valenzuela. Stripped of his land, his heritage, and his dignity, Enrique finally confronted his oppressors, outraging them by telling them to their faces that "Christians . . . are bad men, tyrants, who want only to usurp the land of others and only know how to spill the blood of those who have never given offence."

With a group of followers, he escaped to the Bahoruco Mountains. The enraged Spaniards called him the rebel Enrique, and his followers were condemned as insurgents. Although they were armed only with spears, iron spikes, and bows and arrows, they fought with determination against the Spaniards and their more sophisticated weapons. Time and again, they resisted the Spaniards and made them retreat.

As word of Enrique's victories spread across the island, many Arawaks fled to his refuge and joined him. Acting according to the traditional rights and responsibilities of a paramount chief, Enrique assumed his proper role as protector of his people. He organized his followers, directed their tasks, and trained the military. Village chiefs assisted him. Women, children, and old people were sent to live in caves high in the mountains, where they raised chickens and tended vegetable plots to feed the Indian army. Scouts were posted on all the crags above the passes, and big boulders were rolled into place above the mountain paths. Fighting defensively, Enrique instructed his men to kill Spaniards only in the course of a battle, and otherwise simply to deprive them of their arms. On one occasion, he even spared Valenzuela's life. It was said that Enrique never slept at night and himself patrolled the village until every dawn. For fourteen years, Enrique and his Arawak supporters fought the Spaniards to a standstill.

There was one Spaniard to whom Enrique would still talk—the priest Las Casas. The compassionate Las Casas, who would become known as the Protector of the Indians, met with Enrique in his mountain stronghold. Two months later, the two men appeared before the Spanish authorities and negotiated a truce between the Indians and the government. The long rebellion came to an end, but only after the Spaniards agreed to Enrique's terms: the guarantee of freedom for all the remaining Arawak people.

There were few of them left. Of all the millions who had inhabited the islands in 1492, only handfuls had survived. On Hispaniola, four thousand Arawaks remained to follow Enrique to a settlement at the base of the Cibao Mountains, where the Spaniards let them live in peace and security. By 1542, fifty years after Columbus had first come upon them, the Arawak population was down to two hundred, and the Spaniards were replacing their labor with that of black slaves imported in chains from Africa. By 1552, the Indians on Hispaniola had become extinct.

"If we Christians had acted as we should . . ." Las Casas wrote sadly.

The Calusas of Florida

Northwest of the Arawaks and Caribs of the West Indies, in the southern part of the Florida peninsula on the mainland, was another proud and determined Indian nation, that of the Calusas, who also fought hard against the Spaniards. Possessing one of the most unusual civilizations in North America, the Calusas built their capital city, known as Calos, on huge shell mounds on the peninsula's southwest coast in the area of San Carlos Bay, near present-day Fort Myers.

Few places on earth could have been more benign or beautiful than southern Florida. In the coastal waters and the marine meadows, there was such an abundance of food that dense Indian populations, as well as intricate cultures, arose without the use of agriculture. The Calusas were maritime oriented, but they did more than fish: they farmed the sea. They created systems of lagoons for oyster beds and stone holding pens for sea turtles, mullet, and other fish with which the waters teemed.

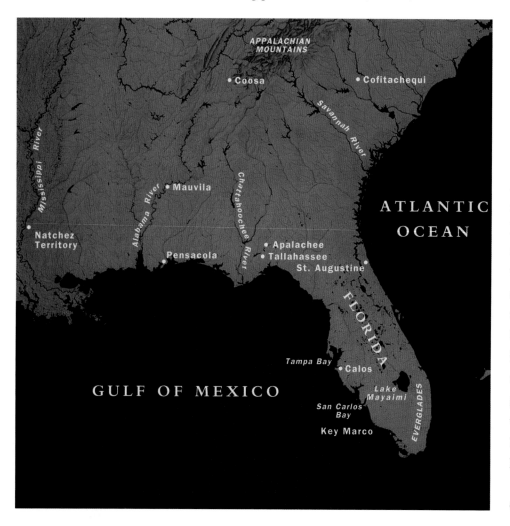

Centuries before the arrival of Europeans, the Calusas extended their influence across southern Florida to the Atlantic coast and Lake Okeechobee (which they called Mayaimi) in a trade and communications network that stretched for hundreds of miles through the mangrove swamps and interior hammocks and saw-grass prairies of the Everglades. In time, they dominated all the tribes in the southern part of the peninsula and held sway over some fifty tributary towns. In addition, Calusa traders, experienced in long-distance sea travel, journeyed in canoes—usually large, shovel-nosed double canoes that, lashed together like catamarans and equipped with a sail, held up to fifty men—to Indian coastal towns in the Florida Keys, the Bahamas, and Cuba.

From his grand statehouse at Calos—in which he could enter-

From Galicia.

F. Delfinum.

I

tain two thousand guests—the Calusa king, a hereditary paramount chief who was believed to have supernatural powers and ruled with unquestioned authority, commanded not only a standing army but the operations of a variety of public works. As revealed in modern times by infrared photography, the Calusas built numerous canals for transportation and trade through the difficult terrain, bisecting present-day Pine Island with a canal and cutting other waterways to give their traders and warriors access to the Lake Okeechobee region and the lands beyond. The Calusas also built islands. Many Calusa towns literally rose from the coastal waters on large, man-made islands piled up from mounds of shells and protected by seawalls. To help withstand the hurricanes that swept in from the Caribbean, they planted mangrove trees as windbreaks for their homes, temples, and other buildings on the mounds.

The grandeur of their ceremonial center at Key Marco, an island of shell on the west coast, was legendary. Covering fifty acres, it was intersected by nine canals leading inward to its midpoint from the sea. At the island's southern end, a massive seawall jutted out into the water, serving as a break against storms. Within the island, the Calusas constructed three lagoons, connecting the largest to a canal that led to a central pyramid mound, eighteen feet high, that commanded a view of the whole island and supported a temple on its summit. At the base of the pyramid was a central court,

This De Bry engraving, based on a drawing by Jacque Le Moyne de Morgues, an artist who accompanied a French expedition in the 1550s, depicts Indian life and the flora and fauna of the mainland territory Ponce de León named Pascua Florida (for the Easter Feast of Flowers). Before the coming of the Europeans, Florida was the home of numerous Indian nations, including the powerful Calusas, who inhabited the southwestern coast of the peninsula, making a comfortable living from the sea.

OVERLEAF: *Searching for gold, slaves, and the mythic life-giving waters of the Fountain of Youth, Ponce de León arrived in Florida in 1513. Driven off by the Calusas, he returned with two hundred colonists in 1521, only to be rebuffed again and be mortally wounded by another Calusa force. This nineteenth-century painting by the American artist Thomas Moran shows the Spanish explorer's first expedition in the forested Timucuan country north of the Calusas.*

flanked by water tanks and terraced gardens. Canoes carrying goods and tribute from distant nations plied along Key Marco's canals; specialists created religious and functional objects; and off the coast and in the lagoons, Calusa fishermen hurled their nets and farmed the waters.

In the warm climate, most buildings had no walls, but were simply raised platforms with poles supporting thatched roofs. With abundant food from the sea, as well as game, roots, and wild fruits and berries from the land, the people had time for leisure activities. Many were sophisticated artisans, creating among other objects some of the finest wood carvings produced by Indians anywhere in North America. At the same time, a principal concern of the Calusas was keeping life pure and unpolluted. A host of rules of behavior existed to maintain the purity and harmony needed for the survival and well-being of individuals and the whole community. Offenses that endangered that harmony might result in illness, a storm, or some disaster that the Calusas interpreted as the displeasure of an evil god or force. Ceremonies and rituals, including a human sacrifice to a deity, were sometimes considered necessary to set things right and restore harmony.

The Calusas undoubtedly first heard of the Spaniards—of their ships that moved like houses on the water, their firearms, and strange and brutal conduct—as early as the time of Columbus, for Indian traders in large canoes could have crossed to the mainland from the islands, bringing the news. At length, the ships of the bearded strangers began to appear off the Florida coasts, and the reports of the white men became real. Here and there along the peninsula, the big ships paused, and armed groups of slave-catching Spaniards came ashore, kidnapping Indians to take back to sell as laborers in the Caribbean island mines. Word of the whites' aggressiveness spread from town to town among the Calusas, whose revered and aged chief—later known to the Spaniards as Carlos—lived in the nation's capital at Calos. Believing that something had thrown their world out of balance and had sent this new threatening force against them, Carlos and his people regarded the Spaniards as an enemy to be fought.

Carved masks like the one in this watercolor painting were important elements in the spiritual life of the Calusas. This one is from Key Marco, an important Calusa economic and ceremonial center.

The explorer Juan Ponce de León was the first known European to be driven off by the Calusas. Ponce had accompanied Columbus to the West Indies on his second voyage in 1493. A leader in the suppression of the Indians on Hispaniola, he had then conquered Puerto Rico, enslaving its Indian population, becoming governor of the island, and growing rich as a plantation owner. In 1512, he received royal permission to explore to the north, and he sailed the next year. History says that he was in search of a wondrous spring on an island called Bimini which Puerto Rican Indians had assured him would restore a man's youth, but it is likely that he was also bent on finding more gold and a new source of Indian slaves.

He failed to find the fabled Fountain of Youth but officially revealed to the Old World the presence of the land he reached in 1513, which he named Pascua Florida for the Eastertime Feast of Flowers in the April season when he stepped ashore. His first landings were on the Atlantic coast of the peninsula in the domains of Timucuan and Ais Indians. Both regarded him as a slave catcher, and after fierce skirmishes, during which Ponce managed to kidnap a few people, the Indians drove him away. Sailing south, he rounded the Keys and tried to land in the heart of the Calusas' territory at San Carlos Bay on the west coast. Carlos's tough, canoe-borne warriors, in two days of desperate fighting on the beaches and around the Spanish ships, forced Ponce to withdraw, with only nine struggling Calusas whom his men had captured to take back to Puerto Rico.

More Spanish intruders entered Calusa waters in 1517, this time as members of a crew on a storm-tossed vessel who claimed they only wished to take on water. Detecting more hostile motives, the Calusas attacked them and, after inflicting some casualties, drove them away. In 1521, Ponce, now sixty years old, appeared again, this time leading two hundred Spanish settlers who intended to establish

Somewhat mysteriously, Key Marco—where this dramatic wolf mask was found—was abandoned by the Calusas shortly before Ponce de León first reached Florida. There is evidence that some of the buildings were burned, and it is possible that the site had become too vulnerable to Spanish slave raiders from the Caribbean islands.

In 1895, archaeologists discovered a vast number of Key Marco artifacts submerged in the swampy area at the site of the ancient Calusa town. Although the objects were hundreds of years old and many had been made of wood, the mud had preserved them almost perfectly, as evidenced by the still-intact details of this carved wooden tablet.

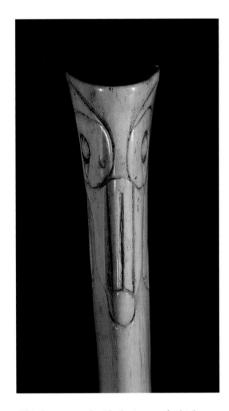

This bone, carved with the image of a bird, was among many decorated pins and awls found at Key Marco.

a colony in Carlos's territory. The Spaniards landed and managed to erect a temporary settlement before a large force of Calusas attacked them. Although the Spaniards' horses and firearms helped the colonists hold off the Indians, the Calusas, fighting with poisoned darts and arrows, inflicted large losses on the Europeans and seriously wounded Ponce in the thigh. The Spanish leader gave up a second time and with the survivors of his failed colony sailed to Havana, where he died of his infected arrow wound.

In the following years, the Calusas were able to maintain their kingdom. Spanish ships, bound for Spain laden with treasure from Mexico and other conquered Indian countries, followed the winds and current northward through the Straits of Florida. Often, they were wrecked in storms, and their crews and passengers were cast ashore on the Keys and the southern Florida coast. Many were captured by the Calusas or the inhabitants of one of their tributary towns and sent to Carlos, who killed or enslaved them or sacrificed them to the gods. The salvaged cargoes of the wrecked ships, often consisting of large quantities of gold and silver, were also sent to Carlos, who traded some of it to other tribes throughout Florida, further enhancing his power and prestige.

Eventually, it led to the undoing of his son and successor, Carlos II. In the years after Ponce, the Spaniards kept coming but avoided the Calusas' country. Farther north, they invaded the lands of Timucuan nations along the Gulf coast and became embroiled in religious warfare with some French Huguenots who had established a fort and settlement in the northeastern part of the peninsula. In 1565, Spaniards under Pedro Menéndez de Avilés, after building a fort at St. Augustine that would become the first permanent white settlement in the United States, wiped out the French.

Menéndez, a fanatically devout Catholic and aggressive empire builder intent on establishing the power of Spain and the Church throughout Florida, founded garrisoned posts along the peninsula's Atlantic coast and, assisted by Jesuit priests, made plans to convert Florida's Indian nations to Christianity. From the beginning, he had a particular interest in the Calusas and in the Spanish castaways whom they were reported to hold captive. One of them was believed to be his own son. In addition, there was the lure of the gold and other treasure recovered from the wrecked ships and now kept from the Spaniards by the Calusas.

In 1566, Menéndez sailed into the Calusa harbor on the southwest coast and was permitted to come ashore. The new Calusa leader, Carlos II, whose father had driven Ponce de León away almost half a century before, was only twenty-five years old, but in the art of diplomatic maneuvering he was the equal of Menéndez. The youthful ruler would have had reasons for agreeing to meet the Spaniards. For one thing,

Like the town of Key Marco, the Calusa nation itself eventually disappeared. Objects like this wooden feline effigy, photographed from two angles, are all that is left of the once-great Calusa culture.

he could see the power of the white men, with their superior weapons, growing stronger in Florida, threatening the Calusas with the same fate as that of the Arawaks. If he became a trading partner of the Spaniards, he could reason, he might strengthen his position and avert such a fate. In addition, while the Calusas still dominated southern Florida, their Timucuan enemies farther north had begun to grow in power by their acquisition of valuable Spanish trade goods. The development was weakening the Calusas' hold over their far-flung tributary towns, and Carlos could have believed that a trade partnership with the Spaniards might enable him to increase his prestige and maintain his authority over his empire. Finally, he was curious about the Spaniards' religion and wanted to learn—and, if desirable, to acquire—the secrets of their gods for himself.

Flanked by a guard of three hundred archers, Carlos sparred diplomatically with Menéndez, exchanging gifts and trying to keep the upper hand. Menéndez temporarily outwitted him, however, by luring him and twenty of his men aboard one of his ships and holding them at gunpoint until the Calusas released all the Christian castaways they were holding. Although some of the Spanish women who were living in Calusa towns with their Indian husbands and half-blood children refused to return to white society, Carlos readily had his people deliver to Menéndez all the rest of the captives (who seem not to have included Menéndez's missing son), as well as some of the gold and silver bullion that the Indians had salvaged from the wrecks.

It was now Carlos's turn to ask for something. To bind his relations with the Spaniards, he proposed to make Menéndez his brother by having him marry his sister. Startled, Menéndez balked at the idea, but the issue threatened to create a crisis, and the Spanish leader finally agreed to the union.

The next day, the Calusas and Spaniards joined in a celebration at the Calusa statehouse to formalize the alliance. Although uncomfortable and planning to avoid consummating the marriage, Menéndez continued to placate Carlos, arriving at the statehouse with a display of pomp that included a Spanish flag, two hundred soldiers, a dancing dwarf, and the music of two fifes, drums, three trumpets, a harp, and a violin. Carlos, in turn, brought with him fifty chiefs; a great number of relatives, including brothers, uncles, and aunts, some of whom were ninety or a hundred years old; a troupe of male tumblers; and a choir of five hundred girls who seated themselves outside the statehouse and sang "all in great harmony."

There was much feasting, music, dancing, delivery of compliments—and mirth occasioned by embarrassing gaffes on the part of Menéndez. At one point, he publicly extolled the virtues of a Calusa lady who he thought was Carlos's wife only to discover that he had addressed the wrong person. When he tried to make amends by flattering the right lady, he did so with such ardor that both Carlos and his wife became agitated, thinking that Menéndez had designs on her. Only with difficulty was the proper and dignified Spanish leader able to reassure them of his innocent intentions.

At the end of the evening, as Menéndez prepared to depart, he shocked Carlos by revealing that he had no intention of taking his new wife with him. After considerable arguing, during which the Calusa leader suggested that he would not oppose the conversion of the Calusas to Christianity if Menéndez honored the marriage to his sister and took her with him, the Spanish leader gave in. At the harbor, he had her baptized Doña Antonia, and the next day, with his new wife and a number of other Calusas, he sailed for Havana, where he promised Carlos he would have the Indians instructed in the white men's religion.

In Cuba, Doña Antonia was placed in the care of a lieutenant in charge of Florida affairs, who was instructed to educate her in Christian doctrine. Then Menéndez departed for four months. During his absence, several of the Calusas in Havana died of disease. Doña Antonia became lonely and depressed, then angry at the husband who had paid no attention to her and had left her in the strange city. When Menéndez came back, she begged to be sent home, and Menéndez was glad to comply.

When Menéndez and Doña Antonia returned to Calusa territory, relations between the Spaniards and Carlos soured. The Calusa ruler and his religious leaders ridiculed, threatened, and finally rejected a Jesuit missionary whom Menéndez sent to convert them. At the same time, the people reacted strongly against a blockhouse that Spanish troops built in their capital city. For a time, Doña Antonia was held hostage to gain the Indians' obedience. Then in a breach of diplomatic faith, Menéndez opened trade relations with the Calusas' enemies, the Tocobagas, who lived just to the north. Doña Antonia and her brother were furious. "[Menéndez] has two hearts," she charged. "One for himself and one for Tocobaga, but none at all for [me] or [my] brother."

Determined now to drive the Spaniards out of his country, Carlos increased his threats. When he tried to seize a Spanish ship, Menéndez lost patience and ordered his execution. The young chief, with twenty of his principal men, was seized by trickery and beheaded, leaving the Calusa empire stunned and leaderless. The Spaniards installed a more pliant Calusa, whom they called Don Felipe, as Carlos's successor, but in the Indians' eyes he had no right to the position, and they refused to acknowledge him. Supported by the Spaniards' arms, he became a hated despot and caused the deaths of fifteen chiefs who opposed him. Finally, the Spaniards caught him plotting against them and killed him, along with fourteen of his followers.

The Calusas had now had enough of the white men. In an act of desperation, they burned their capital of Calos and fled from the island on which their ancestors had built the town. Without the food and labor which the Indians had been forced to supply them, the Spaniards abandoned the post and left the Calusa country. Enraged and frustrated, Menéndez and other Spaniards proposed exterminating the whole Calusa nation or impressing its people into slavery. The prospect of opposition by the Spanish court, as well as the impracticality of the notion, made this impossible, however, and the Spaniards gave up the area, persuading themselves that as a barren, nonagricultural region, unable even to grow corn for their colonies, it had nothing of value for them.

Left to themselves, the Calusas returned to the ruins of their town, named a proper successor as their head chief, and continued their old ways. A century later, they established amicable relations with more benign Spanish authorities in Florida and, opening trade with Spaniards on the peninsula as well as in Cuba, which they could reach in their boats in twenty-four hours, gradually adopted various Spanish customs. Nevertheless, although they became known in Florida as "the Spanish Indians," they never adopted Christianity. White men's diseases, running wild among all of Florida's Indians, eventually reduced their numbers drastically, ending their strong, independent chiefdom and accomplishing what Menéndez had failed to do. In the eighteenth and nineteenth centuries, small, surviving groups of Calusas joined migrant bands of Creeks and others who were entering Florida from the north. With them, they became the Seminole and Miccosukee Indian nations of today.

The Resistance to de Soto

From Florida, the Spaniards in the sixteenth century kept constantly on the move, seeking new lands, gold, and Indians to convert or enslave. The *Requerimiento,* read in Spanish by conquistadors to uncomprehending Indians, was a formal prelude to conquest:

> We ask and require you . . . to acknowledge the Church as the ruler and superior of the whole world, and the high priest called the Pope and in his name the King [of Spain] as lords of . . . this terra firma. . . . [If you submit], we . . . shall receive you in all love and charity, and shall leave you, your wives and children, and your lands, free without servitude. . . .
>
> But if you do not [submit] . . . we shall powerfully enter into your country, and shall make war against you. . . . We shall take you, and your wives, and your children, and shall make slaves of them . . . and we shall take away your goods and shall do you all the harm and damage we can.

The start of the de Soto expedition at Tampa Bay in 1539, as envisioned by Seth Eastman, an early nineteenth-century American artist

A De Bry view of a hunting technique commonly used by the Indians in the Southeast. To creep close to their quarry, hunters disguised themselves as deer, cloaking themselves in the hides and heads of animals they had previously killed.

In the summer of 1539, the conquistador Hernando de Soto, who had been one of Francisco Pizarro's sternest lieutenants in the destruction of the Incan empire in Peru, set out in search of more treasure and gold hidden among still-unknown Indian empires on the mainland. This time he had a license from the Spanish king to "conquer, pacify, and people" what is now the southeastern part of the United States. Landing above the Calusa country on Florida's west coast with an army of six hundred soldiers, one hundred servants, two hundred horses, herds of pack animals and swine, and trained attack dogs—terrifying greyhounds paid the wages of soldiers— he would adhere closely to the letter and spirit of the *Requerimiento*.

De Soto was entering the lush and fertile country, the wooded mountains, green valleys, and swampy bottomlands of the southeastern chiefdoms—inheritors of the Mississippian civilization. Dozens of sovereign Indian nations, including the ancestors of tribes that would later become known to white men as the Choctaws, Chickasaws, Cherokees, Muskokees (Creeks), and Natchez, carried on the traditions of mound building and of paying religious honor to the sun. Hundreds of towns lined the rivers: towns with statehouses and the homes of chiefs on the mounds; large plazas for ceremonies and other public gatherings; cleared playing fields for ball games; and carefully tended agricultural fields spreading into the distance.

The nations were ruled from their principal towns by paramount chiefs who were assisted by members of noble lineages in administering the affairs of state. Other towns, ruled, in turn, by local chiefs assisted by local elites and councils of elders, were often vassals of the paramount chiefs, paying tribute in maize, deerskins, woven mantles, salt, and other commodities to the capital and supplying manpower for large armies that defended the nation against rivals. Within each town, whether it was autonomous or part of a larger political entity, clans—extended families guided by the

But if you do not [submit] . . . we shall powerfully enter into your country, and shall make war against you. . . . We shall take you, and your wives, and your children, and shall make slaves of them.

—THE SPANISH *REQUERIMIENTO*

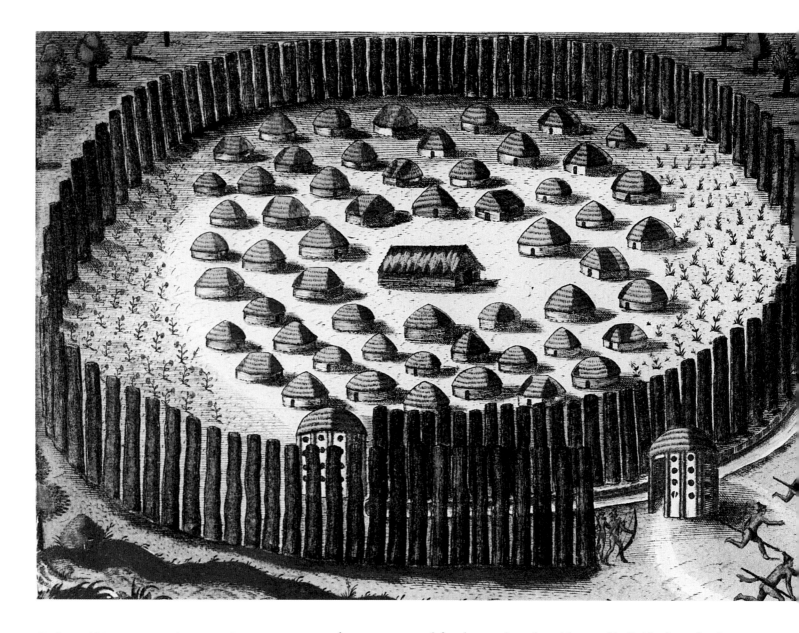

De Soto and his men encountered remnants of the great Mississippian cultures that had flourished in the Southeast for hundreds of years. Many still consisted of politically and religiously centralized chiefdoms ruled by priests, nobles, and paramount chiefs. The long structure in the center of this De Bry engraving of a Timucuan town in Florida was a "town hall," or statehouse, for the chief and his councillors and served also for ceremonies and community meetings. It was surrounded by the dwellings of the villagers and by a palisade for protection from enemies.

most respected women—cared for the needs and problems of individuals, enforcing the rules of community conduct and maintaining the peoples' purity and harmony with the universe.

Throughout this ancient world, from Florida to Texas, for the next four years de Soto and his army cut a path of unparalleled destruction.

First, they marched through the densely populated Timucuan country, the lands of strong chiefdoms stretching across north-central Florida. Entering one town after another, plundering them of their food stores and valuables and threatening torture and death to those who resisted submission, they seized men and women, commoners and members of the ruling classes alike, and took them along as burden bearers, clamped in great iron neck collars and linked together by chains. Stories of the Spaniards' barbarism spread among the Timucuas, and some of the chiefs got their people out of the way of the terrible new enemy or fought back in sharp guerrilla engagements.

In agriculture, Timucuan women worked side by side with the men, as this engraving shows. While the men broke up the ground, the women dug holes into which they dropped seeds of beans and maize.

Despite casualties, de Soto marched ahead, seizing food, impressing Indians as guides and servants, and forcing chiefs to swear submission to the Christian pope and the Spanish king. Occasionally, he met defiance. Refusing to come to meet the Spaniards, the paramount Timucuan chief of Acuera instead sent a fiery message which was interpreted for de Soto:

> I am king in my land, and it is unnecessary for me to become the subject of a person who has no more vassals than I. I regard those men as vile and contemptible who subject themselves to the yoke of someone else when they can live as free men. Accordingly, I and all my people have vowed to die a hundred deaths to maintain the freedom of our land. This is our answer, both for the present and forevermore.

Although he searched, de Soto failed to find the patriot Acuera chief, whose warriors harassed and ambushed the Spaniards. Fourteen of the whites were slain and many more wounded by the Acuerans before the frustrated de Soto marched out of the area.

Based on a Le Moyne drawing, this De Bry engraving pictures some of the ways in which the Florida Indians cured their sick. At right, a man lying on his stomach inhales the smoke of burning seeds with medicinal properties. The Indian on his back at left is having blood taken from his forehead, while the man at center rear is smoking tobacco to help combat an infection.

Farther on, in another Timucuan chiefdom, the Spaniards had more difficulties. Bursting into a large town, they tried to force the inhabitants into submission. The people fled in panic, running toward the principal building, where the chief and his military leaders resided. Before the chief could organize resistance, the Spaniards surrounded the building and, blocking its doors, threatened to burn it down and kill all those who were huddled inside. Surrendering, the chief was held prisoner, and the next day was ordered by de Soto to persuade the leaders of two neighboring chiefdoms to come in and

The paramount chiefs of the southeastern Indian nations were often treated as divine beings. De Bry titled this engraving "the recreational walk of the [Timucuan] king and queen."

submit. One of them did so, but the second one, heaping scorn on the chief who had sent him de Soto's demand, castigated the Spaniards as "sons of the devil" (in the Spanish translation) who "go from land to land killing, robbing and sacking whatever they find, and possessing themselves of the wives and daughters of others . . . without shame of men or fear of any god."

Nevertheless, after de Soto sent another delegation to see him, the chief seemed to have an abrupt change of mind and, appearing suddenly to recognize the Spaniards' military supremacy, allowed them to enter his principal town and house themselves in its buildings. For four days, the army feasted on the town's food supplies while the chief planned his strategy to destroy the invaders. Summoning warriors from throughout his chiefdom, he ordered them to keep carrying food, water, and wood to the Spaniards so they would become used to the presence of so many Indians in town. Then he instructed the interpreters to persuade de Soto to join him on a plain outside of town to observe a display of the abilities of his army, which he would then put at their disposal. Meanwhile, he arranged that at a given signal, the Timucuan warriors would turn their weapons on the Spaniards and drive them from their country.

Unfortunately for the chief, one of the interpreters betrayed the plan to de Soto. Instead of seizing the chief, the Spanish leader schemed to turn the plot to his own advantage. On the appointed day, both armies met on the plain, supposedly in friendship,

Timucuan women return to their town, bringing in baskets filled with game, fish, and produce from their fields.

to demonstrate their respective skills. Suddenly, de Soto gave a signal, and the Spaniards attacked the Timucuas, seizing the chief and driving the warriors back toward a lake. Pursued by two hundred cavalrymen and lancers, many of the Indians were slain on the field. Jumping into the lake, the others swam toward the center as the Spaniards surrounded

R.Holata Outina.

the body of water. Throughout the day, de Soto's men discharged their crossbows and harquebuses at those in the lake, trying to force them to surrender. By nightfall, not a single Indian had yielded. At length, as the Spaniards continued their harassments in the dark, the first Timucuan tired of the long trial of treading water and gave himself up. Then another surrendered. By dawn, almost fifty had allowed themselves to be dragged from the water. Throughout the morning, the Spaniards kept up a relentless vigil, and by noon, all but seven exhausted Indians had surrendered. Exasperated, de Soto ordered the soldiers to enter the water and take them by force. The seven were dragged to shore by their hair and thrown upon the bank. They had been in the lake in water over their heads for thirty hours. Three of them were only eighteen years old.

The chief was imprisoned, and the hundreds of Timucuas taken from the water were chained and distributed among the soldiers as slaves. For seven days, the chief sat silently and almost without life, lulling his captors into complacency. Then seated

Another De Bry engraving, based on a Le Moyne eyewitness drawing in Florida, depicts a Timucuan army departing for war against an enemy. In the center of the massed warriors is their paramount chief, Outina, and at their head are war and religious leaders.

An early seventeenth-century depiction of de Soto's men, with horses and firearms, trapping helpless Indians on the bank of a river.

beside de Soto he suddenly lunged at the Spanish leader, landing a tremendous blow on his face with his fist, at the same time letting out a roar "that could be heard for a quarter of a league around." In an instant, he was killed by the swords of a dozen Spaniards. De Soto lay unconscious for more than a half hour, bleeding through his eyes, nose, and mouth. Both his front and back teeth had been loosened, and two had been knocked out. For weeks, he had to wear a face plaster.

The enraged Spaniards fell upon the Timucuas, killing them indiscriminately. Many were roped around the neck and held tightly like cattle, while swordsmen thrust and slashed at their heads, extremities, and bodies, lopping off pieces of their flesh until the victims died. Others were tied to stakes in the plaza and shot full of arrows. "It was very fortunate for our men that most of the Indians were in chains or other confinements," wrote a Spanish chronicler of the expedition, "for they were valiant and spirited people, and had they found themselves free, would have done more harm. With all that, imprisoned as they were, they tried to do everything they could; and for this reason the Spaniards killed each of them, not permitting a single one to live, which was a great pity."

At length, the Spaniards left the Timucuas' country and entered that of the Apalachees, a rich agricultural chiefdom centered at the site of present-day Tallahassee. De Soto and his men wintered there for six months, again seizing the Indians' stores of food and fighting off repeated Apalachee attacks. Finally, still in quest of gold, they moved north through what are now Georgia and South Carolina, leaving

After ravaging the lands of the Timucuas, de Soto entered the territory of their northern neighbors, the Apalachees, where his troops wintered for six months, living on the stores of those people. Here, Apalachees are seen at work, according to the text accompanying De Bry's engravings, mining for gold in the streams. Later, history tells us the metal was probably copper. The "mining" seems to occur by gathering the sand up in hollow pipes and depositing the contents on the creek bank.

behind them a trail of burned and looted towns, tortured and murdered Indians, and crippled or destroyed Mississippian chiefdoms.

In April 1540, the expedition reached the country of Muskokean-speaking Kasihtas, ruled by an elderly woman chieftain. Stories of the Spaniards' brutality had preceded

An eighteenth-century view of de Soto's men burning an Indian village. In the background, Spaniards fire on the inhabitants who are trying to flee across a river in large canoes to safety.

them, and in their principal town of Cofitachequi, near present-day Camden, South Carolina, the Indians made preparations to cope with the strangers. Food stores were gathered together and hidden so the Spaniards would not be able to steal them, and the aged chief was secreted in a town far distant from de Soto's path. The Spanish army, the Kasihtas hoped, would proceed through their lands quietly and without trouble.

When de Soto arrived on the banks of the Wateree River opposite Cofitachequi, he was greeted by the lovely young niece of the old chieftain, who crossed the river with eight of her ladies in a large canoe. Covered by a great canopy adorned with ornaments, her craft was towed by a second canoe manned by many paddlers and carrying six principal Indians. The niece, who was now the ruler of the town, was wearing fine clothing of spun mulberry bark. Although her name is not known, de Soto was so taken by her beauty that he called her the Lady of Cofitachequi. Paying her respects to the Spanish leader, she seated herself upon a chair which her subjects had brought for her and, wrote one of the expedition's chroniclers, conversed with de Soto "in the formal language of diplomacy, no other man or woman of her people saying a word." At the conclusion of their meeting, she unfastened a great strand of pearls, "as thick as hazelnuts," from around her neck and presented it to de Soto, hoping that he would spare Cofitachequi.

If anything, the sight of the pearls drove everything from the Spaniards' minds except a determination to acquire more of them. Entering the town, the army feasted on corn and plundered the Indians' graves at the great temple mound, taking from them chests of pearls which the Europeans learned were buried with the dead. Hand-

This computer-generated re-creation of a Coosa village suggests how it might have looked at the time of de Soto's arrival in July 1540. The tall temple mound looming in the background was a hallmark of the Mississippian civilization of chiefdoms like that of the Coosas.

ing fistfuls of the pearls to his soldiers, de Soto directed them to make rosaries on which to pray. Then demanding to see the old chieftain so he could have her declare her submission, he forced her twenty-one-year-old adopted son to lead a contingent of soldiers to her hiding place. Torn between a desire to save Cofitachequi and to protect his mother, the young guide paused outside the town to give the Spanish soldiers time to eat. As he waited, he grew morose. Sitting contemplatively, he gave long and profound sighs, then began to remove his arrows, one at a time, from his sheath. Observing that the Spaniards were not watching him, he suddenly pierced himself in the gullet with the long, daggerlike head of one of the arrows, inflicting a mortal wound and dying instantly.

When the Indian bearers were asked by the Spaniards why the youth had taken his life, they explained that the act of guiding the soldiers to his mother's location was unworthy of the love she bore him. De Soto was never able to find the hiding place of the old woman, and on May 13, after seizing the Lady of Cofitachequi to take with them as a prisoner to safeguard their passage through the country, the Spaniards resumed their march. Soon afterward, the Lady managed to escape, taking with her a large part of the plundered pearls.

Continuing on, the de Soto army turned westward and crossed the Appalachian Mountains. In July, it traveled down a broad river and entered the territory of the wealthy Coosa chiefdom.

The Ashes of Coosa

Composed of many thriving tributary towns, the Coosa domain extended southwestward through parts of present-day Tennessee, Georgia, and Alabama. After struggling through the forested mountains, the Spaniards were delighted by the rich agricultural fields of the Coosa countryside and amazed by the splendor of the Mississippian nation's towns. Carried on a litter and accompanied by a thousand leading men in great feathered headdresses, the twenty-six-year-old paramount chief of the Coosas met de Soto outside his principal town and escorted the Spaniards into the

capital, which was located apparently on the Coosawattee River in the northwestern part of present-day Georgia.

De Soto and his men remained there for more than a month, while the young chief, anxious about threats of war from rival, neighboring chiefdoms, courted the favor of de Soto. Soon, however, the arrogance of the Spaniards caused resentment, and relations cooled. The young chief traveled with de Soto the length of the Coosa province and finally managed to escort him out of it. The Spaniards departed with stories of Coosa wealth and the lushness of the countryside that in time became legendary in Spain. The Coosas would not be forgotten.

De Soto's army, meanwhile, pushed forward into the territory of another powerful Mississippian chiefdom, that of the Mobiles. At an initial meeting, arranged by the

Although it is assumed that Mississippian effigy pots like this one had spiritual functions, their meaning is uncertain because so much knowledge and tradition was lost in the turmoil of disease and destruction that wiped out whole Indian nations after the Europeans arrived.

The climax of the Mississippian culture produced elaborate ceremonial works of beauty. This three-headed pot was found in Tennessee.

Mobiles for the Spanish leader to meet their paramount chief, Tascalusa, de Soto seized the chief and made him accompany the Spaniards as they made their way down the Alabama River on rafts to Mauvila. At that important Mobile town, they expected to come on large stores of food. Instead, they found a fortified town surrounded by a strong, defensive wall with towers and, inside the town, the nation's leaders gathered in a council. Tascalusa persuaded de Soto to allow him to enter the town to confer on the Spaniards' behalf with the tribal leaders. In fact, the chiefs, having reports of Spanish behavior, had gathered from throughout the region for a war council. The town was filled with fighting men, and the houses were stockpiled with weapons. Soon after Tascalusa entered the town, de Soto discovered the nature of the chiefs' meeting and demanded that Tascalusa come out. He did not. Instead, a Mobile war captain emerged and delivered a defiant message from the chiefs:

These effigy figurines were found at Etowah, an important Mississippian commercial and cultural center in the region of present-day Georgia. It is believed that de Soto's expedition visited the Etowah chiefdom after leaving the territory of the Coosas.

Who are these thieves and vagabonds who keep shouting 'come forth, come forth' . . . with as little consideration as if they were talking with some such person as themselves? . . . No one can endure longer the insolence of these demons, and it is therefore only right that they die today, torn into pieces for their infamy, and that in this way an end be given to their wickedness and tyranny.

The war captain was struck down with a Spanish sword. Instantly, thousands of Mobile fighters spilled over the walls of the town, engulfing the Spaniards and forcing them to retreat. De Soto rallied them, and a tremendous battle ensued. The Spaniards retreated, advanced, and retreated again. Finally, the determined Spanish

soldiers broke through the town's fortifications with battle axes and drove the Mobiles into the houses. Ordering the buildings set on fire, de Soto kept the army's trumpets, fifes, and drums blaring as a wind spread the flames, smothering the entire town in thick smoke.

And yet the Mobiles fought back ever more desperately. Thirsty Spanish soldiers tried to drink from a nearby pond, but it was red with the blood of the dead. Mobile women strove frantically beside the men. "The Mobile," a Spanish soldier later said, "fought with a desire to die."

Finally, at sunset, after nine hours of battle, it ended. Eyewitness accounts of the number of Mobile dead ranged from twenty-five hundred to eleven thousand. The dead littered the streets between the charred remains of burned buildings. Even the Spaniards reeled in shock. One soldier emerged from the silence of the aftermath frozen "like a wooden statue" until he died. A Mobile man hanged himself by his bowstring rather than be left to survive alone.

De Soto's army, counting only two dead, stayed in the area for a month while the wounded healed. The surrounding Indian nations watched as the Spaniards slowly

The bloodiest encounter between de Soto's men and Indians occurred at Mauvila in the territory of the Mobiles. Thousands of Mobiles were killed when the Spaniards broke through the town's defensive wall and set fire to the Indians' buildings. Here, we see de Soto's force invading an Indian town.

regained their strength and then renewed their march. The army wintered in the territory of the Chickasaws, who kept up a guerrilla siege of the Spaniards for four months. In April, de Soto struck off again and reached the Mississippi River. He spent the rest of the year of 1541 among chiefdoms on the east side of the river and eventually found himself across the wide, muddy waters from temple pyramids rising above the towns of the Natchez nation, another inheritor of the Mississippian culture.

The paramount chief, Quigaltam, the Great Sun of the Natchez, was also the spiritual head of the nation's religious aristocracy. Treated as a god, he was carried on a litter so his feet would not touch the ground. His head was flattened according to Natchez custom, and tattoos of black, red, and blue designs were etched across his body. As the autocratic leader of a nation whose economic and military influence spread in all directions along the Mississippi, he expressed contempt when de Soto summoned him to his camp. "[I am] not accustomed to visit anyone," he replied. "On the contrary, all of whom [I have] knowledge visit . . . and serve . . . [me] and obey [me] and [pay me] tribute."

But de Soto would never see the wealth of the Natchez. On May 21, 1542, he died from illness. After further exploration west of the Mississippi, de Soto's army returned to the river, intending to construct boats and sail to the Gulf of Mexico. On the river, they

After the French settled Louisiana in 1699, a colonial governor, Antoine Simon Le Page du Pratz, made this drawing of the Great Sun, or paramount chief of the Mississippian-culture Natchez nation, being carried on a litter by his subjects to a harvest festival. Years earlier, the de Soto expedition had witnessed similar protocol in many Mississippian chiefdoms throughout the South.

were confronted by a flotilla of a hundred painted Natchez canoes arrayed in battle formation. Fighting men, seated under canopies, dressed in vivid colors to match their canoes, and wearing white and varicolored headdress plumes, forced the Spaniards out of the Natchez territory. One tribe after another picked up the pursuit and drove the soldiers down the river to the Gulf. On July 18, 1543, the de Soto expedition mercifully came to an end. But its consequences on the Indian nations of the Southeast were to be permanent.

Sixteen years later, in August 1559, another Spaniard, Tristan de Luna, with five hundred soldiers and a thousand colonists, sailed along the Pensacola coast of west

Florida. De Soto's veterans had kept alive tales of a verdant province, where one day's travel would take a man through twelve towns and food was abundant— the land of the Coosa chiefdom. Luna had been sent forth to establish a colony and to make use of the legendary wealth of the Coosas to supply Spanish settlements along the Atlantic coast.

But as they moved north, those who had been there with de Soto did not find the land they remembered. The few towns they saw were small and poor. In one of them, the remnant of a once-thriving Coosa town, a woman told the Spaniards, "[Our] town had once been great, but . . . some Spaniards . . . [came here] earlier and made [it] the way it [is]."

The capital of Coosa was an even larger shock. Instead of five hundred houses, there were no more than fifty. Temple mounds stood in decay; cornfields were overgrown and abandoned. No chief borne upon a litter greeted them; no retinues of men in feathered headdresses lined the roadways. The people were gone.

A sick Spanish slave, left by de Soto in the care of the young Coosa chief, had spread an epidemic of a European disease against which the Indians had had no defense. It had swept through the southeastern nations, decimating chiefdoms—in many cases, taking the lives of the majority of the Indian populations. At the same time, food stores had been depleted by de Soto's marauding army and had left whole towns with severe shortages.

Paramount chiefs had been undermined by what was seen as a social and religious failure. Knowledge had been lost as elders had died suddenly. Societies were without their political, religious, and military leaders; organization and authority had collapsed; and peoples had become demoralized.

De Soto's short stay had set in motion a series of events that brought an end to the once-great chiefdoms of the Southeast. Civilizations that had flourished for centuries had swirled into oblivion in less than twenty years. Decades later, from the ashes of Coosa, Cofitachequi, and several other nations, a new union of towns would join together to become the powerful Creek Confederacy. It would constitute regional power for two hundred years.

But that was in the future.

A nineteenth-century engraving pictures the remains of a once-thriving Mississippian center in the area of present-day Georgia. The silent cluster of earthen mounds, which had been surmounted by religious structures and the homes of chiefs, is not unlike the depopulated scenes that Tristan de Luna encountered during his visit to the Coosa territory less than two decades after diseases spread by de Soto's expedition had devastated the region.

It was very fortunate for our men that most of the Indians were in chains or other confinements, for they were valiant and spirited people, and had they found themselves free, would have done more harm.

—CHRONICLER OF DE SOTO EXPEDITION

CHAPTER 4
EUROPEAN

EXPANSION

Pueblo Encounters

Throughout the sixteenth and seventeenth centuries, other European powers followed in the wake of Spain in invading the Indian lands of North America. To most leaders of the Indian nations, the appearance of the white men of whatever country raised complex problems, causing tribes to choose between loss and gain and walk a fine line of survival. The Spaniards and other Europeans clearly had superior weapons, and they often demonstrated that they were more than eager to take Indian lives. But Europeans also possessed valuable goods, including firearms for hunting and warfare, and many Indian leaders believed that if they could make peaceful trading alliances with them, they could gain power in their regions.

What leaders of Indian nations did not understand, often until it was too late, was the way the Europeans viewed Indians. They were not white or Christian. They were savages—wild and brutish—in the minds of many, a dangerous and unfeeling commodity for the slave markets. The end result of the dehumanizing of Indian peoples was that Europeans would negotiate and cooperate with Indian nations as long as they had to, or felt it was in their self-interest to do so. Once a European community in North America was strong enough to dominate an area, however, the diplomatic agreements it had made with Indians became meaningless. The Europeans saw no reason to apply rules of honor to people they considered savages. Indian nations, on the other hand—though they had long-standing traditions of trade and diplomacy among themselves—were totally unprepared during the early periods of contact with Europeans to understand their mind-set. Often, by the time the Indian leaders realized that their only hope lay in war, the war was already lost.

For much of the sixteenth century, Spain continued unabated in the forefront of the Europeans' invasion.

OVERLEAF: *A 1577 painting by the artist John White, a member of Martin Frobisher's expedition to Baffin Island, shows Inuit men in kayaks trying to drive the Englishmen away from their homeland.*

Prayer bowls, like this one from Zuñi, hold cornmeal and other items used during sacred ceremonies to help bring rain. The figures on the bowl are those of a badger, a thunderbird, tadpoles, and a frog. The raised parts of the rim represent the four cardinal directions.

Like all traditional Pueblo peoples, the Hopis of Arizona are agriculturalists and strictly observe religious ceremonies to help ensure successful harvests. The central piece across the forehead of this Hopi tablita headdress—worn in a women's ceremony in October—represents corn, the people's basic crop.

While conquistadors from the West Indies like de Soto and Menéndez scourged the Indian nations of Florida and the Southeast, other Spanish expeditions marched north from Mexico to enter the Indian domains of the present-day American Southwest, a rugged, beautiful, and very-long-inhabited land. By A.D. 1300, it will be remembered, the Anasazis—or, as the Hopis called them, the Hisatsimom—had dispersed from their cliff towns like Mesa Verde, some going to the Hopi and Zuñi towns, but thousands of others traveling east to New Mexico's Rio Grande Valley. There, the various migrating groups, speaking different languages or dialects—Keres or the Tanoan Tewa, Tiwa, or Towa tongues—settled down in some eighty towns.

Like their Anasazi ancestors, these Indians, whom the Spaniards later called Pueblos (the Spanish word for "towns"), built compact houses of adobe and stone, practiced intensive desert agriculture, and maintained a theocratic form of government, led by religious societies whose priesthoods made policies, directed community affairs, and oversaw an annual round of meticulously observed religious ceremonies and prayers. Religion permeated all of life. Every day, every month, and every year, each member of a community—men, women, and children—had a role to play in maintaining harmony with the spirit world. Each individual, like the corn that was the lifeblood of their nations, was part of a delicate balance. In 1540, the Spanish conquistador Francisco Vásquez de Coronado shattered that balance.

Twelve years earlier, an ill-fated Spanish venture in Florida, commanded by a one-eyed, red-bearded adventurer named Pánfilo de Narváez, began a chain of events that led to Coronado's destructive expedition. Narváez, who was eager to emulate Cortés's success in Mexico, landed with an army of four hundred men near Tampa Bay in 1528 and got off to a violent start when he sliced off the nose of a Timucuan

Among the Zuñis, Hopis, and other Pueblo
peoples, apartmentlike buildings housed
extended families, with clans and lineages
occupying adjacent rooms or sections. The
closeness of the people in their daily living
helped to strengthen the social networks within
the community. Here, a young Hopi-Tewa
woman, in a photograph taken about 1890,
grinds corn in the presence of other members of
her family.

chief who had displeased him and threw the chief's aged mother to the Spaniards'
mastiffs, which tore her apart and killed her. Thereafter, his expedition, pursuing ru-
mors of gold, marched north, floundering through swamps and dense forests in the
Florida peninsula and losing more than 150 men to disease and attacks by angry
Timucuan warriors. The expedition finally disintegrated in frustration and defeat.
Hoping to extricate themselves and sail to the safety of a Spanish settlement on the
Mexican coast, the sick and dispirited men built a fleet of small boats, only to become
separated and lost in storms in the Gulf of Mexico. In November 1528, after suffering from hunger, thirst, and a broiling sun that drove many of them mad, eighty unarmed and naked survivors were cast ashore on the Texas coast, where they were
enslaved or killed by local bands of Indians.

Eventually, the number of those who were still alive and living as slaves was reduced to five. Led by Alvar Núñez Cabeza de Vaca, who had been the Spanish king's
agent on the expedition, four of them escaped from their captors in 1534 and for two
years wandered from one tribe to another across the present-day American Southwest
and the Mexican state of Sonora. During their journey, in which the Indians often
treated them as holy people with strong spiritual powers, they heard repeated stories
of what they understood to be rich and opulent cities of a kingdom that lay to their

north. There, the Indians seemed to tell them, people lived in multistoried palaces with doors inlaid with jewels, drank from goblets of gold, and dressed in garments of the finest linen.

When Cabeza de Vaca and his companions finally reached a Spanish settlement in Mexico, their reports of this wondrous new Indian kingdom, apparently richer than Tenochtitlán or Peru, fired the imaginations of the Spaniards. In 1539, a Franciscan friar, Marcos de Niza, guided by one of Cabeza de Vaca's fellow survivors, a black Moorish slave named Estevanico, was sent to reconnoiter the northern territory and discover if the stories were true. In the frontier country of the Opata Indian nation just south of the present-day Arizona-Mexico border, Fray Marcos directed Estevanico with three hundred Mexican-Indian followers to go out ahead and find the first of the rumored cities.

From time to time, Estevanico sent back messages to the friar with reassuring word that he was approaching Cíbola, the first of seven towns of the fabled kingdom.

In truth, Estevanico was nearing Hawikuh, an important town of the Zuñi nation in the arid country of what is now western New Mexico. Wearing rattles, bells, and feathers on his wrists and ankles, and assuming the authoritative role of the powerful spiritual person that Indians had thought him to be when he had traveled across the Southwest with Cabeza de Vaca, he sent a messenger to the Zuñi town governor with the gift of a ceremonial gourd rattle that he had acquired during his wanderings three years before. The Zuñi, in a rage, recognized the rattle as part of the medicine of the spiritual leader of an enemy nation, and as soon as Estevanico and his large Indian following arrived, the Zuñis seized him as a spy, or friend of their foes, and held him overnight under guard. The next

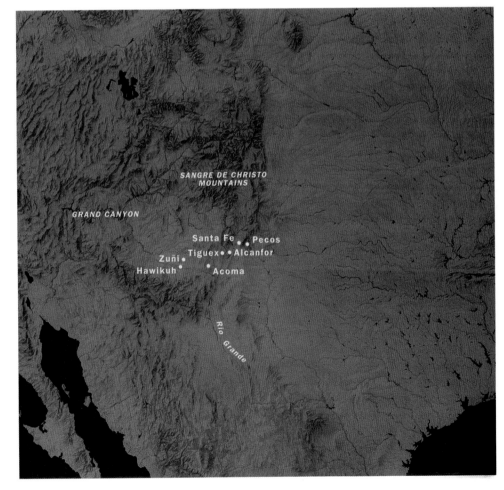

morning, his followers were attacked, and, although some escaped, many of them were killed. In the confusion, Estevanico tried to run away, but was overtaken and slain.

The frightened survivors fled back to Fray Marcos with news of Estevanico's death. The Franciscan hesitated in fear, then with two Indian companions stole forward for a hasty look at the Zuñi pueblo. Endowed with an enormous imagination, the friar gazed at the stone-and-mud-plastered town of terraced buildings, bathed in the golden rays of the sun, and hurried back to the viceroy of New Spain, who had sent him on the mission, reporting that everything that Cabeza de Vaca and Estevanico had said was true. With his own eyes he had seen "house doors studded with jewels, the streets lined with the shops of silversmiths." Moreover, he said, the northern Indians whom he had met had confirmed that this was only the first and smallest of seven wealthy cities of the province of Cíbola, which the Franciscan thought must be the legendary seven lost cities of Antilia, established supposedly by refugee bishops who had fled from the Moors in Spain and settled somewhere on the western side of the Atlantic Ocean. Although it was a piece of romantic medieval mythology, the tale was still firmly believed by many fifteenth- and sixteenth-century Europeans.

Fray Marcos's exciting news was what the viceroy was hoping to hear. The next year, 1540, he dispatched Coronado, the thirty-year-old governor of the northern Mexican province of New Galicia, with an expedition of 230 mounted troops, 62 foot soldiers, a company

Despite more than four centuries of contact with Europeans, Pueblo life and culture survived with great continuity. This photograph of Zuñi governor Balawahdiwa was taken in 1885, but the scene was probably quite similar when Estevanico and Fray Marcos de Niza's expedition encountered Zuñi Pueblo and its governor in 1539.

of priests and assistants, and almost a thousand Mexican Indians, to explore and seize the province of Cíbola.

Guided by Fray Marcos, the army of conquistadors reached Hawikuh, where the Spaniards were furious to discover that the Franciscan's opulent city of gold and jewels was, instead, a muddy desert town of stone buildings and ladders. Angrily, Coronado sent the friar back to Mexico, writing the viceroy that Fray Marcos "has not told the truth in a single thing he said." But the army needed food after its long march, and the Zuñi town at least had abundant supplies of corn and beans.

Frightened by the sudden appearance of the strange host with its fantastic animals and weapons, the Zuñis at first withdrew defensively within their walls and ignored Coronado's signals of peace. For the first time, the Zuñis were seeing horses, whose long heads and big teeth made them certain that they ate people. When at length the Spaniards began to advance toward the walls of the town, alarmed Zuñi priests rushed out and, sprinkling a line of sacred cornmeal on the ground, warned the Spaniards not to cross over it with their fearsome beasts. Ignoring the warning, the Spaniards quickened their pace. Sounding their war horn, the Zuñis let fly a stream of arrows, which was answered by the Spaniards' shout of "Santiago," the war cry for St. James, Spain's patron saint, which they had used in battle against the Moors. The sudden explosions of Spanish guns and the charge of horses and men with long lances routed the Zuñis, and the battle was quickly over.

While the Spaniards fed themselves from Zuñi stores, the defeated Indians sent runners to other Zuñi towns with tales of the awesome powers of the newcomers.

Lured by tales of the wealth of the seven mythical cities of Cíbola, Coronado and his men catch their first glimpse of one of the fabled towns—the Zuñi pueblo of Hawikuh.

Soon curious delegations from towns throughout the region began to arrive, bringing gifts to what the Indians suspected might be the white deities whom their prophecies said would one day appear among them from the south.

That suspicion was soon ended. Still hoping to find another Peru, Coronado sent off exploring parties in all directions, trusting that somewhere else in this northern country he would find a city with jeweled doors and golden streets. One of the parties, led by Pedro de Tovar, discovered the ancient mesa-top towns of the Hopis, with more corn but, again, no treasure. Other soldiers, under García López de Cár-

This fragment from a kiva wall painting of about A.D. 1450, a century before Coronado's expedition, depicts a kachina, a Puebloan spiritual being.

denas, came on the Grand Canyon and stared in frustration at the stupendous barrier that blocked their further progress. And a third group, captained by Hernando de Alvarado, marched east and entered the country of the many towns of the Anasazi descendants, or Pueblos, along the Rio Grande. Once more, in this region that the Spaniards called Tiguex for its Tigua, or Tiwa, Pueblo inhabitants, there was no gold, but the rich, watered fields and numerous settled towns amply stocked with food and supplies made the location an ideal wintering place for the Spaniards.

Alvarado and his men continued on to the most easterly of the Pueblo towns, Pecos, whose governor and war chief—the latter a man the Spaniards called Bigotes (Whiskers) for his long mustache— had been among those who had journeyed to Zuñi to assure Coronado of their desire for friendship. At Pecos, Alvarado met two slaves of the inhabitants, a Wichita Indian named Ysopete and a Pawnee

whom the Spaniards called the Turk, "because," according to a sixteenth-century chronicler of the expedition, "he looked like one." The homelands of both men, who had possibly been captured in battle by the Pueblos or traded to them by Apaches, were on the plains of present-day Kansas, where parties from Pecos sometimes went to hunt buffalo. Hoping slyly that the white men, who seemed so interested in gold, might help free them and return them to their people, the Turk regaled Alvarado with marvelous accounts of a province near his home called Quivira, whose lord "took his afternoon nap under a great tree on which were hung a number of little gold bells, which put him to sleep as they swung in the air" and where "everyone had their ordinary dishes of wrought plate, and the jugs and bowls were made of gold."

To prove that he was telling the truth, the Turk claimed that he himself had possessed a gold bracelet which Bigotes had taken from him. Believing the Turk, who offered to lead the Spaniards to the riches of Quivira, Alvarado demanded that Bigotes give him the bracelet. When the Pecos leader denied any knowledge of it, Alvarado flew into a rage and accused him of lying. The affair quickly became a crisis. Alvarado demanded that Bigotes and his companion, the town governor, whom the Spaniards called Cacique, accompany him back and let Coronado settle the matter. When the two men refused to go, Alvarado put them, as well as the Turk and Ysopete, in chains and, fighting off the outraged warriors of the town, marched them to Coronado, who held them as prisoners throughout the winter.

In the meantime, Coronado had led his army from Zuñi to Tiguex on the Rio Grande, where he took over the Tiwa Pueblo town of Alcanfor near present-day Bernalillo. Ordering all Indians to leave, he turned over the empty buildings to his men for the winter. His high-handedness angered the Pueblos, who had welcomed the Spaniards with friendship and now felt insulted. Worse was to come. As the cold weather approached, Coronado commandeered warm clothing and winter food supplies from all twelve Tiwa towns in the vicinity, even forcing Indians to "take off their own cloaks" and give them to the soldiers. Facing starvation and suffering in the freezing weather ahead, the Pueblos complained to the Spaniards, only to be met by further demands. The arrogant treatment of several town chiefs and the rape of an Indian woman by a Spanish soldier brought relations between the Pueblos and the Europeans to a breaking point.

Certain now that their unwanted guests were mortals like themselves, the Indians turned against them, attacking the Spaniards' horse herd to weaken the power of the white men's army. Although Coronado ordered swift and severe punishment, the revolt, known as the Tiguex War, spread quickly. For more than three months, the

ALEX SEOWTAWA/ZUÑI
"Right after the Pueblo Revolt [of 1680], this place was set on fire and we retreated to our stronghold up here at Dowayalanay, which means ancient mountain or cold mountain. But this one particular priest, he went along with us Zuñis to live up there for quite some time. The other Pueblos that teamed up with the Spaniards thought we killed this priest. They came to get even with us, but the priest wrote in Spanish on a buckskin that he's alive, but he would rather be with the Zuñi people. So he threw the message down from the top and they read his message and they returned back."

Spaniards, shouting their battle cry of "Santiago," waged merciless war against defiant towns, killing their Pueblo defenders and burning captured Indians at the stake. At the Tiwa town of the woman who had been raped, the Spaniards fought their way into the buildings and smoked the people out of their hiding places in the kivas. Choking, the Indians staggered into the open, where they were seized, hauled to the town plaza, and tied to two hundred stakes that Coronado had ordered erected. Then with Bigotes, the Turk, and the other two prisoners from Pecos man-acled and forced to watch what would happen to them if they, too, defied the Spaniards, the anguished townspeople were set on fire and burned to death.

In horror, Tiwas fled from other villages, some seeking refuge in the snowy heights of the Sangre de Cristo Mountains, choosing death from freezing rather than at the hands of the Europeans. Others crowded into the large, fortified pueblo of Moho and resisted a Spanish siege that lasted for fifty days and claimed the lives of two hundred Tiwas. During the resistance, the Indians' water ran out, and thirty Indians died when a well they were digging caved in on them. Finally, the desperate survivors tried to escape in the night, but were intercepted by the Spaniards. Many Pueblos were slaughtered, and others were drowned trying to cross the icy waters of the Rio Grande. A few who were captured alive were distributed as slaves to the soldiers. A second town, where Tiwa refugees had clustered, was also taken, and more than a hundred women and children were made prisoner. The surviving men were burned at the stake, and the town was set afire.

In the spring, Coronado prepared his army for another long march and, accepting the Turk's assurance that he would lead them to the wealth of the kingdom of Quivira, set off for the northeastern plains. Guided by the Turk, who continued to rave about the wonders the Spaniards would see, the expedition made its way past herds of buffalo to the broad Kansas grasslands. It proved to be another disillusionment. When the Turk's Quivira turned out not to be another Indian empire but a village of tall, beehive-shaped grass lodges belonging to seminomadic Wichita Indians of the plains, Coronado was enraged. His men strangled the Turk, and the disgusted army returned to another profitless winter in the empty Tiwa pueblos. In the spring, Coronado, who had been injured in a fall from his horse, abandoned his quest and, borne in a litter between two mules, led his army gloomily back to Mexico. In his wake, the Tiwas returned to what was left of their towns on the Rio Grande and again sought the peace and harmony with their spiritual world that the Spaniards had disrupted. Originally anxious to please and win the friendship of the white strangers, the Pueblos had learned better about them and welcomed their departure with relief.

Fray Marcos has not told the truth in a single thing he said.

—CORONADO

Approach to Pueblo Acoma

Wittick

An 1883 photograph by Ben Wittick of the southern approach to Acoma shows women bringing water in traditional earthenware pots up the narrow and rugged trail from a cistern to the mesa-top Sky City, one of the oldest continually inhabited towns in the present-day United States.

Acoma: The Sky City

For almost sixty years after Coronado's retreat, the Spanish leader's report discouraged further interest in the northern regions, and few white men ventured back to the Pueblo country. Undisturbed save by several unofficial forays by small parties of Spanish priests, fortune hunters, and slave catchers, the towns returned to their ancient routines. But eventually, in Mexico, a new generation, anxious to repeat the glorious triumphs of Cortés and Pizarro, talked again of the lands and people whom Coronado had visited. There were rumors of mines that Coronado had missed, of fortunes to be made in the mysterious lands beyond the Rio Grande, and of Indian souls to be saved in the towns of Tiguex. Finally, the Spanish court, recognizing a need to secure the northern border of New Spain, authorized the viceroy's appointment of one of the wealthiest men in Mexico, Don Juan de Oñate, the middle-aged son of a governor and the husband of a granddaughter of Cortés, to occupy the land of the Pueblos for the king and establish a permanent frontier colony in the northern provinces. "Your main purpose," the viceroy's instructions to Oñate read, "shall be the service of God our Lord, the spreading of His holy Catholic faith, and the reduction and pacification of the natives of the said provinces." An ominous new day had begun for the Pueblos.

Oñate organized a large expedition of colonists, troops, Franciscan friars, supply carts, and cattle and in 1598 led it north to the Rio Grande. After claiming possession

Situated atop a four-hundred-foot-high mesa, the buildings of Acoma were virtually inaccessible to outsiders. Possibly because of its formidable location, early encounters with Europeans were brief and peaceable until Juan de Oñate's mission to colonize Spain's northern territories reached the town in October 1598. Oñate's conquest of Acoma was among the bloodiest and most savage of the European invasion of the Puebloan country.

"once, twice, and thrice" of all the "lands, pueblos, cities, villas, of whatsoever nature now founded in the kingdom and province of New Mexico . . . and all its native Indians," he continued upriver to the Pueblo towns. As he moved from one pueblo to another, requisitioning food and taking formal possession of each town, he was welcomed hospitably by the people, who, having reestablished harmony with their spiritual world, showed no desire for revenge for the cruelty of Coronado. At one town, delegations of leading men from many pueblos met with Oñate in a great kiva, at his direction kissing his hand and that of one of the Franciscans and agreeing

courteously—though probably uncomprehendingly—to become vassals of the Spanish king and the pope.

Near the juncture of the Chama and the Rio Grande, Oñate halted and, like Coronado, ordered the Indians to evacuate one of their towns for his men. The Indians moved out without resistance, and Oñate renamed the town San Juan and proclaimed it the capital of his new colony. Then, anxious to find the riches that Coronado had missed, he rode off with an exploring party on a circular tour of the province. At the same time, the friars began visiting the different pueblos, erecting crosses and, without interference from polite but disapproving Pueblo religious leaders, preaching to throngs of curious townspeople. Their work was abruptly halted by an outburst of resistance at the pueblo of Acoma that threatened the future of the newly founded colony.

Built in mesa country between the Rio Grande Valley and the Zuñi towns in western New Mexico, Acoma—or, as its inhabitants knew it, Aku (Sky City)—sat in timeless isolation high in the dry air atop a rock, almost four hundred feet above its irrigated fields and farming settlements on the desert floor far below. More a part of the sky than of the earth, it was one of the most ancient Pueblo towns and had been occupied for at least five hundred years. In 1540, it had been visited by Coronado's captain, Hernando de Alvarado, on his trip from Zuñi to the Tiguex towns. Although the pueblo's guards had turned him away at first, the town leaders had ultimately greeted Alvarado in friendship and given him presents of turkeys, tanned deerskins, cornmeal, turquoises, pine nuts, and bread. The Spaniards noted with awe the town's almost impregnable position, which was later described by the chronicler of the expedition:

LESLEY DAVID/HOPI

"The Spaniards were here to make us stop our religion, our ceremonies, and all that we practice to this day. And they tried to stop us from that. A long time ago we used to have a symbol which is a circle, which unites; it's a never-ending circle that we had combined together, all the Indians are combining that circle, there's no way out. And when the Spaniards came, the missionaries came, they brought the cross, which is a symbol of separation. And that's where the people separated and went into all the different directions. And to this day they're all over the four corners of the earth."

The village was very strong, because it was up on a rock out of reach, having steep sides in every direction. . . . There was only one entrance by a stairway built by hand. . . . There was a broad stairway for about 200 steps, then a stretch of about 100 narrower steps, and at the top they had to go up about three times as high as a man by means of holes in the rock, in which they put the points of their feet, holding on at the same time by their hands. There was a wall of large and small stones at the top, which they could roll down without showing themselves, so that no army could possibly be strong enough to capture the village. On the top they had room to sow and store a large amount of corn, and cisterns to collect snow and water.

Spared from attack by the Coronado expedition, Acoma was visited during the next fifty years by one or two of the small, unofficial Spanish parties that explored the region. In 1598, the pueblo's leaders learned of the arrival in the Rio Grande towns of a disturbingly large new group of Spaniards—the Oñate colonists—and heard unsettling reports of their demands that all the pueblos submit to their headman and his priests. Concerned that this time there might be trouble for Sky City, a young Acoma man named Zutacapan urged the town to prepare for war against the invaders and gathered a band of warriors to ready the pueblo's defenses. A leading elder named Chumpo disagreed with Zutacapan, reminding the warriors that many thought that the white men were immortals who could not be defeated in battle. Appealing to the

Pots like this one were used by the people of Acoma to store food and water. The pots' unusual shape gave them a low center of gravity, making it easier for women to balance them on their heads when carrying them from a cistern to the top of the mesa. Many Acoma women continue to practice the ancient art of pottery making and are skilled and artistic potters.

pueblo's sense of honor, he argued that if the people treated the Spaniards fairly, they would receive the same treatment in return.

Chumpo's pacifist reasoning prevailed, and on October 27, Oñate and his men, who were on their exploring tour of the province, arrived at Acoma and were welcomed peacefully. Allowed to ascend the mesa and enter Sky City, they fired a salute, a Spaniard reported, "to the wonder and terror of all the savages," after which

Oñate demanded and received the usual pledge of submission. The Indians provided their guests with corn, turkey, and water, as well as food for their horses, and Zutacapan offered to lead Oñate into a kiva. The idea of climbing down a ladder from the kiva's roof, however, into the silent and mysterious darkness of the underground religious center seemed to unnerve Oñate. Suspecting that the Indians were plotting to kill him, he declined the invitation. Soon afterward, he and his men left the pueblo to continue their tour, and the Acoma people felt relieved that they had followed Chumpo's counsel.

About a month later, Juan de Zaldivar, a nephew of Oñate who was hurrying after his uncle's expedition with reinforcements, appeared at the base of Acoma's mesa and demanded food for the expedition's troops. Agreeing this time with Zutacapan, who did not like Zaldivar's haughty manner and once more counseled resistance, the Pueblos refused to give the Spaniards food. Zaldivar offered them hatchets and other articles in trade, however, and they finally agreed to sell him some cornmeal, but explained that grinding the amount of corn he required would take the Acoma women three days.

After waiting for three days, Zaldivar became restless and, forcing his way past the pueblo's guards, led sixteen of his men wearing steel helmets and armor up the steps and finger- and toe-holds onto the mesa-top streets of Acoma. There, Zutaca-

The prolonged contact between the Spanish and Pueblo peoples in the American Southwest left numerous marks on the Indians' life. This fine example of a bowl made at Acoma, or possibly Laguna Pueblo, shows a strong Spanish colonial influence on the traditional Pueblo art form.

pan and other leaders, startled to see the Spaniards inside their town, told Zaldivar that the cornmeal was ready and directed him to send his men to different houses to collect it. No one has ever agreed on what happened next. The Indians blamed the Spaniards, and the Spaniards blamed the Indians for the sudden explosion of violence. Apparently some Acoma men, carefully watching the movements of the Spaniards, took offense at the white men's rude treatment of the Indian women, considering it a violation of the pueblo's hospitality. When, finally, a Spaniard stole a turkey from an old woman and brushed her aside roughly, the Indians' anger burst its bonds, and Zutacapan and the men of the pueblo came to her defense.

The Spaniards, who later contended that Zutacapan and other Indians had deliberately planned and started the fight, opened fire, but were overwhelmed and defeated in the battle that ensued. Zaldivar and all but four of his men were killed, one of them leaping to his death from the mesa. The four who escaped joined their companions waiting below and hurried off with them to carry the doleful news to Oñate. The Acoma losses were never recorded, but the nation had little time to mourn. Within a month, Oñate declared a "just" war and sent a punitive expedition, headed by Zaldivar's brother, Vicente, against the pueblo.

On January 22, 1599, Vicente Zaldivar and his seventy-man force gathered below the mesa. While most of the soldiers engaged the pueblo's guard at the entrance to the trail of steps as a diversion, twelve Spaniards, dragging a cannon, hoisted themselves stealthily up the rock wall at the rear of the mesa. When they reached the top, they turned the cannon against the town and blasted the adobe and stone houses to pieces. At the same time, the main Spanish force brushed past the guards and, swarming up the steps, poured into the town. Falling back in shock, but defending the pueblo, house by house, the Acomas fought back desperately for three days, rushing time and again through fire and smoke to hurl their bodies against the mouth of the cannon to try to contain its deadly blasts.

When it was over, of the pueblo's approximate population of six thousand, more than eight hundred had been killed. Five hundred women and children and eighty men were taken back as prisoners to the Rio Grande, where Oñate subjected them to a quickly convened court at the Inquisition.

The Acomas were judged guilty of treason, and their punishment was merciless. All the Indians, men, women, and youths, were indentured for twenty years as personal servants of the Spanish officials, the leading colonists, and the missionaries, in reality becoming slaves. In addition, the men were sentenced to public mutilation. As a lesson to the other pueblos, the mutilations were conducted in towns along the Rio Grande, where Oñate had chopping blocks set up in the plazas. Held in place on the

Although the Spaniards were able to reconquer the Pueblos' country after the Indians' revolt of 1680, the Pueblos eventually outlasted Spain in North America. The resolute face of the Acoma woman in this twentieth-century photograph by Edward Curtis reflects both the pain her people have endured and the determination with which they have survived.

block, each Acoma man had one foot cut off. Two Hopi men who happened to be at Acoma during the fighting and were also brought back as prisoners had their right hands chopped off and were sent back to their homes to show their people what to expect if they questioned the Spaniards' authority.

In time, Sky City was rebuilt, but life was never the same again, there or among any of the Pueblo nations. Oñate and the secular and religious authorities who succeeded him—ruling after 1610 from a new capital town of Santa Fe—brought the Pueblos under a tyranny so intolerable that in 1680 they united in a successful revolt under a San Juan pueblo religious leader named Pope, killing twenty-one missionaries and about four hundred Spanish colonists and forcing all the rest to flee back to Mexico. For twelve years, the Pueblos were free again, able to practice their own religion without fearing the Spaniards' punishment.

Although the Spaniards returned and in 1692 reconquered the province, they had learned a lesson and were never again as severe in their treatment of the Pueblos as they had been before the 1680 revolt. By the early years of the eighteenth century, Spain, no longer as rich and powerful as it had once been, was dependent on Pueblo troops as auxiliaries of their own forces to protect the northern borders of New Spain against the threats and incursions of other European powers, as well as of Apaches and other raiding tribes. But the Pueblos, too, had learned a lesson. Although the priests had become much more tolerant about the Pueblos' practice of their own religion, the tribes never again allowed white men to know enough about the beliefs and practices of their spiritual life to undermine and destroy it. By fighting through the years to guard their religion, the people of Acoma, the Sky City, and the other Pueblo nations of the Southwest kept it relatively intact, so that today it is still, to a remarkable degree, the basis of the harmony and balance of the everyday life of the Pueblo towns.

Our land, our religion, and our life are one. . . . It is upon this land that we have hunted deer, elk, antelope, buffalo, rabbit, turkey. . . . It is from this land that we obtained the timbers and stone for our homes and kivas. —HOPI

A Clash in the Arctic

Far to the north of the arid Pueblo country, meanwhile, other confrontations with white men, also lethal to native groups, had been occurring. One of them took place on Baffin Island in the Arctic, whose barren loneliness would seem to have had little attraction for Europeans intent on finding wealthy empires or establishing permanent colonies.

Guarding the approaches to present-day Hudson Bay, Baffin Island, the fifth largest island in the world, was the home of Inuit peoples, known later to most of the outside world as Eskimos. Preceded by ancestors of earlier Arctic cultures, they had lived on the mountainous island for hundreds of years, sharing a northern way of life with other Inuit peoples whose homelands partly girdled the polar regions from Siberia eastward to Greenland. Living in close attunement with the natural and spiritual demands of the stern environment, they followed a seasonal routine of hunting, fishing, and gathering wild foods from the land, the sea, and the island's freshwater rivers and lakes, while coping with

Known more commonly to the rest of the world as Eskimos, the Inuit peoples of Alaska, northern Canada, and Greenland accommodated to a difficult life in an unforgiving terrain. Igloos, constructed of ice blocks by Inuit like those encountered by Martin Frobisher on Baffin Island, were used only as temporary winter dwellings or bases for hunting.

Most Inuit settlements were located on coasts or rivers, and marine animals provided an important food source. This illustration shows an Inuit harpooning walrus on the ice.

OVERLEAF: *An 1821 illustration pictures Inuit children dancing to the beat of a hand drum.*

hazardous storms and terrain, extremes of climate, and the Arctic's alternating periods of long days and long nights. In 1921, Knud Rasmussen, an Arctic explorer, recorded an ancient Inuit spirit song, expressing the influence of the unique and difficult environment on the peoples' soul:

> There is fear
> In the longing for loneliness
> When gathered with friends,
> And longing to be alone.
> Iyaiya-yaya!
> There is joy
> In feeling the summer
> Come to the great world,
> And watching the sun
> Follow its ancient way.
> Iyaiya-yaya!
> There is fear
> In feeling the winter
> Come to the great world,
> And watching the moon
> Now half-moon, now full,
> Follow its ancient way.
> Iyaiya-yaya!
> Where is all this tending?
> I wish I were far to the eastward.
> And yet I shall never again
> Meet with my kinsman.
> Iyaiya-yaya!

In the summer of 1576, a small band of East Baffin Inuit arrived at their usual seasonal encampment on

The making of watertight skin boats, called kayaks by the native peoples of the North American Arctic, is at least two thousand years old. Kayaks like the one pictured in this 1824 illustration were a remarkable technological achievement and an indispensable means of transportation for the Inuit. Here, an Iglulik Inuit in West Baffinland returns to his village after a day of hunting.

an island off the northern shore of a great bay that extended for 150 miles into the southern part of Baffin Island. It was the time of the thaw and the breakup and movement of the pack ice, the time to fish the rich seawaters and on the main island hunt the caribou that came down to the coastal salt licks. It was the euphoric time of plenty and regeneration. But for the small band of Inuit setting up their customary camp on Niountelik Island, this summer would be very different.

Years before, when it was first recognized with certainty that North America was a continental landmass barring the way from western Europe to the markets and products of China and the East Indies, seaborne expeditions from England, France, and Portugal had begun to compete with those from Spain, searching for a water passage that would allow ships to sail directly through the continent from the Atlantic to the Pacific oceans. Explorations along the more temperate areas of the Atlantic coast failed to find such a route, and some mariners and their financial backers, searching farther and farther north, began to think that a Northwest Passage (as distinct from Magellan's long, indirect Southwest Passage around Cape Horn), if found, would be through the Arctic waters and islands of North America's northern coast—the territory of the Inuit.

In June 1576, Martin Frobisher, an Englishman backed by private investors in London, set sail for the North American Arctic in search of the elusive passage.

Moving among masses of broken pack ice, he found his way into the great bay on the southern part of Baffin Island, wondering if it was the entrance to the Northwest Passage. When the Inuit in their summer camp on Niountelik Island sighted his sails, they swarmed out to his ship in their kayaks, welcoming the Englishmen in friendship and offering to trade fish and sealskin clothing for European goods. Aboard Frobisher's vessel, one of the Inuit by sign language agreed to guide the explorers farther up the bay through what the Englishmen understood were straits leading into the Pacific Ocean. Indicating, however, that he first had to return to his camp, the Inuit boarded the ship's small skiff with five of Frobisher's men, who were instructed to take him to the island but not to leave the skiff or get out of sight of the ship. For some reason, they disobeyed.

Although the ship signaled them frantically, the men rowed out of view around the island's shoreline and never reappeared. Convinced that they had been captured, Frobisher felt that the remaining thirteen members of his crew were too few to risk a fight on shore. Satisfying himself by seizing one hapless Inuit and his kayak to retaliate and to provide proof to the world where he had been, he sailed back to England. On the way, the despondent Inuit bit off half his tongue and, arriving in England, died.

Of more interest to Frobisher's investors was a piece of mineral that he brought back from the bay and that, after several assays, was deemed to contain gold. With plans to mine the ore and with Queen Elizabeth among his new investors, Frobisher returned to the bay at Baffin Island the following summer at the head of a greatly enlarged expedition that included a complement of soldiers. Landing in July, Frobisher erected a cairn on a hill to assert England's possession of the area and then opened trade with a group of Inuit who suddenly appeared at the cairn. Each side was wary of the other, but all went well until the trading was finished. As the Inuit departed, Frobisher and the master of his ship, deciding to acquire interpreters for their expedition, suddenly tried to seize two of

The Inuit created a variety of functional garments for protection against the harsh conditions of their environment, using skin for water resistance and fur against the cold. Pictured here is an Inuit sewing kit, with a needle, awl, and thimble made of walrus-tusk ivory.

the Inuit who were straggling behind the others. They lost their grip
on them, and, breaking free, the
Inuit attacked the two Europeans fu-
riously, one of them wounding Frobisher with an arrow in the buttock.
Spilling from their shore boats, the
English soldiers came to Frobisher's
help, capturing one of the Inuit and
forcing the others to flee.

With their captive, the English
sailed to a large island in the bay,
where they found an empty village
whose inhabitants had apparently
fled at their approach. Inside the
houses, they found pieces of English
clothing, which they assumed had
belonged to the five men who had
disappeared the year before. Determined to punish the Inuit, even
though they had no proof that their
assumption was correct, they returned to the site the next day, led by
the ship's master (taking the place of
the painfully wounded Frobisher)
and with forty soldiers eager to do
battle. Dividing the force into two
units, the ship's master kept one of
them in two boats along the shore
and sent the other overland looking
for the Inuit. Beneath a range of
mountains, the overland group came
on eighteen Inuit men, women, and
children who ran for the shore. The
soldiers fired their harquebuses to
signal the other group, then chased
the Inuit families, who reached their

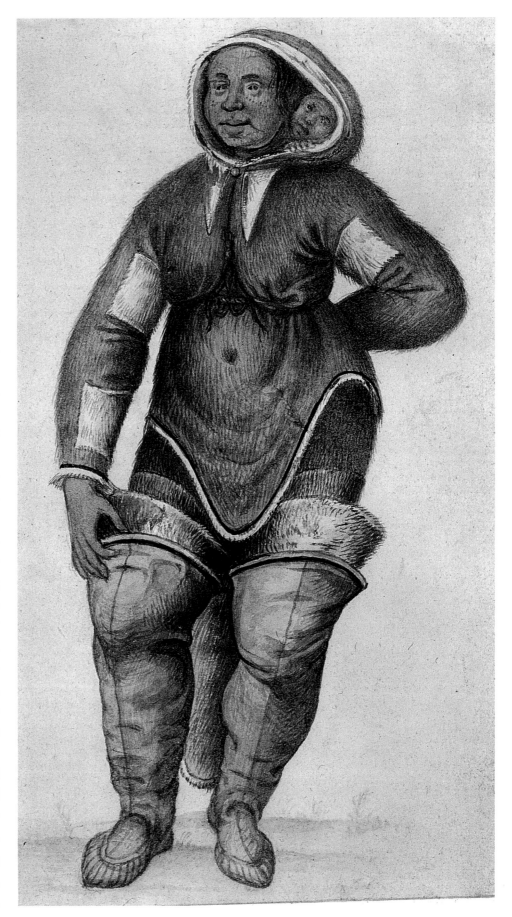

own boats, two umiaks, and tried to escape in them to the open water.

They were quickly cut off by the arrival of the soldiers in the boats. Forced back to the rocky coast, the Inuit landed on a craggy cliff that jutted into the sea. By now, both the foot soldiers and the sea party were upon them, and a savage battle began. The Inuit men, with their women and children huddled against the rocks, resisted with bows and arrows and darts, fighting with a fury that surprised the English. Finally, riddled with wounds and out of arrows, the Inuit men began to throw themselves headlong from the rocks into the sea. Some scrambled over the rocks, slippery with blood, and escaped. One woman, with a baby at her back, crouched helplessly against the rocks. Mistaking her for a man, a soldier leveled his piece and fired, wounding the baby in the arm. At that, the woman shrieked hysterically and was captured and taken aboard ship. There, the expedition's physician put a salve on the child's arm, which the woman fiercely wiped away.

On shore, the soldiers sacked the Inuit summer camp and named the site of the slaughter Bloody Point. Meanwhile, expedition members set to work mining and loading their ships with the island's ore, which they believed contained gold.

An old engraving shows a ship surrounded by the craft of friendly Inuit like those who first welcomed Frobisher.

OVERLEAF: *Kidnapped by Frobisher on his second expedition, the Inuit man seen on the previous spread in a watercolor by John White is garbed in traditional summer dress and posed with a bow. Although he survived the trip back to England with his white captors, the Inuit died soon after arriving there. John White also painted the portrait of the Inuit woman and her child whom the English abducted at Bloody Point. Wounded by Frobisher's men, the child stays warm inside its mother's hood. Like the male captive, both the mother and child died soon after reaching England.*

Four days after the battle, they were confronted by a group of Inuit survivors, who from some distance away set up a piteous outcry and pleaded for the return of the captured woman and her child. In response, Frobisher ordered the woman taken to a high hill so that the desperate members of her family could see her. Then he offered to trade her, the child, and the Inuit man he had captured for the five missing Englishmen from the previous year's voyage. The Inuit assured him that they were still alive, but despite their efforts, the Englishmen could not be produced.

In August, no longer pursuing his quest for a Northwest Passage, Frobisher sailed back to England with the three captive Inuit and some two hundred tons of ore. Aboard the ship, he placed the Inuit man and woman together as if they were animals, and for the entertainment of his men hoped they would display publically how they mated. The reality was that the married woman and her child were from one village and the man from another—all kidnapped by members of an alien culture with complete disregard not only for the complex system of social relations that defined Inuit life, but for the basic humanness of the captives. It was a cruel notion, thwarted by the dignified conduct of the Inuit couple who, adhering to their cultural codes, disappointed their European captors. After reaching England, all three Inuit died. Their full-length portraits, sober reminders across the centuries of their courage and suffering, still exist, painted in watercolor before they left Baffin Island by an English artist, John White, who was a member of Frobisher's expedition.

The following summer, Frobisher made a third and last voyage to Baffin Island, this time at the head of a fleet of fifteen vessels carrying prefabricated building materials and supplies for a permanent mining camp of 120 colonists. The voyage was a stormy one, however, and his grandiose plans went awry when one of his ships foundered with many of his supplies. After wandering off course, he finally reached the bay of Baffin Island. This time, no one came forward to greet the ships. The Inuit had had enough of the white men and stayed determinedly far away from them. Frobisher had created a lonely world. Finding no one with whom to barter for the trade goods he had brought, he became angry at "the brutish and uncivil people" who concealed themselves from him. The weather, too, was against him. It snowed heavily during the summer, and early ice packs threatened to close the bay. Hurrying to load his ships with ore from the mine, he returned to England at the end of August. There, he received a final blow. Further studies of the ore he had been bringing back from Baffin Island revealed that it was worthless. The company of investors that had backed his voyages collapsed, and the Baffin Island venture that had been disastrous for the Inuit people ended.

Centuries later, the Inuit recounted the story of the five white men whom a frightened and impatient Frobisher had deserted on his first voyage and the years they had lived among the island people. It was said that one spring they outfitted an umiak with a mast and sails and departed, never to be seen again.

The Chesapeake Mission

By the sixteenth century, much of North America's Atlantic seaboard from present-day southern Maine to North Carolina had long been the home of many large and small nations who shared a somewhat similar cultural heritage and spoke different dialects of a common Algonquian language. They included such people as the Wampanoags, Massachusetts, Mahicans, Montauks, Raritans, Nanticokes, Kiskiacks, Chesapeakes, Secotans, and dozens more.

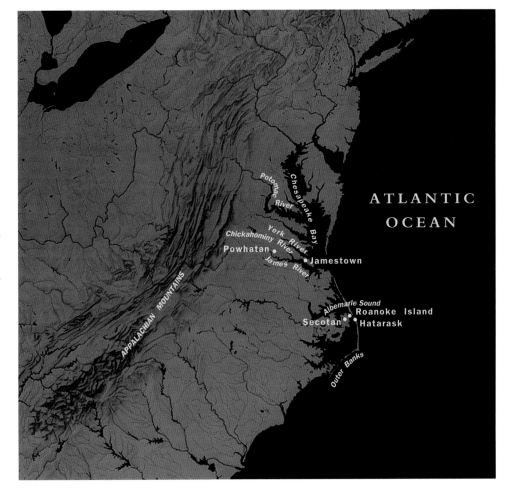

Among these groups, the Kiskiacks of Virginia were a Tidewater people whose territory of woodlands, marshes, and grassy fields near the future site of Williamsburg extended along the humid southern shore of the York River toward the lower Chesapeake Bay. The bountiful region was densely populated with towns of independent nations much like their own, well supported by farming, hunting, fishing, and the gathering of shellfish, nuts, berries, and other wild foods. The bay and rivers were abundant with fish, oysters, and crabs, and at times the sky was filled with flocks of migrating ducks and geese, which the Indian hunters lured to within killing distance by decoys and calls from their blinds.

In 1561, the crew of a Spanish ship exploring the lower reaches of Chesapeake Bay kidnapped a young Kiskiack man, a member of a family that ruled over the towns in the area, and took him to Spain. From there, he was taken to Mexico, baptized Luis de Velasco after the name of the viceroy, who had become his patron, and given to the Dominicans to receive a Christian education. For several years, he studied hard and obediently, winning the trust and admiration of his mentors—though apparently harboring a secret determination to return to his homeland and his own people. That opportunity seemed to come in 1566, when he learned of a new Spanish expedition preparing to return to his country. Proposing that the Dominicans accompany the expedition and establish a mission for the Kiskiacks, he promised to help them win converts if they would take him along.

The scheme worked, but unfortunately the expedition, with Don Luis (as he was known) aboard, lost its way in bad weather and, aborting its plans, sailed to Spain. After two years in Spain, the Kiskiack youth was taken to Havana. In 1570, he again suggested that the Spaniards send a missionary expedition to his people, this time winning the approval of the Jesuits, who agreed to let him go with them as a guide and interpreter. No soldiers were included in the party, for the Jesuits felt that their conduct often set bad examples for the Indians.

In September, the group of eight missionaries, led by Father Juan Baptista de Segura, the Indian Don Luis, and a Spanish boy, was put ashore near present-day Jamestown Island on the James River. Proceeding overland to the York River, they put up a temporary shelter in the country of the Kiskiacks. Don Luis stayed with the priests for two nights, then, giving them a number of pretexts—that he would prepare the village of Axacan, ruled by his brother, for their arrival; that he would bring back food to the priests; that he would return with his brother and other town leaders—he left, promising to come back within eight days. After the allotted time had passed and he had not returned, the anxious priests went looking for him and found him back among his people.

For five months, while the Jesuits established their mission, they pursued Don Luis and, with missionary zeal, demanded that he return to them. But he had come home, and he refused to listen to the priests. Finally, resenting their aggression and attempts to force the white man's beliefs and ways of life on his people, he led his brother and a small group of Kiskiacks to the mission and killed all the Spaniards, except the boy, whom Don Luis's brother adopted.

That spring when a Spanish supply ship from Havana approached, Don Luis dressed a number of Kiskiacks in the Jesuits' habits and paraded them on the beach so that from a distance they would appear to be the priests. The ruse failed to work, however, and after scattering those on shore with fire from the ship's guns, and fighting off Indians who tried to come aboard from canoes, the Spaniards sailed away with two Kiskiack captives whom they had seized in the struggle. The Spaniards now knew that the priests were dead but that the Kiskiacks held the Spanish boy.

The following spring of 1572, Pedro Menéndez de Avilés, on his way back to Spain from Havana with a company of Spanish soldiers, put in at Kiskiack country to punish the Indians for the murder of the priests and to retrieve the boy. Within an

The artist-explorer John White, who had been with Frobisher at Baffin Island in 1577 and painted portraits of the Inuit captives, later (1585–86) visited tribes of the North Carolina coast, producing vivid watercolor scenes of their life. This view by Theodore De Bry, the popular sixteenth-century Flemish engraver, was copied from a White painting and depicts many of the ways in which the Indians harvested the abundant marine resources of the coastal sounds and rivers.

hour of their arrival, they engaged in a fight with the Kiskiacks, killing many of them and capturing the principal chief of the area, who was an uncle of Don Luis, together with five leading men and eight other Indians. Returning to their ship with the captives, the Spaniards were followed by canoes filled with grieving Indians. Claiming that the Spanish boy was living with another important chief, they promised to secure his release if the Spaniards would free their own kidnapped chief and the other captives.

Menéndez granted them time to find the boy, and he was finally produced. The Spaniards, however, went back on their word. With the youth safely on shipboard, Menéndez's men opened fire on a large group of Kiskiacks crowded together on the shore, killing a number of them and scattering the rest. Then as the frightened survivors watched helplessly from hiding, the Spaniards hanged their chief and the other captives from the yardarm of their ship and sailed away. It was the Indians' last view of the Spaniards, who made no further attempt to settle in the area of Chesapeake Bay.

So ended the story of Don Luis and the Europeans. Or did it? Some accounts claim that his sister was the mother of the man whom the English would know as Powhatan, who in the following years became the ruler of a strong confederacy that united all the towns in that part of Virginia and represented them in their dealings with John Smith and the colonists at Jamestown. But there is evidence also that Don Luis was actually the half brother of Powhatan and, remaining among his people, took the name Opechancanough, meaning "He Whose Soul Is White." If so, he finally had his revenge against the Europeans, for in 1622, fifty years after Menéndez hanged the Kiskiacks, the fierce revolt of the aged Opechancanough almost wiped out the white men's colony at Jamestown.

Secotan and Roanoke

South of Chesapeake Bay, along the present-day North Carolina coast, were the lands of three allied Algonquian nations, the Chowanocs, Weapemeocs, and Secotans. The first two dwelled permanently in towns on Albemarle Sound and, like the Kiskiacks, along rivers, while the Secotans spent part of the year on the outer barrier islands and part on the mainland, with the Atlantic coastal waters forming one side of their territory and the tangled gloom of the Little Dismal Swamp the other.

It was a world of beauty and plenty. Carefully tended gardens surrounded each town, providing bounteous harvests of squash, two varieties of beans, pumpkins, sunflowers, amaranthus, tobacco, and three strains of corn that sometimes produced two crops a year. The rivers and broad sounds that lay between the Outer Banks and the mainland swarmed with fish that the Indians harvested with spears, nets, or weirs of reeds constructed across streams and estuaries. In season, the people gathered tur-

This John White watercolor of 1585 is a bird's-eye view of Secotan, the principal town of the Secotan Indians of the North Carolina coast. It portrays various aspects of the Secotans' culture, including their types of housing; fields of corn, tobacco, and pumpkins; methods of food preparation; and areas for ceremonial fires and dances.

Their greene corne.

Corne newly sprong.

Their sitting at meate.

the place of solemne prayer.

hovse wherin the Tombe of their Herounds standeth.

SECOTON.

tles, shellfish, nuts, berries, roots, and other wild foods, and hunters with bows and arrows pursued deer, bears, and small game. In the Secotan territory, camps that drew population to the windy outer islands in the summer were concentrated near inlets between the islands and at other favorite fishing locations.

In July 1584, two small British vessels hove into sight and dropped anchor off one of the inlets, at the outer island known to the Secotans as Hatarask. The ships were on a private reconnaissance expedition backed by the rising English courtier Walter Raleigh and some of his friends. Heralding England's determined entry into the race for North American colonies, they were exploring for a site suitable for a profitable English settlement.

Following the example set by Spain, the members of the expedition took formal possession of the region for the English Crown. It was an act that reinforced and helped make permanent the observance by Europeans of the Doctrine of Discovery,

A Carolina coastal man and woman and some of their food — boiled corn, fish, and shellfish — pictured for European readers by De Bry from a John White painting.

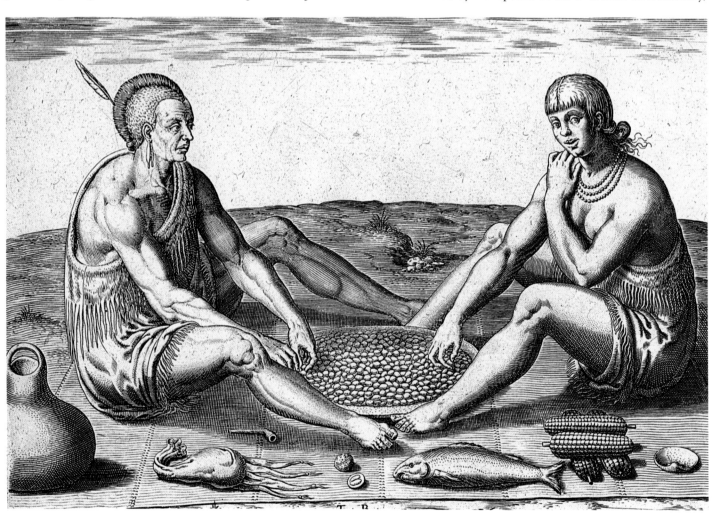

Buckes . . . hares, fishe, divers kindes of fruites, melons, walnuts, cucumbers, gourdes, pease . . . and their countrey corne, which was very white, faire, and well tasted.

—ENGLISH CHRONICLER

a legal fiction used to justify the idea that the title to lands in the Americas belonged to the European nations that discovered, claimed, or conquered them. Ignoring the resident Indian nations and their claims to ownership of the lands on which the white men found them, the doctrine in European eyes became a double-edged device. It abruptly made independent Indian nations and their territories dependencies of a European power, and at the same time established which power—because of its prior claim of possession or conquest—had the right to the territory in question. Until the Dutch in the seventeenth century deliberately purchased land from Indian tribes in the area of present-day New York City to protect their claims against those of imperial rivals, no European power, racing to acquire colonial possessions in North America, took serious notice of the Indians' rights as the actual owners of the land.

At their landing site on the Outer Banks in 1584, the English were met by Granganimeo, the head chief of the Secotans on nearby Roanoke Island and the brother of Wingina, the paramount chief of all the Secotan towns. Granganimeo arrived with forty or fifty of his men, "very handsome, and goodly people, and in their behaviour as mannerly, and civill, as any of Europe," the English noted. The next day, Granganimeo allowed his people to trade with the white men, and the English reported that "there came downe from all parts great store of people, bringing with them leather, corall, divers kindes of dies [to trade] for our hatchets, and axes, and for knives, and would have given us any thing for swordes; but we would not depart with any." The trade was conducted with enthusiasm and goodwill on both sides, and Granganimeo in a show of friendship delivered a vast supply of food to the ships, including "buckes . . . hares, fishe . . . divers kindes of fruites, melons, walnuts, cucumbers, gourdes, pease, and divers rootes, and fruits very excellent good, and of their Countrey corne, which was very white, faire, and well tasted."

The Secotan Indians of the North Carolina coast cooked their food in large earthenware pots, like this one shown in a watercolor by John White. Thomas Hariot, an English chronicler, noted that the Indians cooked with care and ate with moderation. "I would to God that we followed their example," he wrote.

In this John White watercolor, a group of coastal Indians, some with gourd rattles, are shown around a fire. The English chronicler Thomas Hariot believed the scene was of a ceremony following the safe return of a war party.

At Roanoke Island, the expedition members landed at Granganimeo's town, where they were further entertained. From there, they explored the barrier islands and others within the sounds and in September, accompanied by two Indians from Roanoke—Manteo, the relative of a chief, and Wanchese—who agreed to go with them to instruct the expedition members in the Secotans' language and culture, sailed back to England. On the way, one of the ships detoured north to explore Chesapeake Bay, but received a hostile reception in the Kiskiack country from Indians who doubtless were still angry at all whites for the brutalities of Menéndez and the shipboard hanging of their chief and his fellow prisoners. The English seem to have had several of their men killed and wounded before they abandoned their exploration of the bay area and followed the other vessel back to England.

The expedition's reports of the coastal country of the Secotans and their neighbors aroused enthusiasm in London. Raleigh bestowed on that part of the continent the name Virginia in honor of the Virgin Queen, Elizabeth, and she, in turn, knighted the courtier and gave support to the establishment of an English colony among the Secotans. In the spring of 1585, a second expedition of seven ships and a large military detachment commanded by Ralph Lane, a fortifications expert and a veteran of service in Ireland, left England to erect a fortified settlement in the Secotans' territory.

The ships became separated by storms and privateering diversions to New-foundland and the Caribbean, but

at the beginning of July, Lane and 108 soldiers were landed on Wococon, one of the outer islands. After sending word of their arrival to the Secotans' paramount chief, Wingina—now known as Pemisapan—at Roanoke Island, Lane and some of his men set off in a pinnace to explore the Secotans' mainland villages. At the town of Aquascogoc, they stopped to trade. After leaving, they discovered that a silver cup was missing. Lane was furious at the apparent theft of so valuable an object by the Indians, and although dependent on them for food, he wheeled his men about and, determined to teach the Secotans to fear the English, attacked and burned their town and its vital surrounding cornfields and forced the inhabitants to flee to other towns.

Despite the Secotans' shock and anger, Lane persuaded Pemisapan that he had acted with good reason. The chief at length agreed to supply the English with corn and gave Lane permission to build a fort and adjoining cottages on Roanoke Island, where the English leader and his soldiers could spend the winter while the ships and the rest of the party returned to England for reinforcements and supplies. During the fall, Lane and his men erected the fort and rude cottages and continued their explorations of the region. One group, sent to Chesapeake Bay, received a friendly recep-

Another of White's watercolors depicts a Secotan dance. According to Hariot, dances like this one, accompanied by feasts, were held several times a year, attracting guests from neighboring villages and nations.

Secotan women wore skirts of dressed and ornamented deerskins. They cut their hair short in the front and wore earrings made from bone or polished pearls. "They love to walk in the fields and along rivers, watching the deerhunting and the fishing," Hariot wrote.

OPPOSITE: A shaman, or medicine man, painted by White. The Europeans called them "sorcerers" or "conjurors" who were "very familiar with devils," but also admitted their gift of prophecy and their ability to "go against the laws of nature."

tion from the Chesapeake nation, whose lands lay south of those of the Kiskiacks and who had not been involved in the conflicts with the Spaniards. The English exploring party wintered with the hospitable Chesapeakes and returned to Lane with good reports of those Indians and their country.

Meanwhile, relations between Lane's men and the Secotans and the other coastal nations were deteriorating. Although the Secotans' surplus of corn was fast disappearing, the Englishmen put continuing pressure on the Indians to trade their precious supplies, raising widespread resentments and anger. Lane's arrogance and stern military attitude did not help matters. In Chawanoac, the principal town of the Chowanoc nation, where he went exploring, he seized the paramount chief, Menatonon, believing a false rumor that the Indian possessed information about a gold mine. After the alarmed Chowanocs paid him a ransom, Lane released the chief, but kidnapped his son to ensure the tribe's obedience and, taking him to Roanoke, held him a prisoner in leg irons.

To avert warfare between the Indian nations and the whites, the Secotan chief, Pemisapan, called a council that agreed to help the English by constructing fish weirs and planting gardens of corn for their sole use. But in April, the disastrous outbreak of a European sickness that swept through the Indian population dashed the chances of peace.

"[W]ithin a few days after our departur from everie . . . towne, the people began to die very fast, and many in short space," wrote an Englishman, "in some townes about twentie, in some fourtie, in some sixtie, & in one six score." The Secotans blamed the English for the sickness. "They were perswaded it was the worke of our God through our meanes, and that wee by him might kil and slaie whom wee would."

Pemisapan's father and brother died in the epidemic, along with hundreds of others, and through it all, as if unfeeling, the English kept up their incessant demands for the Indians' corn. Finally, Pemisapan was swayed by his councillors and spiritual leaders, who persuaded him that the very existence of the people was imperiled by the English invaders. A plan of war was devised, and late in May Secotan warriors began to gather at Roanoke. Men from the other confederated coastal nations were due to arrive and join the Secotans on June 10. But one of Pemisapan's men revealed the plot to the English, and Lane struck first. On June 1, 1586, he led a group of soldiers to Dasemunkapeuc, the Secotan mainland town where Pemisapan was staying, and sent a messenger to him requesting a council. When the chief appeared, accompanied by a number of subchiefs, the soldiers shot them down. Pemisapan was hit twice, but rose and tried to run toward some woods. Two of the English soldiers pursued him, and one finally knocked him to the ground and cut off his head. Lane's men

The flyer.

followed up by slaughtering the people of Dasemunkapeuc and quelling all opposition. The deaths of the nation's chief and leading men demoralized the other towns and left the Secotan world stunned and in mourning.

Ten days after the murder of Pemisapan, Sir Francis Drake's English fleet that had been attacking Spanish ships and possessions in the Caribbean and Florida arrived at the outer islands and made contact with Lane and his men. The colonists were almost out of supplies, and their morale was low because no relief ship had come. Agreeing to take them back to England where they could reorganize to establish another settlement at a different place, Drake evacuated them from their fort and cottages on Roanoke Island, and on June 18 they sailed away from the death and tragedy of the Secotan country.

Despite the bad experiences of Lane's colony, Raleigh the next year, 1587, sent out a third expedition, this time intent on establishing a permanent colony of English families. Under the leadership of John White, the artist who had been with Frobisher at Baffin Island in 1577 and had accompanied Lane on Raleigh's second expedition to the Secotans' country in 1585–86, 118 men, women, and children set out

for the lands of the Chesapeake Indians, well north of the Secotans and reported by the previous year's exploring party as likely to be much friendlier to the English than the subjects of the late Pemisapan.

The master of the ship carrying the colonists, however, put in at Roanoke Island in midsummer and refused to go on to Chesapeake Bay. The colonists went ashore and, finding the island deserted, repaired and occupied the fort and cottages that Lane and his men had abandoned. Knowing that it was too late in the year to plant, and fearing that the Secotans would not trade food to the settlers, John White left his daughter and newborn granddaughter, Virginia Dare—the first English child born in North America—and sailed back to England, planning to return in three months with more supplies.

OPPOSITE: *The wife and daughter of the principal chief of Pomeiooc are shown by the artist John White wearing chains of freshwater pearls around their necks. The woman holds a gourd "filled with a pleasing drink," and the girl carries a doll given to her by members of the English expedition.*

Once in England, however, the emergency of the Spanish Armada delayed the possibility of White's return to Roanoke that year. Meanwhile, the principal supporter of the Roanoke colony, Sir Walter Raleigh, lost favor at court, public interest and financial backing eluded White, and it was not until three years later, in 1590, that he was able to return to Roanoke with supply ships.

When he got there, the island was silent and without a sign of Indians or the colonists. Almost everything connected with the settlement was gone. Where the houses had stood, only a wooden palisade remained. Carved on some trees were the words CRO and CROATOAN, suggesting that the settlers had gone to the outer island village of Croatoan at present-day Cape Hatteras. White prepared to go in search of them, but a heavy storm, blowing up along the coast, drove

White's portrait of a woman and her baby in Pomeiooc, a town on Pamlico Sound near Secotan.

the ships far out into the Atlantic Ocean. The captain would not risk going back, and White returned, heartsick, to England, never learning the fate of his family and the other members of what became known as the Lost Colony. For 120 years, no other white colony was attempted in the area, and the Secotans were given a respite in which to rebuild their society before they had to fight again for their survival.

The Powhatan Confederacy

In the years following the Secotans' troubles with the English, a notable development occurred among the Indian nations farther north, in the Chesapeake Bay region of present-day Virginia. Nine Algonquian nations on the western side of the bay, most of them ruled by relatives of Don Luis, the Kiskiack, formed an alliance that marked the beginning of a formidable Indian force known as the Powhatan Confederacy. Led by a strong, charismatic statesman named Wahunsonacock—though he was popularly known as Powhatan for the name of his own nation and its principal town— the confederacy, by conquest and persuasion, rapidly gained power. By 1607, Wahunsonacock ruled what, in effect, was a small empire of approximately thirteen thousand people, members of thirty-one tribes, extending from the Potomac River almost to Albemarle Sound and westward from Chesapeake Bay to the falls of the principal rivers at the present-day cities of Richmond and Fredericksburg. To exert authority over this large area, he maintained many homes, traveling between them with an entourage of wives, bodyguards, and civil, religious, and war leaders.

Just below Wahunsonacock in rank were the district chiefs of each of the confederacy's member tribes, many

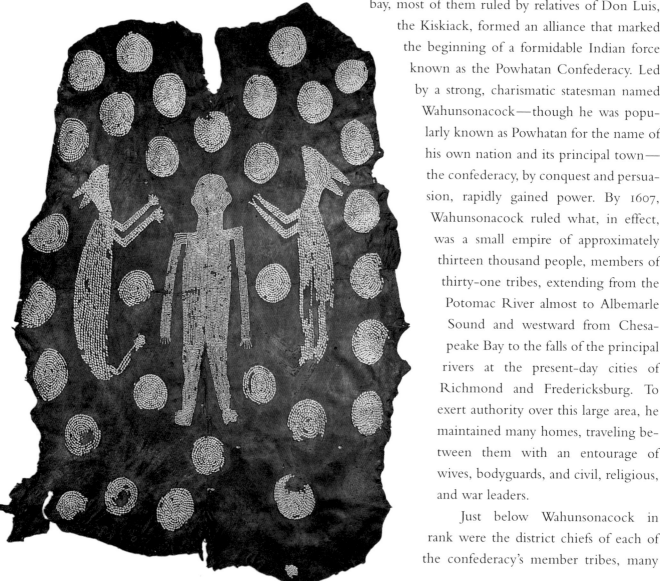

The ceremonial mantle of Wahunsonacock, the paramount chief of the Powhatan Confederacy, was made of the hides of seven white-tailed deer. Over seven feet long, it bore a design created from thousands of shells.

of whom were related to him by kinship or marriage. Among them, his most powerful ally was his half brother, Opechancanough (perhaps the man known formerly to the Spaniards as Don Luis), who had become chief of the Pamunkeys, the largest and strongest Powhatan tribe, able to muster three hundred warriors.

In 1607, a new English colonizing expedition, bypassing the Secotans' territory, sailed into the lower Chesapeake Bay and established a fort and settlement on the James River in the Powhatans' country. To the members of the Indian confederacy, the newcomers were not welcome. From their own past experiences with European priests, seafaring slave catchers, and trader-explorers and the reports that had come to them of the whites' aggressions against the Secotans, Wahunsonacock and his *weroances,* or subchiefs and councillors, viewed the 105 English colonists as threatening invaders.

Two weeks after the Europeans landed, Powhatan warriors attacked

Wahunsonacock sits on a raised platform within a longhouse, smoking his pipe and attended by his councillors and wives. Published in 1612 as an illustration on a map of Virginia, the scene was engraved by De Bry from a description given him by Captain John Smith.

them, testing their strength. The whites' muskets and cannons held off the Indians, and Wahunsonacock soon ordered his forces to withdraw. At their James Fort, however, the colonists—mostly gentlemen adventurers unused to farming or hard physical work—had little to celebrate. When their ship left to return to England for more colonists and supplies, the settlers, with dwindling stores at the fort, recognized their dependency on the Powhatans for food. That summer, the whites lived largely on sturgeon, seacrab, and rations of wormy wheat and barley. The inadequate diet, com-

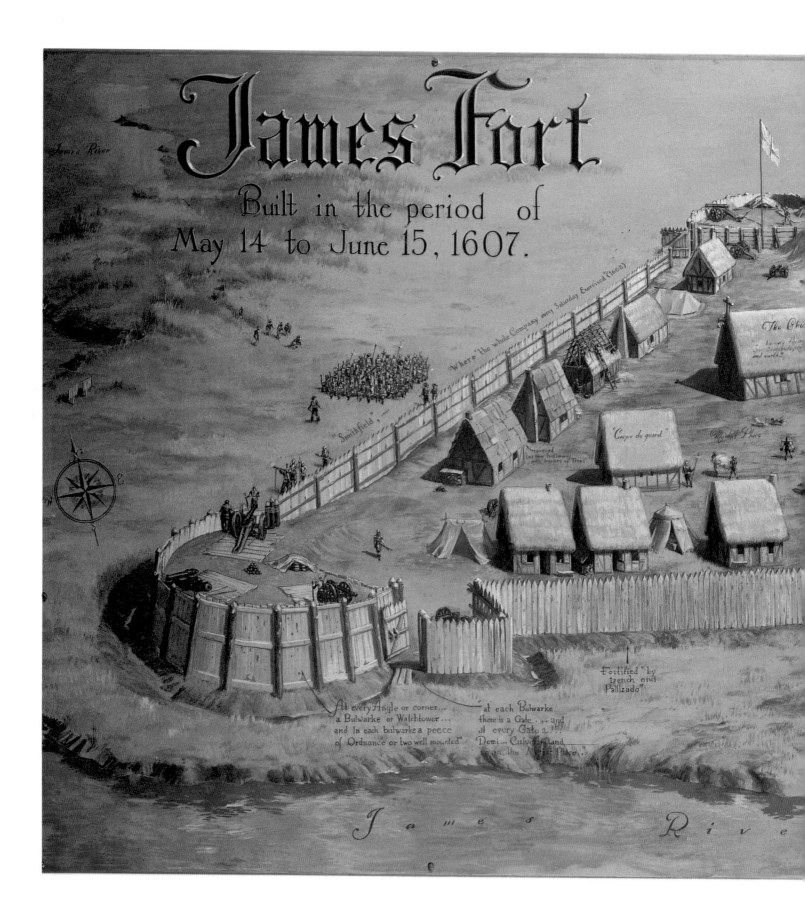

James Fort

Built in the period of
May 14 to June 15, 1607.

bined with the heat, the hard work, and the use of the brackish James River for their drinking water, felled almost the entire colony with various sicknesses, and by September half of the settlers had died. For a while, the survivors were saved from starvation by the compassion of some local Powhatans, who took pity on their plight and brought them "such plenty of their fruits, and provisions, as no man [was in want]."

During the fall, Captain John Smith and several other members of the colony went upriver by boat in search of Indians with whom to trade for food. At the town of Kecoughton, the Powhatans wished only to trade for the white men's muskets and swords and, when refused, treated Smith's party with scorn. The meeting ended in a fight, in which Smith's men killed several Indians with a volley of musket fire. Driving back the others, the Englishmen filled their boat with corn from the Indians' stores and left them hatchets and trinkets in exchange.

Smith's bullying for corn, which continued at other towns during the ensuing month, did not go unnoticed by Wahunsonacock and his subchiefs. Finally, losing patience, he ordered his half brother, the Pamunkey chief Opechancanough, to capture and bring John Smith to him. In mid-December, while Smith was exploring the Chickahominy River, he was seized by Pamunkey warriors and taken to Wahun-

How they tooke him prisoner in the Oaze 1607

C·S·

C·S·

C·Smith bindet fighteth with the Kin[g] all his company.

As relations worsened between the Powhatans and the English colonists, Wahunsonacock ordered the capture of John Smith. This engraving from Smith's General Historie of Virginia *depicts the battle in a swamp on the Chickahominy River in mid-December 1607, in which he was taken prisoner by Pamunkey members of the Powhatan Confederacy.*

A fanciful illustration of Pocahontas saving John Smith's life. Although it is more likely that her father, Wahunsonacock, never intended to kill Smith and, in fact, treated the English captive with respect, Smith's dramatic version of his rescue, written many years later, received wide acceptance and is still believed by many people.

sonacock. The Powhatan leader could see that the English were poorly equipped to survive in their settlement and might soon be swept away by starvation. Recognizing shrewdly, however, that, if helped, the colony could be a valuable member of the confederacy as a source of weapons and metal for knives and other goods, he treated Smith with respect, feasting him for several days, probably adopting him ceremonially as a son, and then returning him to James Fort. (No one knows the truth of the well-known story of Smith's being saved from death by Wahunsonacock's daughter, Pocahontas, after his capture. Smith's first writings on his experiences in Virginia made no mention of his having been threatened by the Powhatan leader or of the melodramatic Pocahontas episode. It was only sixteen years later, when Smith was composing his memoirs for a wide audience, that he told the story. Then, in fact, he related no fewer than three occasions when beautiful women saved him at the last moment from a horrible death.)

On January 2, 1608, a ship arrived at James Fort with supplies and more colonists from England. Five days later, a fire destroyed the new supplies, as well as stores of corn that the English had received from the Indians. Wahunsonacock, however, now regarding the colony as a protectorate of the confederacy, would not let it starve and temporarily supplied it with food. For a while, relations between the English and the Powhatans ran smoothly. Smith and Christopher Newport, the master of the colony's

supply ship, visited Wahunsonacock, bringing him "a suit of red clothes, a white greyhound and a hatte" as presents from King James. Then placing on the chief's head a crown that Newport had brought with him from England, they persuaded the Powhatan leader to bend his knee in imitation of a coronation ceremony and proclaimed him king of the Powhatan empire under James I. It is questionable whether Wahunsonacock, a proud man in his sixties, grasped the meaning of the Englishmen's words, for he was no novice in politics and would not have welcomed being demoted to the king of a vassal state under another king.

Having secured peaceful relations with Wahunsonacock, Smith, still in desperate need of corn for the colony, was emboldened to renew his intimidation of individual towns and their leaders. In January 1609, he entered the capital town of the Pamunkey nation and demanded that its powerful chief, Opechancanough, sell him corn. When the chief refused to do so, Smith seized him by the hair and held him with his pistol pointing at him while his men took the corn they wanted. Smith then ordered the chief to pledge good behavior and pay the colony a regular tribute in corn. If the Pamunkeys refused to comply, Smith promised to load his ships with their "dead carkasses" and boasted that "warres" were the "chiefest pleasure" of the English.

Smith's high-handedness encouraged similar conduct by other colonists, and, despite Wahunsonacock's efforts to avoid hostilities, the individual Powhatan tribes could no longer be restrained. The whites' aggressions

A nineteenth-century painting depicts John Smith and Christopher Newport, the master of the Virginia colony's supply ship, presenting a crown to Wahunsonacock. To the Indian leader, the strange coronation was a ceremonial recognition by the English of his power as head of the Powhatan Confederacy, but for the colonists, the crowning signified the submission of the Indian "king" to their own monarch, James I of England.

C Smith taketh the King of Pamavnkee prisoner 1608

When a fire destroyed the Jamestown colonists' food stores, the English resorted again to seizing corn from the Indians. This engraving from Smith's history of the colony shows him holding Wahunsonacock's brother, the powerful Pamunkey chief Opechancanough, by the hair and demanding at gunpoint the payment of a regular tribute of corn in exchange for his life.

led to Indian resentments and retaliations, and in the fall of 1609, full-scale war broke out. Although at first the English enjoyed success, they were ultimately routed by Opechancanough's Pamunkey warriors. Gaining the upper hand, the Powhatans laid siege to James Fort and came close to annihilating the English. In the meantime, John Smith had been injured by an accidental explosion of gunpowder and taken back to England.

The Powhatans eventually ended their siege, and, reinforced by hundreds of new colonists who arrived in the summer of 1610, the English went on the offensive. For a year, wearing their full battle armor, they fell on the Powhatan tribes, killing men, women, and children in attacks heightened by a crusading religious feeling against the non-Christian Indians. Despite large losses, Wahunsonacock refused to capitulate, and the hostilities went on.

In 1613, the English captured the old chief's daughter, Pocahontas, and offered to ransom her for all the English prisoners held by the Powhatans. The Indians released their prisoners, but the English continued to hold Pocahontas. While a captive, she was instructed in English custom and the Anglican religion and was baptized Lady Rebecca. And though already married, she revealed that she had fallen in love with John Rolfe, one of her English captors and teachers.

In March 1614, the weary Wahunsonacock, hoping to see his daughter again, finally agreed to peace, which was sealed a month afterward by the marriage of Pocahontas and John Rolfe. Two years later, the couple, with their infant son, sailed to

England, accompanied by a group of Powhatans, including Tomocomo, a trusted aide to Wahunsonacock, who had instructed him to count the people in England. In London, Pocahontas was a sensation. The "right-thinking savage" from Jamestown, as the colony was now known, was shown off in the best circles, had her portrait painted, and was even presented to the king. Tomocomo, it was said, gave up trying to count the people almost as soon as he landed.

Pocahontas was never to see her native country again. In March 1617, as the group left England to return to Jamestown, she and her son became sick. Their ship put into Gravesend, where she died of smallpox and was buried on March 21. She was twenty-two years old. Her son was dropped off at Plymouth, where he was raised during the next eighteen years.

A long and bloody war between the Powhatans and the Virginia colonists ended in 1613 after the abduction of Wahunsonacock's daughter, Pocahontas, by the English. For her release, the English demanded that the Indians free all their white captives. The Powhatans met their side of the agreement, but Pocahontas remained with the English. She was schooled in British custom and religion and baptized Lady Rebecca. This idealized version of her baptism at Jamestown hangs in the U.S. Capitol in Washington, D.C.

The news of Pocahontas's death, together with Tomocomo's report of the number of people in England—"Count the stars in the sky, the leaves on the trees, and the sand upon the seashore," Tomocomo is supposed to have told the Powhatan leaders on his return—were heavy blows to the aging Wahunsonacock. Resigned, perhaps, to the realization that the Powhatans could never rid themselves of the white men and would ultimately become their subjects, he abdicated the leadership of the confederacy, which was already in tatters, and died the next year.

Married to the English colonist John Rolfe, Pocahontas, now known as Lady Rebecca, crossed the Atlantic in 1616 with her husband and infant son to London where, in fashionable lace cuffs, starched shoulder collar, brocaded velvet mantle, and tall beaver hat, she sat for this portrait, probably by the young Dutch artist Simon Van de Pass.

Wahunsonacock's defeatism was not shared by his more combative half brother, Opechancanough, who succeeded him and quietly revitalized both the traditional culture and the military power of the Powhatans. Aided by his close adviser, a shaman and war captain named Nemattanew, Opechancanough planned the destruction of the entire English colony, whose plantations and new settlements were now expanding up the rivers and across the lands of the Powhatan peoples. By 1622, the English population had swelled to more than a thousand, and the number of plantations had risen to almost fifty. The time was approaching when Opechancanough would have to make his move.

In March, that moment came. An Englishman murdered the chief's adviser, Nemattanew. Two weeks later, Opechancanough struck, launching surprise attacks against settlements and plantations along the James River. On the first day, the Powhatan warriors killed 347 colonists, more than a quarter of the white population. The London Company, which had founded the colony and still oversaw its fortunes, ordered the immediate extermination of all the Powhatans, forbidding the making of peace on any terms.

OPPOSITE: A lurid nineteenth-century version of Opechancanough's warriors falling on Virginia colonists in 1622.

The war lasted for a decade, although most of the fighting occurred within the first three years. The English knew that Opechancanough was the leader and strategist of the uprising, and they put a bounty on his head. In a desperate plot to kill him in 1623, they invited him and hundreds of leading Indians to a grand peace conference. At its conclusion, the English served glasses of wine, which they had poisoned, and proposed a toast to "eternal friendship." The Indians drank, and most of them almost immediately dropped dead. English soldiers at the conference killed the rest. Whether Opechancanough had attended and escaped, or was never at the meeting, is not known. But he was not killed and the next year led eight hundred warriors in a two-day battle against the English musketeers. Although the Powhatans finally withdrew, the English recognized the confederacy as still a potent force. There was little fighting after that, and peace was finally made in 1632.

The cessation of hostilities sealed the fate of the confederacy. With peace came a massive colonial expansion that the Indians could not stop. Twelve years after the war ended, the desperate Powhatans, squeezed into small parts of their former homeland, saw no hope but a return to war.

In the spring of 1644, the aged Opechancanough, carried into battle on a litter, again launched a surprise attack against the settlements

and burgeoning tobacco plantations of the English. The Indians killed five hundred colonists, but this time the population of whites in Virginia was too large, and there was no hope of defeating them. The Powhatan warriors struggled bravely for two years for the last of their lands. Finally, the doughty nonagenarian Opechancanough was captured. He could not walk without help, and, without his servants to hold his eyelids open, he could not see. His captors exhibited him publicly. Then one of the English guards shot him in the back and killed him. It was the end of the Powhatan Confederacy, which had tried and failed to save the Indians' lands from the tide of English expansion.

Patuxet

In the part of the continent now known as New England, meanwhile, waves of English colonists were threatening the lands of other Indians. From southern Maine to Long Island Sound, that region in the early part of the seventeenth century was dotted with the agricultural villages and seasonal hunting, fishing, and gathering camps of dozens of local and regional native groups, all sharing, with small variations, the same culture, Algonquian language, and political, economic, and religious ways of life.

Most of the villages were small, independent, and egalitarian, composed of a number of extended families and headed by a village chief, or sachem, who served as spokesman and counselor, but lived like everyone else and had no coercive powers over the people. Other villages, either voluntarily or by conquest, were united in alliances or confederacies, led by grand sachems and their councillors. Among most of the peoples, families and villages were held together by strong matrilineal clans, and it

was not unusual for a sachem, even one presiding over an alliance of many villages, to be a woman.

In the villages, often located at junctures of streams or above riverbanks, the families lived in small, circular wigwams or breadloaf-shaped longhouses, both covered with slabs of bark or woven mats and erected adjacent to the Indians' cultivated fields of maize, kidney beans, squash, Jerusalem artichokes, pumpkins, tobacco, and other crops. In the spring and summer, village groups traveled to root-gathering and berry-picking grounds, to estuaries and favorite sites along rivers for fish runs, and to tidal marshlands and the coast to collect mussels, scallops, clams, oysters, and lobsters. After the fall harvests, they moved inland to the forests, where the members of a number of villages would cluster together while their hunters gathered meat for the winter, trapping, netting, and killing with longbows and arrows a great variety of game animals and birds, from black bears, deer, and squirrels to Canada geese, swans, and turkeys.

Throughout the year, the people's relationship to the spiritual world dominated everyday affairs. Everything in creation had a spirit to which the people were bound and with which they tried to live in harmony. Over all was a Master of Life, or Creator, but through their dreams or with the aid of a village shaman, known in the Algonquian languages as a powwow, individuals sought contact with the spirits of familiar creatures or natural forces that could advise, cure, or assist them. The powwows, who could be men or women, often held great power, employing magic, hypnosis, medicinal herbs, and psychological astuteness to maintain their position as intermediaries between the people

A computer-generated image of trim longhouses of bent sapling frames covered with bark or mats shows what the principal village of the Wampanoag, Montaup, in the area of present-day Rhode Island looked like in about A.D. 1620.

Utilitarian objects, like this beautifully carved, double-headed turtle bowl produced by a Niantic Indian in the region of present-day Connecticut, were common trade items among New England tribes like the Wampanoags.

and the world of the spirits on which everything in the life of an individual or a village depended.

In addition to local resources, most villages had long had access to valued products from other areas, carried on trails or by canoes over a network of trade routes that linked the different parts of the region. From village to village moved articles of exchange: hides and furs, wooden bowls and earthenware pots, chestnuts, berries, dried fish, and other foods, and eagerly sought white and purple beads made from certain shells by a few coastal tribes on Long Island Sound and known as wampum.

During the sixteenth century, the growing presence of European fishermen and the frequent appearance of seafaring explorers and fur traders on the continent's North Atlantic coast introduced to the trade network metals, manufactured ornaments, utensils, cloth, colored glass beads, steel weapons, and other European goods. The acquisition of the new articles, many of them endowing their Indian owners with new power and prestige, aroused jealousies and the desire to have access to, and be favored by, the white men, particularly among the rival sachems of the confederacies. At the same time, many of the coastal villagers who had direct contact with the European traders learned the dark side of those contacts: white men kidnapped Indians, were arrogant and rude

Carved about 1650, this handsome feast bowl of the Nipmuck tribe of Massachusetts is one of the oldest surviving wooden items made by New England Indians.

to Indian civil and religious leaders and to Indian women, and they introduced horrible sicknesses that depopulated whole villages.

Among those who had experienced both the good and the bad side of the European seamen and traders were the allied villages of the Wampanoag, or Pokanoket, Confederacy, which by the early part of the seventeenth century extended from the eastern side of present-day Rhode Island's Narragansett Bay, across southeastern Massachusetts to Cape Cod. On the western shore of Cape Cod Bay were the inviting harbor and village of Patuxet, one of the thriving centers of the Wampanoag Confederacy.

In the year 1614, an English sea captain named Thomas Hunt kidnapped twenty-four Indians along the New England coast and took them to Malaga, Spain, to sell as slaves. Subsequently, monks ransomed some of them, including a Patuxet Indian named Tisquantum, or Squanto, who was in his midthirties. Tisquantum worked as a servant for the monks for three years and then managed to escape to England, where he became the friend of a wealthy English merchant named John Slaney. Slaney had Tisquantum instructed in the English language and, in 1619, arranged for his passage to Newfoundland. From there, Tisquantum was able to make his way back to the country of the Wampanoags, only to find that in his absence epidemics of white men's diseases had swept through his homeland, devastating his tribe and others and completely wiping out the population of his own village of Patuxet. The site of Patuxet was deserted and silent, its gardens overgrown. In

Kidnapped by English mariners in 1614 and sold as a slave in Spain, Tisquantum, a Patuxet Indian from the site of the future colony of Plymouth, escaped servitude and made his way to England and finally back to his Massachusetts homeland. Later, he acted as translator and negotiator between the Indians and the English colonists and taught the Pilgrims how to plant corn and fertilize it with fish, as seen in this illustration.

After enduring their initial North American winter, the Pilgrims encountered their first Indian—Samoset, an Abenaki from Maine who, to their surprise, greeted them in English which he had learned from European fishermen on the coast. Samoset later returned to Plymouth colony with Tisquantum, who amazed the Pilgrims by also addressing them in English.

the place of family and friends, Tisquantum found only their skulls and bleached bones lying in the grass and among the remains of the wigwams.

Leaving the area, the last of the Patuxets, he roamed the countryside looking for food and shelter and finally joined a village of Wampanoags who had survived the sicknesses. Sometimes he met Usamequin, the portly and dignified grand sachem of the Wampanoag Confederacy, who lived in a village on a peninsula which the Indians called Montaup on the eastern side of Narragansett Bay. The population losses from the epidemics had gravely weakened the Wampanoags, and Usamequin's enemies, the Narragansetts, who lived on the western side of the bay and had escaped the deadly path of the epidemics, had recently driven the Wampanoags off bay islands and were threatening to take even more territory from them. Listening attentively to Tisquantum's wondrous accounts of the white men's wealth and power across the seas, Usamequin was quick to perceive that he could use the support of such allies in his efforts to halt the Narragansetts.

The year after Tisquantum's return, in December 1620, a small English ship, the *Mayflower*, sailed into Patuxet Harbor, setting ashore 102 Pilgrim colonists who re-named the deserted site Plymouth. The winter was a hard one for the fledgling settlement. Disease and starvation reduced the Pilgrims' number by a half. No Indian people came forward to assist them, and none could be found. In March 1621, however, a tall, handsome Abenaki Indian from the Maine coast named Samoset, who had learned English from European fishermen and had been living as a guest at Usamequin's village, appeared at Plymouth, startling the colonists with the words, "Welcome, Englishmen." He told the Pilgrims about the plague that had depopulated the area in which they had settled. "There is neither man, woman, nor child remaining, as indeed we have found none," commented William Bradford, the colony's historian, "so that there is none to hinder our possession or to lay claim unto it."

Soon afterward, Samoset returned to the Plymouth colony with Tisquantum, whose familiarity with the English language—learned in England and better than that of Samoset—again surprised the Pilgrims. Later, on the same day, the Wampanoag grand sachem, Usamequin, arrived from his village of Montaup, forty miles away. With him were his brother Quadenquina and sixty warriors. With Tisquantum and Samoset interpreting for them, the colonists learned that Usamequin was known more commonly by the name Massasoit and that he ruled over eight large villages and about thirty smaller ones. He was, wrote Bradford, "a very lust [*sic*] man in his best years, an able body, grave of countenance, and spare of speech. . . . His face was painted with a deep red like mulberry and he was oiled both head and face."

Entering one of the colony's cabins, Massasoit exchanged formal greetings with the Pilgrims' governor, John Carver, ate a meal with the English, and concluded a peace treaty with them in which both sides agreed to aid each other in the event of an attack by a third party. From Massasoit's point of view, the alliance with the English and their thunderous guns would help him regain his strength against the Narragansetts.

Once established, peaceful relations were furthered by Tisquantum, who remained in his ancestral homeland with the Pilgrims and taught them how to plant and where to fish. In the fall, twenty acres of Indian corn stood at Plymouth.

A romanticized version of the first meeting between the Pilgrims' governor, John Carver, and the Wampanoag chief, Massasoit. The two men agreed to a peace treaty in which each promised to aid the other in the event of an attack by a third party.

RAMONA PETERS/WAMPANOAG

"For us the Wampanoag, the people of the first light, thanksgiving is something that we hope to be on all levels through the creation, to know who we are and what we are and what our capacities are. In order to say a true thanks to the Creator you have to know what you are. And that is a personal endeavor. To know your gifts and then to be able to share them. When we met the English, we made that offering. And of course it would take time for them to know who we are and what we are, to be able to be in thanksgiving. If you think about it, we gave them unconditional acceptance and love and nurturement. Otherwise they would have been massacred at the beach. That was an ability of my people of which I am most proud. But to say thank you for the love you receive from another group of people and to peacefully and happily coexist with us, that did not happen. And it still isn't happening. That is the only thing that we can lament about, is not to be received for who we are. For we are the people of the first light. The new and original thought of the Creator is on that light."

Learning of the Indians' traditional custom at the time of harvest, the Pilgrims decided to have a holiday of thanksgiving and invited Massasoit to share their bounty. The grand sachem arrived with ninety of his people, who provided five deer for the communal feast. For three days and nights, the festivities continued, as prayers, singing, and Wampanoag ceremonies alternated with shooting contests, wrestling matches, footraces, and English and Indian games. When it ended, the Pilgrims and Massasoit's people promised to make the feast an annual celebration of their harvests and friendship.

It was a promise that could not be kept. For a while, the treaty of alliance benefited both sides. Massasoit's friendship with the English protected his people from the Narragansetts, and he gained wealth and prestige. On the other hand, the peace with Indians, supported by Massasoit, gave security to the colony and let it grow and flourish. But Massasoit made many land concessions to the expanding English population, and although he tried to preserve harmony and goodwill during his lifetime, the relationship between the Indians and the whites changed. After forty years of peace, which grew ever more tenuous and difficult to maintain, Massasoit died in 1662. By then, a new, covetous generation of English settlers had spread across the Wampanoags' lands, their authoritarian government, courts, laws, and religious leaders were asserting stern and disrespectful rule over the Indians, and Massasoit's hard-pressed people were seething with resentments.

A depiction by the American artist Howard Pyle of the death of Massasoit's son and heir, Wamsutta, known to the whites as Alexander. Many Wampanoags believed that the English had poisoned the young chief. Wamsutta was succeeded by Massasoit's fiery younger son, Metacom, whom the English called King Philip.

OPPOSITE: *When the Pilgrims' first corn crop ripened in the fall of 1621, the colonists invited Massasoit and his Wampanoag people to share in the harvest. With long-standing traditions of ritual feasts and thanksgiving ceremonies of their own, the Wampanoag guests brought gifts of food to their hosts. The feasting and festivities lasted for three days and nights.*

King Philip

When Massasoit died, his eldest son, Wamsutta, known to the English as Alexander, succeeded him. Wamsutta did not share his father's tolerant attitude toward the white settlers, and to the English authorities, he often seemed haughty and disloyal. He had scarcely been in power for a year when he was taken under guard to Plymouth for questioning by the English. During his interrogation, he became sick and, leaving his two sons as hostages with the Puritans, was allowed to return home. On the way back to his village, he died. The English claimed he died of illness. Most Wampanoags believed that he had been poisoned or had died of bitterness over his rude treatment by the English.

The leadership of the Wampanoags passed to Wamsutta's younger brother, Metacom, known to the Puritans as King Philip. The confederacy that he would head was a world away from the one into which he had been born twenty-four years before. By 1662, some forty thousand English colonists lived in New England, about twice the size of the Indian population. Wherever the English were most densely settled, the Indians were precariously surrounded and outnumbered, their shrunken and depleted hunting lands allowing them little choice for livelihood but to work for the English as laborers and servants alongside slaves. Zealous Puritan authorities, with no

TALL OAK/NARRAGANSETT

"When the first Europeans arrived, Columbus and his crew, he came and he called us Indians, because of the obvious reason, he thought he was lost in India. But what did we call ourselves before Columbus came? That's the question so often asked. And the thing is in every single tribe, even today, when you translate the word that we each had for ourselves, without knowledge of each other, it was always something that translated to basically the same thing. In our language it's Ninuog, or the people, the human beings. That's what we called ourselves. So when the Pilgrims arrived here, we knew who we were, but we didn't know who they were. So we called them Awaunageesuck, or the strangers, because they were the ones who were alien, they were the ones that we didn't know, but we knew each other. And we were the human beings."

regard for the laws or customs of sovereign Indian nations, vigorously prosecuted Indians for hunting and fishing on the Sabbath, using Indian medicines, or entering into non-Christian marital unions. In Plymouth itself, where Massasoit's people and the struggling Pilgrims had once joined to give thanks in their own ways, Indians now faced a sentence of death for denying the Christian religion.

King Philip took an uncompromising stand against the English and their aggressions. Tall and slim, he had been raised as a hunter and warrior and was at home in the forests. At the same time, he was an able orator with an agile mind that often outwitted his opponents in councils. The colonial authorities, whom he infuriated, called him sly and calculating, but he was also quick to anger and was unrelenting as an enemy. Unlike his father, he spoke out defiantly against the white men's attacks on the Indians' culture, religion, and property and denounced their repressive laws. He warned that their expansion and the taking of Indian lands would continue until the Indians had no country left. Time and again, he was hauled before the English authorities at Plymouth and charged with treachery. Each time, he stood his ground, vehemently denying the charges, and was returned to his village at Montaup.

In 1671, amid rumors of an Indian conspiracy, the Puritans again called Philip to Plymouth for questioning. Although he was forced to surrender his weapons, acknowledge the sovereignty of the king of England, and promise to pay an annual fine of a hundred pounds, he continued to speak out forcefully for Indian lands and the freedom of the Indians to live by their own teachings and government. At the same time, recognizing that the Indians' only hope lay in a war that would drive all the English out of the country forever, he planned secretly for a coordinated uprising by the Wampanoags and other New England tribes.

During the next four years, while managing to assuage the whites' fears about him, he appealed to neighboring tribes for support. While some of the Indians, particularly the young warriors, approved of his idea, he had difficulty persuading others. The leaders of many villages and allied groups were already too tied to the English to risk war, while others who had been enemies of the Wampanoags refused to accept joining forces under Philip.

In 1675, three of Philip's people, including one of his closest advisers, were hanged by the English for a crime allegedly committed against a converted Christian Wampanoag. Enraged, Philip protested that Wampanoag sovereignty had been violated and proclaimed that the English had no right to involve themselves in affairs between Indians. His fiery oratory raised his followers to a readiness for war. The Wampanoags had suffered their last insult.

And yet hostilities came unexpectedly, before Philip had completed his plans or fully formed a coalition of the tribes. On June 20, 1675, a group of angry young Wampanoag men came into Swansea and, after shooting some cattle and terrifying the white population, ransacked the village for three days. Finally, an English youth shot at one of the Indians and wounded him. Word spread quickly among the Indian villages, and the next day war erupted as if by a signal. In a series of furious attacks that seemed brilliantly orchestrated, the isolated towns of Rehoboth, Taunton, Dartmouth, and Middleborough were caught by surprise and burned to the ground. The powerful Nipmuck Indian nation, along with the Pocumtucks, Pocassets, Sokokis, and Hassanamesitts, joined Philip and the Wampanoag alliance.

The sudden attacks caused hysteria among the whites. Christian Indians in "praying towns," established by missionaries in various parts of New England to keep them secure from the influence of the unconverted, were deemed suspicious and herded onto offshore islands, where they were imprisoned under military guard. Still, Indian victories mounted. Fifty-two of the ninety English settlements were burned or otherwise damaged, and it was reported that Indian troops hung upon the fringes of other English towns "like the lightning on the edge of clouds." Although aided by trusted Christian Indians and Mohegan mercenaries from Connecticut, the frustrated English militia was outmaneuvered at every turn.

After their capture or surrender, most of Philip's followers were sold into slavery, as seen in this illustration. The slaves went either to buyers on the mainland or to large plantations in Bermuda, the Bahamas, or the Caribbean. Philip's own wife and child were among those sold as slaves in Bermuda.

From Massachusetts, the war spread to other parts of New England. Along the Maine coast, the Saco, Wawenoc, Kennebec, Pigwacket, and Arosaguntacook Indians joined in the attacks against the whites. And even the Wampanoags' former enemies, the Narragansetts of Rhode Island, plunged into the war after the English,

unsure of the Narragansetts' sympathies, attacked and burned a fortified town, killing more than six hundred neutral Narragansett men, women, and children, who, the Boston divine Cotton Mather later recorded, were "terribly Barbikew'd."

The devastating massacre suffered by the Narragansetts was followed, however, by a series of setbacks and losses that destroyed Philip's winter food supplies and demoralized the Wampanoag allies. Many of the Indians who had been fighting worried about their untended gardens and returned to their villages. Others lost heart and surrendered, only to be sold into slavery in the West Indies by their Puritan captors. Plymouth alone shipped five hundred Indian prisoners to the Caribbean slave markets.

By the spring of 1676, the tide had turned against Philip. As though they were trailing a wounded animal, troops hunted him down. His war for freedom and sovereignty disintegrated into a struggle for survival. In April, Canonchet, the veteran sachem and war leader of the Narragansetts, was captured and executed by an English firing squad. Before he died, he declared proudly: "I like it well. I shall die before my heart is soft or I have said anything unworthy of myself." His body was quartered and burned, his head sent to colonial officials in Hartford.

The war was not yet a year old, but the early Indian victories were only a memory. As summer approached, the allied Indian army was starving. The English militia and their scouts hounded Philip's men. On one occasion, English troops stole into an Indian camp and killed three hundred of his people who had sought rest in a hiding place near a falls. Some of the fleeing Indians managed to reach their canoes, but in their panic left their paddles behind and were swept over the falls to their deaths. For the next two months, the Indians evaded capture. But the noose was tightening. In August, a Massachusetts force fell on Philip's camp, killing or capturing 173 Indians. Philip narrowly escaped being taken, but among those captured were his wife and nine-year-old son. In Plymouth, the clergy decided their fate, sending them on a slave ship for sale in Bermuda. Philip was grief stricken when he learned the news. "My heart breaks," he told a companion. "Now I am ready to die."

Philip chose where he would die. He returned to the old Wampanoag capital at Montaup, where his father, Massasoit, had fed and entertained the Pilgrims. In the dawn of August 12, 1676, an English army surrounded the sleeping camp. Moments later, King Philip was dead—shot through the heart by an Indian mercenary. His head was cut off and displayed on a pole in Plymouth for the next twenty years. His finery, so admired by the English—his enormous wampum belts, red blanket, and clothing—were given to the Indian who killed him.

In later years, a Christian Pequot Indian preacher in New England named William Apes remarked about Philip's struggle, "During the bloody contest, the pious fathers wrestled hard and long with their God, in prayer, that He would . . . deliver their enemies into their hands. . . . Nor could they, the Pilgrims, cease crying to the Lord against Philip, until they had prayed the bullet through his heart. . . . If this is the way they pray, that is, bullets through people's hearts, I hope they will not pray for me."

King Philip's War was the most devastating war ever fought on New England soil. It cost the English six hundred lives, twelve hundred homes, and eight thousand cattle. The Wampanoag, Nipmuck, and Narragansett nations lost three thousand lives. Only one hundred Narragansetts and several hundred Wampanoags were reported to have survived the war. The smaller tribes were virtually extinct, or their surviving members had fled north into Canada. Hundreds more had been shipped as slaves to the Caribbean, Spain, Portugal, the Azores, Algiers, and Virginia and the other southern colonies. The Indian power in southern New England no longer existed.

OPPOSITE: *The death of King Philip in August 1676 spelled the end of Indian freedom and power in New England. Only fifty-five years before, the Wampanoag Confederacy had joined the struggling Plymouth colony in a thanksgiving feast celebrating the survival of the Pilgrims in the Indians' country.*

I like it well. I shall die before my heart is soft or I have said anything unworthy of myself.

—CANONCHET, NARRAGANSETT SACHEM

CHAPTER 5
THE CAULDRON

Deer Hides and Slaves

The Sewees, a small nation of Siouan-speaking Indians who lived along the Santee River and on some of the sea islands of the coast of present-day South Carolina, were a kind and trusting people. When English colonists arrived in their country in 1670 to establish a settlement that eventually became the city of Charleston, Nicholas Carteret, one of the settlers, wrote that the Sewees "ran" enthusiastically "up to the[ir] middle in mire and water" to carry the white people ashore from their ship, then "stroaked [them] on the shoulders with their hands," to convey their pleasure and friendship. At the same time, they cried, "Bony Conraro Angles" ("English are very good friends"), expressing the warmth of their feelings for the newcomers with bits of words they had picked up from earlier contacts with maritime traders and Spanish missionaries.

A short time later, the Sewees, along with neighboring coastal tribes, twice helped save the fledgling colony, aiding the English to repel Spanish attacks from Florida and supplying the settlers with food when famine threatened them. Soon enough, however, events turned harshly against the Sewees. By 1700, they were almost extinct, suffering, according to a contemporary account, a uniquely tragic end.

After the arrival of the whites, the Sewees had been decimated by smallpox and other European diseases that they had caught from the settlers. Wave after wave of deadly fevers depopulated the Sewee villages and shattered their society and culture. But trade with the English was to prove even more calamitous to them. For more than a century previously, coastal Indians had been trading with whites, and the Sewees were well aware of the value of having a trading partner in their midst. Almost from the moment that they

OVERLEAF: *The ambush of General Edward Braddock's English army in the woods of western Pennsylvania by French forces and their Indian allies in July 1755 during the French and Indian War.*

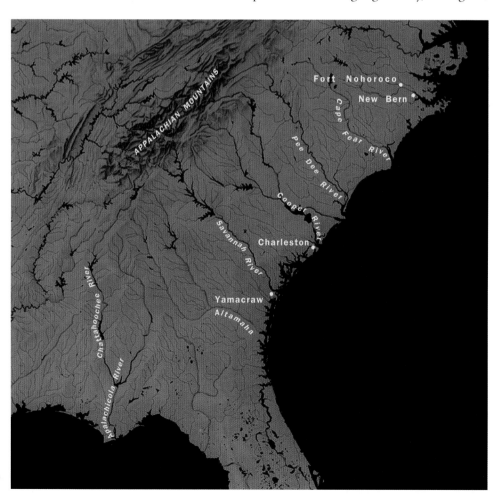

carried the colonists ashore on their backs and set them down on firm ground on the day of their arrival, trade had begun with them. After the "stroaks" of welcome, according to Carteret, the Indians "brought deare skins, some raw, some drest, to trade with us, for which we gave them knives, beads, and tobacco and glad they were of the Market."

Thereafter as the English colony, centered around the settlement at Charles Town, took root, a trade for deer hides and furs flourished. It was not long before greedy English traders abused and corrupted the trade, plying Indians with cheap rum to make them drunk and cheat them out of the products of their hunt, murdering Sewees who demanded fairness, and creating resentments by high-handedness and insults. In time, the Sewee hunters learned that the traders sold their deer hides and furs in England for twenty times the top price they paid the Indians. It was the final blow to the Sewees' trusting nature. Seething with anger at the deceit of the traders, the Sewee council made a decision that determined the nation's fate forever.

In the year 1701, John Lawson, a surveyor visiting the now-thriving commercial center and port of Charles Town, heard that the Sewees had lost nearly all their population and described what a trader told him had happened to them. The Sewees, Lawson wrote, noticed that ships arriving from England came into view each time at the same spot on the horizon. "[Seeing] that the ships came always in at one place . . . made them very confident that [that] way was the exact road to England,"

In 1736, Philip G. F. von Reck, a German visitor to James Oglethorpe's new colony at Savannah, Georgia, drew this watercolor of what he titled "a festival" in a nearby village of Yuchi Indians. Hanging in the interior of the shelter appear to be guns, which the Yuchis would have acquired in trade or received from English colonists in the Carolinas whom they had helped in slave raids against other tribes.

he said, "and seeing so many ships come thence, they believed it could not be far." At a meeting of their council, they embarked upon a plan to sail to England, where they could establish their own relationship directly with that nation and be paid what the traders received.

Preparations were begun at once, with the utmost secrecy. A fleet of canoes "of the best sort, and biggest size" was built. "Some Indians," Lawson related, "were employed about making the canoes, others to hunting, every one to the post he was most fit for, all endeavours tending towards an able fleet and cargo for Europe. . . . In a small time they had gotten a navy, loading, provisions, and hands ready to set sail."

All able-bodied men and women boarded the craft, filling the canoes with the most valuable goods their nation possessed, including their hopes and dreams of just

treatment. At last, the flotilla was launched into the surf, leaving behind on the shore only the old, sick, and very young. The big canoes made their way past the Charles Town wharves and into the open road of the ocean, heading directly for the point on the eastern horizon where the merchant ships from England always appeared.

Perhaps they left in the hurricane season of autumn, or perhaps it was a summer storm that enveloped them. Whatever it was, a mighty gale blew up that swallowed the canoes and bore many of the Sewees to a grave in the open sea. Those who survived were the less fortunate. They were snatched from the waves by a passing English slave ship and sold in a West Indies slave market.

Back in their homeland, Lawson in 1701 saw the handful of remaining Sewees. "Nothing affronts them more," he wrote, "than to rehearse their voyage to England." Soon afterward, the remnants of the once-kind and trusting nation were absorbed by other tribes, and the Sewees, like many other small nations of the southeastern coastal regions, ceased to exist.

From 1680 to 1730, in addition to the commerce in deer hides, furs, and rum, the Indian slave trade was a mainstay in the economy of the proliferating Carolina settlements. During that period, countless thousands of men, women, and children of dozens of Indian nations were enslaved by the English colonists, seized by them in raids or purchased for the slave markets from Indians who had captured them from other tribes, usually at the instigation of the English. At first, the slave traders pretended humanitarian goals, explaining that buying Indian prisoners saved them from the worse fate of being tortured by their captors. But the traders soon dropped all pretense and, deliberately pitting one tribe against another with offers of guns, powder, and cheap English textiles and manufactured goods, encouraged Indian slave-catching raids against weaker tribal rivals and intertribal wars waged mostly for captives to sell to the whites. On top of the waves of epidemics that swept through the Indian villages, the destructive impact of the slave trade disoriented numerous nations and engulfed the Indian world from the southern Atlantic seaboard to the Mississippi River in dislocations and turmoil.

The first Indian victims were the members of a host of coastal tribes easily accessible to English raiding parties. The effects of enslavement and disease emptied villages of survivors, who abandoned their ancestral homelands and fled inland to other tribes for safety. At the same time, the English pursuit of the policy of "divide and conquer," inducing tribes to war upon each other for captives to sell as slaves, led to the disappearance of many nations—the Cusabo, Wimbee, Edisto, Stono, Kiawa, Coosa, Isaw, Wanniah, Sampa, Ashepoo, Elasie, and many others—whose remnants were absorbed by interior tribes.

OPPOSITE: *Tribes often fought back against the invaders. This sketch by Baron Christoph von Graffenried depicts his torture after he, John Lawson, and their black servants were captured by Tuscarora Indians in 1711. The year before, Graffenried had helped establish New Bern, a colony of German Palatine and Swiss settlers, on lands belonging to the Tuscaroras in the region of present-day North Carolina. Although the Tuscaroras spared Graffenried, they burned Lawson at the stake and tried unsuccessfully to drive the Europeans from their lands. Defeated, they migrated north to Pennsylvania and found refuge among their fellow Iroquois.*

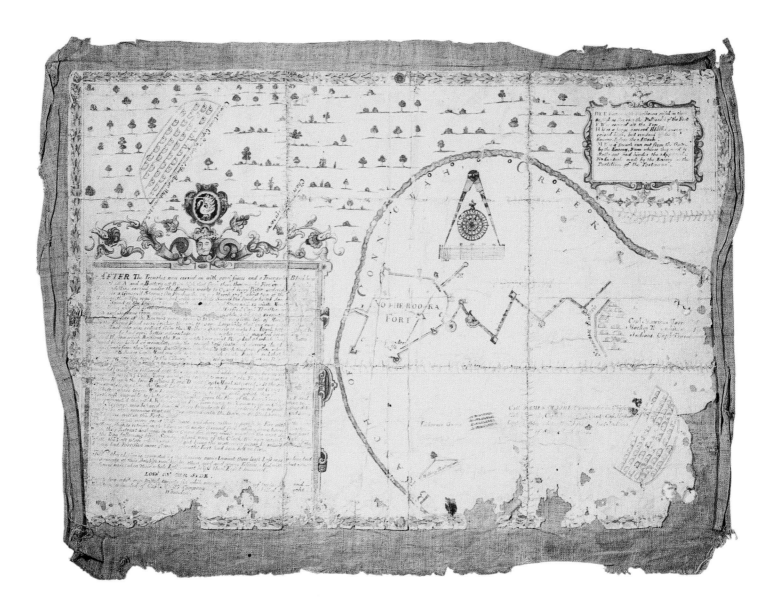

It took several expeditions and the combined forces of colonists and Indian allies of many different tribes to defeat the Tuscaroras. This 1713 map of an expedition of thirty whites and a thousand Indians from South Carolina against the Tuscaroras' "Fort" Nohoroco (center) in the bend of Contentnea Creek in North Carolina shows three of the colonists' camps (upper left and lower right). After a furious assault, the Tuscarora stronghold fell. Some of its surviving defenders escaped, but most were taken to Charleston as slaves.

Sometimes, the English made and fought in the wars, aided by Indian allies to whom they promised some of the slaves and spoils for themselves. The result was the same: a division of Shawnees, who at that time lived along the Savannah River, helped the colonists utterly destroy and enslave the Westo nation, which then disappeared almost without a trace. Later, in 1712–13, Yamasees, Catawbas, Cherokees, and a mixed group of smaller tribes helped slave traders and settlers in North Carolina defeat the Iroquoian-speaking Tuscaroras. Long the object of repeated raids by English slave catchers, the Tuscarora villagers finally gave up and emigrated north to Pennsylvania and protection offered them by their relatives, the five Iroquois tribes of the League of the Hodenosaunee. When the fighting with the Tuscaroras was over, the tribes that had helped the English fared little better. In 1715, the Carolina colonists turned on the Yamasees, who fled to Florida, but not before warfare with the English overcame their allies, the Catawbas, and obliterated the

Waxhaw, Congaree, Sugeree, Santee, and other coastal nations that had assisted the whites in defeating the Tuscaroras.

When the supply of Indian slaves became exhausted along the coast, the traders turned to the interior tribes, sometimes traveling up to six hundred miles themselves to acquire slaves, but more often encouraging Indian nations to war on more distant ones and bring back captives to sell to the whites. A notable exception was slave-raiding campaigns into Spanish-held Florida by an army of fifty South Carolina colonists and a thousand Creek, Apalachicola, and Yuchi Indian allies led by James Moore, a Carolina governor and slave dealer, in the first years of the eighteenth century. Moore and his troops ravaged missions, burned Franciscan priests at the stake, and almost wiped out the survivors of the original Apalachee, Timucua, and Calusa Indian populations of Florida. In 1704, Moore returned to South Carolina with more than six thousand captives for the slave markets—Christian Indians whom his army had seized at the Spanish missions.

Gradually, to meet the colonists' seemingly insatiable demand for slaves, tribes throughout the Southeast, including the Chickasaws, Choctaws, Creeks, Hitchitis, Cherokees, and Muskokean groups, became enmeshed, to a greater or lesser degree, in the machinations of the trade. Many of the Indian slaves were kept for the home economy in the southern colonies or were shipped to Pennsylvania, New York, or New England. But thousands were sent to the expanding English sugar plantations in the Bahamas, Barbados, and Jamaica and to Bermuda and various other markets in the Caribbean. Suffering

Tomochichi, a chief of the Lower Creeks, and his nephew, Toonahowi. In 1733, Tomochichi, who lived at the Creek town of Yamacraw on the lower Savannah River and was a friend of the English, sold his land to Oglethorpe for what became the colony of Savannah, Georgia. This engraving was made from a portrait painted the following year by William Verelst when Tomochichi and his nephew accompanied Oglethorpe to London as part of a Creek delegation to meet King George II and Queen Caroline.

from disease, starvation, and a strange environment and subjected to brutal conditions of labor, few Indians shipped to the West Indies survived their first year of servitude, necessitating a steady demand for replacements.

After 1730, the supply of Indian slaves among tribes relatively easy to reach was depleted, and most inland sources had become too hard to reach or were protected by the French in Louisiana. The tempo of the trade decreased rapidly, and the importing of African slaves to take the place of the Indians expanded dramatically. Yet, in spite of the fact that the majority of Indian slaves had been exported, the slave labor structure of the American South by then had been built on the backs of Indian people. Even in 1730, one-quarter of all the slaves in South Carolina were still Indian, and in a few colonies the proportion was considerably higher. By that time, the names of dozens of southeastern Indian nations, fallen victim to the disruptions and violence of the colonial slave trade, were scarcely remembered, and their surviving members, if there were any, were wanderers among strangers, trying to put their world together again.

A late eighteenth-century painting shows a British trader, William A. Bowles, with Creek Indians at his trading post on the Chattahoochee Apalachicola River near the Georgia–West Florida boundary. The artist, who may have been Bowles himself, depicts the post as a thriving agricultural center in the country of the Lower Creeks.

The Fur Trade

You gave birth to us, for you brought us the first iron.

A FOX CHIEF TO FRENCH TRADER NICOLAS PERROT,

IN THE REGION OF WISCONSIN, 1669

While the economy of the southern colonial expansion was being driven by the trade in hides and human beings, French, Dutch, and English traders in the North were engaged in a commerce centered on beaver, martin, ermine, otter, lynx, and other furbearing animals that were abundant in the wooded homelands of the Indian nations of the Northeast and the region of the Great Lakes. By the seventeenth century, the fur trade with the easternmost tribes was already playing an important role in the mercantile economies of rival European nations. From beaver hides, for example, came felt, and when felt hats came into fashion in Europe and raised a demand by hat-

They never made an accumulation of skins of moose, otter, beaver, or others, but only so far as they needed them for personal use.

—BRITISH TRADER, SPEAKING

OF INDIAN HUNTERS

ters for the exceptionally fine-grade beaver pelts from the North American wilds, the Indian fur trade offered fat profits for Europeans who engaged in it.

At first, there were few signs of the profound changes the fur trade would bring to the lives and cultures of the Indian suppliers. To many northern tribes, like the Montagnais and Naskapis of the Labrador peninsula, the Micmacs of the present-day Canadian Maritime Provinces, and the Maliseets and Abenakis of what is now Maine, the fur trade was initially merely an extension of a seasonal round of food-gathering—largely by hunting, trapping, and fishing— that they had followed for centuries. At various times of the year, these Indians still regularly hunted beaver, fox, rabbit, otter, and other

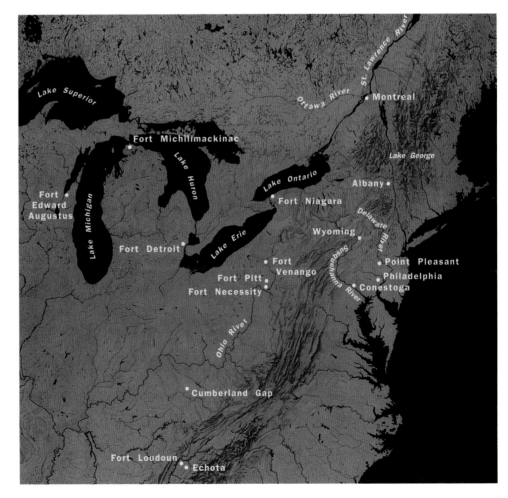

Sauvage de la Baye de hudson

This Indian hunter, portrayed in 1796 by the French artist Grasset de Saint Sauveur, could have been a member of the Montagnais, Cree, or another tribe with whom the French and British traded for furs in the interior of eastern Canada from Labrador to Hudson Bay.

small furbearing animals. In winter, they split into multifamily units and in the deep forests hunted the larger game, including moose, caribou, and bear. Late spring was their season for coming together again, when their villages rejoined for ceremonies, social activities, courtship, games, feasting, and trade. It was a routine to which the European fur traders adapted, accepting, in addition, a relationship in which the Indians' traditions, and not those of the Europeans, set the standards and conduct of the exchange.

In the first half of the seventeenth century, French traders, based in Montreal, moved up the St. Lawrence and Ottawa rivers and across the Great Lakes to the upper Mississippi Valley, forming fur-trading partnerships along the way with Ottawas, Hurons, Ojibwas, Menominees, Potawatomis, Mesquakies (who became better known as Foxes), and numerous other inland tribes who supplied them with furs from the forests, lakes, and rivers of the continent's heartland. Not all the tribes and bands did the actual hunting; many, like the Hurons and Ottawas—and especially the five New York Iroquois nations after they had exhausted the supply of beaver on their own lands—filled the role of monopolistic middlemen, acquiring pelts by trade or force from more distant tribes or from those who occupied the best fur countries, and then selling them profitably to the whites.

In 1670, when the British established the Hudson's Bay Company to vie with the French monopoly in present-day Canada,

A decorative detail from a 1777 map of Canada pictures the principal commerce of that part of North America at the time—bargaining for furs.

the northern tribes skillfully played the traders of the two powers off against each other and made use of the competition between them to get the highest prices for their furs. The payments the Indians received—guns, powder, balls, hatchets, blankets, cloth, kettles, knives, mirrors, awls, needles, beads, paints, combs, and other European manufactured goods—vastly changed their material culture. At the same time, however, since the Europeans depended on the stability and goodwill of the Indian nations for the furs, the traders in the beginning did little overtly to disturb the tribes' traditional customs or threaten their societies and lands.

In this work by Peter Lindestrom, a lively scene of warfare forms the backdrop to a quieter depiction of friendly trade in the late seventeenth century between Swedish colonists and Lenape Indians, whom the whites called Delawares for the river where many of them lived.

This 1612 engraving, embellishing Champlain's map of his explorations in the Northeast, showed little concern for realism in depicting Indians. The woman and child and the warrior at the left with shield, bow, and club were supposed to be Montagnais, and the mythic pair at the right were allegedly from somewhere on the New England coast. Images such as these formed long-lasting visions among stay-at-home Europeans of what Indians looked like.

But the fur trade, which originally conformed to the cultural customs of the Indian nations, inevitably changed and had an increasingly adverse impact on the tribes. Many Indian nations, for instance, gradually found it more lucrative to trade with the white men than to pursue old economic activities. Some of the agricultural nations stopped planting and let their fields lie fallow and overrun with weeds, while hunting societies lost the rhythm of their lives. Traditional trade networks and practices were disrupted, jealousies and feuds were aroused, and the ability of tribes to control the behavior of their members was undermined by the diverting presence of the Europeans.

In addition, village, clan, and family cohesion and discipline broke apart as individuals, eager for economic gain and prestige, put personal goals ahead of the values and well-being of the group. Some Indians, seduced by the Europeans' wealth and

OPPOSITE: *Early in the eighteenth century, religious orders such as the Ursuline nuns of Quebec taught European embroidery techniques to the Indians they converted. Floral embroidery would seem at least partly responsible for the development of floral beadwork designs, which are still found in different forms among the tribes of the eastern United States, the Plains, and much of Canada. Perhaps no people mastered floral beadwork to the extent that the Chippewas did. This Ojibwa (the original form of Chippewa) bandolier bag was fashioned after a European shoulder bag, probably for trade.*

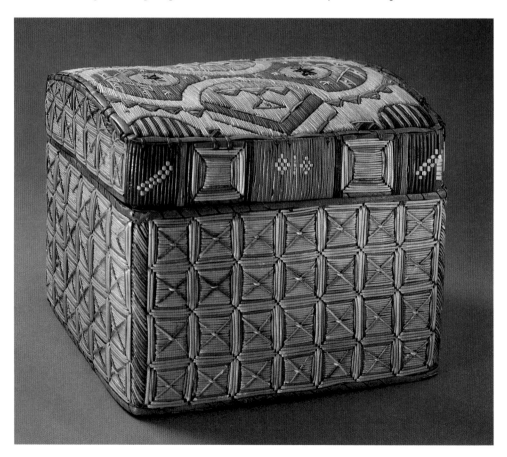

This handsome trunk-top box was made by a Micmac Indian in eastern Canada in the early part of the nineteenth century. Its sides, formed by bands of birchbark, are sewn together with spruce root and decorated with porcupine quillwork. Finely crafted birchbark boxes and other articles were often made by northeastern Indian women to trade to the Europeans.

power and defying the counsel of tribal civil and spiritual leaders, left their homes and families to try to enter the white men's world and live and travel with the traders. At the same time, bands and nations that once traded for mutual benefit were forced into cutthroat competition—even hostility—as hunters, under pressure to produce more furs, encroached on the hunting lands of others.

Meanwhile, ancient tribal and personal spiritual values and sacred relationships with the land and animals also changed or were abandoned. Noting the disappearance among some Indian hunters of an acknowledgment of brotherhood with the animals they hunted, and gratitude to them for giving their lives that humans might not go hungry or unclothed, a British trader wrote:

> [Before], they
> killed animals only
> in proportion as
> they had need of
> them. They never
> made an accumulation
> of skins of moose,
> otter, beaver, or
> others, but only so far
> as they needed them
> for personal use.

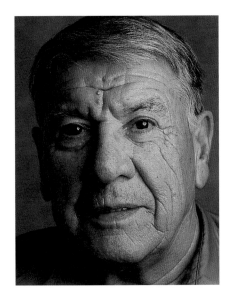

ANTHONY FRANCIS/MICMAC

"It was once related to me by an elder in our community that he identified one instance where the Micmacs were trading for guns, and the way they used to trade is that they used to stack the furs up to the length of the gun. And there were standard-length guns at that time. But then, when the traders, the European traders, realized that they could get this pile of furs up to the length of the gun, they lengthened the gun. They made these guns longer. And they were up to six feet at times, and then the hunting was not as good when this started happening. The Indians were greatly offended by these kinds of practices."

Within decades, species of animals were all but wiped out in entire regions. Guns, steel traps, and the intensive hunting caused a depletion of wildlife, which at times resulted in the Indians' starvation.

Alcoholism also became a problem. Adherence to tribal authority and traditions—maintained in the past by the reasoning of elders and clan relatives, the mediation and teaching of spiritual leaders, or, if need be, by public ridicule and shame or even ostracism from the group—was eroded by the widespread use of liquor, with which many traders plied Indians to make it easier to cheat them. Alcoholism became rampant among many nations engaged in the fur trade and, with epidemics of smallpox, tuberculosis, and other diseases, ripped apart family and tribal structures.

Long the setting of peaceful, interconnecting trade networks among the tribes, much of North America by the mid–eighteenth century had been turned by the fur trade largely into a continent of uprooted and stressed Indian nations. The driving force of European expansion had cut away at Indian cultures, traditions, and the people themselves. From the Appalachian frontier to the Mississippi Valley, stability and age-old systems of conduct had collapsed. Warfare, stemming from the fur trade and the competitiveness of the Europeans, and in deadliness unlike any the tribes had ever encountered in the past, became endemic, obliterating or decimating many nations, like the Wenros, Conoys, Petuns, Neutrals, Eries, and Susquehannocks, dispersing others, like the Hurons, Ottawas, Mahicans, Nanticokes, and Shawnees, and causing

A romantic Frederic Remington portrayal of an Indian and trapper greeting each other somewhere in western Canada.

Tempting an Indian with trade goods—a common scene in the fur countries of the North and West. Among the European-produced goods, many, such as cloth, metal cookware, and tools, made life easier for the Indians, but others, like guns and rum, disrupted and destroyed their societies.

a chain reaction of collisions, displacements, and flights of terrified tribes, seeking new homes and safety from deadly war parties, armed with traders' guns, who would control the source and supply of furs as far west as present-day Iowa and Minnesota.

For the Indian nations, it was a period of unprecedented violence. The most devastating wars were waged by the Iroquois, the suppliers of furs first to the Dutch at Albany and then to the English until their own lands were depleted of beavers. Then for three bloody decades, beginning in 1649, they fought to open routes for themselves to western and northern fur regions and take the furs and their sources away from the Hurons and their allies and friends who supplied the French. Theirs were wars of annihilation. Father Jerome Lalemant, a French Jesuit missionary among the Hurons, described the Iroquois warriors:

> They come like Foxes through the woods. They attack like lions.
> They take flight like birds, disappearing before they have really
> appeared.

Thousands of Indians died before the Iroquois' so-called Beaver Wars ended.

SIR*JOS*JEBB.

As a result of the seemingly insatiable European demand for furs, vast areas of North America were overhunted. Some nations, like the Iroquois—one of whose warriors of the eighteenth century is pictured here—waged war on less powerful tribes to acquire new hunting grounds or to become middlemen between those still able to supply furs and the European traders.

As the fur trade moved west, it left behind an enduring trail of still another tragedy. Nations that had trapped and hunted their lands to exhaustion had also grown dependent on the guns and cloth and other goods the traders had paid them. Now the traders and their goods were gone. Unable to return to their original economies and bereft of income from the whites, many of the former fur-trade nations in the East became pariahs, sunk in poverty, alcoholism, and despair. The best any of them could hope for, said a Frenchman in Canada, was "to forget what was past for their own preservation."

The Walking Purchase

Few Europeans of the eighteenth century understood the role that whites played in bringing destruction and chaos to so many of the ancient cultures and civilizations of the Indians' world. And in their hunger for land they continued to bring more.

In Pennsylvania, a lasting friendship, begun in 1682 between William Penn, the colony's founder, and a division of the Lenape, or Delaware, nation, whose villages extended across present-day southeastern New York, New Jersey, Delaware, and southeastern Pennsylvania, was deteriorating rapidly. Thomas Penn, William's son, produced a deed allegedly signed by his father and three Lenape chiefs in 1686. It ceded to the colony all the Lenape lands around the forks of the Delaware River, west of Neshaminy Creek in Pennsylvania "as far as a man can go in one day and a half."

The fifty-year-old deed had never been walked. Believing that the land cession would be a small one, the Lenapes agreed that the deed should be honored to end any dispute over its boundaries before settlers overran even more of their lands. Pennsylvania, on the other hand, applied anything but honorable thinking to the settlement. Its leaders advertised for athletes, offering land incentives and money to whoever could go the longest distance in the allotted time. Agents were sent out to find the fleetest men, and three were finally selected. They were trained for nine days over the terrain they would walk, while workers slashed and cleared brush from the path they would follow.

What was called the Walking Purchase was consummated on August 25, 1737.

OPPOSITE: The lures of the fur trade uprooted many Indian peoples, creating a new class of "hang around the fort" Indians who benefited from the presence of the Europeans. These colorfully dressed Ottawas, veterans of the fur trade, were painted at Fort Michilimackinac in upper Michigan in the eighteenth century.

OVERLEAF: Benjamin West's painting of William Penn's apocryphal treaty with the Lenape Indians under the Shackamaxon Elm at Philadelphia in 1682. Although the event never occurred and its story probably stemmed from land purchases made from the Indians in 1683, Penn's fair and honest treatment of the Lenapes became an American legend. In contrast, the shameful displacement of the Lenapes by the Pennsylvania colonists a generation later is almost unknown.

When the walk began, crowds of spectators lined the path, cheering on the participants—who loped rather than walked. From the sidelines also, Lenapes called repeatedly to the athletes to walk, not run. Of the three athletes, only one lived through the ordeal, and he fell prostrate at the end of the day and a half. He had covered sixty-four miles, securing for the whites approximately twelve hundred square miles of the Indians' lands.

Embittered, the Lenapes for a while refused to move, especially when the original deed, questioned as a fraud, disappeared. Pennsylvania and the League of the Hodenosaunee, however, had previously agreed that the Iroquois would mediate all affairs between Pennsylvania and its Indian population. The powerful League took Pennsylvania's side and forced the weaker Lenapes to resettle in refugee areas it had established for dispossessed tribes at Wyoming (present-day Wilkes-Barre, Pennsylvania) and Shamokin on the upper Susquehanna River. These Hodenosaunee refugee centers would ring with the laments of many displaced and homeless nations, driven from their ancestral lands by European colonists or the Indian wars of the fur trade: Nanticokes, Saponis, Piscataways, Shawnees, Mahicans, Tutelos, and many others. In 1748, a Moravian missionary in Bethlehem, Pennsylvania, made note of a number of Nanticoke refugees passing by "on their way to Wyoming." They had come from their original homes on the Eastern Shore of Maryland and were carrying the bones of their dead in their arms so that they would not have to leave them behind.

The French and Indian War

To most of the Indian nations of the Appalachian frontier and the Ohio Valley, the conflict which the English colonists called the French and Indian War, beginning in 1754, was little more than a continuation of the turbulence that had been wrack-

Lapowinsa, chief of the Lenapes who signed the fraudulent Walking Purchase treaty in 1737, was forced to move his band westward from the Delaware River to a new home on the Susquehanna.

OPPOSITE: *Iroquois canoes and their uses are portrayed in this early English illustration. Included are views of thirteen men in a long canoe of elm bark; portaging a canoe; navigating rough waters; paddling a canoe while standing upright; the scheme of a birchbark canoe with eight seats; and an Indian "oar," or paddle.*

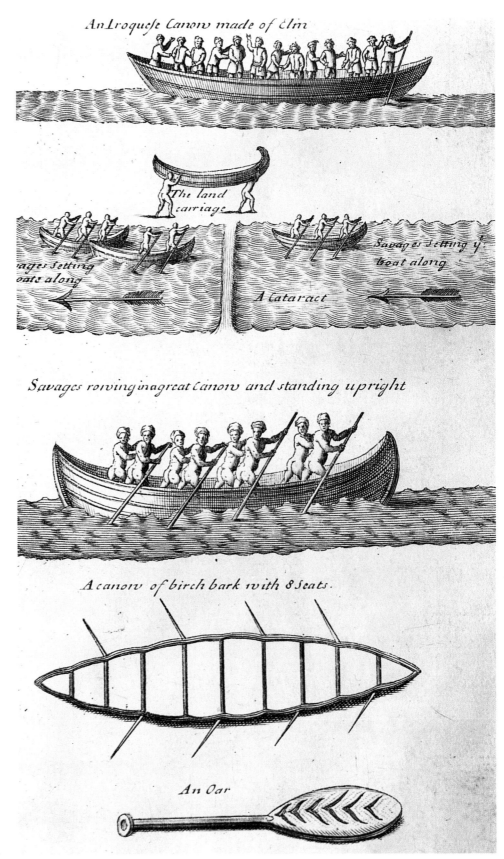

ing the tribes and their relations with the expanding white population and with each other.

Escalating from years of smaller wars and skirmishes between the British and their colonies aided by Indian allies on one side and the French and their tribal supporters on the other, the conflict was a final struggle of the two European imperial powers for possession of North America. Most tribes recognized it as a war without profit for themselves and tried to stay neutral, but many bands were unable to avoid being dragged in to fight as auxiliaries of one side or the other.

The immediate cause of the war was French moves to build forts in the upper Ohio Valley, a large area claimed also by Virginia and the British Crown, which had granted half a million of its acres to the Ohio Company for the development of English settlements. Insisting, on the other hand, that the Ohio Valley belonged to France, which needed it for "a free and certain passage" from its centers in eastern Canada to its possessions on the Mississippi River, French officers minced no words in maintaining that "It is our absolute design to take possession of the Ohio—and, by God, we will do it!"

In the winter of 1753–54, Virginia sent the twenty-one-year-old

surveyor and frontier militia officer George Washington to the area to warn the French fort builders to leave. He failed to persuade them to withdraw, but, of almost equal importance, both he and the French officers with whom he dealt showed concern over the loyalty and support that Indian tribes would give their respective forces in the event of hostilities. The Ohio country was filled with the bands of many tribes, some of which had previously favored the French and others the English. But in large measure, they were refugee bands who lived in the region by sufferance of the League of the Hodenosaunee (which, like the British and French, also claimed possession of the Ohio country), and they found it difficult to act independently of the Iroquois chiefs. Since the League wanted no part of the whites' quarrel, persuading Indians to fight in their behalf loomed as a major problem for both European powers.

Prior to Washington's arrival, a powerful Seneca chief named Tanacharison, or the Half King, the League's spokesman for Iroquois settlers who had moved to the Ohio country, as well as overseer of the dependent refugee Delaware bands in the region, proposed to the French commandant that the French and English both withdraw and let the League rule the area as a buffer district between the two European powers. In response, the French officer, losing his temper, rendered his cause little benefit by shouting at the dignified Seneca statesman, "I am not afraid of flies or mosquitoes, for the Indians are such as those. I tell you, down that river [the Ohio] I will go. If the river is blocked up, I have the forces to burst it open and tread under my feet all that oppose me. I despise all the stupid things you have said." He then flung at the Half King a string of wampum that signified friendship and kicked it around in a gesture of contempt.

When Washington reached the

OPPOSITE: *This depiction of Iroquois traveling in the snow and making a winter camp illustrated the writings on Indian customs and practices by a French Jesuit missionary, Joseph François Lafitau, who lived at a mission for Canadian Iroquois near Montreal for almost six years early in the eighteenth century. In the foreground, Indians, whom the engraver forgot to clothe in furs despite the cold weather, carry their goods on their backs or pull them in toboggans. Others in the background prepare camp, cutting wood, making a fire with a drill, and setting up a kettle.*

A distorted, early French version of North American Indians, this 1664 engraving shows an exotically garbed Huron of the Great Lakes in sandals, striped hose, and fringed apron, smoking a pipe.

A 1664 French rendition of a muscular, tattooed Iroquois warrior, posed in classic European style and, though holding a war club, looking deceptively unfearsome.

area, he found a ready welcome and assurances of friendship for the English from the insulted Seneca chief. Injury was added when, in Washington's presence, another French officer tried to get the Half King so intoxicated that he would be unable to travel on with Washington, as he had promised to do, but would remain with the French, who could work to persuade him to supply Iroquois auxiliaries to the French forces. The Frenchman was unsuccessful, and the Half King went on with Washington.

Nevertheless, the Seneca chief's friendship did not imply the League's military support for the English, and Washington returned to the Virginia government concerned that the French would muster western and Canadian Indian allies, while the Iroquois and the tribes they controlled would abandon the English. "Without Indians to oppose Indians, we shall have little hope for success," he told the Virginia governor.

In April 1754, Washington returned to the Ohio Valley with 120 men to protect a company of 40 Virginia frontiersmen who were building an English fort at the strategically important forks of the Ohio, the site of present-day Pittsburgh. Still friendly to the English, the Half King had joined the builders to offer his advice and the support of his warriors—mostly local Seneca émigrés known as Mingos, a Delaware term for "Stealthy Ones"—in case the French interfered. Before Washington arrived, however, an overwhelming French army of 500 troops and Indian auxiliaries appeared at the forks and forced the small group of Virginians to surrender the post, which the French renamed Fort Duquesne for the French military commander in North America.

Slipping away, the Half King and his Indians met Washington's militiamen and joined them in an attack on the camp of a small detachment of French soldiers, killing the commanding officer and nine of his men. When the French officials learned of the affair, they complained that the attack had been unprovoked, calling the killing of the officer the "assassination" of an envoy who had been bearing a message to the English, and blowing up the episode into an international controversy that some accepted as the event that actually began the French and Indian War.

Soon after the confrontation, the Half King and his Indians left Washington, who chose a location known as the Great Meadows to build his own palisaded post, which he named Fort Necessity. The site was a poor one. The fort was on low ground, commanded on three sides by nearby wooded hills. Before he departed, the Half King had advised the youthful Washington against using the site, and he was proven correct.

On July 4, 1754, a French army of 650 regulars and Indians, inflamed by their officers to avenge Washington's "assassination" of the party of the alleged French envoy, attacked Fort Necessity. The French had had success in gaining Indian support, particularly from bands who were their trading partners in Canada or were under the influence of French missionaries. Among those accompanying the French soldiers were Wyandots, Ojibwas, Abenakis, Nipissings, Ottawas, Algonquins, and Iroquois, the last from French missions among the Onondagas and Mohawks. After fighting inconclusively all day in a pouring rain, however, the Indians informed the French commander that they intended to leave for their homes the next day. Faced by their withdrawal, the French offered Washington honorable surrender terms. Unable to sustain a siege, Washington accepted and, turning over his fort to the French, marched his small, bedraggled army back to Virginia.

The following year, the French at Fort Duquesne were able to rally Indian allies again to assist in stopping another and more serious English threat to their hold on Ohio country. This time, a larger Indian force of hundreds of Ottawas, Ojibwas, Miamis, Potawatomis, Menominees, Shawnees, Hurons, Delawares, and pro-French Senecas were instrumental in helping the French rout Major General Edward Braddock's redcoated grenadiers in the deep woods near the Monongahela River on July 9, 1755.

Braddock, who had a habit of insulting the tribes, had only eight Indians with his army. Prior to his disastrous wilderness march to try to capture Fort Duquesne, he

OVERLEAF: *The Seven Years' War between England and France also enmeshed their colonists and many Indian tribes in North America, where the two imperial powers battled for control of that part of the world in a conflict that the English colonials called the French and Indian War. In this scene, Indian allies of the French are shown preparing to burn a pro-British Onondaga captive at the stake.*

OPPOSITE: *This portrait of Kanagagota (Standing Turkey), the Head Beloved Man, or principal chief, of the Cherokees, known to the English colonists as Old Hopp of Chote, was painted in London by Francis Parsons when the chief visited England with other Cherokees in 1762. Parsons misunderstood his name and titled the portrait* Cunne Shote, *corruptions of the first part of the chief's name and that of the Cherokee capital, Echota.*

had unwittingly caused the refugee bands of Shawnees and Delawares finally to take up the hatchet against the English by informing the Delaware head chief, Shingas, arrogantly that after he drove the French from the Ohio country, only the English—and "No Savage"—would inherit and inhabit that land. It took the English three more years following Braddock's defeat to gain possession of the area. In 1758, a large, new army under Brigadier General John Forbes, accompanied by several bands of Iroquois, Catawba, and Cherokee warriors who had been won to the English side, built a road across the rugged, forested mountains of Pennsylvania and marched over it to Fort Duquesne. Outmanned and isolated, the French burned the fort and departed, leaving the forks of the Ohio to the British, who promptly built a new post on the site, which they named for their prime minister, William Pitt.

Meanwhile, Braddock's defeat had left the English frontier settlers exposed to the French and to raids by their Indian allies, whose morale and aggressiveness had risen with the belief that they had chosen the winning side. With more than five thousand anxious whites abandoning their cabins and fields and withdrawing east to safety in more settled areas, an embassy had been sent to the Cherokee nation, long friendly to the English, to seek help in protecting Virginia's border against the Shawnees and other pro-French tribes.

One of the East's largest and most powerful nations, the Cherokees lived in towns that extended across interior parts of South Carolina, northern Georgia, western North Carolina, and portions of Virginia and present-day Kentucky, Tennessee, and Alabama. For years, their strength and distance from the European coastal colonies had spared them from much of the turmoil and demoralization of other nations and had allowed them to remain intact under their traditional leadership. From their capital at Echota, they governed with a combination of clan-based democracy and pre-Columbian Mississippian religious doctrine.

At the start of the war, French agents, often working through friends among the Creek nation, tried to persuade the Cherokees to attack the English. Although many Cherokees had complaints against the English traders, and a pro-French party arose within the tribe, headed by an influential chief of the town of Tellico named the Man Killer, most Cherokees followed their Head Beloved Man, or principal chief, Old Hopp of Chote, in remaining loyal and friendly to the English.

Like the Iroquois, however, the Cherokees at first tried to be neutral in the white men's war. But they, too, were unhappy about the incursions of the Shawnees and other tribes into the border areas, which they regarded jealously as their own, rather than as the property of Virginia, the French, or anyone else. In their meetings with the English negotiators after Braddock's defeat, they promised to send war

Based on archaeological excavations, this illustration shows Fort Loudoun, which the British built in 1756 to help protect Cherokee territory from the French. English abuses against Cherokee people, however, followed the fort's construction, causing many Cherokees to desert the English in favor of the French, and eventually Cherokee warriors attacked and captured Fort Loudoun.

parties to help defend Virginia's border, but in return won agreement from the English to build forts in the frontier country to protect the Cherokees from their enemies.

Beginning to make good on their promise, the English, in 1756, built Fort Loudoun to help guard the Cherokees' territory, and for a while, pro-English Cherokee groups prepared war parties to fight the French. But a series of atrocities perpetrated by English settlers against the Cherokees within their own country, together with resentments of anti-Indian prejudice by British officers and anger at continued cheating by the British traders, cooled what little enthusiasm existed for becoming involved in the Europeans' struggle. In 1758, when the nation sent a war party into Pennsylvania to accompany General Forbes's march against Fort Duquesne, all but a handful of the warriors deserted the British and returned to their homes almost before the campaign got under way.

Within the Cherokees' country, meanwhile, tensions increased, and relations between the English and the Indian nation got out of hand. Murders of Indians were followed by the killing of white families and the burning of their homes and crops. Armed skirmishes between Cherokee war parties and white militia groups became common as attacks by one side brought on reprisals by the other. Finally, in May

1759, an assault by English officers on some Cherokee women whose husbands were away on a hunt led to widespread clashes and the preparation by the government of South Carolina for a large-scale Indian war.

In October of the same year, Oconostota, the Great War Chief of the Upper Cherokees and a staunch friend of the English, hoping to defuse the situation and restore peace, led a party of thirty-one important Cherokees, all of them town chiefs, to Charles Town. Instead of treating with the delegation, however, the governor of South Carolina, anxious for glory, had them all arrested and sent to Fort Prince George, another post which the English had built on the Cherokee frontier. There the Indians were imprisoned in a small barracks room intended for six members of the garrison.

When other pro-British Cherokee chiefs pleaded for the release of the prisoners, whom the English now termed "hostages," the South Carolina governor agreed to free Oconostota and several others, but only on the delivery to him of substitute Indians, whom he executed. This was the last straw. Infuriated Cherokee warriors began the long-threatened war, laying siege to Fort Prince George and attacking frontier settlements from Virginia to Georgia.

The war spirit was fierce on both sides. After the successful defense of one stockade, during which several Cherokees were slain, the militia commander wrote the South Carolina governor that "We had the pleasure, during the engagement, to see several of our enemy drop; and we have now the pleasure, sir, to fatten our dogs with their carcasses, and to display their scalps, neatly ornamented, on the top of our bastions." At Fort Prince George, meanwhile, when the besieging Cherokees killed the post's commander, the enraged garrison, in retaliation, slaughtered the imprisoned chiefs, some of whom were murdered while bound in shackles.

As the war raged on through 1760, the British sent a force of twelve hundred regulars into South Carolina to assist the provincials. The army marched through the Cherokees' country, sacking and burning towns, cornfields, and granaries, cutting down the Indians' orchards, and killing and capturing a small number of Cherokees. Near present-day Franklin in North Carolina, Cherokee warriors engaged the troops in battle, killing twenty soldiers and—though finally withdrawing themselves—forcing the Royal Scot and Highland regulars to retreat.

A computer-generated re-creation depicts the Cherokee capital of Echota on the Little Tennessee River among the wooded mountains in the area of present-day eastern Tennessee, as it may have looked at the time of the French and Indian War. Fort Loudoun was just to the west.

The Three Cherokees came over from the head of the River Savanna to London. 1762
& their Interpreter that was Poisoned.

Ostenaco, also known as Outacite or the Man Killer, stands at left with a hatchet and wampum belt in this group of Cherokee chiefs who went to London to meet King George III in 1762. Inaccurate in its details, this engraving was based partially on the earlier portraits by John Verelst of the Mahican and three Mohawk chiefs who visited London in 1710. The Englishman eyeing the group was the Indians' interpreter.

After breaking the siege at Fort Prince George, most of the Bristish troops left the Carolinas. Meanwhile, Cherokee warriors led by Oconostota captured Fort Loudoun. In 1761, the British sent in more men who, assisted by Chickasaw allies, defeated a large Cherokee force. Following the engagement, the troops marched again through the Cherokees' country, reducing fifteen towns to ashes and once more burning the Indians' fields and granaries. In advance of the troops, some five thousand Cherokees fled into the mountains, where they faced starvation.

The campaign broke the morale of the weary Cherokees, who sued for peace. The English, too, had had enough fighting, and a new governor, meeting in Charles Town with Cherokee peace chiefs, finally brought the war to a close in November 1761.

On another front of the French and Indian War, meanwhile, the British had been hard at work, trying to win support against the French from the Iroquois tribes of the League of the Hodenosaunee in New York. Land swindles, British condescension, reports of better treatment by the French, and a host of territorial conflicts with the different English colonies had eroded the League's traditional friendship for the British. In 1754, commissioners from most of the English colonies met with the Iroquois leaders in Albany, ostensibly to try to satisfy the Indians' grievances. Instead, the commissioners, jockeying among themselves for advantages for their colonies, consummated sly new land deals, which eventually gave the tribes further grievances.

At the same time, the commissioners got a stern lecture from the almost eighty-year-old Chief Hendrick of the Mohawks, who told them that whereas the English had "thrown us behind [their] back and disregarded us," taking the Indians' land and debauching their warriors with rum, the French, "a subtle and vigilant people," were "ever using their utmost endeavors to seduce and bring our people over to them." Drawing attention to the strength which the unity of the League had given the Iroquois tribes, Hendrick urged the colonies to gain strength against the French by following the example of the Iroquois and uniting as they had done.

The notion was not new to Benjamin Franklin, one of the commissioners from Pennsylvania, who had brought to the Albany Congress a plan for union of the colonies. Franklin admired the Iroquois League, and undoubtedly it had influenced his thinking. "It would be a strange thing," he wrote, "if Six Nations [the Tuscaroras were now members of the League] of ignorant savages should be capable of forming a scheme for such an union, and be able to execute it in such a manner as that it has

The drama and fury of colonial border warfare, inherent in seizing Indian lands, were conveyed to nineteenth-century non-Indian readers by books with gripping pictures like this one by the popular American illustrator Felix Darley.

Benjamin Franklin, who had served as a
colonial Indian commissioner and had met with
Iroquois leaders, was inspired by the example of
the League of the Hodenosaunee. Although his
plan for uniting the colonies, presented in 1754,
was not adopted, it later influenced Franklin's
draft of the Articles of Confederation of the new
United States in 1777.

subsisted ages and appears indissoluble; and yet that a like union should be impracticable for ten or a dozen English colonies, to whom it is more necessary and must be more advantageous, and who cannot be supposed to want an equal understanding of their interests." Nevertheless, although the Albany Congress voted to accept Franklin's plan of union, none of the colonies ever ratified it.

During the war, some of the Iroquois bands went their own way, as we have seen. Groups of French-influenced Mohawks, Onondagas, and Senecas sent war parties against the English, while in the Ohio country, the Half King's western, non-League Senecas, or Mingos, helped George Washington. Even old Hendrick himself, a good friend and relative by marriage of Sir William Johnson, the British commissioner of northern Indian affairs in upper New York, actively joined the English side, bringing four hundred Mohawk warriors to assist Johnson's campaign in the summer of 1755 against the French in the Champlain Valley. At Lake George, on the eve of a battle with a large force of French and their Indian allies, the aged Hendrick

The Mohawk sachem Hendrick, standing beside a tree carved with crosses representing enemies he had slain or captured in battle. A loyal friend of the British, Hendrick was one of the four "Indian Kings" who had had their portraits painted in London in 1710 (see pages 51–3). In 1754, when he was in his seventies, he urged the English colonies to gain strength and defeat the French by forming a union among themselves like that of the Hodenosaunee.

This illustration of a Hodenosaunee council meeting accompanied the publication of Lafitau's study of Iroquois customs in 1734. Strict rules of procedure and courtesy were followed in the Grand Council of the Hodenosaunee, and interruption of a speaker was not allowed.

looked over his small body of Mohawks and commented, "If they are to fight, they are too few; if they are to die, they are too many." The next day, Johnson won the battle, but Hendrick and many of his Mohawks were killed in the fierce fighting. Finally, four years later, when the British appeared to be the certain victors in the war, a large number of Mohawk and other Iroquois warriors helped another English army capture Fort Niagara from the French.

By that time, the members of the League of the Hodenosaunee were facing a crisis of their own. Located strategically between the centers of French and British colonial governance, they had risen to power and wealth by playing the two European rivals against each other, enacting the role of a neutral third force but threatening each side that, if they were given reason to do so, they would join or favor the other. With the defeat and withdrawal of France from North America, the situation would change. No longer could the Iroquois have their way with the British officials by threatening to side with the French. Surrounded by English colonies and forts, and without a countervailing European force with which to threaten the British, the League had lost a powerful diplomatic weapon.

Pontiac's Resistance

The departure of the French forces from North America and the turning over of their frontier forts to British troops at the end of the war also stunned the western and Great

Lakes Indian nations that had sided against the English. British officers and Indian agents tried to establish friendly relations with the pro-French tribes, but received no help from Sir Jeffrey Amherst, the imperious commander in chief of British forces on the continent, who had a haughty contempt for Indians and their cultures and regarded them as inferior and "wretched" people. "The only true method of treating the savages," he instructed his officers in the field, "is to keep them in proper subjection and punish, without exception, the transgressors."

Amherst also ordered an immediate end to the traditional French practice of maintaining friendly relations with Indians by giving those who called at the forts powder and lead for hunting when they had run short, emergency provisions for their families when game was scarce, and a little clothing or small gifts for goodwill. "I do not see why the Crown should be put to that expense," he told an Indian agent, denying his recommendation to continue the liberal French methods of treating with the Indians.

The enforcement of Amherst's stern Indian policies, particularly the denial of guns, powder, and lead to hunters trying to provide for their families, enraged the western Indians, and none more so than a powerful forty-year-old war chief of the Ottawa nation named Pontiac, whose people had been loyal trading partners and war allies of the French for almost a century and a half. A fiery orator and daring military strategist, Pontiac had gained widespread prominence among the pro-French western nations for his qualities of leadership during the French and Indian War. Fiercely antagonistic to the British, he was angered not only by Amherst's new policies, but by the flood of English settlers who, surging westward after the defeat of France,

A nineteenth-century painting of the Ottawa chieftain Pontiac, by John Mix Stanley.

Despite a long siege, depicted here in a painting by Frederic Remington, Pontiac's warriors were unable to take Fort Detroit. Their rebuff contributed to the collapse of the joint efforts of many tribes to drive the English colonists east of the Appalachian Mountains.

were overrunning the Indians' lands in western Pennsylvania and the Ohio country.

In 1762, Pontiac was influenced by a Delaware prophet named Neolin, who, conveying a message he had received from the supernatural world, preached that the tribes should unite and return to their old Indian ways, giving up their trade with whites and renouncing the use of alcohol and white men's trade goods. If they did so, he promised that they would regain their former strength and happiness and be able to drive the Europeans from their lands. Translating the prophet's words into action, Pontiac led the forming of a widespread alliance of the western and Great Lakes nations to capture the English forts and force the whites out of their country.

Chippewas, Ottawas, Potawatomis, Menominees, Hurons, Delawares, Shawnees, Senecas, Foxes, Mingos, Kickapoos, Mascoutens, Weas, Sauk, and Miamis, all responded eagerly to his call, joining in a concerted uprising against the British positions over a vast area of the West. While Indian forces under Pontiac himself laid siege to Fort Detroit, and Delawares, Shawnees, and Mingos began a siege of Fort Pitt, other tribes in less than two months captured every other British Ohio Valley or

CHARLES DAWES/OTTAWA

"In convincing people that he had a chance for success Pontiac had to have a battle plan. And he was so successful with it that today his tactics and his strategy are being taught at the United States Military Academy at West Point. That's how successful it was. In World War II some of his tactics were duplicated by General MacArthur in the Pacific, where he didn't attack every island that was Japanese held. . . . What he did was island hop. He took strategic points away from them and left them out there stranded. And that way he only had to fight in certain areas and islands until he isolated them. Pontiac did the same thing. When he started taking the British forts, he took them one by one—cut off the security of the colonists. Then they were on their own. His vision was that once we get the last one, once we get Detroit, we will just kind of herd them ahead of us like ducks or geese right back to the Atlantic Ocean. A brilliant idea. A brilliant strategy."

Great Lakes post, with the exception of Fort Niagara, from Forts Edward Augustus and Michilimackinac in Wisconsin and northern Michigan, respectively, to Fort Ouiatenon on the Wabash River in present-day Indiana and Fort Venango in western Pennsylvania.

The unforeseen rebellion spread panic and a renewed burst of anti-Indian hatred among the whites' frontier settlements. At Conestoga, Pennsylvania, twenty Christian Susquehannock Indians, the last survivors of their nation—more than half of them old people and little children—struggled to live peacefully under the protection of the Pennsylvania government. On December 14, 1763, during a heavy snowfall, a mob of border ruffians, known as the Paxton Boys for their home in the nearby district of Paxton and led by a hysterical elder of the Presbyterian Church, murdered six of the Indians. Although the rest were spirited away safely to Lancaster and put in a strongly built workhouse for their protection, the Paxton Boys followed them there and two days after Christmas hacked their way into the workhouse with axes and, unopposed, butchered them all. John Penn, an eyewitness, later described the massacre:

> Those cruel men . . . by violence broke open the [workhouse] door, and entered with the utmost fury. . . . When the poor wretches saw they had no protection . . . nor could possibly escape, and being without the least weapon for defence, . . . they divided into their little families, the children clinging to the parents; they fell on their knees, protested their innocence, declared their love to the English, and that, in their whole lives, they had never done them injury; and in this posture they all received the hatchet! Men, women, and little children were every one inhumanely murdered!—in cold blood! . . . The bodies of the murdered were then brought out and exposed in the street, till a hole could be made in the earth, to receive and cover them.

In the West, Pontiac's war went on, but his great alliance began to falter. Independent Indian nations were unused to acting in concert. Having scored successes, some war parties saw nothing else to accomplish and went home. Others met frustrations and grew tired

Pontiac's early victories stirred anti-Indian fear and hatred along the frontier. The brutal massacre of twenty Christian Susquehannock Indians at Conestoga and Lancaster, Pennsylvania, in 1763 by a mob known as the Paxton Boys was the worst incident of the vigilante violence.

of the conflict. Still others found important reasons to return to their families and villages. At the same time, Amherst organized massive frontier expeditions to retake the forts and utilized a more sinister and successful type of warfare against the tribes. To Colonel Henry Bouquet, one of his frontier officers in Pennsylvania, he wrote, "Could it not be contrived to send the small pox among the disaffected tribes of Indians? We must on this occasion use every stratagem in our power to reduce them."

Bouquet replied that he would try to follow Amherst's advice and added that he would even like to hunt "the vermin" with dogs. In response, Amherst wrote him that "You will do well to try to inoculate the Indians by means of blankets, as well as to try every other method that can serve to extirpate this execrable race. I should be very glad your scheme for hunting them down by dogs could take effect, but England is at too great a distance to think of that at present." A few weeks later, when Amherst dispatched reinforcements to Fort Detroit, which had continued to hold out against Pontiac's warriors, he told their commander to treat the Indi-

Sinclair's Lith Phil.ª

ans "not as a generous enemy, but as the vilest race of beings that ever infested the earth, and whose riddance from it must be esteemed a meritorious act, for the good of mankind."

In the spring of 1764, the Shawnees and Delawares investing Fort Pitt caught smallpox, apparently from blankets which the fort's commander had presented to an Indian delegation that had entered the post to discuss peace. The scourge spread rapidly, raging through villages and undermining the ability of the affected bands to continue the war. Elsewhere, British reinforcements were gaining the upper hand, and the alliance continued to crumble. One by one, the Senecas, Sauk and Foxes, Menominees, Miamis, and other tribes made peace with the English. The Indian sieges at Fort Detroit and Fort Pitt both collapsed. In 1765, two years after it had begun, Pontiac's rebellion was over. General Amherst left the world of the Indian nations and returned to England. Pontiac, defeated and shunned by the tribes that had once rallied to his side, wandered eventually with a handful of loyal followers into the Illinois country. There, in April 1769, he was murdered by a disgruntled Peoria Indian.

Meanwhile, in 1763, shaken by the immensity of the Indian uprising, the British Crown had made a gesture in the tribes' behalf. By royal proclamation, all the country west of the Appalachian Mountains was reserved as hunting grounds for the Indians. All settlers were directed to withdraw from unceded lands west of the mountains, and future purchases of land in that region were prohibited unless approved in a public meeting between the Indian owners and representatives of the British government. As expected, the proclamation, which raised an immediate protest by settlers and land speculators in the

The Menominees, an Algonquian nation of the Great Lakes region, were members of Pontiac's coalition. A Menominee of a later day, this chief named Markomete, which the whites understood meant Bear's Oil, had his portrait painted when he visited Washington, D.C., with a Menominee delegation to sign a peace treaty with the United States in 1831.

The Lenape, or Delaware, Indians, driven from their own lands and repeatedly pushed westward by the advancing Europeans, played leading roles in Pontiac's alliance. Their prophet Neolin had influenced Pontiac. When hostilities commenced, Delaware warriors joined Shawnees and Mingos in attacking Fort Pitt. To combat them successfully, the British called for a parley and gave them blankets infected with smallpox. This elderly Delaware chief, Tishcohan, had been one of the signers of the notorious Walking Purchase treaty in 1737 that had ousted his band from its Delaware Valley homeland.

colonies, proved unenforceable. With the collapse of Pontiac's war, whites again poured over the mountains onto Indian lands.

Border Warfare

In 1773, to protest a British tax on tea, American patriots dressed up as Mohawk Indians and dumped 342 chests of tea into Boston Harbor. To the colonists, the "Indian" perpetrators of the Boston Tea Party were a symbol of a newly emergent freedom. But to Indians who were aware of the event, the spectacle of the whites using them to symbolize bravery and freedom smacked of hypocrisy, and the irony of the masquerade was not lost on them. In the coastal colonies, now far from the tensions of the frontier, Americans used the images and symbols of the Indians to represent their own defiance and bravery; in the interior, Indian people, at the same time, were being attacked and slain for the same attributes.

As events in the colonies swirled toward revolution against the British king and Parliament, a new wave of American settlers was moving west through the Cumberland Gap, crossing the Appalachians in defiance of the king's proclamation line. Following the Wilderness Road pioneered by Daniel Boone in Kentucky, they invaded a vast intertribal hunting ground shared and depended up on for buffalo, elk, deer, bears, turkeys, and other game by Shawnee, Iroquois, Delaware, and Cherokee hunting parties.

The friction that developed between the Indians and the white invaders led quickly to another border crisis. The frontiersmen and their families viewed the Indians as obstacles to be driven away or eliminated and believed—usually correctly—that no court would try a white man for killing a "savage." An escalating cycle of violence erupted as the Indians resisted desperately, attempting to retain their food-gathering grounds and retaliate for the killing of their people.

In 1768, the League of the Hodenosaunee tried to end the conflict. Asserting ownership of the contested land and authority to speak for its Indian occupants and

In the Boston Tea Party of December 16, 1773, the rebelling colonists made the Indian into a symbol of their own resistance to tyranny. Dressed as Mohawks, they protested unreasonable British taxes, dumping chests of tea into Boston Harbor.

In the years preceding the American Revolution, settlers followed the Wilderness Road pioneered by Daniel Boone and streamed into the Indian hunting grounds of Kentucky. This romantic scene of Boone escorting settlers through the Cumberland Gap into the Indian lands west of the Appalachians was painted by the American artist George Caleb Bingham.

users, who were either Iroquois or peoples they regarded as their dependents, they sold their own and the other tribes' claims to all the country south of the Ohio and Susquehanna rivers to the English, freeing the Kentucky hunting grounds and a large area of western Pennsylvania for white settlement. The Shawnees and other western tribes were furious at being sold out and refused to accept the Iroquois' action.

As another Indian war seemed inevitable, Cornstalk, the leading Shawnee war chief, appealed to the whites, detailing his people's grievance: "We never sold you our [Kentucky] lands which you now possess . . . and which you are now settling without ever asking our leave, or obtaining our consent," he argued. "We live by hunting and do not subsist in any other way—That was our hunting ground and you have taken it from us. This is what sits heavy [on our] hearts and on the hearts of all nations."

His appeals were unheeded. Competing with Pennsylvania for control of the northwestern trans-Appalachian lands, Lord Dunmore, Virginia's royal governor, supported the settlers, who, he later explained, "do not conceive that government has any right to forbid their taking possession of a vast tract of country . . . which serves only as a shelter to a few scattered tribes of Indians. Nor can they be easily brought to entertain any belief of the permanent obligation of treaties made with those people, whom they consider as but little removed from the brute creation."

As settlers continued to press westward and the Indian hunters refused to be dispossessed, the border warfare went on, bringing human tragedies to Indians and whites alike. At the mouth of Yellow Creek on the Ohio, fifty miles west of Fort Pitt and the new town of Pittsburgh that was growing up around it, was the encampment of a prominent Cayuga-Mingo sachem named Tachnechdorus, also known as John Logan, who had long been a friend of the English. On April 30, 1774, while Logan was away on a hunting trip, a party of white men appeared at Yellow Creek and, without provocation, murdered all thirteen members of his family. Filled with grief and a desire for revenge, Logan and a small group of warriors, in retaliation, wiped out a settlement of white families. It started a new chain of attacks and counterattacks and aroused a determined war fever in Virginia.

That fall, Lord Dunmore marched an army of three thousand Virginia militia into the contested country and on October 10 defeated Cornstalk's Shawnees, together with allied Delawares, Wyandots, and western Iroquois, or Mingos, in a hard-fought battle at Point Pleasant near the juncture of the Kanawha and Ohio rivers. The Indians retreated north of the Ohio River, and the following month, Cornstalk was forced to sign a treaty with the British, formally relinquishing the Indians' hunting grounds in Kentucky.

Fighting with Cornstalk's forces at Point Pleasant was John Logan, who during the battle purportedly took thirteen scalps in retribution for the murdered members of his family. At the close of the war, he dictated to Simon Girty, a British agent, the following message to Lord Dunmore, which, published years later by Thomas Jefferson in his *Notes on the State of Virginia,* became famous as "Logan's Lament":

> I appeal to any white man to say, if ever he entered Logan's cabin hungry, and he gave him not meat; if ever he came cold and naked, and he clothed him not. During the course of the last long and bloody war, Logan remained idle in his cabin, an advocate for peace. Such was my love for the whites, that my countrymen pointed as they passed, and said, "Logan is the friend of white men." . . .
>
> Col. Cresap, the last spring, in cold blood, and unprovoked, murdered all the relations of Logan, not sparing even my women and children. There runs not a drop of my blood in the veins of any living creature. . . . Who is there to mourn for Logan?—Not one.

The American Revolution

As tensions between the colonies and Great Britain reached the breaking point, the interracial turbulence on the frontier threatened to become part of the new strug-

That was our hunting ground and you have taken it from us. This is what sits heavy [on our] hearts and the hearts of all nations.

—CORNSTALK

George Washington, painted by John Trumbull in 1790. Oneida and Tuscarora Indians helped Washington's troops at Valley Forge. Later, Washington sent an army against the pro-British Iroquois, devastating their country.

gle between the whites. The Hodenosaunee Confederacy and its dependent nations in the west, the Delawares and Shawnees, wanted no part of the fight. Traveling to Pittsburgh with other leading chiefs to meet with the Americans in the fall of 1775, Cornstalk carried a message of peace and friendship to the American frontier settlements from his sister and clan mother, who, with the other Shawnee clan mothers, exercised considerable power over the nation's important decisions, including those concerning war or peace. His sister wrote the Americans:

> Brother, I have spoken to our headmen. . . . I have exhorted them and all our Nation to keep fast of your Friendship. . . . I would come up myself but have been lately delivered of a son. . . .
>
> Brother, if the white people entertain designs to strike us I beg you will tell me—I depend upon you that I may remove out of danger with my children.

At the conference, both sides—each for its own reasons—called for the neutrality of the Indian nations. The newly emerging American government realized that it

Iroquois Indians at Independence Hall, Philadelphia. In May 1776, a delegation from the League of the Hodenosaunee visited the Continental Congress and, while officially recognizing the fledgling union of the colonies, told the Americans that the Iroquois would remain neutral in the Revolutionary War.

could not fight on different fronts against a combination of British and Indians and hope to win. And the Indian leaders knew from experience that in the end it was the Indian nations that suffered most severely from involvement in the white men's conflicts. The council concluded with American assurances that Indian borders and neutrality would be respected and that no effort would be made to recruit Indian fighting men.

In May 1776, a Hodenosaunee delegation traveled from Albany to Philadelphia, where its members spent a month lodged in Independence Hall above the chamber in which the Continental Congress was meeting. British efforts had been mounting to induce the Iroquois tribes to abandon their neutrality and join the English against the colonies. It had worried Washington, and despite the agreement made at Pittsburgh and the efforts of the American Indian agents and of most delegates to keep the League neutral, Washington and other colonial leaders urged winning active Iroquois support before the British did so.

"In my opinion," Washington argued, "it will be impossible to keep [the Indians] in a state of neutrality . . . and I submit it to the consideration of Congress, whether it would not be best to immediately engage them on our side." Washington proved persuasive. Unknown to the Iroquois delegates, who were never informed of the action taken in the very room beneath their feet, Congress passed a resolution authorizing Washington to raise an Indian contingent for the American army. The resolution, a blatant breach of the promise given the tribes at Pittsburgh the previous

The Mohawks' charismatic leader Theyendanegea, or Joseph Brant, painted by the British artist George Romney. Despite the professed neutrality of the Hodenosaunee confederacy, Brant was dedicated to the British cause and rallied support for the Crown throughout the war.

Theyendanegea, Joseph Brant, The Mohawk Chief

Both the Americans and the British considered Indian allies essential to their Revolutionary War efforts. A large and powerful confederacy commanding strategic territory close to the colonies, the Hodenosaunee were particularly well lobbied, and both sides found allies among the Six Nations. Here, British General John Burgoyne attempts to persuade the Hodenosaunee to embrace the English cause and join his 1777 campaign in the region that is now upper New York State.

[The] eagle . . . is able to see afar. If he sees in the distance any danger threatening, he will at once warn the people of the League.

—FROM THE GREAT LAW OF
THE HODENOSAUNEE

fall, ignored the sovereignty of the Hodenosaunee council and negated the careful diplomacy which others had been conducting for months.

George Morgan, the chief American negotiator who had met with the Indian nations at Pittsburgh, was distressed by the news. "I apprehend it may occasion hostilities against our frontier settlements to our infinitely greater damage than the value we can possibly expect from the service of [a few Indians who] may engage themselves [in the American army]," he said. But while the Continental Congress was undermining the diplomatic efforts of American agents, so too were forces within the Iroquois League working to end the Hodenosaunee commitment to neutrality.

Earlier in the critical summer of 1776, the Mohawk chief Theyendanegea, better known to the whites as Joseph Brant, returned from a visit to England. Brant, whose sister, Molly, had married the British Indian commissioner, Sir William Johnson, was the son of a prominent Mohawk family with close and long-standing ties to the British. He had received an exceptional education at white schools and, at thirty-four, was a charismatic Indian leader with outstanding abilities and a strong will.

Passionately pro-British, Brant traveled among the Six Nations, delivering a message that was contrary to the decision of the League's council to stay neutral. Arguing that the rebellious colonies were aggressive and expansive, he maintained that if they won, they would overrun the Indians and dominate the continent. The only hope for the sovereignty and survival of the Iroquois, he insisted, was to fight on the side of the Crown.

At the same time, the Oneidas and Tuscaroras were pulling in the opposite di-

rection. Strongly influenced by anti-British colonial missionaries, and moving away from their traditional culture and authority, they were drifting toward an outright alliance with the Americans. (During the bitter winter of 1777–78, the two tribes would make clear where their sympathies lay when some of their members brought lifesaving blankets and corn to Washington's cold and starving troops at Valley Forge.) The open defiance of the council's neutrality imperiled the unity forged by the Great Law, and above the League members loomed the threat of a civil war.

In January 1777, an epi-
demic struck Onondaga, the seat
of the Hodenosaunee government. A message
was sent to the authorities of the new United States:

> We have lost out of [our] town by death ninety, out of which are three
> principal [chiefs]; We the remaining part of the Onondagas do now
> inform our Brothers [the Americans] that there is no longer a council
> fire at the Capital of the Six Nations. However we are determined to
> use our feeble endeavors to support peace through the Confederate
> Nations but let this be kept in mind that the Central Council fire is
> extinguished . . . and can no longer burn.

*If they are to fight, they are too
few; if they are to die, they are too
many.* —CHIEF HENDRICK

It was a serious blow to the confederacy. Political decisions could not be made until
the condolence ritual was performed, and in the chaos and uncertainties of the war that
ceremony could not take place. "Times are altered with us Indians," an Onondaga am-
bassador later explained during a meeting with the Marquis de Lafayette, as the League
splintered and came apart. "Formerly the warriors were governed by the wisdom of the
[chiefs], but now they take their own way and dispose of themselves without consult-
ing [the chiefs]. While we wish for peace and they are for war, brothers, they must take
the consequences . . . they have long since forsaken our council fire."

The Americans and British both knew that the fighting men of the League
might supply the key for victory or defeat. Both sides worked aggressively to exploit
the weakened Indian confederacy. The British warned the Iroquois that they would
lose their country if they did not fight against the Americans. Without the authority
of the Grand Council, the Senecas and other Iroquois people (except the Oneidas and
Tuscaroras) gathered at Oswego in the early summer of 1777 at the invitation of the
British to determine whether to join the English forces.

Blacksnake, a tall, slender, young Seneca warrior, raised to value both leadership in war and skillful diplomacy, listened closely as Joseph Brant argued for an alliance with the British. "Brant came forward," Blacksnake asserted in an interview
many years later, "and said that if we did nothing for the British . . . there will be no
peace for us. Our throats will be cut by the Red Coat man or by America . . . 'I
therefore say,'" he quoted Brant, "'we should go and join the father . . . this is the
only way for us.'"

Blacksnake's uncle Cornplanter, the Senecas' respected war captain, rose to challenge Brant. Cornplanter was a father and husband who provided well for his family

by hunting and trading. A veteran of the French and Indian wars and
of all the critical council decisions of his time, he
was thoroughly opposed to becoming involved in another white man's quarrel that would bring only death and misery to the Indian nations. "War is war," he reminded his
listeners. "Death is death. A fight is a hard business. . . .
Here America says not to lift our hands against either
party—I move therefore to wait a little while to hear
more consultation between the two parties." In utter
disbelief, Blacksnake and the others watched as Brant
rose irately to his feet and ordered Cornplanter to be
quiet and then called him a coward.

The following day, the predominately Mohawk and
Seneca gathering, reacting angrily against the implication
that they, too, might be stigmatized as cowards—and supplied
with kegs of rum by the British, who hoped to gain control over them
by making them drunk—agreed finally to fight with the English. Cornplanter
reluctantly accepted the majority will and rallied the warriors to unity. The forces of
war were now unleashed along the entire Indian-colonial frontier, spreading westward to the trade centers in the Illinois country and south to the lands of the Cherokees, Chickamaugas, and Creeks in present-day Tennessee and Alabama.

Unlike the Seneca war chief Cornplanter, Cornstalk, the Shawnee leader, had not
yet resigned himself to the inevitability of fighting. In a bold attempt to prevent his people from being dragged into the conflict, he and another leading Shawnee went on a
peace mission to the American fort at Point Pleasant, the site of Cornstalk's defeat by
Lord Dunmore in 1774. Regarding the two Indians as still hostile to the colonists, the
Americans seized them and threatened them with death. "When I was young and went
to war," Cornstalk told them, "I often thought each might be my last adventure, and I
should return no more. I still live. Now I am in the midst of you, and if you choose,
[you] may kill me. I can die but once. It is alike to me whether now or hereafter."

Ball-headed war clubs like this Iroquois example were common to tribes from the eastern plains all the way to the Atlantic Ocean prior to the arrival of Europeans. Sculpted from solid wood, war clubs were treated with great reverence by their owners. Later, after the introduction of metal goods and weapons, the war club developed into the more familiar "tomahawk" form.

These beautifully beaded Iroquois moccasins are covered in a floral design probably learned from early contact with Ursuline nuns in Quebec.

When Cornstalk's young son, anxious about his father's arrest, hurried to the fort, the Americans imprisoned him also. "My son," Cornstalk tried to reassure him, "the [Creator] has seen fit that we should die together. . . . It is his will and let us submit; it is for the best." The next day, a company of soldiers entered the prison and shot Cornstalk and his son to death. As the other Shawnee tried to escape through the chimney, the soldiers pulled him down and murdered him with axes. It was a costly error for the Americans. The angry Shawnees abandoned their peace sentiment and neutrality and joined the side of the British.

Meanwhile, on August 6, 1777, a force of eight hundred American militiamen and about sixty of their Oneida allies was ambushed by an army of English troops, Tory units, and some four hundred Iroquois warriors, led by Joseph Brant, at Oriskany Creek in New York's Mohawk Valley. A part of British general John Burgoyne's unsuccessful campaign to win the war, the battle was fiercely fought, and before Brant's Indians and the English withdrew, they had claimed the lives of nearly five hundred Americans and their Oneida allies at a loss to themselves of about a hundred Iroquois and a similar number of Tories and British soldiers. From the Iroquois point of view, the battle reflected the beginning of a tragic civil war among the once-united Hodenosaunee.

As the colonists' Revolution progressed, Indian forces hurt the Americans badly, destroying economic and military resources and demoralizing frontier settlements. General Washington sent an American army against the one Iroquois nation still holding officially to a policy of neutrality—the Onondagas. After the Americans ransacked their capital and seized Onondaga women as captives, many of the warriors of that nation, too, abandoned neutrality and plunged angrily into the war as allies of the British.

Committed to crushing the pro-English Iroquois, who under Brant and British officers continued to raid and terrorize frontier settlements, Washington in August 1779 sent Major General John Sullivan and an American army of about three thousand men into Hodenosaunee country. As Sullivan carved a swath of destruction through the Six Nations, setting fire to villages and crops, a stream of Iroquois refugees fled to hiding places ahead of his troops. Sullivan's officers and men, meanwhile, wrote in awe of the prosperity and highly civilized appearance of the deserted towns they were destroying:

> The Indians live much better than most of the Mohawk River farmers their Houses very well furnished with all necessary Household utensils, great plenty of Grain, several Horses, cows and waggons. . . .

> The town, which consisted of one hundred and twenty eight houses, mostly very large and elegant . . . encircled with a clear flat which extends for a number of miles, where the most extensive fields of corn were and every kind of vegetable that can be conceived. . . .

> There are a great number of apple and peach trees here, which we cut down [and] destroyed. . . .

Of the more than thirty principal Seneca, Cayuga, Onondaga, and Mohawk towns that existed before

War is war. Death is death. A fight is a hard business. —CORNPLANTER

This computer-generated image of a Hodenosaunee village in what is now New York State was re-created from the vivid descriptions of members of Major General John Sullivan's American forces. While Joseph Brant's pro-British Iroquois sacked the Oneida and Tuscarora homelands, the Americans attacked and destroyed all but two of the Senecas' towns.

General Sullivan's campaign, only two of the larger Seneca towns remained unscathed. In retaliation for their alliance with the Americans, the Mohawk leader Joseph Brant burned the villages of the Oneidas and Tuscaroras. Every Hodenosaunee nation suffered in the war, along with the refugee nations that lived among them.

In addition, since it was already fall when the destruction and burning stopped and the soldiers marched away, there was no time to replace the lost crops. With the arrival of winter, the tragedy heightened. It was the coldest season in living memory. The snow fell five feet deep. Many freezing, homeless Iroquois died of hunger, cold, and disease.

The war continued until 1783, when the British gave up the struggle and recognized the new United States of America. As they had been warned by Cornplanter and other leaders who had originally urged them to be neutral, the Indian nations gained nothing from the conflict, and lost much. Deserted by the British and forced out of their New York lands by the victorious Americans, Joseph Brant and his Mohawk followers were joined by other pro-English Iroquois, as well as by Tutelos and smaller refugee groups, and moved to Canada, where their descendants still live. Those who remained in the original Hodenosaunee territory fared little better. After the war, their landholdings were whittled down by swindling land speculators or were taken from them to be given as land grants to veterans of George Washington's army as compensation for their service in winning liberty for the white population of the new nation.

OPPOSITE: *The Revolutionary War brought great suffering to the Hodenosaunee nations, who turned against each other and in the end were devastated by the Americans and abandoned by the British. Their age-old village life, observed by Lafitau and pictured here only a few decades earlier, would never be the same.*

CHAPTER 6

LOSS OF THE

EAST

Of Utmost Good Faith

The utmost good faith shall always be observed toward the Indians; their lands and property shall never be taken from them without their consent; and in their property, rights, and liberty they never shall be invaded or disturbed unless in just and lawful wars authorized by Congress; but laws founded in justice and humanity shall, from time to time, be made, for preventing wrongs being done to them and for preserving peace and friendship with them.

THE NORTHWEST ORDINANCE, ENACTED BY CONGRESS IN 1787

OVERLEAF: *In this painting by Cornelius Krieghoff, Chippewas prepare to hunt caribou.*

Throughout the years of the Revolution, settlers, speculators, and agents of land companies had continued to push westward into the Indian countries beyond the Appalachians. When the Indians resisted the invasion of their hunting grounds and the threats to their people and villages, the Americans usually laid all the blame for the Indians' hostility on British or Loyalist intrigues rather than on themselves and called on state and local militia units to help them. The result was a series of border conflicts during the Revolution that flamed along the frontier from the Great Lakes to Georgia.

In the forests north of the Ohio River, Shawnees, Delawares, Miamis, Potawatomis, and others, armed and supplied by the British commander at Fort Detroit, often helped the English as allies, but fought primarily to defend their lands. Three times, expeditionary forces of Virginia and Kentucky riflemen, led by George Rogers Clark, campaigned through the western region to try to secure it from the British and the Indians, the

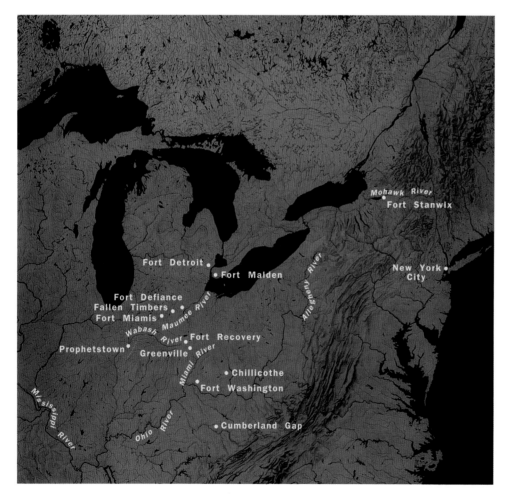

second time, in 1780, burning Chillicothe and other principal Shawnee towns in Ohio. Clark was successful in wresting control of the area from the British, but his attacks on the Shawnees loosed terrible retaliatory raids against the American settlements in Kentucky that threw them into chaos and diverted men and resources from the war against England.

Farther west, meanwhile, a combined force of Spaniards and American frontiersmen destroyed a Sauk and Mesquakie (Fox) town in the Illinois country. At the same time, in Kentucky and Tennessee and along the frontiers of the Carolinas and Georgia, where the Cherokees, Shawnees, and elements of the Creek and Chickasaw nations felt that their future lay better with the British than with a victory by the aggressive colonists, warfare between the Indians and forces of settlers and frontiersmen raged on year after year almost without interruption.

An early nineteenth-century painting by George Winter shows a group of Indiana's Potawatomis resting in the Wabash River country near what is now Logansport.

And yet, despite the Indians' resistance, which to the Americans characterized Kentucky and the country beyond the mountains as a "dark and bloody ground," the land-hungry settlers kept coming. As early as 1776, the Shawnee war captain Cornstalk, who traveled south from western Pennsylvania across Kentucky to a meeting with Cherokee leaders, described what was happening in the lands he had been forced to cede to the whites only two years before: "When we passed through the country between Pittsburgh and our nations, lately Shawnee and Lenape [Delaware] hunting grounds, where we could once see nothing but deer and buffalo, we found the country thickly inhabited and the people under arms," he said. "We were compelled to make a detour of 300 miles. . . . We saw large numbers of white men in forts; and fortifications around salt springs and buffalo grounds."

When the Revolution ended, the tempo of westward migration increased. Em-

Pea-Walk-O, a young Potawatomi woman. George Winter painted this portrait in 1837, just before her people—no longer able to resist the whites' overrunning of their Indiana lands—were forced to move west of the Mississippi River.

Mas-Saw, a Potawatomi woman who had inherited the rank of chieftain and shows a mixture of Indian and white influences in her dress. She wears earbobs, a blue-and-orange crepe shawl, a cape decorated with silver brooches, and a necklace of strings of dark beads. According to the artist, Winter, she "was a woman of no common mind and ability; her influence among the Indians was very observable."

igrant families by the hundreds pushed into western Pennsylvania and went beyond, floating down the Ohio River in flatboats to establish new settlements along the banks, all the way to the Mississippi River. Others poured into the lands south of the Ohio. By 1790, Kentucky had a white population of seventy-four thousand, and Tennessee and the frontier regions beyond it thirty-six thousand. In another ten years, more than three hundred thousand people had followed Daniel Boone's old trace through the Cumberland Gap, and Boone himself, finding Kentucky too populated, had migrated to the western side of the Mississippi River in what is now the state of Missouri.

At the Treaty of Paris that formally ended the American Revolution in September 1783, no attention was paid to Indian rights or interests. The British, who had promised to protect tribal land rights, simply sold out their Indian allies, ceding their lands to the United States and Spain with no consideration for the sovereignty or the rights of possession of the resident Indian nations. The United States, in turn, operating under a theory of conquest underlying the Paris peace treaty, claimed not only political sovereignty over the Indian lands surrendered by the British, but actual ownership of the land itself.

The new American nation believed that it had beaten both the British and the Indians, although it had defeated no tribe, and although even after Sullivan's destruction of the Iroquois towns, Joseph Brant and furious pro-English Iroquois warriors had been able to storm back in 1780, 1781, and 1782, terrorizing and laying waste almost fifty thousand square miles of colonial-inhabited territory between the Mohawk and Ohio rivers. But in winning the war with Great Britain, the Americans assumed that they had also conquered the Indians and could treat their lands as prizes of the conquest. Bankrupt from the war and owing back pay to the Continental soldiers, the government used Indian lands to give the veterans military land bounties instead of cash.

An encampment of Potawatomis at Crooked Creek, Indiana, painted by Winter before the ousting of the Indians to make way for white settlers.

For a while after 1783, adhering to the theory of conquest, the government of the Articles of Confederation treated the Indians with a heavy hand. Pressures from land companies and prominent speculators, as well as the Indian-hating sentiments along the frontiers, fueled the government's drive to secure Indian acceptance of the American land demands. Between 1784 and 1789, government negotiators coerced Indian leaders in the East and the country north of the Ohio—known to the new nation as the Northwest Territory—into signing a number of cession treaties that not only reduced the Indians' land base, but undermined their national sovereignty. Vast areas of Indian land, now regarded as public land, passed into white ownership, and tribes were forced to live within small reservations. At the same time, the questionable methods of coercion, bribery, or deceit by which these treaties were usually negotiated by the government, the insufficient authority or misrepresentation of many of the Indian individuals who signed the treaties, and the enormous loss of lands and resources resulting from the cessions caused the majority of Indian people to denounce the agreements.

Fort Stanwix, an important fort in what is now upper New York State. In 1777, during the Revolution, its colonial garrison contributed to Burgoyne's defeat by halting a British force advancing toward the Mohawk Valley and a union with Burgoyne. At Fort Stanwix, also, the Iroquois nations were pressured into signing two unfavorable treaties, in 1768 selling lands in the Ohio Valley and in 1784 surrendering additional territory.

In the wake of the Revolution, no Indian groups suffered more than the Iroquois nations. Shattered by their own war losses and forced relocations, abandoned and insulted by the British, who, ignoring them, had ceded sovereignty over their lands to the United States, and divided among themselves without the powerful, united structure of the League of the Hodenosaunee to speak for and protect them, the different tribes—even those who had sided with the colonists—were set upon by rapacious land companies and speculators and by the American government itself. After calling a treaty meeting at Fort Stanwix in upper New York State in 1784, ostensibly to establish peace between the United States and the Six Nations and their dependent tribes, the American delegates were urged by James Duane, a former member of the Continental Congress's Committee on Indian Affairs, to undermine whatever self-confidence remained among the Iroquois by deliberately treating them as inferiors, rather than equals.

"Instead of conforming to Indian political behavior We should force them to adopt ours—dispense with [wampum] belts, etc.," Duane said. "I would never suffer the word 'Nation' or 'Six Nations,' or 'Confederates,' or 'Council Fire at Onondago' or any other form which would revive or seem to confirm their former ideas of independence, to escape . . . they are used to be called Brethren, Sachems & Warriors of the Six Nations. I hope it will never be repeated . . . they should rather be taught . . . that the public opinion of their importance has long since ceased."

The American delegates took Duane's advice. They pointedly brushed aside acknowledgment that there was any such thing as an Iroquois Confederacy; seized Iroquois hostages and conducted negotiations literally at gunpoint; threatened military action against women and children in the Iroquois villages; and treated Indian spokesmen in an arbitrary, high-handed manner, intentionally insulting them and threatening a continuation of the war against them. In the end, although the Iroquois considered themselves unconquered in war, their negotiators were forced to cede all their lands west of New York and Pennsylvania, including territory occupied by their western dependents, and accept a reservation of diminished area in New York for themselves. In the following two years, American commissioners made similar treaties, first at Fort McIntosh near Pittsburgh in 1785 and the next year at Fort Finney on the Ohio River, using bribery, threats, alcohol, and manipulations of unauthorized representatives to attempt to wrench land away from Delawares, Wyandots, Ottawas, Chippewas, Shawnees, and other Ohio nations.

Incensed by their treatment, the Iroquois and the Ohio tribes publicly repudiated the treaties as fraudulent. In addition, the western nations turned with contempt on the members of the League of the Hodenosaunee, attacking the "cowardice" of their former allies and protectors in the face of the Americans' pressure and condemning the Iroquois' sale of their west-

The utmost good faith shall always be observed toward the Indians; their lands and property shall never be taken from them without their consent.

—THE NORTHWEST ORDINANCE, 1787

Hodenosaunee (Iroquois) signatures on the 1768 treaty at Fort Stanwix, acknowledging their receipt of ten thousand dollars for the sale of Ohio Valley lands. The drawings next to the names represent clan membership. Joseph Brant's name is fourth from the top in the second column. It reads "Joseph Thayendanegea," a combination of his baptismal and Mohawk names.

As the frontier moved westward, the Hodenosaunee were no longer able to stand between the advancing white settlers and the Ohio and Great Lakes tribes like the Ottawas and Chippewas. Shown in this portrait from the early nineteenth century is No-Tin, a Chippewa chief.

ern satellites' lands at the Fort Stanwix meeting. "The Chippewas and all these Nations who live on those Lands Westward, call to us and ask us, Brothers of our Fathers, where is the place you have reserved to us to lie down upon?" an Iroquois speaker chided his fellow councillors in arguing against acceptance of the Fort Stanwix treaty. At the same time, the more powerful Ohio tribes, no longer counting on the leadership of the Iroquois in resisting the expanding whites, began to form their own defensive confederacy.

To more sober heads in the American government, both the Iroquois and the Ohio tribes still represented formidable military powers, and when delegations of resentful leaders from their nations began to arrive in Philadelphia, airing grievances over unfair treatment and tales of fraud in achieving the treaties, members of Congress began to experience a change of attitude. The acquisition of Indian lands was still high on the list of government priorities; public lands to survey and sell to settlers were almost the only assets available to the government. At the same time, no one relished an Indian war with the capable Iroquois or Ohio tribes.

Far from the tensions of the frontiers, and persuaded particularly by the oratory and talented statesmanship of the Iroquois, the government gradually changed its policy, abandoning the theory of ownership of Indian land by right of conquest and accepting, instead, a more just position, expressed first in the Northwest Ordinance of 1787, which Congress passed for the governance of the land north of the Ohio River. Declaring that "The utmost good faith shall always be observed toward the Indians," the act asserted that the tribes' lands and property would never be taken from them without their consent, implying a return to the prewar British policy that recognized that the Indians possessed the right

Large peace medals, to be suspended from ribbons around the neck, were often given by government officials to important Indian men at treaty councils to symbolize agreements of peace and friendship. This medal, picturing President George Washington and an Indian, was given to Tarhee (The Crane), a Wyandot chief in the Ohio country, in 1793.

to the soil, even while a non-Indian power maintained sovereignty over them. Two years later, Henry Knox, secretary of war in George Washington's first administration of the new constitutional government, spelled out more explicitly what would become America's enduring official (though not always observed) position: the United States would recognize that the Indian nations held legal title to their lands until the government by just negotiation, or a just war, extinguished that title.

In theory, it sounded fine. The United States, in great need of funds to finance the new central government, would send commissioners to the tribes to negotiate fairly as equals for the purchase of Indian lands, which the government could then sell at a profit to land-hungry whites, bringing money into the national treasury. (Until the Andrew Jackson administration of the 1830s, in fact, revenues from the sale of public lands acquired from Indians remained a large part of the government's annual income.) In practice, on the frontier, however, it rarely worked. From the beginning, few, if any, tribes—as in Ohio—were willing to sell their lands at any price, and the frustrated government negotiators in the field again turned to dealing fraudulently with unauthorized tribal members, bribing or making some of them drunk to secure their *X*'s on treaty papers or forging their marks on official documents of cession without the Indians' knowledge. In other cases, white settlers, frontiersmen, and speculators, hoping to profit from the exploitation of Indian lands, got out ahead of the government negotiators, squatting illegally in territory still unceded by the Indians, provoking Indian attempts to drive them away, which then caused military forces to come to their support and dispossess the Indians by force or by punitive treaties that the government imposed on the defeated tribes.

The Iroquois nations, meanwhile, had gone into a political, economic, and social decline which the change in American governmental policy could not stem. During the 1790s, speculators and land companies continued to pressure the tribes, employing the unsavory array of now-proven practices—bribery, alcohol, hard-sell tactics, deceit, and threats—to gain control of what remained of the Iroquois lands. By 1797, the Mohawks, Oneidas, Onondagas, and Cayugas retained only small bits of land in New York State. That same year, the Seneca chiefs were deceived into selling all their territory except for eleven small reservations totaling two hundred thousand acres in the western part of New York and northwestern Pennsylvania.

Torn into factions by humiliated and quarreling leaders, shorn of hunting grounds, and living in poverty and sickness on small islands in an encroaching sea of hostile white settlements, the Hodenosaunee were in a crisis of survival. The very fabric of their once-great democracy beneath the Tree of Peace was unraveling.

Handsome Lake

As the eighteenth century neared its close, many of the Senecas, the strongest of the wavering Iroquois societies, wondered whether there was any future for themselves in their traditions as Hodenosaunee. Ignored by their former dependents and allies in the Ohio country, they had lost the tribal and personal self-assurance of leadership. In despair, many of them had turned to alcohol, making the nation appear dissolute and depraved in the eyes of unfeeling whites. Without hindrance, Philadelphia Quakers and missionaries of other Christian denominations had come to attempt, in their terms, to "save them" by changing their beliefs and values and by teaching them to farm like whites and to live like them, spread out on private homesteads with farms rather than in tightly knit settlements clustered around communal longhouses. That way they were out of sight of each other so the Indian men would not be embarrassed by being seen "doing women's work" in the fields, and old patterns of community living were shattered.

Among the Senecas, Sagoyewatha (He Who Keeps Them Awake), known to the whites as Red Jacket, a noted orator and defender of his people's traditions,

A reluctant supporter of the British during the Revolution, the Seneca orator Red Jacket became a principal spokesman for his people after the war. Although he signed treaties ceding large portions of the Seneca homeland, he was a staunch defender of traditional ways and an outspoken critic of Christianity. This engraving, from a painting by Seth Eastman, shows Red Jacket wearing a peace medal of solid silver presented to him by President Washington in 1792.

tried to hold off the missionaries, on one occasion responding contemptuously to an overeager representative of the Boston Missionary Society:

> Brother, we have scarcely a place left to spread our blankets; you have got our country, but are not satisfied; you want to force your religion upon us. . . . Brother, you say there is but one way to worship and serve the Great Spirit; if there is but one religion, why do you white people differ so much about it? Why do not all agree, as you can all read the book? . . .
>
> We are told that your religion was given to your forefathers, and has been handed down from father to son. We also have a religion which was given to our forefathers, and has been handed down to us their children. We worship that way. It teacheth us to be thankful for all the favors we receive; to love each other; and to be united. We never quarrel about religion.
>
> Brother, the Great Spirit has made us all; but he has made a great difference between his white and red children; he has given us a different complexion, and different customs. . . . Since he has made so great a difference between us in other things, why may we not conclude that he has given us a different religion? . . .
>
> Brother! We do not wish to destroy your religion, or take it from you. We only want to enjoy our own.

In those trying times, Red Jacket was unable to halt the forces that were luring his demoralized people to change. As Seneca warriors and statesmen had been left without an army or a country, so were the nation's spiritual leaders and teachers losing adherents to the Hodenosaunee traditions.

Meanwhile, Cornplanter, the distinguished Seneca war chief who had fought reluctantly on the British side during the Revolution and had suffered the destruction of his towns by the Sullivan expedition, had relocated his band in several settlements along the Allegheny River, straddling the New York–Pennsylvania border. Concluding that he would have to accommodate to the victors, he had become a trusting friend of the Americans, had signed the 1784 agreement at Fort Stanwix and other unpopular treaties and land sales, and, although he had not become a Christian, had welcomed to his towns the Quakers and other teachers of agriculture and of the whites' ways of living.

Among the refugee Senecas residing in Cornplanter's principal town of

DANIELLE SIOUI/HURON

"What destroyed our culture the most was the coming of the missionaries and the coming of the fur trade at just about the same time. They tried to destroy our beliefs. . . . The language has been almost completely lost due to the fact that by sending us to private schools, and the Catholic religion—not only Catholic, almost all the Christian religions—prohibited us from speaking our own language. And by prohibiting us to speak our own language, then we had to adapt to the French language so we could communicate better with the French, and become more alive. And by doing so, then they were entering into our lives very, very fast. So what was going on in the background was a big loss of identity. A loss of culture."

Jenuchshadego, or Burnt House, on the Allegheny was his half brother, Handsome Lake, a warrior and hunter whom the defeatism of the times had turned into a confirmed drunk. Like so many other Senecas, he had seen his society and culture slowly crumble, his nation's military and political power reduced to impotence, and his own ability to do something about it vanish. Now in his sixties, an escapee from depression to whiskey, he was a sick and dissolute man, seemingly beyond rescue.

Then on June 15, 1799, something extraordinary happened. Handsome Lake lay on his bunk, wretchedly ill from an alcoholic binge, fearing he was about to die and

During a visit to New York City in 1796, Cornplanter, the great Seneca war chief, posed in his finest regalia for this splendid portrait by F. Bartoli. A British ally during the Revolution, Cornplanter had become a firm friend of the Americans.

worrying that the Creator regarded him as "evil and loathsome." Suddenly, those out-side his cabin heard him exclaim "*Niio!*" ("So be it!") and, fearing that he was dying, sent for Cornplanter. Handsome Lake was not dying, however, but had received the first of three intensely spiritual visions, in which he was instructed by the Creator how to halt the demoralization and destruction of the Hodenosaunee.

Like the Great Law of the Peace Maker, who had guided the Hodenosaunee Confederacy centuries before, the Creator's message, as Handsome Lake revealed it to the dejected Iroquois peoples, showed them a way to rebuild themselves and revi-talize their societies. In essence, the Creator told them to renew their hearts and minds by reviving their traditional ceremonies and returning to their old ways. Known today as the Gaiwiio, or the Good Word, the message encompassed a code of conduct, which the people called the Code of Handsome Lake and which told them not to drink, gamble, or beat or abuse one another. But the visions that Handsome Lake experienced were long and vivid, and the Creator's message was one of intricate detail concerning how the people should behave. Although the code contained ele-ments of Quaker influence, on the whole it represented a revival of traditional Iro-quoian values and morals.

Traveling first among the Seneca towns and reservations and then to the other Hodenosaunee nations, Handsome Lake, now a reformed advocate of abstinence, spread the Good Word, and wherever people accepted his code, communities and families were uplifted and their morale restored. In 1815, at the age of eighty, Hand-some Lake died while visiting the Onondagas. Just before his death, he addressed a crowd outside his cabin:

> I will soon go to my new home. . . . Whoever follows my teachings will follow in my footsteps and I will look back upon him with out-stretched arms inviting him into the new world of our Creator. Alas, I fear a pall of smoke will obscure the eyes of many from the truth of Gai-wiio but I pray that when I am gone that all may do what I have taught.

Although the following years continued to be times of trouble for the Ho-denosaunee, marked by additional land loss, cultural erosion, and intensified evangel-ical pressure, Handsome Lake's message, adopted and practiced by growing numbers of Iroquois, served as a sustaining counterweight to defeat. Motivating a profound re-generation of Hodenosaunee society, based on the traditional beliefs and ceremonies of the Great Longhouse, the Good Word ensured through the decades that the League and the culture of the Iroquois peoples had the strength to survive, even until today.

**LEON SHENANDOAH/
ONONDAGA**

"Well, I think what people should think of is the message that came from the Creator, and they must do three things, the things that he laid down—there must be peace, we must love one another, regardless of where they're from, who they are, what color they are, we were all made from the Creator. We were all created from one man. There's no separation. So I have learned that I must love all people that walks on this Mother Earth, regardless of what color they are."

The Struggle for Ohio

While the treaty of 1783 had ended the war between Great Britain and the Americans, it had not halted the war by Britain's western allies—the Shawnees, Miamis, Chippewas, and other Indian nations of the Ohio country and the lower Great Lakes—against the Americans who continued to invade their lands north of the Ohio River. The collapse of the Iroquois political and military power left the western tribes suddenly more vulnerable to the Americans. But although the British had ceded sovereignty over the Northwest Territory to the United States, they had refused to leave the area (citing, as an excuse, American violations of other provisions of the treaty), and in the Indians' struggle against the American settlers, the tribes continued to receive encouragement, as well as arms, food, and other supplies, from English and Canadian officials at Detroit and other forts in the region to which the British still clung.

This night scene of Menominee Indians in canoes on Wisconsin's Fox River shows them spearing salmon by the light of torches. The painting was made by the Canadian artist Paul Kane, who visited the Menominees in 1845.

Among the many problems facing the new government of the United States, none was more thorny than the question of how to achieve peace with the western tribes. The government wanted and needed their lands, but it neither desired, nor could it easily afford, a large-scale war against the Indians. Moreover, many Americans in the East, including anti-Federalist opponents of George Washington's administration, would oppose such a war as an immoral invasion of the Indians' country for the benefit of speculators and "land jobbers," as well as a dangerous and costly buildup of the new central government's military power, which they feared would become a threat to the people's own hard-won liberties.

The differences of opinion bothered Washington, who himself speculated in western lands and had written earlier to the Congress of his concern over how to "induce them [the Indians] to relinquish *our* territories and remove to the illimitable regions of the West." At the same time, Washington and other federal officials blamed fanatic, Indian-hating frontiersmen and their attacks on Indian villages for

Dakota Sioux women of the present-day Minnesota region playing a dice game in which they tossed marked plum stones in a bowl, trying for combinations of seven. The illustration is based on a watercolor by Seth Eastman, a talented American army officer who served in the Dakotas' country in the early part of the nineteenth century.

This painting by Eastman shows how Indian women in the Great Lakes area camped on scaffolds to protect their crops from birds and animals as harvest time approached. As the Indian nations of the Ohio and Great Lakes regions began losing their traditional homelands, centuries-old seasonal rounds had to be abandoned.

much of the trouble in the Ohio country, calling them "lawless adventurers" and "banditti" and describing their squatting on Indian lands as the stealing of government property—lands which, when legally ceded, could instead have been sold by the government for the national treasury.

On the Ohio frontier, meanwhile, events throughout the 1780s swept both Indians and the United States toward the major conflict that Washington hoped to avoid. Following the fraudulent post-Revolution treaties, which American negotiators had tried to impose on the western tribes at Forts McIntosh and Finney, the Indians—with the assistance of British agents—attempted to establish a confederacy whose leaders could negotiate an acceptable treaty with the Ameri-

cans to make peace and establish a permanent boundary between the white settlers and the Indians' country. In effect, it would have created what the British desired— an Indian buffer state between the expansion-minded United States and the British possessions in Canada.

The effort, for the time being, foundered over differences among the tribes as to where the boundary should be, but two freewheeling American expeditions of frontier bullies and brawlers that simultaneously invaded the Indians' lands roused the tribes to fury and ended all notions they might have had of agreeing to a peace. One expedition, composed of more than a thousand Kentucky volunteers, led by

George Rogers Clark, started up the Wabash River toward where the tribes were meeting, trying to decide whether to confederate. Clark became drunk and disorganized, hundreds of his men deserted, and the rest called off the expedition and returned home "in vile disorder" without seeing action. The second expedition, however, some eight hundred Kentucky frontiersmen, sacked and burned Shawnee villages on the Miami River, torturing, murdering, and scalping Indian victims and leaving behind them a trail of savagery and brutality. The enraged Shawnees were quick to seek revenge. Deciding with their war chief, Blue Jacket, that there could be no peace negotiations with the Americans, they crossed the Ohio River and raided settlements in Kentucky.

Meanwhile, the American Congress set about organizing the Northwest Territory for governance and for the survey and sale of its ceded lands to settlers. Maintaining the validity of the dubious land cessions which it had wrung from the Indians at the contested treaty meetings, the government in 1789 built Fort Washington on the north bank of the Ohio River in country the Miami Indians still claimed as their own. White settlements—the beginnings of the city of Cincinnati—soon sprang up in the neighborhood of the fort, sending parties of furious Miami and Shawnee warriors once more on the warpath.

Under the overall command of Little Turtle and Blue Jacket, the war chiefs, respectively, of the Miamis and Shawnees, the Indians struck again and again, laying waste homes and farms, slaying white families in their cabins and fields, seizing captives and livestock, and attacking flatboats as they came down the Ohio filled with new settlers and supplies. The Indians' angry effort to drive the settlers and the protecting fort from their lands created a crisis for the Americans. Major General Arthur

During the first ninety years following the Revolutionary War, virtually all Indian land in the Ohio Valley and Great Lakes areas was ceded by tribes in more than 150 American and Canadian treaties, many of them fraudulent. Typical was the treaty signed by this "Grand Council" of certain Chippewa bands and American officials at Fond du Lac, Wisconsin, in 1826.

When we passed through the country between Pittsburgh and our nations, lately Shawnee and Lenape [Delaware] hunting grounds, we found the country thickly inhabited and the people under arms.

— CORNSTALK

St. Clair, a veteran of the French and Indian War and the Revolution, whom Washington had named the first governor of the Northwest Territory, tried to make peace with the tribes, but the Indians rebuffed the messengers he sent to their villages, refusing to discuss any agreement with him save the withdrawal of all permanent American settlements north of the Ohio River.

To St. Clair, the situation called for military action against the tribes, especially when reports told of mounting incidents of attacks by Chickasaws and other western Indians against Americans, and it began to appear that the boldness of the Ohio tribes, if not quelled, might ignite a general Indian war. Hurrying to New York City, the seat of the federal government, St. Clair won the approval of Washington and his secretary of war, Henry Knox, for a brief and limited but hard-hitting campaign to destroy the military power of the offending tribes and provide an example for other Indians on the frontier. Returning to Fort Washington, St. Clair assembled an expedition of regulars and Kentucky and Pennsylvania recruits, totaling some 1,450 men, and placed them under the command of Brigadier General Josiah Harmar, a hard-drinking officer who had served with Pennsylvania troops during the Revolution, though he was unknown to Washington.

Harmar's expedition was a disaster. The Indians "should be made to smart," St. Clair had instructed him. Instead, after struggling through the Ohio forests, up the Miami River watershed, and looting and burning the hastily evacuated Indian center of

An Indian Family in the Forest, *painted by Cornelius Krieghoff, showed the conical form of shelter, often covered with bark, that was in common use throughout the northeastern woodlands.*

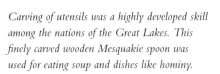

Carving of utensils was a highly developed skill among the nations of the Great Lakes. This finely carved wooden Mesquakie spoon was used for eating soup and dishes like hominy.

Kekionga on the Maumee River at the site of present-day Fort Wayne, Indiana, Harmar's troops, in a fierce encounter beginning on October 19, 1790, were twice lured into costly ambushes and cut up by Miamis and Shawnees under Little Turtle and Blue Jacket. After two days of desperate fighting, during which 183 Americans were killed and some of their units sent fleeing in panic from the battlefield ("For God's sakes retreat. . . . There are Indians enough to eat you up!" screamed one mounted militiaman to a terrified group of infantry), Harmar ordered a withdrawal that turned into a disorderly flight from the Indians' country.

The exultant Shawnees and Miamis, now confident that they could drive the Americans from their lands, quickly reoccupied their villages and sent out hunting parties to replenish their food supplies for the winter. In January, Blue Jacket and some two hundred warriors went south, commencing a new series of raids against the American settlers and the traffic on the Ohio River. As the white frontiersmen fought back, atrocities mounted on both sides, and the warfare reached new extremes of cruelty. At the same time, in the north, the tribes moved down the Maumee River, establishing a new center for their villages at the confluence of the Auglaize and Maumee rivers, which put them closer to the Lake Erie routes to their British supporters at posts like Fort Detroit. Even as they took the war to the American settlers, most Indians believed they would soon have to deal with another American army, and they were right.

When Washington received news of the debacle of Harmar's expedition, he was not surprised. "I expected little from it from the moment I heard he was a drunkard," he told Knox. Nevertheless, for the security of the fearful settlers and land developers in Ohio, as well as the honor of the nation, he felt he would now have to punish the western Indians severely. Concluding that Harmar had simply been an incompetent officer and that all

This Mesquakie storage bag was woven from wool and basswood fiber around 1890.

that was needed was an abler and more experienced commander, he ordered General St. Clair himself to organize and lead a new expedition against the Indians.

St. Clair fared worse than Harmar. Fifty-seven years old, a member of Washington's staff during the Revolution, and now grown wealthy as a Pennsylvania property owner and land speculator, he was enormously heavy, snobbish, and given to bouts of temper tantrums, asthma, and gout. An influential Federalist and friend and political supporter of the president, he refused to accept advice from his fellow officers and proved to be no more competent in the field than Harmar had been.

Departing on October 4, 1791, from Fort Hamilton, a newly built post on the lower Great Miami River, he started toward the Indian villages on the Maumee with an army of twenty-three hundred regulars and short-term recruits, most of them undisciplined and half-trained, as well as badly armed and ill supplied by corrupt government contractors. Equipped with eight artillery pieces and accompanied by two hundred camp-following women who were listed as "cooks," the expedition lumbered north at a pace of less than five miles a day. As militia enlistment terms ended, men drifted away and returned home. Many others deserted. By November, the army had dwindled to fourteen hundred men. Despite the urging of his junior officers, St. Clair, who was frequently sick or suffering from gout and had to be carried on a litter, put out no scouts ahead of the troops. Stopping to build a small advance post along the way, the expedition at length reached an upper tributary of the Wabash River and, on November 3, camped on both sides of the stream.

Unknown to the Americans, parties of Indian scouts, one of them led by a youthful Shawnee warrior named Tecumseh, had been spying on the army from the woods and reporting its progress to Little Turtle and Blue Jacket almost since St. Clair had departed from Fort Hamilton. The two war chiefs, at the head of an allied Indian force composed of members of fourteen western tribes, had bided their time, waiting for the Americans to camp on a site advantageous for an Indian attack. The location St. Clair had chosen on November 3, a large clearing surrounded by creeks, heavy underbrush, and swampy grounds, was such a site, and Little Turtle and Blue Jacket, with a thousand warriors, lay hidden in the deep woods only a mile or two away.

At dawn the next morning, with piercing yells, the Indian force, led by the thirty-nine-year-old veteran war strategist Little Turtle, launched an attack against St. Clair's men. Emerging from the forest and coming at the Americans from three sides, the Indians charged first into the camp of the militiamen, taking them by surprise and killing many of them with hatchets and knives as they tried to fight back. Fleeing in panic, the survivors raced across the stream to St. Clair's main camp on a small plateau, spreading fear among the troops that were gathered there. A moment later, the Indians charged onto the plateau, engaging the Americans again in furious hand-to-hand fighting.

The fierce struggle lasted for three hours. Dazed and wearing only a tricorn hat and a greatcoat over his underwear, St. Clair tried to hoist himself onto his horse, but gave it up when both his horse and his orderly were killed. In the confusion, he attempted to give orders, but no one would listen to him. Around him, his officers and men were dropping by the score. Some of the artillerymen managed to fire their pieces, but the shots went high. A moment later, Blue Jacket and a group of Shawnees and Delawares, the latter fighting under their war chief, Buckongahelas, swarmed over the battery and killed the gunners. At last, St. Clair and some five hundred survivors fled together like a frightened "drove of bullocks," as one of them later recalled, down the road which they had recently hacked from the forest in their march from the south.

On November 9, what was left of the shattered army stumbled back into Fort Washington, having covered in only four days the distance it had taken them five weeks to travel during their advance. Behind them, the defeated men had left 623 dead officers and men of the original 1,400 members of the force, 24 dead civilian teamsters and sutlers, all eight of their artillery pieces, all the expedition's supplies and equipment, and all but two of the camp-follower "cooks." It was the greatest military defeat a United States army would ever experience from Indians, its casualties dwarfing in number even the approximately 250 members of Custer's command who died at the Little Bighorn in 1876. In addition to the dead, 271 of St. Clair's men were seriously wounded. Later it was discovered that the Indian casualties were 21 killed and 40 wounded, making the battle also one of the most one-sided defeats in the history of the army.

The members of the Indian coalition celebrated their great victory, then returned to their homes to hunt and prepare for the winter, reinforced in their expectation that the Americans would soon give up trying to hold on to the country north of the Ohio River. It was easy, at first, even for many fearful whites to believe that the Indians might be right. The near annihilation of St. Clair's army, all but stripping the region of troops, panicked the American settlements and land-development companies and temporarily halted emigration to Ohio. In the months following the battle, Indian war parties led by Tecumseh and other warriors renewed their raids, underscoring their determination to force the whites to leave. "The savages," wrote an anxious investor in the Ohio Land Company, "believe them Selves invincible and have much cause of triumph."

Then, suddenly, in the summer of 1792, word came down the Ohio River, filtering into both white settlements and Indian villages, that another American army, bigger and more powerful than the first two, was assembling at Pittsburgh to force the submission of the western Indians. Unlike Harmar and St. Clair, moreover, its commander was a competent, respected Revolutionary War figure, General "Mad Anthony" Wayne, the hero of the battle of Stony Point.

Wayne's assignment was actually a tentative one, depending on a still-unfolding chain of events that had begun in the East on the heels of St. Clair's disaster. News of the rout had shocked Washington, Congress, and the general public. Although Washington was convinced that the western Indians were now at war with the United States and would have to be defeated, he was restrained by a widespread sentiment in the Congress and among the public in the East in favor of making peace with the western tribes and stopping the invasion of their lands. To get Congress to vote funds for the building and supplying of a large, new federal army of five thousand regulars to cope with the situation in Ohio, he had to agree first to try to make peace with the Indians.

In the spring of 1792, Secretary of War Knox, following through in good faith, tried unsuccessfully to get word to the Miamis and Shawnees that the United States wished to talk peace with them. Six messengers were sent to the tribes, and all were killed as spies. Finally, the government enlisted the Iroquois as intermediaries, and in the summer an Iroquois delegation, headed by Red Jacket, journeyed to a large gathering of almost a thousand Indians from a dozen western tribes that met at the Shawnee villages on the Auglaize River.

This also failed. The western Indians were in no mood to listen to anything but an American agreement to a complete withdrawal from all lands north of the Ohio

This portrait, believed to be that of Tecumseh in white men's clothes, may be the only known true likeness of the great Shawnee leader. Done by an unknown artist, it was obtained by the Chicago Natural History Museum in the late nineteenth century from a descendant of explorer William Clark and General George Rogers Clark, both of whom fought against Tecumseh in the conflicts of the Ohio Valley.

When an Iroquois delegation headed by Red Jacket attempted to negotiate on behalf of the Americans with the Shawnee, Miami, and other nations in the Northwest coalition who allied themselves to resist encroachment in the 1790s, the stormy, controversial leader was humiliated by the western tribes in attendance. The scene is depicted here in a painting called The Trial of Red Jacket, by John Mix Stanley.

River and, in addition, a promise by the United States to pay the Shawnees for taking their former hunting grounds in Kentucky. Condemning the Iroquois for not helping them defend their lands, the western tribes hooted at and humiliated Red Jacket, who finally gave up. Winning an agreement from the tribes to listen to American representatives at a council the following summer, he returned home.

In the meantime, Congress appropriated more than one million dollars for the new federal army, and, with forty-seven-year-old Wayne as its commander, the new force of regulars—termed the Legion of the United States—trained for months, first at Pittsburgh, then at Legionville, Fort Washington, and Hobson's Choice on the Ohio River, waiting for orders to march north against the Indians. By the summer of 1793, Wayne had whipped his army into shape and was anxious to lead it against the Indians. But three American commissioners were scheduled to attend the conference the western Indians had agreed to the year before, and Knox told Wayne to wait while one more attempt was made to negotiate a peaceful settlement. "The sentiments of the great mass of Citizens of the United States are adverse in the extreme to an Indian War," he reminded Wayne. "The favorable opinion and pity of the world is easily excited in favor of the oppressed. . . . If our modes of population and War destroy the tribes the disinterested part of mankind and posterity will be apt to class the effects of our Conduct and that of the Spaniards in Mexico and Peru together—."

Wayne fretted impatiently, but obeyed orders. Meanwhile, the three commissioners started for the Indian villages on the Maumee River, where the conference was to be held. Fears for their safety held them short of their destination, however, and they never did reach the Maumee or deal directly with the western Indians. Instead, they exchanged messages with tribal spokesmen, using British and Iroquois intermediaries to carry their proposals and responses back and forth. Nothing went well. The Americans admitted that the United States had erred originally in assuming that they had won title to the Indians' lands by right of conquest. Now they were willing to give up all claims to lands north of the Ohio River except for heavily settled areas and others developed and sold by land companies around Cincinnati and the Scioto and Muskingum rivers. For these tracts, the United States would pay the tribes fifty thousand dollars in trade goods and an annuity of ten thousand dollars.

After two weeks of meetings, the Indians sent back a blunt response. Their position had not changed; the Americans must withdraw from *all* lands north of the Ohio River. Regarding the offer of payment, they suggested that the Americans use that money instead to resettle elsewhere the whites who were now squatting on the Indians' lands.

There is evidence that the Americans knew all along that the peace effort would fail and pursued it only to convince public opinion in the United States and abroad that, as Secretary of State Thomas Jefferson put it, "peace was unattainable on terms which any of them would admit." At any rate, the American commissioners informed the Indians that there was no point in continuing the negotiations. Sending off a coded message to Wayne, "We did not effect peace," which by previous arrangement with Knox was an order to the legion commander to begin "vigorous offensive action," the delegation left for home.

At that point, Wayne's carefully made plans went awry. He marched his troops to an advance post, which supposedly had been stocked with provisions and supplies for the rest of the way to the Indian villages on the Maumee. For some reason—the corruption or incompetence of the civilian contractors or the deliberate sabotage of James Wilkinson, a rival American general who was later revealed to have schemed to get rid of and succeed Wayne—the supplies were not at the post. It was already late in the fall, and Wayne could not go on with troops who might starve. Infuriated, he postponed the campaign until the following year, busying his troops during the winter by having them build two more advance posts along his line of march through the Indians' country—one, which became known as Greenville, at the site of the pres-

Sell a country! Why not sell the air, the clouds and the great sea, as well as the earth? Did not the Great Spirit make them all for the use of his children? —TECUMSEH

OVERLEAF: *General Anthony Wayne's mounted Legionnaires overwhelm Blue Jacket's allied Indian force at Fallen Timbers along the Maumee River on August 20, 1794. The battle, pictured here by Rufus Zogbaum, ended organized Indian resistance in the Ohio country.*

ent town of the same name in western Ohio, and the other, Fort Recovery, at the location of St. Clair's defeat on the Wabash River, where Wayne had taken some of his men to bury the remains of the American dead.

It was July 1794 before he finally got his supply problems in hand and was ready to commence his long-delayed offensive. In the meantime, British officials in Canada, fearing that Wayne might threaten their position at Fort Detroit, had sent troops to reactivate Fort Miamis near the present site of Toledo, Ohio, below the Indian villages on the Maumee River. The near presence of the British troops, coupled with inflammatory, anti-American remarks by Canada's governor, asserting that England would soon go to war again with the Americans and restore the lost hunting grounds to the Indians, had emboldened the tribes. Tired of waiting for Wayne to make a move, some twelve hundred allied warriors, led by Blue Jacket, on June 20 attacked Fort Recovery, Wayne's most forward post. After an initial success in ambushing some of the garrison, the Indians were driven off by cannon fire and retreated with heavy losses.

The setback worried some of the Indians, including Little Turtle himself.

Through the reports of scouts, he was aware that Wayne, whom he called "the chief who never sleeps," was a far abler opponent than Harmar or St. Clair had been and that the new American army was better trained and more formidable than the ones the tribes had previously faced. A trip to Fort Detroit to find out what aid the Indians might expect from the British forces increased Little Turtle's concern. Following the truculence of the Canadian officials, London had counseled restraint, sending them orders to keep the Indians friendly without becoming involved in their wars. Now Little Turtle sensed that, despite all the earlier assurances, the Indians could not count on British military assistance. Returning home and learning that Wayne had begun his march toward the villages on the Maumee, he told the council of the allied tribes that, without help from the British, the Indians could not beat Wayne and that it was time to make peace with the Americans, for no matter how many Long Knives (their term for the Americans) the Indians killed, there were always more coming after them.

When some of the other Indians called Little Turtle a coward and wondered whether he had become too old or had been listening too long to the Americans, he split with his old partner, the more belligerent Blue Jacket, who was sure that the Indians could defeat Wayne. Although Little Turtle resigned from his position of leadership, he nevertheless announced that he would not leave the coalition, but would take the Miamis into battle with the other tribes.

In the first week of August, Wayne, at the head of his legion of twenty-two hundred infantry regulars and fifteen hundred Kentucky militia cavalry, reached the Auglaize and Maumee rivers. The Indians had abandoned their villages, and Wayne's men set them on fire and trampled the gardens and fields of crops. At the confluence of the two rivers, the heart of the Shawnee-Miami community, Wayne built

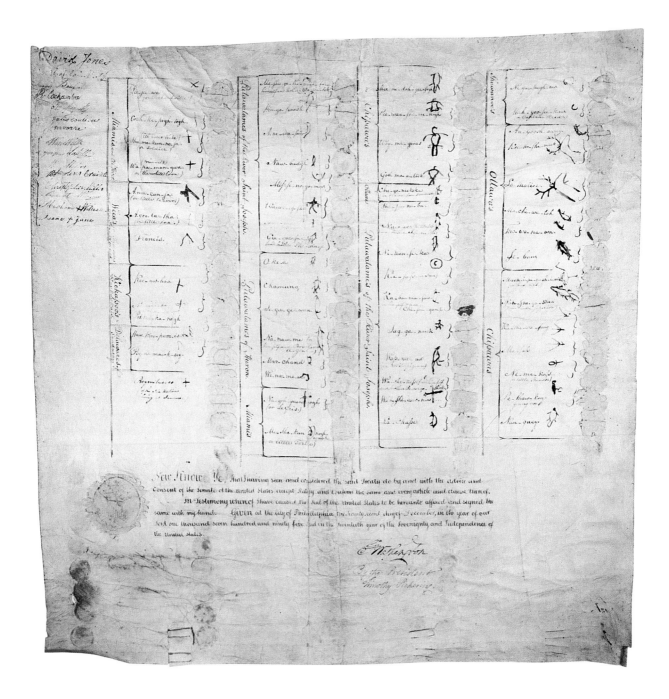

The signature marks of some of the eleven hundred Indian chiefs and warriors who signed the Greenville treaty of peace in 1795. Forced on the tribes by General Wayne, the treaty extinguished the Indians' title to almost two-thirds of the land of present-day Ohio, part of Indiana, and the sites of what became Detroit, Chicago, and other important midwestern cities.

another post, which he named Fort Defiance, then started down the Maumee in search of the Indian army.

With Blue Jacket now at their head, fourteen hundred warriors of the allied nations were waiting to intercept the Americans in the woods bordering three sides of a large clearing along the Maumee where a tornado had blown down many large trees. In the woods on his left side, Blue Jacket had stationed the Miamis and Delawares; in the center, the Ottawas, Potawatomis, and other Great Lakes tribes; and on the right, his own Shawnees, the Wyandots, and a seventy-member contingent of white militiamen, painted and dressed like Indians, who had come from Canada to help the tribes.

Early on the rainy morning of August 20, Wayne's army, led by 150 Kentucky cavalrymen followed by four infantry regiments, came into the clearing from the

*Our lives are in the hands of the
Creator. We are determined to
defend our lands, and if it be his
will we wish to leave our bones
upon them.* —TECUMSEH

A calumet, or peace pipe, smoked by the parties
during the Greenville treaty negotiations in
1795. One impatient American observer at the
meeting was irritated by the "tedious routine"
occasioned by the Indians' traditional custom of
insisting that everyone present take a turn at
smoking the pipe as a representation of their
sincerity in accepting the peace.

fourth side. As the Americans picked their way across the fallen timbers (which became the name of the battle), the Ottawa and Great Lakes Indians, ignoring Blue
Jacket's plans, charged prematurely from their hiding places, howling and yelling, and
fell on the Americans. In the confusion, the cavalry and then the front ranks of the
infantry gave way and began to flee. Wayne, astride his horse, rode through the
milling men, ordering his officers to shoot those who ran, and the panic ended. Reforming their lines, the Legionnaires successfully fought off the Ottawas.

Meanwhile, the tribes on both flanks had begun firing, revealing their positions to
the Americans. A series of bayonet charges by Wayne's men soon dislodged the Indians
from their hiding places. Finally, an American sharpshooter killed the Ottawas' principal
war chief. Unable to retrieve his body, the Ottawa warriors fled, starting a general withdrawal from the battlefield by the other tribes. Within an hour after the start of the fight,
it was over. The Americans, who lost thirty-one killed and about a hundred wounded,
counted only forty dead and severely wounded Indians. But Blue Jacket and the allied
tribes had suffered a crushing defeat at Fallen Timbers that put them at Wayne's mercy.

If there was any hope that the British would help the Indians, it was quickly
dashed. From the battlefield, the beaten warriors fled five miles down the Maumee
to seek safety at Fort Miamis, the reactivated British post. The fort's commander,
however, refused to open the gates to let them in and ordered his men to shoot any
Indian who tried to clamber over the palisades. When the American troops approached, the Indians abandoned their attempts to get into the fort and continued
their panicked flight down the Maumee, finding safety finally on the western shore
of Lake Erie, where Wayne's men did not follow them.

The next year, the coalition tribes assembled again, this time at Wayne's headquarters at Greenville. On August 3, 1795, some eleven hundred Shawnee, Delaware,
Ottawa, Potawatomi, Wyandot, Miami, Chippewa, Kickapoo, Wea, Piankashaw, and
Kaskaskia chiefs and warriors heard the terms of a peace treaty that Wayne had drawn
up for the losers at Fallen Timbers. Under its provisions, the tribes gave up almost
two-thirds of present-day Ohio, a sliver of southeastern Indiana, and sixteen strategic
areas in the Northwest Territory, including the sites of the modern cities of Detroit,
Toledo, Chicago, and Peoria, Illinois.

One by one, the tribes agreed to the terms. The Indians' struggle for the land
of what eight years later would become the state of Ohio had ended, and a
pattern had been established for the American nation's
further expansion westward.

Tecumseh and Tenskwatawa

The defeat at Fallen Timbers, the betrayal by the British, and the terms of the Greenville treaty took the heart out of many of the western Indians who had been fighting for so long to save their lands. Some of the older chiefs and members of their bands followed the lead of Little Turtle, becoming friends of the American government and doing what they could to learn and adopt the white man's ways. Abandoning hunting and war, they turned to agriculture and even to the dress and religion of their white neighbors.

Though demoralized and seemingly powerless, the majority of Indians, however, rejected acculturation and struggled to hold on to their traditional ways of life. The depletion of furbearing and game animals, resulting from new waves of settlers who overran the ceded lands and even areas still owned by the Indians, made it harder for the hunters and their families to obtain from whites the trade items on which they had come to depend. Parties of young men ranged farther and farther from their villages in search of pelts and meat, disrupting family life and village ceremonial calendars. With diminishing fur and food resources, the bands were forced to rely increasingly on treaty-promised government annuity payments and credit from traders, leading to a cycle of Indian indebtedness to whites and a loss of dignity.

Their dependency gnawed at the young men, whose cultures had esteemed hunters and warriors. With dwindling opportunities to prove themselves and win honors from their people, they turned in frustration to drink, trading scarce resources for alcohol. The normally peaceful and well-ordered rhythms of their villages were shattered as drunken warriors vented their rage on one another and on their families. Time-honored customs of respect and obligations between kinsmen were undermined. Communal sharing and assistance waned. Promiscuity increased. Alcohol weakened physiological resistance, and epidemics of white men's diseases, with which traditional cultural knowledge could not cope, swept through the bands.

In the dark years of hopelessness, two Shawnee brothers, Tecumseh and

Disheartened by the loss of land and lives in the years after the Revolution, the surviving Indian peoples struggled to hold on to their traditions in the face of alcohol, defeat, and dependency. This drawing by the Seneca artist Jesse Cornplanter, descendant of the great Seneca chief, depicts the drinking and troubled times among demoralized Indians at Cornplanter's village before the Handsome Lake revival.

Lalawethika, the latter seven years younger and totally unlike Tecumseh, arose to revitalize and reunite the demoralized tribes with what began as essentially a religious movement. Tecumseh, whose name conveyed a Shawnee allegorical phrase meaning "Celestial Panther Lying in Wait," was born in 1768 and was raised as a hunter and warrior. During the post-Revolution warfare in Kentucky and Ohio, he had gained a reputation among the tribes as a skilled and daring war chief and a bitter foe of the white settlers. A handsome, powerfully built man, he had fought bravely at Fallen Timbers, and the next year had refused to participate in the humiliating Treaty of Greenville. His brother, who had lost his right eye in a childhood accident, had begun drinking as a teenager and had grown to manhood with deep psychological and emotional problems. An alcoholic who was unable to care for himself properly and had to

The Shawnee Prophet, Tenskwatawa (The Open Door), brother of Tecumseh, holds his mystery, or medicine, fire, and sacred string of beans which followers touched to show their acceptance of his teachings. He was in his fifties, forgotten after Tecumseh's death and living in Kansas, "silent and melancholy," when he sat for this portrait by George Catlin in 1830.

rely on Tecumseh to feed his family, he was looked down upon by others and had been given his name, which meant "Rattle" or "Noisemaker," because of his bragging that covered his helplessness.

On a spring night in 1805, living in Indiana as a sickly member of Tecumseh's band, Lalawethika fell into a trance and experienced a divine revelation that changed the course of his life. Like Handsome Lake and a number of other visionaries and prophets who appeared at the time among the disheartened Indian nations, Lalawethika reported that he had gone to the spirit world and seen the Creator, who had told him to change his bad ways and become a teacher who could carry the Creator's messages to the people and lead them along the right path.

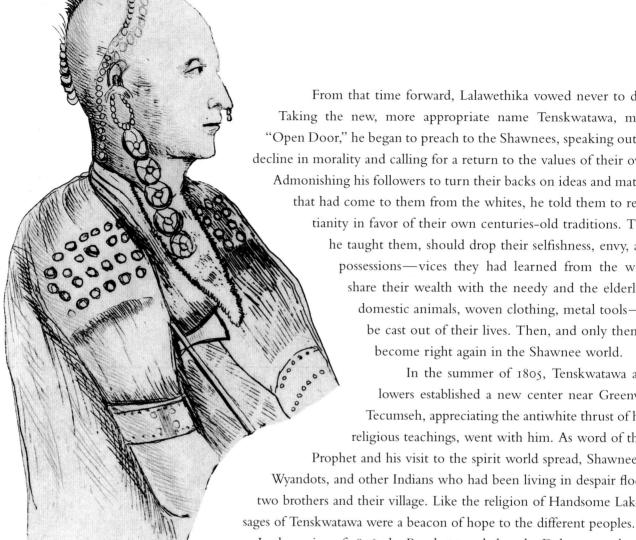

The Shawnee Prophet's teachings rejected the influences of white culture on the Indian nations. Included were manufactured items brought to the Indians by traders, like the earrings and the trade cloth shirt worn by this Miami man.

From that time forward, Lalawethika vowed never to drink again. Taking the new, more appropriate name Tenskwatawa, meaning the "Open Door," he began to preach to the Shawnees, speaking out against the decline in morality and calling for a return to the values of their own culture. Admonishing his followers to turn their backs on ideas and material things that had come to them from the whites, he told them to reject Christianity in favor of their own centuries-old traditions. The Indians, he taught them, should drop their selfishness, envy, and lust for possessions—vices they had learned from the whites—and share their wealth with the needy and the elderly. Alcohol, domestic animals, woven clothing, metal tools—all should be cast out of their lives. Then, and only then, would all become right again in the Shawnee world.

In the summer of 1805, Tenskwatawa and his followers established a new center near Greenville, Ohio. Tecumseh, appreciating the antiwhite thrust of his brother's religious teachings, went with him. As word of the Shawnee Prophet and his visit to the spirit world spread, Shawnees, Ottawas, Wyandots, and other Indians who had been living in despair flocked to the two brothers and their village. Like the religion of Handsome Lake, the messages of Tenskwatawa were a beacon of hope to the different peoples.

In the spring of 1806, the Prophet traveled to the Delawares, who at the time were accusing a number of their people of witchcraft. Tenskwatawa had nothing to do with their fate, but when the accused were found guilty by the Delawares and burned at the stake, horrified Moravian missionaries working among the tribe blamed their deaths on the influence of the Shawnee Prophet and complained about him to William Henry Harrison, the stiff-necked governor of the Indiana Territory. In an angry letter to the Delawares, Harrison asked, "Who is this pretended prophet who dares to speak in the name of the Great Creator? . . . Demand of him some proofs at least of his being the messenger of the Deity. . . . Ask him to cause the sun to stand still—the moon to alter its course—or the dead to rise from their graves. If he does these things, you may then believe that he has been sent by God."

Harrison had cause to wish he had not written the letter. Soon after its arrival among the Delawares, Tenskwatawa accepted its challenge and announced to his followers that on a certain day he would make the sun disappear and would then bring it back. In some manner—spiritually or from a white man's almanac—Tenskwatawa learned that an eclipse of the sun was due to occur on that date, or it may have been a coincidence. But when, on the appointed day, an eclipse occurred, news of the Prophet's "miracle" traveled like wildfire among the tribes, and many more followers came to live with the Shawnee brothers.

Meanwhile, the steadily growing numbers of settlers in the Northwest Territory increased the demand for lands still held by the Indians. Using deception, bribes, and alcohol, and overlooking the promises of the Greenville treaty to protect the Indians' unceded country, Harrison extracted a series of new treaties from handpicked, aged, and pliable chiefs of the Delaware, Miami, Sauk and Mesquakie (Fox), Wyandot, Ottawa, and other tribes. For the paltry annuities given to these chiefs, who were frequently drunk and lied to during the negotiations, millions of additional acres from western Ohio to present-day Wisconsin and Missouri passed from Indian to white ownership.

As the tribes were forced off their lands, many of the young warriors lost faith in their traditional chiefs who had made the sales and, turning away from them, traveled to Greenville to listen to the Shawnee Prophet. The concentration of their growing numbers, leading to tension and occasional altercations with settlers, together with the increasingly anti-American tone of the Prophet's sermons, alarmed the Indian agent at Fort Wayne, who informed Harrison that Tenskwatawa was a danger to American authority.

To Harrison and officials in the young state of Ohio, the tensions were part of an international crisis that was threat-

We-Wissa, a Potawatomi chief, painted by George Winter at a conference of members of that tribe and U.S. government officials in what is now Fulton County, Indiana. There, the Potawatomis were pressured to vacate lands they had previously ceded and migrate west earlier than required by the terms of the treaty. "The ceding of their lands is merely a weaker power driven from its possession by a stronger," Winter wrote, referring to an action that toward the end of the twentieth century, in upheavals in eastern Europe, would be termed ethnic cleansing.

I am a Shawnee. My forefathers were warriors. Their son is a warrior. From them I take only my existence. From my tribe I take nothing. I have made myself what I am. —TECUMSEH

ening to erupt in a new war between the United States and Great Britain. Despite the fact that Jay's Treaty of 1794 had finally made the English give up their forts in the Northwest Territory, their fur traders and agents, working out of posts on the Canadian side of the border, were still active among the American tribes, supplying their needs and encouraging their anti-American feelings. Refusing to acknowledge the legitimate and profound grievances of the Indians, Harrison and others were quick to assume that the Prophet was a British agent. As relations between the Indians and whites deteriorated further, Harrison sent several emissaries to Greenville, demanding to know the Prophet's intentions.

To placate the Americans, Tecumseh, who was beginning to broaden his brother's spiritual teachings into an Indian resistance movement with political and military overtones, joined Blue Jacket and the Wyandot chief Roundhead in a meeting with the governor of Ohio in September 1807. In the council, Tecumseh emerged as a powerful voice for the tribes, speaking for almost three hours with a skill and passion that would impress all who would hear him, Indians and whites alike, for the rest of his life. Condemning the past treaties between the western tribes and the United States government as fraudulent, he asserted that henceforth the Indians would surrender no more land north of the Ohio River and that, although they had no intention of trying to regain the lands they had already ceded, they would defend their remaining country with their lives. Moved by Tecumseh's eloquent statement of the Indians' point of view, the Ohio officials felt reassured that they were not dealing with British agents.

Nevertheless, the tensions with white neighbors and the antagonism of Harrison made the brothers' position at Greenville in ceded country too vulnerable to an American attack, and in April 1808, they moved to lands still owned by Potawatomis and Kickapoos in northwestern Indiana, establishing a new "Prophetstown" near the junction of the Wabash and Tippecanoe rivers. Indians from many tribes followed them, and like Tecumseh, Tenskwatawa began to speak to them, not only about religious issues, but also about Indian political and military unity.

In June, despite previous British betrayals of the tribes, Tecumseh journeyed to Canada to see what support the English might give him if he had to fight the Americans. His trip, like the one he had made to meet the Ohio governor, reflected his growing role of leadership among the Indians. The movement his brother had begun was acquiring another dimension, based increasingly on Tecumseh's vision of a united Indian defense of Indian lands and cultures. The British urged Tecumseh not to precipitate a conflict with the Americans, but finding him "a very shrewd and intelligent man," who might be useful to them in the future, promised to send supplies to the new village on the Tippecanoe.

During the following year, Tecumseh continued to travel widely, conveying to tribes from the Great Lakes to the Mississippi River a message that combined his brother's revitalization teachings and his own call for united action to halt the cession of Indian lands to the whites. At Prophetstown, during the same period, the large population taxed the food supplies. Deaths from hunger and disease were common, and some of the tribal groups blamed the Prophet and went home.

In need of land to attract settlers who would make Indiana a state, Harrison heard of the adversities and defections at Prophetstown, as well as reports that the influence of the Prophet and his brother was declining, and decided it was a good time to hold a new treaty meeting. In September 1809, he convened a council of "friendly" Miami, Delaware, and Potawatomi chiefs at Fort Wayne and, with the use of small bribes, induced them to cede more than three million acres of lands in central Indiana. The Miamis and Delawares sold their own lands, but the Potawatomis blithely signed away lands they had never occupied.

Tecumseh and Tenskwatawa were outraged by the treaty. More determined than ever to forge a united resistance to the Americans, Tecumseh traveled tirelessly from village to village, proclaiming that Indian lands belonged to all the Indian peoples in common and that no individual chief or tribe had a right to sell any part of them. Tecumseh was not alone in his anger. The Fort Wayne treaty shocked the leaders and members of many of the western tribes and bands. People turned against chiefs who had been friendly to the Americans and came in crowds to listen to the thundering orations of Tecumseh, who now put himself forward unhesitatingly as their leader. The problem, he told the Indians, was that weak individual chiefs could be manipulated by the Americans, and that tribes, acting alone, were not strong enough to resist the whites. The solution was a political and military union of tribes, owning all the land in common, and following his leadership in preserving the remaining Indian land base.

Tecumseh's vision of a Pan-Indian movement, his aspiration to centralized leadership, and the idea of the common ownership of land, all influenced in part by the

In 1808, Tecumseh, Tenskwatawa, and their followers moved from the Shawnee settlement at Greenville to the site of an old Indian town at the intersection of the Wabash and Tippecanoe rivers in Indiana. This computer-generated re-creation shows how the new Indian center, known as Prophetstown, may have appeared at its height before American forces destroyed it after the Battle of Tippecanoe in 1811.

In August 1810, Tecumseh and Governor William Henry Harrison of Indiana Territory met at Vincennes, Harrison's capital. The conference grew so heated that the two leaders, pictured here, threatened each other with violence. For the moment a fight was avoided, but Tecumseh was buying time, building his coalition and seeking help from the British to stop the Americans from taking more Indian land.

example of the United States and the public lands which the states owned in common, clashed with the very essence of tribal political structures. Older chiefs rejected Tecumseh's challenge to their authority and to the autonomous traditions of their sovereign nations. Many young warriors, however, contemptuous of the chiefs who had signed away their lands, aligned themselves with Tecumseh. In the spring of 1810, hundreds of Delaware, Miami, Sauk, Mesquakie, Potawatomi, and Kickapoo warriors joined the Shawnee brothers at Prophetstown.

Again, Harrison became concerned about the unrest, this time worrying that Tecumseh and his followers might attack Vincennes, the Indiana capital. Twice, at Harrison's invitation—in 1810 and 1811—Tecumseh, accompanied each time by a large number of Indians, traveled down the Wabash to join the governor in a peaceful council. At times, the meetings were affable; at other times, the air bristled with hostility as the two strong, willful leaders faced each other.

In the first meeting, Tecumseh, speaking through an interpreter, introduced himself and his vision for the Indians:

> I am a Shawnee. My forefathers were warriors. Their son is a warrior. From them I take only my existence. From my tribe I take nothing. I have made myself what I am. And I would that I could make the red people as great as the conceptions of my mind, when I think of the Great Spirit that rules over all. I would not then come to Governor Harrison to ask him to tear the treaty. But I would say to him, Brother, you have liberty to return to your own country. . . .
>
> The way, the only way to stop this evil is for all the red men to unite in claiming a common and equal right in the land, as it was at first, and should be now—for it never was divided, but belongs to all. No tribe has a right to sell, even to each other, much less to strangers, who demand all, and will take no less. . . .
>
> Sell a country! Why not sell the air, the clouds and the great sea, as well as the earth? Did not the Great Spirit make them all for the use of his children?

Although both meetings ended inconclusively, Harrison was aware of Tecumseh's powerful personality and strong hold over the tribes. After the second council, in August 1811, he wrote to Secretary of War William Eustis:

> The implicit obedience and respect which the followers of Tecumseh pay to him is really astonishing and more than any other circumstance bespeaks him one of those uncommon geniuses, which spring up occasionally to produce revolutions and overturn the established order of things. If it were not for the vicinity of the United States, he would perhaps be the founder of an Empire that would rival in glory that of Mexico or Peru.

No difficulties deter him. His activity and industry supply the want of letters. For four years he has been in constant motion. You see him today on the Wabash and in a short time you hear of him on the shores of Lake Erie or Michigan, or on the banks of the Mississippi and wherever he goes he makes an impression favorable to his purpose.

Nevertheless, Harrison viewed Tecumseh's movement as a peril that had to be destroyed. When he learned that the Shawnee leader planned an extensive visit to southern tribes following the second council at Vincennes, he laid plans to attack Prophetstown while Tecumseh was away. Tecumseh's absence, he wrote Secretary Eustis, "affords a most favorable opportunity for breaking up his Confederacy."

In October 1811, Harrison invaded the Indians' unceded land, marching an army of a thousand men to the Tippecanoe River in the vicinity of Prophetstown. Ignoring the orders of Tecumseh, who had warned Tenskwatawa against starting hostilities—which, before Tecumseh had fully formed his coalition, would be premature—the Prophet launched an impulsive attack against Harrison's camp with some six hundred Winnebagos, Potawatomis, and Kickapoos in the predawn darkness of the morning of November 7. After a furious battle, the Indians were forced to withdraw among the trees, from where they kept up a desultory fire against the Americans throughout the day. By the following day, they had left the area and started for their homes, angrily blaming Tenskwatawa for their failure against the American troops. Leading his men, unopposed, into the deserted Prophetstown, Harrison burned all the wigwams and log buildings and destroyed the Indians' possessions and supplies, including their stores of food.

In the meantime, Tecumseh had been in the South, carrying his appeal to the Chickasaws, Choctaws, Creeks, and others to join his coalition in a war against the Americans. In one town after another, his oratory stirred huge and excited audiences that sometimes included a white trader or Indian agent who reported the passion with which the Shawnee chief spoke. His words "fell in avalanches from his lips," said one of them. "His eyes burned with supernatural lustre, and his whole frame trembled with emotion. His voice resounded over the multitude—now sinking in low and musical whispers, now rising to the highest key, hurling out the words like a succession of thunderbolts. . . . I have heard many great orators, but I never saw one with the vocal powers of Tecumseh."

Clad only in a breechclout and moccasins, with lines of red war paint under his eyes, Tecumseh urged his audiences to stop their intertribal wars, to unite in a single nation as the whites of the United States had done, and to fight together for all

Who is this pretended prophet who dares to speak in the name of the Great Creator? . . . Ask him to cause the sun to stand still—the moon to alter its course. . . . If he does these things, you may then believe that he has been sent by God.

—WILLIAM HENRY HARRISION
ABOUT TENSKWATAWA

their land before it was too late. "Where today are the Pequot?" he demanded. "Where the Narraganset, the Mohican, the Pokanoket and many other once powerful tribes of our people? They have vanished before the avarice and oppression of the white man, as snow before a summer sun. . . . Will we let ourselves be destroyed in our turn without making an effort worthy of our race? Shall we, without a struggle, give up our homes, our lands . . . the graves of our dead and everything that is dear and sacred to us? . . . I know you will say with me, Never! Never!"

Tecumseh's dynamic presence and eloquence, however, could not overcome a cultural rift that was occurring between the western and southern tribes. In the Northwest, hunting remained the basis of tribal economies, and Tecumseh's movement embodied a desire to return to old ways. In the South, where there had been a high rate of intermarriage between the tribes and British traders and other whites, a generation of mixed-blood leaders who had received an education and spoke English had come to power. Although traditional Indians opposed them, they were strong enough to steer the tribes toward the adoption of white ways and peaceful coexistence with the Americans, which they believed was the best strategy for survival. Assisted by missionaries who had moved in among them, many of the southern Indians were fast becoming acculturated, raising pigs, chickens, and cows and harvesting small crops of corn. These Indian farmers were not impoverished like their northern counterparts and had not yet felt the full threat and violence of waves of white settlers.

Pushmataha, the famed Choctaw chief, painted by Charles Bird King in 1824. One of Tecumseh's strongest opponents during the Shawnee's visit to enlist allies among southern tribes in 1811, Pushmataha argued eloquently that making war on the Americans would be futile and suicidal.

Countering Tecumseh's eloquence with fiery oratory of their own, pro-American southern chiefs like the Choctaws' Pushmataha persuaded their people that it would be suicidal folly to make war on the United States, with whom they had no quarrel, and at the same time reminded them that they had long been enemies of the Shawnees and the other western tribes. In the end, only a handful of virulently anti-American Creeks in present-day Alabama pledged to join Tecumseh's coalition, which persuaded him that he was not yet ready to start hostilities.

Returning home early in the spring of 1812, Tecumseh was shocked to find Prophetstown in ruins and his thousand fighting men and their families gone. Tenskwatawa himself had come back to the burned settlement, but when Tecumseh learned what had happened, he flew into a rage, grabbing his brother by the hair and threatening to kill him. From then on, Tenskwatawa lost all influence among the Indians, staying in the shadow of Tecumseh, eventually becoming a wanderer, and dying in obscurity.

The Death of a Dream

Gathering his intimates and leading war chiefs around him, Tecumseh set about rebuilding his coalition. It was not difficult to do. Many of the bands, smarting from their setback at Prophetstown, were already raiding American settlers in angry, un-

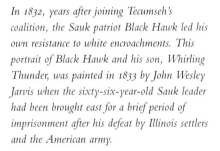

In 1832, years after joining Tecumseh's coalition, the Sauk patriot Black Hawk led his own resistance to white encroachments. This portrait of Black Hawk and his son, Whirling Thunder, was painted in 1833 by John Wesley Jarvis when the sixty-six-year-old Sauk leader had been brought east for a brief period of imprisonment after his defeat by Illinois settlers and the American army.

coordinated attacks of their own. Others, like Black Hawk's following of Sauk and Fox Indians in Illinois, were eager for revenge against the American treaty makers who had robbed them of their lands. Anxious for all-out war, they were ready to act together under Tecumseh.

The British base of Amherstburg and Fort Malden on the Canadian side of the Detroit River, where Tecumseh offered the services of his Indian fighting force to the English in the War of 1812.

The hostility of the western Indians, which the Americans made themselves believe stemmed principally from the intrigues of the British, helped precipitate the long-threatened war between the United States and Great Britain, which began in June 1812. Tecumseh seized the opportunity to achieve his goals with a British alliance and British arms. Accompanied by a force of Potawatomis, Kickapoos, Shawnees, and Delawares, he moved to Fort Malden on the Canadian side of the Detroit River and offered his services to the British. As bands of Wyandots, Chippewas, Sioux, Winnebagos, and Sauk and Fox soon joined him, it seemed that his years of tireless effort were bearing fruit. Impressed by his abilities and the large number of tribal fighting men who had followed him into Canada, the British put him in charge of their allied Indian force.

Besieged by a joint Indian-British army, in which Tecumseh and his forces played important military roles, the Americans surrendered Fort Detroit in the early days of the war. But after a year, little more had been gained, and British losses were mounting. While the British will to honor their commitment to protect Indian lands faded, the Americans constructed new forts to solidify their control of the Ohio Valley. Tecumseh had reason to recall with concern how the British had abandoned the Indians a generation earlier at the end of the American Revolution.

On September 13, 1813, American ships under Commodore Oliver Hazard Perry destroyed the British fleet on Lake Erie and cut the British army in the West from its

A crude 1833 rendition of the death of Tecumseh on October 5, 1813, at the Battle of the Thames. Soon after the Americans, at left, launched their attack, the British commander and his troops abandoned the battle. His Indian allies fought on, but they were overwhelmed and Tecumseh was killed.

supply bases in the East. As a large American force under Harrison advanced on Detroit, the British made preparations to retreat across Canada to the East, abandoning the western country to the Americans. For a while, the British commander Colonel Henry Procter concealed his plans from Tecumseh, who eventually found out. Enraged, the Shawnee chief roared at Procter in front of the other British officers:

> Listen, Father! We . . . wish to remain here, and fight our enemy, if they should make an appearance. . . . You have got the arms and ammunition. . . . If you have an idea of going away, give them to us, and you may go and welcome. As for us, our lives are in the hands of the Creator. We are determined to defend our lands, and if it be his will we wish to leave our bones upon them.

After his death, many whites honored Tecumseh as a heroic and honorable opponent. An example is this imaginative portrayal of the dying Tecumseh, sculpted in marble in 1856 by Ferdinand Pettrich. Actually, no white saw Tecumseh killed, and no Indian ever revealed what happened to his body.

Faced with Harrison's advancing force of three thousand men, Tecumseh nevertheless had to retreat eastward across Ontario with the British for a hundred miles. At the Thames River, Procter halted his withdrawal. Tecumseh would retreat no farther. On October 5, 1813, the Shawnee chief rallied his fighting men as he inspected the lines from horseback. Tecumseh told his men they would be victorious, and he urged Procter to do the same:

> Father, tell your men to be firm, and all will be well.

Tecumseh dismounted and joined his troops in their position in a swampy thicket. In close pursuit, Harrison appeared and in midafternoon launched a cavalry charge against the British regulars in the center of Procter's line. The British collapsed, resisting for only a few minutes before fleeing, with Procter on horseback racing past them in terror as they retreated.

Tecumseh did not run, and neither did his men. These were loyal followers who had supported the Shawnee brothers since the beginning. From a nearby hillside, the discredited Shawnee Prophet watched as the Americans charged his brother's position. Some said that Tecumseh received a gunshot wound to his chest. Most had no idea of when or how he was killed, or of what happened to his body. Thirty minutes after he was last seen alive in the battle, his men disengaged and melted away in the forest.

The battle was over. But something larger than Tecumseh's vision of a unified Indian resistance had ended. Except for a brief, tragic attempt by Black Hawk's Sauk and Fox Indian followers to hold on to their sacred homeland in Illinois in the 1830s, the western tribes' long, armed struggle for their lands between the Ohio River and the Great Lakes had finally been lost.

Where [are] the Narraganset, the Mohican, the Pakanoket and many other once powerful tribes of our people? They have vanished before the avarice and oppression of the white man, as snow before a summer sun.
— TECUMSEH

Removal from the South

By the early nineteenth century, the great Indian nations of the South—the Cherokees, Choctaws, Chickasaws, and Creeks—no longer constituted a military threat to the young United States. Within each nation, deep divisions were growing between those who were trying to maintain their traditions and Indian ways of life and an increasing majority who were embracing the material culture of the whites.

In 1812, the rift among the Creeks turned into a bloody civil war. The Creeks, or Muskokees, had received their English name from early traders who had noted

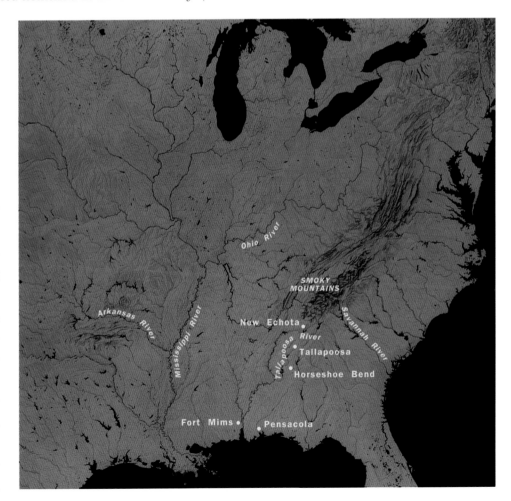

John Trumbull drew this pencil sketch of Hopothle Mico, a leading Creek chief, when a delegation from that nation visited President Washington in New York City in July 1790 to discuss a cession of their lands. Because the Indians feared Trumbull's drawings of them as "magic," he sketched surreptitiously, describing the Creeks as possessing a dignity "worthy of a Roman Senator."

A heroic image of Andrew Jackson, depicted in a lithograph of the 1830s. With Cherokee and Choctaw help he defeated the Creeks, becoming president largely on his reputation as an Indian fighter. Once in the White House, he set in motion the armed removal of the southeastern tribes to lands west of the Mississippi River in the region of present-day Oklahoma.

that their towns lay generally along waterways of the interior. A widespread confederation of the descendants of Coosas and many of the other sixteenth-century Mississippian nations whom de Soto had met or heard about in present-day Georgia, South Carolina, and Alabama, the Creeks had gained importance not only because of their numbers and strength but also because of their geographic position amid the competing empires of Spain, England, and France and their diplomatic skill in playing them off against each other for Creek friendship and influence.

In the years before the American Revolution, the Creeks had reached the height of their power. Their huge inland confederation, still relatively untroubled by white pressure for its lands, could muster six thousand fighting men from a hundred towns.

After the Revolution, their fortunes deteriorated drastically. Southern cotton farmers, land speculators, and poor white settlers moved onto Creek territories, causing the new American government to persuade the Creeks repeatedly to cede strips of their homeland. As the angry history of other borders was repeated, the Creeks split into pro- and anti-American factions.

With the outbreak of the War of 1812, the anti-American Upper Creeks, known as Red Sticks for the red-painted sticks they carried that Tecumseh's followers had said would help them in battle, broke with the pro-American Lower Creeks and joined the British in the war against the United States. On August 30, 1813, a large war party of Upper Creeks overwhelmed the American Fort Mims in southern Alabama and killed more than 350 people within the stockade, bringing swift reprisals from federal troops and militia. Lower Creeks, as well as Cherokees and Choctaws, flocked to assist the Americans against the Red Sticks, and on March 27, 1814, they helped an army of several thousand Tennessee militia, led by Andrew Jackson, almost wipe out the Upper Creeks, under their war chief, Menawa, at

Horseshoe Bend on the Tallapoosa River. More than a thousand Red Stick warriors died fighting or trying to escape. A few months later, Jackson called a treaty meeting with the pro-American Lower Creeks and, despite the help they had given him against their relatives, forced them to cede almost eight million acres, or approximately two-thirds of the territory of the entire Creek nation, to the United States.

The surviving Red Sticks and their families were dispersed and in hiding

George Catlin's portrait of a Creek woman, Tchow-ee-put-o-kaw, wearing a necklace of turquoise disks. By the time he made this painting in 1836, many Creeks had abandoned the traditional style of native-made dress shown here in favor of European clothing.

and had no power to object to the surrender. Eventually, many of them settled among bitterly anti-American Seminoles in Spanish-owned Florida, only to be caught up in border friction between the Seminoles and marauding whites from Georgia, who claimed to identify blacks living among the Seminoles as runaway slaves and tried to recapture them.

The conflicts soon escalated into a vicious racial war. In 1818, Jackson, again at the head of an American army supported by Lower Creek auxiliaries, marched into Florida, attacking the Red Stick émigrés and the Seminoles, burning their villages, and capturing Pensacola and St. Marks from the Spaniards. The war was quickly over, and in February 1819 the chastened Spaniards ceded Florida to the United States.

Merging gradually with the Seminoles who were scattered in villages throughout Florida, the Red Sticks enjoyed little peace under the Americans. By the 1830s, they, along with the Seminoles, were at war again with the United States, resisting attempts by Ameri-

Menawa (The Great Warrior), an Upper Creek chief and leader of the Red Sticks in the Creek War of 1813–14. Defeated by Andrew Jackson at the Battle of Horseshoe Bend, he was shot seven times and believed killed. Somehow, he crawled off the battlefield and recovered, only to surrender and lose his land and possessions. A steadfast opponent of removal, he was relocated with his tribe to what is now Oklahoma in 1836.

A Seminole village in Florida in 1842.

OPPOSITE: *Osceola, the Seminole resistance leader. Until he was treacherously seized at a truce meeting under a white flag, Osceola proved the equal of the U.S. Army. "We disclaim . . . the 'glory' of this achievement of American generalship," wrote one newspaper of his capture. "If practised towards a civilized foe, [it] would be characterized as a violation of all that is noble and generous in war."*

can armies to move them from Florida to the prairies of the western part of the Arkansas Territory (present-day Oklahoma), beyond the Mississippi River. In 1837, after luring him to a parley under a flag of truce, the Americans seized Osceola, originally a member of a refugee Red Stick band and the ablest and boldest of the Seminole leaders. The next year, Osceola died in prison.

The conflict, waged mostly in the peninsula's forests and malarial swamps, was, from the government's point of view, the longest, costliest, and least successful Indian war in American history. Lasting almost seven years, from 1835 to 1842, it cost the army fifteen hundred lives and the United States between forty and sixty million dollars. More than four thousand Seminoles were captured and sent west, but in the end the government gave up in exhaustion, leaving a number of related bands of Seminoles and Mikasukis in the fastnesses of the Everglades, where they continue to live today.

Meanwhile, after the War of 1812, most of the Cherokees, Choctaws, Creeks, and Chickasaws were still in their homelands and intended to remain there. Convinced that tribal survival in the South depended not only on peaceful coexistence with the whites but also on the adoption of white ways, the leadership of the nations made determined efforts to speed the acculturation of their people. Although many Cherokees clung tenaciously to their traditions, a large part of the population of that nation quickly became the most acculturated—or, as the whites called it, "the most civilized"—of the southern tribes.

The process began in earnest with the arrival of Moravian missionaries in 1801, followed by missionaries from the American Board of Commissioners for Foreign

Missions in 1817. The latter settled among the Cherokees and taught them the rudiments of the white man's practice of agriculture, domestic arts, and English reading and writing, as well as Christianity. Acculturation was quickened in the 1820s by the remarkable talents of Sequoyah, a Cherokee veteran of Jackson's army at Horseshoe Bend, who invented a Cherokee alphabet

and reduced the nation's spoken language to writing. Literacy grew at a rapid rate among the Indians, and in 1828 the tribe began to publish a newspaper, *The Phoenix,* with columns in Cherokee and English. It was edited by Elias Boudinot, a well-educated Cherokee who had attended a missionary school in Connecticut.

In the same year, the Cherokees adopted a new political system, basing it largely on the model of the American Republic. At a constitutional convention, tribal delegates established a tribranch government, with a principal chief, a bicameral council, and a court system. John Ross, a mixed-blood leader, was popularly elected principal chief and held the position until his death in 1866. Educated by the missionaries, Ross spoke little Cherokee and dressed like a white southern planter. He owned trading and ferry businesses, as well as a large plantation and slaves. But he was committed to his people, and the full-blood Cherokees were his staunchest supporters. Under his leadership, annuity payments gained in the ceding of lands were used to construct a national capital, New Echota, with imposing buildings for the different branches of the government. Although many Cherokees resented the proliferation of rules and regulations, the advocates of change held sway, creating a strong agriculture-based economy and a sophisticated political system with progressive leaders who could argue the white man's laws.

In varying degrees, the Choctaws, Chickasaws, and Creeks followed a similar road to acculturation, learning from missionaries, educating their young at schools, creating constitutional governments modeled after that of the United

Sequoyah, also known as George Gist or Guess, the inventor of the Cherokee system of writing. His syllabary, or alphabet of syllables, which he holds here, was received at first with skepticism by the Cherokees, but after a demonstration of its ability to convey messages from a family in Arkansas to their Eastern Cherokee relatives, it caught on quickly. In only a few months, thousands of Cherokees were using it.

The front page of the first issue of the Cherokee Phoenix, *published on February 21, 1828, at the Cherokee capital of New Echota. A weekly newspaper printed in both English and Sequoyah's syllabary, it ran until the Georgia militia forced its closure in 1835.*

States, and developing stable agricultural economies. In each of the tribes, prosperous Indian elites emerged, wearing fashionable clothes, living in two-story plantation houses, owning slaves and handsome carriages, and rivaling the lifestyle of their most affluent white neighbors. To non-Indian Northern visitors and writers, the four nations, together with the Seminoles, became known as the Five Civilized Tribes.

To white southerners, however, they were still Indians, and to Georgians especially, their presence within the state, independent of the state government and its laws and occupying huge areas of rich, fertile lands, was intolerable. In 1802, Georgia had ceded its western lands to the federal government in return for a promise to extinguish all Indian land titles in Georgia and eject all Indians from the state. It had not been done, but in 1817 Jackson bribed and coerced several Cherokee leaders into signing a treaty in which a third of the Cherokees' territory was exchanged for a tract of equal

JOHN ROSS/UNITED KEETOOWAH BAND OF CHEROKEE IN OKLAHOMA

"The word 'Keetoowah' basically originated from God, that gave us our name, but the word 'Keetoowah' has always been the name the Cherokee people have called themselves. The word 'Cherokee' does not have a meaning in our language. The word 'Cherokee' came from the words in the Choctaw language meaning the inhabitants of the cave country. And the word 'Keetoowah' means principal people or the chosen ones in our language."

John Ross, the principal chief of the Cherokee nation. By the time he assumed that office in 1828, his people were already under pressure to move westward. From 1830 until 1838, Ross visited Washington, D.C., repeatedly, leading a determined but unsuccessful campaign to prevent the exile of his nation from its ancestral homeland in the Southeast.

324

size in the western part of the Arkansas Territory. Emigration to the new lands was voluntary, and by 1835 nearly six thousand Cherokees had willingly moved west.

At the same time, pressure was also put on the Creeks to give up their lands in Georgia. In 1825, the mixed-blood William McIntosh, the leading chief of the Lower Creek towns who had fought with Jackson against the Red Sticks, accepted a twenty-five-thousand-dollar bribe to persuade the Creeks to cede all their land in Georgia and vast tracts in Alabama in exchange for territory in Arkansas. Opothleyahola, leader of the Upper Creeks who opposed removal, reminded McIntosh that the Creek Council had voted a death sentence for any member of the nation who sold Creek land. Despite the warning, McIntosh and his supporters signed a treaty selling the Creeks' territory, and the Creek Council carried out its death sentence on the signers.

George Catlin painted this portrait of Tahchee, a Cherokee man, in 1836. Shown wearing a turban, a popular headgear among the Cherokees, Tahchee served as a guide for U.S. troops before the removal of the Cherokees in 1838.

Although the fraudulent treaty was rejected by President John Quincy Adams, another one was negotiated in which the Creeks were able to retain their extensive Alabama lands, but were forced to cede their territory in Georgia for acreage in the West. In 1828, some thirteen hundred Creeks migrated voluntarily from Georgia to the new country. The rest of the displaced Creeks joined their fellow Creeks in Alabama, where an English traveler described them as poverty stricken, hungry, and ill clothed, "wandering about like bees whose hive has been destroyed."

The election of Andrew Jackson to the presidency in 1828 was disastrous for the tribes. Jackson was committed to the removal, by force if necessary, of all Indians in the East to the spacious, still little-known "Great American Desert" west of the Mississippi River, which presumably no whites would ever wish to possess. There, his argument went, the tribes could live and develop as they wished, secure from the hostility of whites. Immediately after his election, the Georgia legislature passed a law extending the jurisdiction of the state's police powers, laws, and courts over the Cherokees who lived within Georgia and asked for Jackson's support. The action forced Jackson's hand. Increasing the pressure on the tribes to leave the East, his administration made the removal of the southern Indians a national issue, "the greatest question," some said, "that ever came before Congress, short of the question of peace and war."

In many ways, white American public opinion had changed since the philosophically enlightened period of the writing of the Declaration of Independence and the founding of the Republic. By the early nineteenth century, arrant nationalism and racism had struck deep roots among the majority of white Americans, and the southern Indians would not find safety by modeling themselves and their republics on the idealism of the American revolutionists. Despite their successful efforts to become acculturated, they were still regarded as members of an inferior race, no longer feared but possessing what the whites wanted. Under Jackson, they would fall victim to what in the late twentieth century would become known brutally, but candidly, as ethnic cleansing.

In 1829, gold was discovered on Cherokee lands, and thousands of whites, violating treaties, poured across the Indian nation's borders to stake claims. Removing its troops, the federal government gave a free hand to Georgia officials who, de-

Women of the southeastern Indian nations wove handsome shoulder bags with floral designs of multicolored beadwork. This example, which may have been made near the time of removal, is Cherokee.

Shown here in a computer-generated image is the two-acre main square of the Cherokee capital of New Town, Georgia, renamed New Echota in 1825. In 1835, it was the scene of the signing of a fraudulent treaty by a small minority of Cherokee chiefs who for five million dollars ceded all of the Cherokees' land in the East and agreed to move west. Their fatal action, eagerly accepted by the government as binding on the whole tribe, split the Cherokees and doomed the cause of those who were against removal.

In 1830, the Treaty of Dancing Rabbit Creek dispossessed the Choctaws from lands in Alabama and Mississippi, forcing most of them to move to what is now Oklahoma. To seal the agreement, this six-hundred-year-old pipe bowl from their Mississippian ancestors was used by the Choctaws who signed the treaty.

termined to force the Indians from their state, quickly passed laws making it illegal for Cherokees to mine gold, to testify against a white man, or to hold political assemblies for any purpose other than ceding land, thus making it impossible for a Cherokee to seek justice or the Indians' government to function. Cherokee appeals to Washington had little effect. Ignoring the Indians' plight, Jackson advised a Georgia senator to "build a fire under them. When it gets hot enough, they'll move."

In the fall of 1829, the Cherokee National Council, meeting in violation of the Georgia law, ordered the death penalty for anyone who sold tribal lands. It was too late. On May 28, 1830, Congress passed the Removal Act, directing the forced removal of the eastern tribes to the West.

The Choctaws, whose chief, Pushmataha, had kept his nation on the American side during the War of 1812, were the first to feel the cruelty of the legislation. Employing bribes and coercion, federal negotiators induced the tribe to sign the Treaty of Dancing Rabbit Creek in September 1830, agreeing to give up their lands in Alabama and Mississippi and move to western Arkansas. During the next four years, some four thousand of the thirteen thousand Choctaws who headed west died of hunger, disease, accidents, and exposure to freezing wintry weather on the long, difficult trek to their new homes. Another seven thousand managed to evade emigration, remaining in Mississippi and eventually becoming citizens of that state.

In 1832, the Creeks signed another treaty, this time surrendering all their land in Alabama. Although they were starving and filled with despair, a majority of the people at first refused to move. White land speculators, poor land-hungry families, and cotton planters needing new fields moved in, driving the Creeks from their homes and appropriating their property and livestock. Finally, bands of desperate Lower Creeks began to raid the whites, burning their houses and barns, stealing food, and killing settlers. In a painful reprise of the Creek civil war, McIntosh's old nemesis, Opothleyahola, though he was bitterly opposed to removal, assisted an American army against the troublemaking "hostiles." The government

Choctaw Indian Camp on the Mississippi River, near Natchez in the nineteenth century, by Karl Bodmer.

"rewarded" Opothleyahola by ordering the immediate removal of the entire tribe.

During the summer of 1836, eight hundred Creek "hostiles" in manacles and chains, together with their families, were forcibly removed by the army to western Arkansas (which, by act of Congress, had become the Indian Territory). Soon afterward, Opothleyahola and his followers also departed for the West. It was a terrible journey, in which thousands died along the way. At its conclusion, several Indians wrote to their guards, "We are men. . . . We have women and children, and why should we come like wild horses?" Altogether, it was estimated that the Creeks lost as much as 45 percent of their population of twenty-two thousand during their removal.

With the Choctaws and Creeks removed, the government turned its attention to the more acculturated, and therefore more troublesome, Cherokees. From 1830 to 1838, John Ross made repeated trips to Washington, attempting to forestall removal. He met many times with members of Congress and with President Jackson, with whom he had served during the Creek War, all to no avail. Twice, the Cherokee nation sought the protection of the Supreme Court. In 1831, it sued the state of Georgia to halt the illegal seizure of Cherokee property and to establish that the tribe was not subject to Georgia's jurisdiction. The Supreme Court dashed Cherokee hopes when it ruled in *Cherokee Nation v. Georgia* that the Court did not have jurisdiction in the matter. In his decision, however, Chief Justice John Marshall, an anti-Jacksonian and Federalist of the old school, recognizing the growth of the military power of the United States over that of the Indians, rendered a pointedly relevant, new definition of the relationship of the tribes to the American government. Henceforth, he wrote, they should be considered "domestic dependent nations" whose relationship to the "United States resembles that of a ward to his guardian." Although it implied that the government was obligated to protect the Cherokees, the Jackson administration ignored it.

In 1832, the Cherokees and their missionary and other white supporters brought a second case to the Supreme Court, *Worcester v. Georgia,* stemming from Georgia's arrest and imprisonment of Samuel A. Worcester and other missionaries charged with living among the Cherokees without se-

SAM PROCTER/CREEK

"I want to do something even if it's gonna be in a small way for all the people, for my Muskokee people. When I think about that, I think about Opothleyahola. I think about him, what he did say always comforts me. 'He says even though I'm gone, always remember, mention my name, and one of these days, there'll come a time that Muskokee people will live like they used to.' That's my desire. I know it's gonna happen. It may not be in my day and time, but we have generations and generations going, y' know. We have grandchildrens, and they're gonna have their grandchildrens, and they're going to be here. That's what I think about, that's what my heart lies upon."

Karl Bodmer painted Tshanny, a Choctaw Man, *in the removal period, near New Orleans.*

curing a state permit or swearing allegiance to Georgia. This time, Justice Marshall came down unmistakably on the side of the Indians, ruling that jurisdiction over the Cherokees belonged exclusively to the federal government, and that Georgia had no power to pass laws affecting the tribe. "The whole intercourse between the United States and this nation [the Cherokees]," he wrote, "is, by our constitution and laws, vested in the government of the United States."

The Cherokees were elated, believing that Georgia had been stripped of its power over them and that their lands and laws had been restored to their nation. Despite their jubilation, however, Jackson ignored the Court's decision and encouraged Georgia to do likewise. According to legend, Jackson remarked privately, "John Marshall has rendered his decision, now let him enforce it."

In 1833, the state of Georgia held a lottery of Cherokee land and property. Acculturated Indian leaders, including Ross and John Ridge, the son of Major Ridge, one of the nation's most prominent men, were among those who lost their plantations and had to move their families to Tennessee. Throughout the Cherokee lands in Georgia, full-bloods were evicted from their cabins and robbed of their fields and livestock. At New Echota, the government buildings were given away to holders of winning lottery tickets.

As the situation became more desperate, Major Ridge, his son John, and his nephew Elias Boudinot, who had opposed removal, lost heart and, convinced that bloodshed was the only alternative, changed their position. By 1834, the once-unified Cherokees were dividing into two bitterly distrusting factions, one under Major Ridge supporting removal, the other, led by Ross, opposed to it.

The following year, Ridge traveled to Washington and negotiated a treaty with the government, selling the Cherokees' lands for five million dollars. When he returned home, the Cherokees' National Council unanimously rejected the treaty. Nevertheless, the Ridge faction met secretly in New Echota and, although they knew the consequences, signed it.

A Cherokee man, sketched about 1820. He wears buckskin moccasins and leggings and a coat made from a trade blanket.

"I know I take my life in my hand, as our fathers have also done . . . ," said Elias Boudinot. "We can die, but the great Cherokee nation will be saved. . . . Oh, what is a man worth who will not dare to die for his people? Who is there that would not perish, if this great nation may be saved?"

Despite Ross's angry protests, the United States Senate ratified the New Echota treaty, which gave the Cherokees three years to give up their country and move west. During those years, Ross campaigned tirelessly, but without success, to have the treaty annulled. Meanwhile, although Ridge and his family and followers emigrated to the Indian Territory, the great majority of the Cherokee people, under Ross's leadership, made no

The Cherokee removal in 1838, during which thousands perished on what became known as the Trail of Tears, is pictured by the modern-day Native American artist Brummet Echohawk.

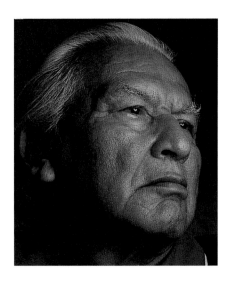

preparations to leave. Finally, in the summer of 1838, General Winfield Scott, who did not relish his assignment, arrived in Georgia with seven thousand troops and orders to remove the Cherokees by any means necessary.

Thousands of Cherokees were rounded up at bayonet point and held by the army at various camps to await the journey west. A few groups took to the forests and mountains and managed to evade the troops. Cherokee traditions tell of many who resisted and escaped and of heroes and heroines who sacrificed for others. One, a proud elder named Tsali, who was known to whites as Charley, killed a soldier who had brutally prodded Tsali's wife with a bayonet in one of the stockades. Escaping, Tsali and his wife and sons fled to join other Indian families who were hiding from the soldiers in the forests and caves of the Smoky Mountains. When General Scott heard of the soldier's death, he ordered troops to hunt down Tsali and his family.

Organizing a band of refugees, Tsali avoided capture, although the troops pursued him relentlessly through the mountains. Finally, when Scott learned that two more soldiers had been killed, he announced in frustration that he would abandon the search for all the other holdouts hiding in the mountains if Tsali and his sons would give themselves up. When he learned of this, Tsali turned himself in to save the rest of the people. A final cruel blow awaited him. The army forced Cherokees of Ridge's treaty party to form the firing squad that executed him, three of his sons, and a brother. True to his promise, Scott ignored some four hundred traditional Cherokees who remained in the mountainous country evading removal. Their descendants are still there today, recognized as the nation of Eastern Cherokees.

When the removal of those who were going west began, the hardships, physical exertions, and emotional trials of what to the Indians became known as the Trail of Tears claimed a heavy toll in lives. Receiving permission to take over the removal from the army, Ross organized the people into thirteen parties. Ross and his wife left Georgia with the last contingent. On the grueling forced march that took the parties an average of six months to complete, Ross's wife was among those who died of hunger, exposure, or despair. It is estimated that of the eighteen thousand Cherokees who were rounded up for the trip, approximately four thousand died in stockades or on the journey.

In the Indian Territory, the Cherokees slowly rebuilt the society and economy they had had in the East. The factionalism remained, however, and in 1839 Major Ridge, his son, and his nephew Elias Boudinot were assassinated for having signed the Treaty of New Echota. Meanwhile, during the winter of 1837–38, the last of the southern tribes, the Chickasaws, were removed to the Indian Territory from northern Mississippi and Alabama. They offered little resistance.

ROBERT BUSHYHEAD/CHEROKEE
"When Tsali gave himself to be martyred for his people, and when he died, he was a victor. He accomplished the thing which was uppermost in his mind, that his people might go free. Had he not done this, after the removal, after the soldiers returned, those hiding in the mountains were going to be hunted down and shot on sight. Now the story continues from there that after the return of the soldiers back into the area here from Oklahoma the Cherokees were set free. They would not be hunted down like animals."

OPPOSITE: *Once removed to the Indian Territory (present-day Oklahoma), the Cherokees began rebuilding their lives. This John Mix Stanley painting records a council of seventeen tribes held in the new Cherokee capital of Tahlequah in 1843 to promote goodwill between the Cherokees and other tribes who had been thrown together in the western country.*

Stand Watie, who had favored removal and was a bitter enemy of John Ross, raised a regiment of Cherokees who fought for the South during the Civil War. Promoted to general, he was given command of all pro-Southern Indian troops, leading them in more battles than were fought by any other Confederate unit west of the Mississippi River. When the war ended, Watie was the last Confederate general to surrender.

The Removal Act was also applied in the North. Many nations between the Ohio River and the Great Lakes were pushed west of the Mississippi River: Pontiac's Ottawas, Little Turtle's Miamis, Tecumseh's Shawnees, Black Hawk's Sauk and Foxes, Delawares, and others were first moved to present-day Iowa and Kansas, then finally into the Indian Territory with the southern tribes. Through the years, some nations, like the Menominees and most of the Senecas, successfully fought off removal, and groups of Miamis and others managed to return and reestablish themselves in the lands they had left.

In the East, five of the Six Nations of the Hodenosaunee still occupy lands that were part of the Iroquois domain before the coming of the Europeans. They, together with tribes and remnant bands overrun by whites from Maine to Georgia before the American Revolution, were little affected by the removal policy. Passamaquoddys, Abenakis, Wampanoags, Pequots, Piscataways, Shinnecocks, Nanticokes, Chickahominys, those who combined to become the Lumbees, and many others lived on in the East, unnoticed. And a division of the Choctaws, as well as Seminoles, Mikasukis, and Tsali's people, the Eastern Cherokees, together with small groups of Indians along the Gulf coast, successfully evaded or resisted removal and are still in the South.

The nations that were removed to the Indian Territory in the 1830s were soon torn apart again by the Civil War. Forced to take sides, some of the tribes raised troops for the South, and some for the North. The Cherokees, Creeks, and Seminoles had men fighting on both sides. Federal and Confederate armies overran the Indian Territory, shattering the prosperity that had begun to develop. When the war ended, Stand Watie, a Cherokee cavalry leader, was the last Confederate general to surrender.

In the following years, the Indians' lands in the territory were reduced, tribal councils outlawed, and the Indian Territory opened to white settlements. In 1907, with its white population far exceeding that of the Indians, the land which the government had exchanged with the tribes for their homelands in the South, to be theirs alone for "as long as the grass grows and the rivers run," became part of the new state of Oklahoma.

Except for its handle, this twill-plaited market basket, made by Eastern Cherokees and woven from split cane, is typical of traditional Cherokee basket making and design.

CHAPTER 7
STRUGGLE FOR

THE WEST

The Other Coast: California

During the eighteenth-century invasions of Indian lands in the East, seaborne European explorers, fur traders, and missionaries were simultaneously discovering—and disrupting—Indian nations inhabiting the lands of the Pacific coast, from the fog-shrouded Aleutian Islands in the north to the warm, oak-covered hills of southern California.

In the Aleutians, the invaders were Russians with their eyes not on lands but on the sleek furs of sea otters and seals that populated the rocky coastline. Invading Aleut villages, they seized the women and children, holding them hostage for months of abuse while they forced the men to hunt otters until they had enough pelts to ransom their families. When one area was hunted to exhaustion, the Russians moved on to a new area, first eastward across the Aleutians, then along the coastline of southeastern Alaska, and eventually to northern California, forcing the expert Aleutian hunters to migrate with them.

Over the years, groups of Aleuts resisted what often amounted to slavery under the harsh rule of despotic Russian masters. In the Aleutian Islands alone, fourteen thousand Aleuts lost their lives from the mid–eighteenth to the mid–nineteenth century, trying in vain to regain their freedom. In time, Russian missionaries converted many of the surviving Aleuts to the Greek Orthodox Church, because, according to one of their traditions, the Aleuts finally became convinced that "any religion which can save the Russians must be very strong."

Southeast of the Aleutians, occupying ruggedly beautiful coastal territories from Alaska's Panhandle to northern California, Tlingits, Tsimshians, Haidas, Kwakiutls, Nootkas, and other Northwest tribes were among the wealthiest of all the

OVERLEAF: In 1834 the artist George Catlin accompanied a regiment of U.S. dragoons on an expedition to the southern plains and recorded this amusing scene of a herd of buffalo, pursued by Comanche hunters, breaking through the dragoons' disciplined line of march.

An Aleut hunter wearing the traditional decorated, wooden-peaked hat that kept the salt spray from his eyes paddles his kayak past a herd of sea lions off one of the Pribilof Islands in the Bering Sea. The scene was painted by Louis Choris, a Russsian artist who accompanied Otto von Kotzebue on a voyage to Alaska in 1816.

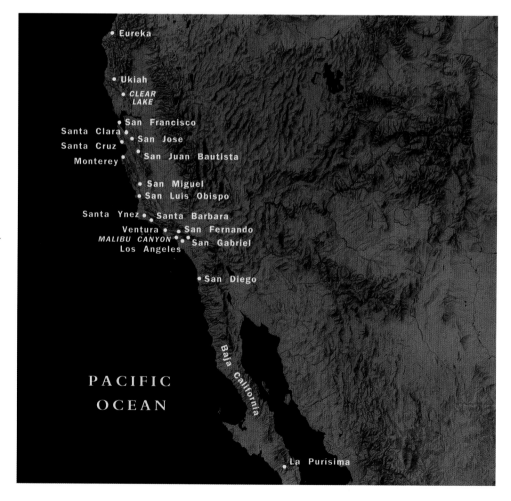

OPPOSITE: This imposing Tlingit warrior, armed with a bow and with a dagger hanging at his side, is clad in a visored wooden helmet, a wooden collar across his throat, and body armor fashioned from cedar slats. Such protective coverings, used by Haidas, Tsimshians, and Tlingits, bore heraldic designs denoting membership in special groups. The drawing was made by Tomás de Suria, an artist with a Spanish expedition under Alejandro Malaspina to the Pacific Northwest coast in 1791.

Inuit effigies of birds, fashioned from wood or parts of birds, honored these creatures whose spirits helped the people. Shown are, above, a carved woodpecker affixed to a dancer's baton by a spring of whale cartilage, which made it peck the staff during a dance, and, below, a charm made from the head of a loon.

The peoples of the coastal and interior Pacific Northwest carved in many different media, including wood, stone, horn, antler, and bone. The figure above of a mother and child, about seven and a half inches high, was made from the antler of an elk by a coastal Chinookan Indian near the mouth of the Columbia River.

Exquisite bowls like the one at right—about eight inches in diameter—were made by peoples of the Northwest from the horns of mountain sheep. The hard, spiral horns were first boiled or steamed to allow them to be shaped, carved, and engraved with designs.

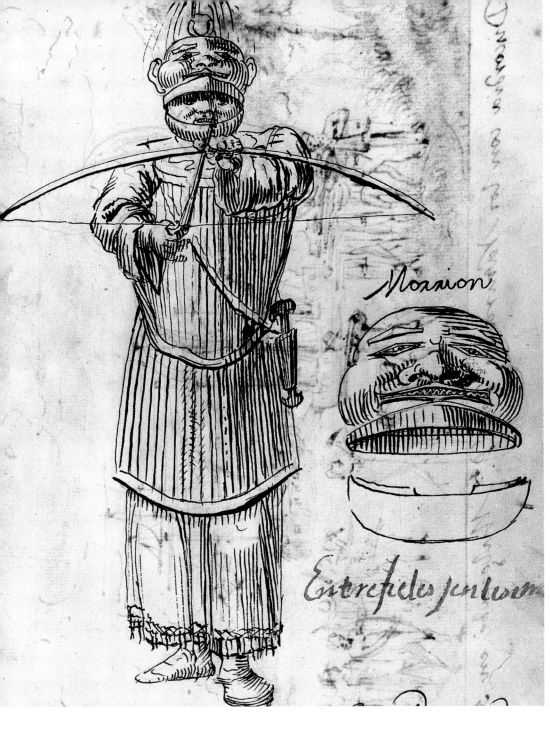

Morrion

Entrefiles jenturin

Indian nations, with a spectacular material culture and powerful leaders. Although they were maritime oriented and practiced no agriculture, they enjoyed huge harvests of fish and shellfish from the sea and rivers, as well as game and wild foods from the lush forests, which enabled them to create prosperous and complex societies. Noted as traders and raiders who plied the coastal waters in large canoes from village to village, they were among the few Indian peoples who put a value on personal wealth, which in their case included captives as well as material goods. Strengthened by a rich spiritual life and the bonds of clans, their societies were powerful enough to withstand the Russians, and—though greatly influenced by white traders, with whom they had occasional armed conflicts—they were far enough from Europe to make it into the twentieth century still in possession of most of their homelands.

This elaborately carved spear is Tlingit in origin. Like other tribes from the Northwest coast region, the Tlingit carved many household and functional objects, including weapons. Spears were used by the Tlingit in war and in hunting sea mammals such as sea otters, sea lions, and fur seals, which provided food, clothing, and other tribal necessities.

habitants de Californie.

This 1822 lithograph of a group of northern California Indian neophytes, probably Costanoans and Coast Miwoks, at the Spanish mission San Francisco was based on a watercolor made six years earlier by Louis Choris, an artist who visited the mission with members of Otto von Kotzebue's Russian naval expedition.

Farther down the coast, in one of the most densely populated areas of North America north of Mexico, were the Indian nations of California. Speaking as many as eighty mutually unintelligible languages, as well as several hundred dialects of those languages, the many different California tribes, with a population of more than three hundred thousand, were divided into "tribelets" and bands—smaller units that lived under hereditary family chiefs or headmen in several thousand separate and politically autonomous communities, ranging from permanent villages to transient camps and wickiup settlements. Although they lived close to each other and often infringed on each other's territory, the relatively small egalitarian units—usually made up of no more than fifty to five hundred persons, and in which a majority generally decided most issues—found it difficult to organize for or wage war. When it occurred—usually over poaching or another infringement of territorial rights, the abduction of women and children, or the avenging of poisoning or other effects of suspected witchcraft—it was small-scale, formal, and quickly over. Often, the men of both sides lined up opposite each other, discharged their arrows at one another, and then returned to their villages.

Like the Northwest coastal nations, the California Indians did not practice agriculture, but lived well by fishing, hunting small game and birds, and gathering an enormous variety of wild foods. Among many of the tribes, acorns from the California oaks, ground and cooked into a soup, mush, or bread, formed the staple of the peoples' diet.

Other favorite foods in California's diverse environments ranged from deer, rabbit, quail, and salmon to buckeyes, sugar pines, and hazelnuts; tules, cattails, and camas roots; ryegrass seeds; and wild plums, grapes, and manzanita berries.

In the south, ranging along the coast from the area of present-day San Luis Obispo to Malibu Canyon, as well as on the Santa Barbara

A computer-generated re-creation of a Chumash village of large domed dwellings built beneath the Coast Range along the southern California shore near present-day Santa Barbara. Constructed of thatched grass, they could each comfortably house a large extended family.

Channel Islands and extending inland to the San Joaquin Valley, were the unusually large villages of the Chumash nation, one of California's biggest tribes. Sometimes containing a thousand or more inhabitants, the villages were composed of ceremonial grounds, semisubterranean sweat houses, cleared playing fields, storage huts, and round thatched dwelling houses, up to fifty feet in diameter and able to hold as many as seventy people.

Most Chumash people were gatherers, hunters, and fishermen. Among those with specialized skills and knowledge were curers, astrologers, canoe builders, basket and bead makers, soapstone carvers, woodworkers, and rock artists. Their outstanding achievements included the making of unique, seagoing plank boats, the carving of steatite figures, and the creation of some of the finest polychrome rock paintings in North America. In addition, the Chumash were at the heart of a regional trading economy that used shell beads for currency, with their manufacture and distribution controlled by their government. Numbering almost twenty thousand people, and speaking at least six Chumash dialects in their extensive territory, they worked, prayed, gave birth, and died on lands that had been occupied and harvested by their ancestors for thousands of years.

In 1769, the Franciscan missionary Father Junipero Serra and a Spanish army reached the country of the Ipai and Tipai tribes in the vicinity of present-day San

The Quechan Indians pictured here were Yuman-speaking farmers who lived in the hot bottomlands along both sides of the lower Colorado River in the area of present-day Yuma, Arizona. After revolting successfully against Spanish settlers in their country in 1781, they avoided Euro-American domination until the United States built Fort Yuma in their territory in 1852. The surrounding land became Fort Yuma reservation in 1884, and the Quechan continue to live there today.

Indians living in the region of present-day Los Angeles were rounded up by the Spaniards and forced to live at the mission San Gabriel, pictured here by Ferdinand Deppe in 1832 after a sketch he had made in 1828. In the foreground at right is a typical thatched hut of the local Indians, whom the Spaniards named Gabrielinos.

Diego and the U.S.–Baja California border and established the first in a chain of twenty-one missions that extended up the coast to San Francisco. When he reached the Chumash territory, Father Serra failed to recognize the complex religious underpinnings of the society that had served the Indians and provided harmony and beauty to their lives for generations. "[B]elieve me," he wrote, "when I saw their general behavior, their pleasing ways and engaging manners, my heart was broken to think that they were still deprived of the light of the Holy Gospel." Beginning in 1772 at today's San Luis Obispo, he founded five missions in the Chumash territory.

Once more, as almost everywhere else in the hemisphere where Europeans invaded Indian countries, missionaries went to work, undermining and destroying the fabric of centuries-old indigenous societies. To Father Serra and the other Spanish missionaries in California—as to the missionaries in Mexico, Peru, Florida, New England, and elsewhere—the only tolerated religion was Christianity. The spiritual life of the Indians was deemed no religion at all, but instead heathen superstition and sorcery.

Serra sent out Spanish soldiers to the Indian villages to gather up all the people and bring them, by force if necessary, into the missions. There, regimented, policed

by the missionaries and troops, and severely punished for infractions or resistance, they were converted, taught trades, and after a period of time, assigned plots of land to become Christian farmers and laborers—in effect, slave workers for the missions and other Spanish interests. Few of the native Californians came to the mission of their own free will. Once they were converted, the recruits, or neophytes, as they were called, were not free to leave. In 1878, as an old man, a Kamia Indian named Janitin from the San Diego area provided an interviewer with a rare recollection of a neophyte's experiences:

> I and two of my relatives went down . . . to the beach . . . to catch clams. . . . We saw two men on horseback coming rapidly towards us; my relatives were . . . afraid and they fled with all speed. . . . It was too late . . . they overtook me and lassoed and dragged me for a long distance . . . their horses running. . . .
>
> When we arrived at the mission, they locked me in a room for a week; the father . . . [told] me that he would make me a Christian. . . . One day they threw water on my head and gave me salt to eat, and with this the interpreter told me that now I was a Christian and that I was called Jesus. . . .
>
> The following day after my baptism, they took me to work with the other Indians, and they put me to cleaning a milpa [cornfield] of maize. . . . I cut my foot and could not continue working. . . . Every day they lashed me . . . because I did not finish. . . .
>
> And thus I existed . . . until I found a way to escape; but I was tracked and they caught me like a fox. . . . They lashed me until I lost consciousness. . . . For several days I could not raise myself from the floor where they had laid me, and I still have on my shoulders the marks of the lashes.

Given Spanish names and dressed in blue uniforms, the neophytes worked in the mission's fields and shops, farming, caring for livestock, tanning hides, and producing candles, bricks, tiles, shoes, saddles, soap, and other necessities for the mission. When punished, they were whipped with barbed lashes; put in stocks, hobbles, or solitary confinement without water; branded; mutilated; or even executed. "The treatment shown to the Indians is the most cruel I have ever read in history," wrote a disapproving friar at California's mission San Miguel to the viceroy of Mexico in 1799. "For the slightest things they receive heavy floggings, are shackled, and put in the stocks,

TONY ROMERO/CHUMASH
"The Chumash never had clocks, never had time, so life was just a paradise here, and when they had to change from Paradise to . . . I call it incarceration. . . . You speak of the churches, all Indian people will tell you there weren't no churches, they were better understood as fortresses where they were housed. . . . There was nothing special about any Indian, unless he was an excellent saddle-maker, somebody that made himself famous by doing what the Spanish taught him to be, or if you're a good plasterer or brickmaker, whatever the chores were, then you were known for your talent, other than that, you were just a plain old Indian."

An illustration by the Russian artist Louis Choris depicts a group of California "Mission Indians," whose attire showed a mixture of European and indigenous influences and who, under pressure from the Spaniards, had all but lost their tribal identity. Here, they are shown, apparently unobserved by the priests, playing the stick game, a traditional gambling game forbidden by the missionaries.

OPPOSITE: *The secularization of the California missions by the Mexican government in 1834 gave little real freedom to the Indians. Thousands had died, and others, left impoverished and destitute by the missionaries, were exploited and ill treated by wealthy landowners who took over the missions' property. This illustration of an Indian in Baja California was made five years after the closing of the missions.*

and treated with so much cruelty that they are kept whole days without a drink of water." For his complaints in behalf of the Indians, the friar was declared insane and taken out of California by a guard of soldiers.

At the missions, Indian men and women, including husbands and wives, were forced to live separately, and unmarried women, who were frequently preyed on by soldiers at neighboring presidios, as well as by Spanish mission personnel, were sequestered in conventlike barracks. Inadequate and strange food to which the Indians were not accustomed, poor shelter and sanitation, disastrous epidemics of malaria, smallpox, and other diseases, despair, punishments, and cultural loss all contributed to a genocidal death rate among the neophytes.

On a number of occasions, desperate but unsuccessful rebellions flared against the Spaniards. In 1775, some eight hundred Ipai and Tipai Indians from nine villages united to burn the San Diego mission. In the uprising, which took a year to put down, a priest and two other Spaniards were killed. Ten years later, an Indian medicine woman named Toypurina led an unsuccessful attempt to destroy the San Gabriel mission east of Los Angeles. Other revolts broke out among the Costanoan Indians at the San Jose, Santa Clara, San Juan Bautista, and Santa Cruz missions and, most spectacularly, among the Chumash Indians at the Santa Ynez, La Purísima, and Santa Barbara missions.

In 1824, the Chumash destroyed part of the Santa Ynez mission and, reinforced by Indians from San Fernando, captured La Purísima, mounting a defense with captured Spanish cannons and swivel guns that held off attacking soldiers. When word of the uprising spread, the Chumash neophytes at Santa Barbara armed themselves and in a several-hour fight drove off a body of troops. After sacking that mission, the Indians fled to the hills. A month later, a cease-fire ended the siege of the Indians at La Purísima, while other soldiers pursued the refugees from Santa Barbara who had been

joined by rebellious neophytes from San Fernando. After a number of skirmishes, a truce was negotiated, and many of the refugees were rounded up and returned to their missions. In the end, seven La Purísima neophytes were executed by the missionaries and soldiers, and four were sentenced to ten years of chain-gang labor.

Finally, in 1834, sixty-five years after the start of the Spanish enslavement of California Indians, Mexico, which won its independence from Spain in 1821, secularized the missions and ended the Church's right to imprison Indian people. Thousands were free to leave. "When all the Mission Indians heard the cry of freedom, they said, 'Now they no longer keep us here by force,'" recalled Fernando Librado, a surviving Chumash. "Some people stayed on the mission lands and some went home to their rancherias. . . ." But thousands more would not see their homeland. At the Santa Barbara mission alone, more than forty-six hundred Chumash names filled the burial registry. Their bodies were put in large pits near the church, denied either traditional or Christian burial.

For the survivors, there would be no return to their ancient, peaceful world. Their original home villages had been destroyed and their

**ED CASTILLO/
CAHUILLA-LUISEÑO**

"The rich embroidery of Indian
cultures throughout California can
offer California's newcomers,
everyone who came after us, an
insight into how to live at peace with
this land. See, I think this land will
change you. I don't think that
outsiders have been able to change it
as much as they thought they had.
Certainly Americans today are much
different than Europeans, and I think
that the lesson for all of us to learn is
that Indian society offers us a way to
live in peace and harmony with this
land, and bring us back to balance.
We've been way out of balance for a
long time. Now it's time to listen to
California's first children, and we'll
tell you how we lived here. We don't
believe we've migrated here. Our
Creation stories tell us that we were
made right here. This land was given
to us. We are now sharing the land
with others, not through our own
choice, but the reality of our lives is
that we must share it, and we're
willing to do that if you are willing to
listen."

lands taken by Mexicans. The missions had been transformed into Mexican rancheros—large private kingdoms overspreading what had been mission properties. Able to do nothing but watch and try to survive the new upheavals, a freed neophyte from the Dolores mission at San Francisco voiced the helplessness that many Indians felt:

I am very old . . . my people were once around me like the sands of the shore . . . many . . . many. They have all passed away. They have died like the grass . . . they have gone to the mountains. I do not complain, the antelope falls with the arrow. I had a son. I loved him. When the palefaces came he went away. I do not know where he is. I am a Christian Indian. I am all that is left of my people. I am alone.

Left with few choices for survival, most former neophytes became feudal serfs, or peons, on the Mexican ranch estates. Then, by the Treaty of Guadalupe Hidalgo that ended the Mexican War in 1848, the United States expanded to the Pacific Ocean. California passed from Mexican to American hands just as gold was discovered in the northern California territory of the Nisenan Indians. The rush of gold seekers over-

whelmed populations of Indians in the interior valleys, foothills, and mountainous areas of California, who for decades had successfully resisted or evaded capture and imprisonment in the Spanish missions. Now a new, and equally deadly, age of peril faced the tribes that had been spared.

Miners trespassed on Indian lands, overrunning hunting and gathering grounds, invading villages, and seizing Indian women. Parties of whites opened fire for sport on defenseless men, women, and children, wiping out entire camps and rancherias of innocent people. Women were hauled back to white settlements to be used as concubines, while Indian children were kidnapped to be sold as slaves. For the whites, it was open season on Indians, whom they contemptuously called diggers, because of their use of a digging stick with which they gathered roots. For the Indians, it was as close to genocide as any tribal people had faced, or would face, on the North American continent.

One of the most sensational massacres was the deliberate work of United States Army forces in California. It occurred in 1850 at Clear Lake, east of Ukiah in the northern part of the state, where two abusive Americans, Charles Stone and Andrew Kelsey, had captured hundreds of Pomo Indians and forced them to work on a cattle ranch they had taken over three years earlier from Mexicans. William Benson, a Pomo chief, later described the conditions of his people's servitude on the Americans' ranch:

> About twenty old people died during the winter from starvation. From severe whipping, four died. A nephew of an Indian lady who was living with Stone was shoot [sic] to death by Stone. . . . When a father or mother of young girl was asked to bring the girl to his house by Stone or Kelsey, if this order was not obeyed, he or her would be whipped or hung by the hands. . . . Many of the old men and women died from fear and starvation. . . .

One day, Shuk and Xasis, two Pomo men working the cattle herds, lost one of Kelsey's horses while trying to rustle a cow for their hungry families. Afraid of the inevitable punishment, they met in council to decide what to do. Chief Benson continued with his account:

> All the men . . . gathered in Xasis' house. Here they debated all night. Shuk and Xasis wanted to kill Stone and Kelsey. They said Stone and Kelsey would kill them as soon as they [found] out . . . the horse was [gone].

The following day after my baptism, they took me to work with the other Indians, and they put me to cleaning a milpa [cornfield] of maize.

—JANITIN, A KAMIA INDIAN

This picture, accompanying an 1839 history of California by Alexander Forbes, a British consul in Mexico, purported to show Indians— possibly Maidus of the northeastern part of the present-day state—inside a semisubterranean earth-covered dance or council house taking a "hot air bath," or purifying sweat.

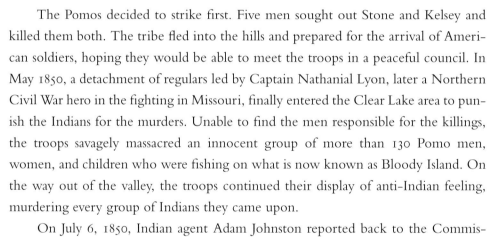

In many parts of California, acorns, converted into various dishes, were a staple in the Indians' diet. In this 1902 photograph, a Hoopa woman in northern California pours water from a basket cup to leach the toxicity from meal she is making from acorns.

The last survivor of the Yahi-Yana tribe, Ishi became an overnight celebrity when he was discovered in the foothills at Oroville, California, in 1911. Viewed as "the last wild Indian," he was taken to San Francisco, where he was studied by Alfred Kroeber and other anthropologists until his death in 1916. In this 1914 photograph, Ishi demonstrates a call which Yana hunters had used to lure rabbits.

The Pomos decided to strike first. Five men sought out Stone and Kelsey and killed them both. The tribe fled into the hills and prepared for the arrival of American soldiers, hoping they would be able to meet the troops in a peaceful council. In May 1850, a detachment of regulars led by Captain Nathanial Lyon, later a Northern Civil War hero in the fighting in Missouri, finally entered the Clear Lake area to punish the Indians for the murders. Unable to find the men responsible for the killings, the troops savagely massacred an innocent group of more than 130 Pomo men, women, and children who were fishing on what is now known as Bloody Island. On the way out of the valley, the troops continued their display of anti-Indian feeling, murdering every group of Indians they came upon.

On July 6, 1850, Indian agent Adam Johnston reported back to the Commissioner of Indian Affairs in Washington on the catastrophic situation in California:

The majority of the tribes are kept in constant fear on account of the indiscriminate and inhumane massacre of their people. . . . They become alarmed at the immence [*sic*] flood of immigration which spread over their country. . . . It was quite incomprehensible to them.

During the following decade, California newspapers, some boastfully, some with a twinge of conscience or shame, documented many of the atrocities. In February 1860, the *Northern Californian* in Union (today's Arcata) published a story, headlined "Indiscriminate Massacre of Indians—Women and Children Butchered," with the details of the slaughter with hatchets and axes of 188 peaceful Indian men, women, and children in their villages on Humboldt Bay. Resenting the newspaper's criticism of the murders, the whites in Union threatened the youthful editor—twenty-three-year-old Bret Harte—and forced him to flee town. Other papers like Eureka's

Fernando Librado, whose Chumash name was Kitsepawit, was born into the California mission system in 1805, lived to see its end, and ultimately worked with anthropologists to record his knowledge of the traditional ways of his people. In addition to his autobiography, he helped produce many volumes on Chumash history and culture before he died in 1916 at the age of 111.

Humboldt Times carried more typical headlines: "Good Haul of Diggers," "Thirty-eight Bucks Killed," "Forty Squaws and Children Taken," "Band Exterminated."

In the 1850s, the demand for agricultural labor was so great that Californians and their courts winked at Indian slavery, though black slavery was banned in the state. A decade later, after post–Civil War legislation outlawed all forms of slavery in the nation, machines and unemployed miners replaced the Indian workforce in California's agriculture. By that time, the barbarities of generations of Spaniards, Mexicans, and Americans, repeated waves of epidemics, years of starvation, overwhelming assaults on the tribes' subsistence, life, and culture, and the complete absence of legal protection had reduced the state's Indian population by 90 percent, from approximately 310,000 in 1769 to 30,000 at the end of the gold rush. (It would drop even further, in 1900 reaching a low of between 10,000 and 20,000, before rising again through the twentieth century.)

In an interview in his old age, the Chumash survivor Fernando Librado, originally from the area of present-day Ventura, exemplified the tenacity of spirit that had sustained the California Indians:

> Upon my last visit to Ventura I saw the last of the Ventura Indians. [They] were living in a tiny hut east of the mouth of the . . . river. . . . One of the old men told me that they were very glad that I was not ashamed to talk the Indian language. They told me to continue in use of it and to keep the beliefs; if I did so, I would live a long time.

Fernando Librado lived to be 111 years old, sadly marking the passing of most of his people:

> I once went over to Donociana's house. . . . I wanted to learn the Swordfish Dance. After the meal I asked her to teach me the old dances, saying, "For you are the only ones left who know the old dances." Donociana began to cry, and I left saying nothing more.

I am very old . . . my people were once around me like the sands of the shore. . . . They have all passed away. They have died like the grass . . . they have gone to the mountains. . . . I am all that is left of my people. I am alone.

—FREED NEOPHYTE FROM THE DOLORES MISSION

Diné: The Long Walk

From Fort Defiance the Navajos started on their journey. . . . Women and children traveled on foot. That's why we call it the Long Walk. It was inhuman because the Navajos, if they got tired and couldn't continue to walk further, were just shot down. . . . They had to keep walking all the time, day after day . . . for about 18 or 19 days . . . through all kinds of hardships, like tiredness and having injuries. And when those things happened, the people would hear gun shots in the rear. But they couldn't do anything about it. They just felt sorry for the ones being shot.

HOWARD GORMAN, A DINÉ ELDER

Far inland from California, the high desert plateaus and red-rock mesas, buttes, and canyons of northeastern Arizona and northwestern New Mexico were home to

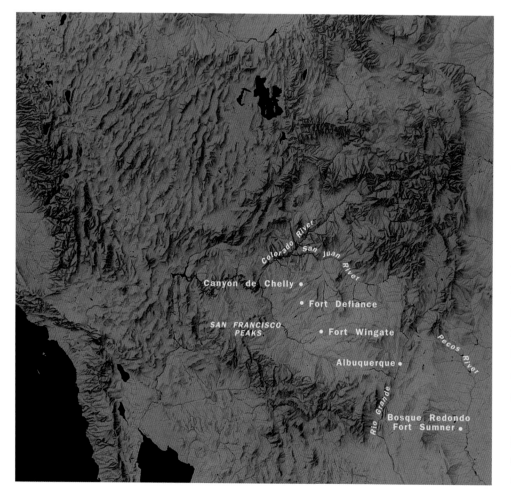

some twelve thousand Athapascan-speaking Diné, or Navajo, people. Recent migrants from the northwestern part of the continent who settled on ancestral lands of the Hopi, Zuñi, and Pueblo peoples in the fifteenth or sixteenth century—just ahead of the arrival of the Spaniards in the Southwest—the Diné adapted quickly. Spanish missionaries pressured the formerly nomadic people to become a nation of pastoral sheepherders. Adopting the new culture, the Diné grew gardens and orchards and built up large flocks of sheep and goats, expressing themselves by weaving beautiful clothing and blankets from the wool of the sheep.

When the white Americans gained possession of the Southwest after the Mexican War, the Diné were expected once again to change

This painting of Diné (Navajo) Indians was made by H. B. Möllhausen, a member of a United States surveying expedition in the Southwest in 1853. Although inaccurate in some details, it shows the handsome, striped "chief's blankets" that were the hallmark of Navajo weaving and were a much sought-after trade item in the mid-nineteenth century.

their way of life. In 1851, the United States built Fort Defiance in the heart of the Diné country. Suddenly, an Indian community that depended on grazing land—a scarce commodity in the arid country—was competing for pasture with the horses, mules, and cattle of the U.S. Army. Manuelito, the determined head chief of the Diné, complained to the steely commander of the fort, Major William T. H. Brooks:

> Your army has horses and wagons, mules and many soldiers. They are capable of hauling in feed for their own livestock. We . . . have only our feet, and must take our sheep and cattle wherever there is good grazing. . . . That land around the fort has been ours for many years.

Maintaining that his troops would continue to use the Indians' pasturage, by force if necessary, Brooks decided to punish Manuelito's defiance before it got out of hand. In May 1858, a detail of soldiers, under orders from Brooks, shot sixty head of Manuelito's livestock and drove off the rest. Marching into the fort, the incensed Diné leader spoke to the major:

> The water there is mine, not yours, and the same with the grass. Even the ground it grows from belongs to me, not to you. I will not let you have these things.

The tension soon led to fighting. In October 1858, troops from Fort Defiance, supported by 160 Zuñi mercenaries, burned Manuelito's village and fields. The blow only stiffened Manuelito's resolve to prevail over the Americans. "We will stop this suffering!" he announced. "I will lead the Diné. We will make war and drive the white men from our land!"

When the Diné were first created, four mountains and four rivers were pointed out to us, inside of which we should live.

—BARBONCITO

The Diné resistance fighter Manuelito, tall and blanket-wrapped, is seen at the far right of this group of Navajo men, photographed about 1883.

On April 30, 1860, a thousand Navajos, or Diné, led by Manuelito and Barboncito, a strong medicine man and war leader, attacked Fort Defiance, almost overrunning it before being driven off. During the next year, Navajo fighting men resisted retaliatory strikes by American troops. Finally, the outbreak of the Civil War caused the withdrawal of soldiers to the East and the abandonment of Fort Defiance.

It was only temporary. By 1863, volunteer regiments from the western states and territories had taken the place of the withdrawn regulars, and newly built Forts Wingate and Canby threatened the Navajos. That year, General James H. Carleton, head of the Military Department of New Mexico, ordered his subordinate, the famous scout Kit Carson, then a commander of New Mexican troops, to remove the Diné to a reservation Carleton had founded called the Bosque Redondo on the sun-baked plains of eastern New Mexico.

Carson's tactic was to drive the Diné from their homeland by destroying their means of survival. His advancing army killed sheep, contaminated wells, and burned or wrecked crops, orchards, hogans, and everything of use or value to the Indians. To avoid capture, the Diné fled from their usual settlements and camps and spread out through their country. Manuelito, Barboncito, Ganado Mucho, and other chiefs led thousands of the people into the Canyon de Chelly and other hiding places in the rugged terrain. Week after week, as fall passed and winter set in, Carson continued to search for them. For the Diné there was no rest. Dinetah, their country, had turned into a place of hiding and danger.

Finally, Carson's men entered the Canyon de Chelly, the heart of the Diné homeland. From the rim of the canyon and hidden recesses in its tall, red-rock walls, the Navajos, hungry and freezing in the wintry weather, watched in horror as Carson's men moved through the canyon, searching for them. Years afterward, Eli Gorman, a Navajo medicine man, described the plight of his father's family, whose hideout in a cave in the side of the canyon was discovered and attacked by the soldiers:

Another shot was heard, and another and another. The firing gradually picked up, and soon it sounded like frying, with bullets hitting all over the cave. This went on nearly all afternoon. Then the firing ceased, but, by that time, nearly all of the Navajos were killed. Men, women, children, young men and girls were all killed on the cliffs. Some just slid off the cliffs. . . . At the bottom were piles of dead Diné; only a few survived. Blood could be seen from the top of the cliffs all the way down to the bottom.

In 1868, the eloquent Diné chief Barboncito, seen here, played a leading role in securing support from General William Tecumseh Sherman and other government negotiators for the Navajos to end their disastrous exile at the Bosque Redondo and return to their homes.

Diné women in front of their hogan, or "home place," the traditional house of their people. The hogan has taken many forms, including this one, the conical forked-pole type, common in the nineteenth century.

Another account of the fighting, passed on to Betty Shorthair, a Diné, by her grandmother, told of four women whose families were starving and, unaware of the presence of the soldiers, had entered the canyon to gather cactus fruit. Startled by the appearance of five white men on horseback, they and other Indians scattered, seeking the safety of caves in the cliff walls. Betty Shorthair's grandmother continued her account:

> Two girls who went into a cave in the cliff were shot down, and they were hanging from the cliff. As my mother's group was running along, there was a woman walking toward them with blood flowing from her hip. She had been shot by the soldiers. It was late afternoon. Another lady was walking along, and they caught up with her. There were many footprints, and still the noise of the guns continued.

As winter deepened, hunger forced hundreds of weakened and poorly armed Diné to surrender. They came in, sick, starving, and cold, to Forts Wingate and Canby, where they were held as prisoners before starting out under guard on a forced march to Fort Sumner on the desolate Bosque Redondo reservation. The three-hundred-mile Long Walk in the winter of 1864 was a tragedy that still weighs heavily upon the Diné people, among whom the voices of those who endured the trek have never stilled:

It was horrible the way they treated our people. Some old handicapped people and children couldn't make the journey, were shot on the spot and their bodies left behind for the crows and coyotes. . . .

[D]aughter got tired and weak and couldn't keep up with the others or go any farther because of her [pregnancy]. So [we] asked the Army to hold up for a while and to let the woman give birth. But the soldiers wouldn't do it. They forced my people to move on, saying they were getting the others behind. Not long after [we] moved on, [we] heard a gunshot. . . .

The pattern of this stunning Diné blanket is a variation of that of the early striped chief's blankets. After the Navajos were released from Fort Sumner in 1868, the interest of non-Indians in their weaving grew quickly, and the art continues to provide a means of income for Navajo women to this day.

Those who survived the Long Walk joined their traditional enemies, the Mescalero Apaches, whom Carleton and Carson had also incarcerated on the Bosque Redondo reservation—a wretched strip of sandy ground along the Pecos River. Most of the trees had been cut down to build Fort Sumner at the reservation, and there was nothing but barren, bad land. The Diné had to dig trenches and holes in the ground as shelters. Cows were slaughtered and their hides used as windbreaks and shades for arbors. The bushes and small trees were quickly used up in fires, and the people were forced to dig up and utilize mesquite roots for firewood.

Without safe drinking water and enough food and blankets, hundreds of Navajos died during the first year at the Bosque Redondo. To General Carleton, the architect and overseer of the Indians' exile, the goal of "reforming" them into whites was worth the price in human suffering. The Bosque Redondo, he wrote proudly to the adjutant general of the army in Washington, was a "grand experiment to make civilized human beings out of savages. Here they . . . discard . . . their ways and learn how to be like white men. . . . To gather them together little by little onto a Reservation away from the haunts and hills and hiding places of their country, and there . . . teach their children how to read and write: teach them the art of peace: teach them the truths of Christianity. Soon they will acquire new habits, new ideas, new modes of life."

To the Indian people held captive there, this process meant something very different. "The surest way to kill a race is to kill its religion and its ideals," said Frederick Peso, whose people, the Mescalero Apaches, shared the Bosque Redondo exile with the Diné. "Can anybody doubt that the white race deliberately attempted to do that? This is to kill the souls of a people. And when the spirit is killed, what remains?"

By the spring of 1865, nine thousand Diné and four hundred Mescaleros were living on rations for two-thirds that number. Many were still dying of starvation and disease. While life at the Bosque was miserable, however, it was even more perilous for

Navajos in Arizona who still resisted. Manuelito and other defiant leaders had never surrendered, but continued to hold out in the canyons. Through the hard winter of 1865–66, they spoke in whispers, afraid to light fires and risk soldiers spotting them. The free Diné lived in fear also of Ute and Mexican slave raiders who trafficked in stolen children. The words the chief Ganado Mucho spoke to Manuelito were remembered:

> My friend, we have withstood hunger and cold for many months. . . . These Utes are growing even more brazen than the Mexicans, and unless some miracle holds them in their own country, I fear they will cause us much more misery than we have known before. I think we should consider taking our people to Bosque Redondo, where they will be safe. . . .

To save their people, Manuelito and Ganado Mucho surrendered at Fort Wingate. But the hope of protection proved illusory. On the march to the Bosque Redondo, Mexican slave traders abducted Ganado Mucho's two daughters. He never saw them again. Then, after reaching the reservation, Ganado Mucho's young son was killed by Comanche raiders.

After years of failed crops, a thousand Diné deaths, and hundreds of desperate Indians escaping from the reservation, the American government came to see the Bosque Redondo as a miserable and costly failure. In May 1868, Washington sent a delegation led by General William Tecumseh Sherman to meet with Diné leaders on the reservation. When he arrived, Sherman was shocked by the deplorable condition of the Diné. "I found the Bosque a mere spot of green grass in the midst of a wild desert," he wrote General Grant, soon to be president of the United States. The Diné, he reported, were "sunk into a condition of absolute poverty and despair." When the meetings with the Indians got under way, the eloquent Barboncito was chosen to speak for the Diné. His words had to be translated from Navajo to Spanish, and then from Spanish to English.

"When the Diné were first created," Barboncito explained to the white visitors, "four mountains and four rivers were pointed out to us, inside of which we should live. That was to be our country and was given to us by the First Woman of the Diné tribe. It was told to us by our forefathers that we were never to move east of the Rio Grande or west of the San Juan rivers and I think that our coming here has been the cause of so much death among us and our animals. When one of our big men dies, the cries of the women cause the tears to roll down to my moustache. I think then of my own country."

By the early nineteenth century, Diné weaving techniques had evolved and designs grown more intricate. This beautiful example is of the serape style, which drew on the Saltillo serapes of Mexico in its design. Classic Period Diné serapes like this one were characterized by elaborate interlocking diamond and terraced zigzag motifs.

Skillfully, Barboncito went on to argue why the return of the Diné to their own country would be in the best interest of the government:

> If we are taken back to our
> own country, we will call
> you our father and mother.
> If you should only tie a goat
> there, we would all live off
> it, all of the same opinion. I
> am speaking for the whole
> tribe, for their animals, from
> the horse to the dog, also
> the unborn. . . . It appears
> to me that the General
> commands the whole thing
> as a god. I hope therefore
> he will do all he can for my
> people . . . and I wish you
> to tell me when you are
> going to take us to our own
> country.

The young Diné girl in this portrait by Edward Curtis wears a velvet blouse and skirt, along with jewelry of coral, turquoise, silver, and shell. The clothing was adapted from what white settlers wore and has now become traditional Navajo dress.

Permission was granted for the return. A treaty outlining new boundaries for the Diné nation and conditions of their release was signed. They could never again possess arms or conduct raids, and their children would have to be educated in white schools. The Diné were given food and sheep to take back with them. The Bosque Redondo was quickly abandoned, and the people began the walk home.

"We told the drivers to whip the mules, we were in such a hurry," said Manuelito. "When we saw the top of the mountain from Albuquerque, we wondered if it was our mountain, and we felt like talking to the ground, we loved it so, and some of the old men and women cried with joy when they reached their homes."

Ever since then, the Diné, or Navajos, have rigorously observed the terms of the treaty they signed in 1868. Today, by far the largest Indian nation in the United States, with a population in excess of two hundred thousand, they occupy the same high desert plateaus and red-rock country from which Kit Carson and General Carleton sent them into exile. And in Canyon de Chelly, still the awesome heart of their homeland, young Diné tour guides daily show visitors where the tragedy leading to the Long Walk of their ancestors began.

The Way of the Plains

For centuries, tens of millions of buffalo roamed the Great Plains, the seemingly endless grasslands rising from the Mississippi Valley westward to the Rocky Mountains. For centuries, Plains nations, many of them engaging in small-scale agriculture along the waterways of the plains, but also hunting on foot, relied on the immense herds for food and for raw materials to provide essentials in their lives. There were no horses yet, on the plains or in any other part of the Western Hemisphere, nor would there be any until Columbus brought the first ones from Spain to the West Indies on his second voyage, in 1493.

The Plains nations in the ancient past had learned the ways of pedestrian nomads on the grasslands, building small, portable tipi dwellings of poles covered with sewn buffalo hides, and using dogs to transport meat and belongings on travois formed by tipi poles that were hitched to the dogs and were dragged along behind them. In the seventeenth and eighteenth centuries, the shock waves of European invasion and expansion in the East began pushing woodland nations west, one against another, forcing some of them onto the plains and creating friction with the nations already living there. The result was an uneasy mix of rooted and uprooted nations—peoples who became known to whites as Crows, Mandans, Assiniboines, Hidatsas, Cheyennes, Shoshonis, Arapahos,

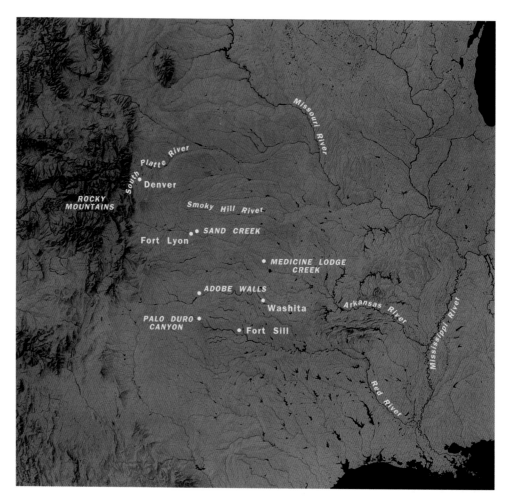

This nineteenth-century print from a painting by Swiss artist Karl Bodmer shows Mandan Indians of the upper Missouri River in the area of present-day Bismarck, North Dakota, using a dogsled in winter.

These Assiniboine men of the northern plains—one with a trade gun and the other with a lance and a buffalo-hide shield—were painted in the summer of 1833 at Fort Union, an American Fur Company post, by Karl Bodmer, who was accompanying Prince Maximilian of Wied-Neuwied on an expedition up the Missouri River to study the western tribes.

Pawnees, Kiowas, Comanches, Arikaras, Sioux, Blackfeet, and others. They spoke many dialects of different language families and learned to communicate with each other by a common sign language.

In 1680, the sudden revolt by the Pueblo Indians in New Mexico (referred to on page 172 in chapter 4) resulted in the flight of Spanish colonists back to Mexico and the abandonment of great numbers of Spanish horses, which were seized by the Pueblos and, by trade or warfare, were widely dispersed northward among tribes throughout the American and Canadian plains. Within seventy-five years, Indian possession for the first time of what some of the tribes called "the big dog" transformed the plains, creating the youngest and to non-Indians perhaps the most familiar of North American Indian cultures—the dramatic and colorful horse culture.

White explorers and fur traders reached some of the tribes so soon after they had acquired their first horses that the Indians could tell them how the sudden change had affected the lives of their people. Typical was an account by Iron Teeth, a Cheyenne woman of the central plains:

My grandmother told me that when she was young . . . [t]he people themselves had to walk. In those times they did not travel far nor often. But when they got horses, they could move more easily from place to place. Then they could kill more of the buffalo and other animals, and so they got more meat for food and gathered more skins for lodges and clothing.

After they got their first horses—which also allowed the Indians to transport longer poles and thus build larger tipis—it generally took a tribe a generation to become fully mounted. At first,

Even before the arrival of the horse on the plains, Indians used many techniques for hunting buffalo, by far their most important food source. The two hunters shown in this George Catlin illustration are disguised in wolf skins, permitting them to creep close to the unsuspecting herd.

Tipis of the Plains tribes, like this Crow Indian lodge below, were sometimes covered by as many as twenty buffalo hides. In later years, as the buffalo disappeared, canvas replaced the hides. In this illustration by George Catlin, made about 1851, the lodge covers are shown painted with the war exploits of one or more of the male occupants.

On the southern plains, Comanche Indians demonstrated their feats of horsemanship for this painting by George Catlin in 1834. Hanging by one heel from a horse running at full speed, a Comanche warrior was shielded from the enemy's view, but was still able to shoot arrows with deadly accuracy. "I am ready, without hesitation, to pronounce the [Comanches] the most extraordinary horsemen that I have seen," Catlin wrote.

only the boldest young men and women dared to ride the new animal. The more fearful older people shifted their belongings from the dogs to the horses, but preferred to continue walking. By the time the old people had died and the youths had taken their place, everyone, especially the members of hunting and war parties, was riding. The famous Absaroka, or Crow, chief Plenty Coups described a special bond that often existed between a Plains Indian warrior and his horse:

> My horse fights with me and fasts with me, because if he is to carry me in battle he must know my heart and I must know his or we shall never become brothers. I have been told that the white man, who is almost a god, and yet a great fool, does not believe that the horse has a spirit. This cannot be true. I have many times seen my horse's soul in his eyes.

Mobile nations with horses, tracking buffalo herds across the vast open spaces of the plains, often crossed paths. Territorial and other disputes arose, and for many warfare became a way of life. In several nations, prestigious warrior societies developed, and courageous warriors brought honor and esteem to themselves and their families. Having lost his father, Running Chief, a young Pawnee Indian, was raised by his mother, who gave him the following advice:

The bronze sculpture above by Frederic Remington conveys the excitement of a Plains Indian warrior getting away with a horse he has captured from an enemy. Introduced to the Indians by the Spaniards in the sixteenth century, the horse had its greatest impact on the nations of the plains, who were able to hunt over greater distances and with increased success, revolutionizing many aspects of their culture.

The five Indians portrayed in this group painting by Charles Bird King were members of a multitribal delegation from nations inhabiting the eastern fringe of the Great Plains—Oto, Kansa (Kaw), Missouri, Omaha, and Pawnee—that visited Washington, D.C., and other eastern cities in 1821.

When you grow up, you must be a man. Be brave, and face whatever danger may meet you. . . . Remember that it is his ambition that makes the man. . . . If I should live to see you become a man, I want you to become a great man. . . . If I live to see you a man, and to go off on the warpath, I would not cry if I were to hear that you had been killed in battle. That is what makes a man: to fight and to be brave.

With the influx of guns, traded from Europeans in the eighteenth century, the plains could have become the setting of a contest of annihilation. But even bitter enemies saw large-scale killing as wasteful and lacking in honor. Instead, the Plains tribes developed a complex, ritualized warfare, in which the mere touching of an enemy, known as "counting coup," brought higher honor than killing. It was a dangerous and

ABOVE RIGHT: *A Plains warrior's coup stick. Warfare among the Plains nations differed greatly from the Indians' wars with the Euro-Americans. In the Indians' highly ritualized contests, "counting coup," or coming close enough to an enemy to touch him with a stick like this one and getting away without suffering injury, was considered more impressive than killing an opponent, since it demonstrated the bravery of the winner and humiliated the person touched.*

A nineteenth-century Plains Indian warbonnet. Headdresses like this were worn only by men of great status, almost always by those who had gained recognition for exploits against enemies. The bonnet is made of the feathers of a golden eagle wrapped in red trade cloth and decorated with beadwork.

respected challenge. Plenty Coups, the Crow chief whose name reflected his many battlefield exploits, recalled the intense pride and exhilaration he felt after counting his first coup:

> We soon reached the timber . . . and drove the enemy back easily. Three days later, we rode into our village singing of victory, and our chiefs . . . came out to meet us singing Praise Songs. My heart rejoiced when I heard them speak my own name . . . I shall never forget it, or how happy I felt because I had counted my first coup.

The Sand Creek Massacre, 1864

For decades, the horse cultures of the Plains tribes flourished. White explorers and fur trappers and traders came and went, followed by missionaries, miners, freighters, and settlers, who crossed the plains on their way to Oregon, California, Salt Lake City, or other destinations west of the territories of the Plains tribes. Although the Americans made no critical demands on the tribes for cessions of Great Plains territory, their increasing traffic drove away game, destroyed wild-food gathering grounds, polluted water sources, and spread measles, whooping cough, and other dread sicknesses among the Indians. Then in 1858 and 1859, gold discoveries on the South Platte River at the foot of Colorado's Rockies started a stampede of whites across the buffalo-hunting grounds of the Cheyenne, Arapaho, Sioux, Kiowa, and Comanche Indians.

As thousands of fortune hunters flocked to Denver and the new mines, the government attempted unsuccessfully to keep the Indians away from the various routes the emigrants were using. Bands of Lakota Sioux were told to stay north of the Oregon Trail route and its South Platte spur that led to Denver. In the south, the army tried in vain to drive the Kiowas and Comanches below a route that ran along the Arkansas River. In the vast sweep of land between the Platte and Arkansas, the Cheyennes and Arapahos found themselves caught by a third route from Kansas to Colorado that ran directly through their traditional hunting grounds, which had

This ledger-book drawing was made by Yellow Horse, a Cheyenne who with other resistance leaders was sent to prison in Fort Marion, Florida. The horse-stealing exploits of Yellow Horse are being celebrated.

been guaranteed to them by a treaty in 1851. In 1861, government negotiators tried to break the treaty and force the two tribes onto a barren reservation in southeastern Colorado, but the Indians refused to go.

    While resistance leaders prepared their warriors for defense of their lands, other chiefs, knowing the strength of the United States and hoping to protect their people from suffering and death, were trying to avoid war at all cost. Cheyenne chiefs Black Kettle and White Antelope had long been committed to friendship with the United States. In 1861, they had been agreeable to breaking the 1851 treaty and going onto a reservation. Then they had traveled to Washington to meet with President Lincoln, who gave Black Kettle a large American flag and White Antelope a peace medal. By 1864, however, aggressions against the Indians by Colorado volunteer troops, bringing reprisals by small groups of warriors, fanned rumors and fears of a large-scale Indian war that would cut off Denver and the Colorado mines from the rest of the country. Panic among the miners and frontier politicians, settlers, and businessmen led them to see all Indians as dangerous.

    Black Kettle and other Cheyenne and Arapaho leaders were concerned and made their way to Denver to meet with Territorial Governor John Evans and the military commander of Colorado, Colonel John Chivington, both of whom hoped to make political capital for themselves by suppressing the Indians. In the white man's city, Black Kettle faced the two men and spoke from his heart.

> All we ask is that we may have peace with the whites. . . . I want you to give all the chiefs of the soldiers here to understand that we are for peace, and that we have made peace, that we may not be mistaken by them for enemies. . . .

Black Kettle and the other leaders left Denver with what seemed to be assurances from Evans and Chivington that they could seek protection by camping near Fort Lyon in southeastern Colorado. But the Cheyenne world was divided. Their warrior society, the Dog Soldiers, wanted to fight for their homeland. They headed north to join the Lakota Sioux and Northern Cheyenne bands who wanted to resist. Black Kettle headed south for the promised safety of Fort Lyon.

On the eve of the Sand Creek Massacre, this delegation of central plains Cheyenne and Arapaho chiefs, headed by the Southern Cheyenne leader Black Kettle (far left, seated), sat for their photograph at Camp Weld near Denver on September 28, 1864. They thought they had made peace with the Americans. Eight weeks later, Colorado troops treacherously fell on their sleeping camp, killing men, women, and children indiscriminately and committing atrocities on the bodies of the dead and wounded Indians.

Among the Cheyennes with Black Kettle was George Bent, the son of a prominent white fur trader, William Bent, and his Cheyenne wife, Owl Woman. George Bent's letters and narrative told the white man's world the Indian side of what happened:

> So now [Black Kettle] broke up our camp on the Smoky Hill and moved down to Sand Creek, about forty miles northeast of Fort Lyon. . . . All the Indians had the idea firmly fixed in their minds that they were here under protection and that peace was soon to be concluded.

But Colonel Chivington's orders, conveyed to his Indian-hating Colorado volunteers, reflected a different point of view:

> The Cheyennes will have to be soundly whipped before they will be quiet. If any of them are caught in your vicinity, kill them, as that is the only way.

By that November of 1864, winter had come to Colorado's High Plains. A huge American flag, President Lincoln's gift to Black Kettle, flapped in the wind from a tall lodgepole in front of the chief's tipi in the village on Sand Creek. At dawn on November 29, the Colorado volunteers, ordered by Chivington to take no prisoners, rode across the dry creek bed into the sleeping Indian village. George Bent was still in bed and described the attack:

Magpie, a niece of Black Kettle, and her husband, George Bent, the son of William Bent, a well-known fur trader, and his Southern Cheyenne wife, Owl Woman. In this 1867 photograph, George Bent, who recorded the Indian side of what happened at Sand Creek, wears moccasins and white men's clothing. Magpie's handsome dress was made from trade cloth and is studded with elks' teeth.

I heard shouts and the noise of people running about the camp. I jumped up and ran out of my lodge. From down the creek a large body of troops was advancing at a rapid trot, some to the east of the camps, and others on the opposite side of the creek, to the west. . . . I looked toward the chief's lodge and saw that Black Kettle had a large American flag tied to the end of a long lodgepole and was standing in front of his lodge, holding the pole. . . .

I heard him call to the people not to be afraid, that the soldiers would not hurt them; then the troops opened fire from two sides of the camps. . . . The women and children were screaming and wailing, the men running to the lodges for their arms and shouting advice and directions to one another. . . .

[White Antelope] saw the soldiers shooting the people, and he did not wish to live any longer. He stood in front of his lodge with his arms folded across his breast, singing the death song: "Nothing lives long, only the earth and the mountains."

Wearing the peace medal he had been given by President Lincoln, White Antelope was shot dead in front of his lodge. Black Kettle ran with his wife toward the creek bed, where people were digging desperately into the sand for protection. Before reaching the creek, Black Kettle's wife was shot. Believing her dead, he ran on without her. George Bent continued his narrative:

Most of us who were hiding in the pits had been wounded before we could reach this shelter; and there we lay all that bitter cold day from early in the morning until almost dark, with the soldiers all around us, keeping up a heavy fire most of the time. . . . They finally withdrew, about 5 o'clock. . . . As they retired down the creek, they killed all the wounded they could find and scalped and mutilated the dead bodies which lay strewn all along the two miles of dry creek bed.

As the survivors crawled out of hiding in the fading light, they found the horrible carnage—their village destroyed, winter food stores and blankets plundered, and their loved ones, even babies and pregnant women, ripped open and savagely mutilated by Chivington's soldiers. With other Indians, the wounded George Bent tried to keep warm on the frozen plain:

ROBERT SIMPSON/SOUTHERN CHEYENNE

"In the early morning hours of November 29, 1864, just about the sun time, two women were out picking up wood when they saw what they thought was buffalo, but it wasn't buffalo, and they kept looking and they heard shots, and they put down their sticks and started screaming and running towards the main camp. Everybody came running out of their tipis to see what was going on, and my great-great-grandfather Chief White Antelope ran out, he had no weapons or nothing on him, he raised up his hands and he said, 'Stop, we're at peace, we're at peace.' And they wouldn't stop shooting."

That night will never be forgotten as long as any of us who went through it are alive. It was bitter cold, the wind had a full sweep over the ground on which we lay, and . . . no one could keep warm. . . Many who had lost wives, husbands, children, or friends, went back down the creek and crept over the battleground among the naked and mutilated bodies of the dead. Few were found alive, for the soldiers had done their work thoroughly.

Black Kettle found his wife with nine bullet wounds in her body. Miraculously, she was alive. But more than 150 Indians had been slaughtered. Eventually, the survivors struggled across the plains to a camp of the Cheyenne Dog Soldiers on the Smoky Hill River, where they were clothed, fed, and given horses. Black Kettle's feelings were of betrayal and bitterness. "I once thought that I was the only man that persevered to be the friend of the white man," he said. "But since they have come and cleaned out our lodges, horses, and everything else, it is hard for me to believe white men any more."

Lieutenant Colonel George Armstrong Custer. A graduate of West Point, he made a reputation as a flamboyant young cavalry officer in the Civil War. In 1868, at age twenty-eight, he fell on Black Kettle's slumbering village of Southern Cheyennes at the Washita River, killing more than one hundred peaceful Indians, including the chief, and acquiring the enduring enmity of many of the Plains tribes.

That night will never be forgotten as long as any of us who went through it are alive. . . . Many who had lost wives, husbands, children, or friends, went back down the creek and crept over the battleground among the naked and mutilated bodies of the dead. —GEORGE BENT

OVERLEAF: *A painting by Robert Lindneux of the massacre at Sand Creek, Colorado Territory, on November 29, 1864. Colorado volunteers, whipped to a frenzy of hatred against Indians by their fanatic commander, Colonel John M. Chivington, are shown thundering into the unsuspecting camp of Southern Cheyennes and Arapahos, who had understood they would be safe if they camped here. At his tipi in the center, rear, Black Kettle raised an American and a white flag in an unsuccessful attempt to halt the attack.*

When the American Civil War ended, the government, under pressure from easterners who were sick of fighting and repelled by stories of Sand Creek and other immoral military actions against the western Indians, tried to find peaceful solutions. In 1867, it called together the tribes of the southern plains, including the Southern Cheyennes, and at a treaty meeting at Medicine Lodge Creek, Kansas, set aside two large reservations for them in the western part of the Indian Territory. Many of the bands, including the Cheyenne Dog Soldiers and various factions of the Kiowas and Comanches, wanted nothing to do with reservations. Despite his loss, however, Black Kettle saw no hope in resistance. Late in the fall of 1868, he brought his beleaguered band of Southern Cheyenne survivors into a camp on the Washita River on one of the new reservations. Most of the young men had meanwhile left him to join Indians who were resisting, leaving mostly Cheyenne women, children, and elderly with the chief.

As Black Kettle settled down peaceably, the United States sent out columns of soldiers to scour the southern plains and bring in the Indians who would not go voluntarily onto the reservations. In November, the 7th Cavalry, led by Lieutenant Colonel George Armstrong Custer, followed a Cheyenne raiding party to Black Kettle's village. "This party going to Black Kettle's village . . . ," George Bent explained, "made it appear that Black Kettle's band was hostile, though these Cheyennes were not of his band."

At dawn on November 27, 1868, Custer's troops charged into Black Kettle's sleeping village. George Bent was not there, but from Indian relatives and tribal eyewitnesses, he was able to describe the second surprise attack on the band, almost four years to the day after the first one, and the death, this time, of its ill-starred chief:

> Black Kettle mounted a horse and helped his wife up behind him and started to cross the Washita River, but both the chief and his wife fell at the river bank riddled with bullets. . . . The soldiers rode right over Black Kettle and his wife and their horse as they lay dead on the ground, and their bodies were all splashed with mud by the charging soldiers.

Black Kettle, his wife, and 101 other peaceful Southern Cheyennes were killed that day. In his quest for peace, the chief had unwittingly twice led his people to slaughter. Over the ruins of his village on the Washita, words he had spoken in one of his many councils with whites lingered like an epitaph in the freezing air:

> Although wrongs have been done me, I live in hopes. . . . All my

This Catlin painting of a Comanche village in Texas shows women stretching and scraping buffalo hides before sewing them together to make covers for their tipis, which were up to twenty-five feet in diameter, a way of life only a memory when Ten Bears made his famous speech at Medicine Lodge Creek in 1867.

friends, the Indians that are holding back—they are afraid to come in; afraid to be betrayed as I have been. . . .

Death Throes on the Southern Plains

In the last year of the Civil War, the North's top military leaders—Generals Grant, Sherman, and Sheridan—waged total war against the South, pounding it into submission without letup. Four years later, the same three men—Grant now as president, Sherman as general in chief of the army, and Sheridan as commander of all the troops on the plains—applied the same strategy of total, uninterrupted pressure to force the last free Indians of the southern plains to do what the government wanted them to do: to go willingly onto reservations, out of the white man's way, where missionaries and educators could turn them into whites.

After Custer's massacre of Black Kettle's Cheyennes at the Washita, Sheridan ordered all holdout Kiowa, Comanche, as well as Cheyenne and Arapaho, bands to go on the new reservations or face annihilation by the army. Shaken by the cruelty of Black Kettle's fate, most of the bands gradually came in. But after a while, the reservation seemed like a prison to them, and by 1870, the Kiowas and Comanches especially were full of complaints and ready to rebel. Deprived of their hunting lands, fed broken promises by Washington and dictatorial reservation officials, and often sick, cold, and starving because of inadequate, spoiled, or shoddy supplies provided by government swindlers, many Indians remembered the oratory of the aged Comanche chief Ten Bears at the Medicine Lodge Creek treaty meeting in 1867:

Wun-pan-to-mee (The White Weasel), a Kiowa woman of the southern plains, painted in the 1830s by George Catlin.

> You said that you wanted to put us upon a reservation, to build us houses. . . . I do not want them. I was born upon the prairie, where the wind blew free and there . . . were no enclosures and everything drew a free breath. I want to die there and not within walls. . . . The white man has the country we loved, and we only wish to wander on the prairie until we die.

The Kiowa patriot Satanta photographed during one of his periods of captivity. Known as the Orator of the Plains, he spent much of his life fighting U.S. government efforts to force the Kiowa and Comanche nations onto reservations. In 1878, during his final imprisonment, he died in a mysterious fall from a window. Prison guards claimed he jumped to his death, but the Kiowa people believed he was murdered.

Another impassioned voice at Medicine Lodge Creek had been that of Satanta, or White Bear, a great Kiowa chief:

I love the land and the buffalo, and will not part with it. . . . I want the children raised as I was. I don't want to settle. I love to roam over the prairies. There I feel free and happy, but when we settle down we grow pale and die. . . . A long time ago this land belonged to our fathers; but when I go up to the river I see camps of soldiers on its banks. These soldiers cut down my timber; they kill my buffalo; and when I see that, my heart feels like bursting. . . .

This is our country. We have always lived in it. We always had plenty to eat because the land was full of buffalo. We were happy. . . . Then you came. . . . We have to protect ourselves. We have to save our country. We have to fight for what is ours.

Both Ten Bears and Satanta had finally gone onto one of the reservations, Ten Bears peaceably, Satanta against his will. Seized by Custer, he had been taken as a prisoner to the reservation, where General Sheridan soon allowed him to be released. A burly fifty-year-old giant with jet-black hair falling to his shoulders, Satanta was brave and impatient, a restless adventurer and raider, and, to white men, a fierce and determined enemy. With Lone Wolf, another militant war chief, and Kicking Bird, who,

Big Tree, a young Kiowa war chief, was ordered arrested in 1871 by General Sherman for participating in an attack on a mule train in Texas. Sentenced to be hanged, he was paroled instead after eastern humanitarians and other Indian leaders protested the harsh sentence. He lived on the Kiowa reservation in the Indian Territory (later Oklahoma) until his death in 1929.

Quay-ham-kay (The Stone Shell), a Kiowa described by the artist, Catlin, as a "fair specimen of the warriors of this tribe." His jaw is painted with vermilion, and he wears a headdress of eagle feathers and necklaces of white and colored beads, in the traditional manner recalled by Satanta at Medicine Lodge Creek.

on the contrary, favored peace with the Americans and accommodation to reservation life, Satanta contended for leadership of the Kiowas.

From time to time, Satanta stole away from the reservation, leading raiding parties into Texas and Mexico to look for food and supplies. Because of chronic shortages of promised government rations and other necessities, the forays were often the only way to survive. In May 1871, joined by three other Kiowa leaders—mustachioed seventy-year-old Satank (Sitting Bear), honored as the head of a society of the Kiowas' ten bravest warriors; Big Tree, a youthful war chief; and Mamanti (Sky Walker), a medicine man—Satanta led a raiding party into Texas and attacked a mule train of ten freight wagons carrying corn. The Indians killed seven of the twelve teamsters, plundered and burned the wagons, and captured forty-one mules.

The raiders just missed attacking a smaller train that was escorting General Sherman, who had come to Texas to learn for himself how well the Indians were being pacified. When he was told of the attack on the mule train, Sherman was furious and hurried to Fort Sill on the Kiowas' reservation. There, he and the agent summoned Satanta and the other chiefs, who had just returned from their raid, and asked them what they knew about the affair. Satanta announced defiantly that it was he who had led the raid:

> The white people are preparing to build a railroad through our country, which will not be permitted. . . . More recently I was arrested by soldiers and kept in confinement for several days. But that is played out now. There is never to be any more Kiowas arrested. I want you to remember that. Because of this, I led [our young men] to Texas — to teach them to fight.

Sherman ordered Satanta, Satank, and Big Tree arrested. After a sudden flare-up of the Indians' tempers and a wild tussle between the chiefs and the whites, in which Sherman came close to getting shot, the three chiefs were jailed at the post and then

BILLY EVANS HORSE / KIOWA

"My grandmother told stories about how good a man Satanta was to his family. . . . As a father he was just like any other father, he had four children, he had sons, and when he came home he wasn't the warrior, the so-called hostile or whatever other label they gave him, he wasn't that kind of person. He was a father that was caring for his family, he tried to make sure that they were comfortable, and when he had to leave he told them, 'I have to go on long journeys.' He even had a song he sung, and he told his brother, 'I have to travel up to the far north and if I don't come back,' he said, 'don't cry for me because my bones will be devoured by the wolves.' He was that kind of a man."

sent under guard in wagons to Texas to stand trial for the murder of the teamsters. On the way, Satank sang the death song of the Koitsenko, the honored warriors' society that he headed. As the wagons rolled along the road, he proclaimed to those who knew his native tongue:

> Tell them that I am dead. I died the first day out, and my bones will be lying on the side of the road. I wish my people to gather them up and take them home. See that tree ahead? I shall never go beyond that tree.

As the wagons neared the tree, Satank managed to wriggle out of his manacles, having previously chewed his wrists to the bone. Suddenly producing a knife that he had been able to hide under his blanket, he lunged at one of the guards, hurling him off the wagon. The other guards drew their guns and shot the Kiowa leader dead. Satank's last request, to have his body taken home, was denied. His remains were deposited at Fort Sill.

In Texas, Satanta and Big Tree were convicted by a white jury and sentenced to be hanged. Influential reformers in the East, however, who supported the policy of winning over Indians by nonviolent means ascribed the Kiowas' action to "influences irresistibly evil" of the military in the West and with the help of members of Grant's administration persuaded Governor Edmund J. Davis of Texas—a pro-Union Texas judge and officer in the federal army during the Civil War—first to commute the sentence of the Kiowas to life imprisonment and then to release them on parole.

Sherman reacted with fury. As the two chiefs were returned to the reservation, the man who had once marched a Union army from Atlanta to the sea wrote hotly to the Texas governor: "I believe in making a tour of your frontier, with a small escort, I ran the risk of my life, and I said to the military commander what I now say to you, that I will not again voluntarily assume that risk in the interest of your frontier, that I believe Satanta and Big Tree will have their revenge, if they have not already had it, and that if they are to have scalps, that yours is the first that should be taken."

Satanta and Big Tree now found that the buffalo-hunting bands, both those that were still free and those that frequently left the reservations to join them on hunts, were facing a new crisis. In 1871, an eastern tannery had developed a method to produce a superior leather from buffalo hides, creating a sudden demand for the hides. The price of buffalo hides had shot up, and almost overnight the southern plains had filled with hide hunters, killing buffalo by the hundreds of thousands. It was an obscene period. Between 1872 and 1874, the hunters, many with new, high-powered

Sharps rifles, slaughtered almost four million of the great beasts, shipping their hides east and leaving the unused carcasses rotting on the plains. The Indians could see the herds getting smaller or disappearing from different areas, and mixed with their anger at the waste was a great fear, for they still depended on the buffalo for food, as well as materials for clothing, shelter, and other articles used in everyday life.

The whites saw what was happening as an unexpected blessing. In destroying the buffalo herds, the hide hunters were wiping out the Indians' food supply. To avoid starvation, the bands would have to go onto the reservations and accept government-issued rations. The government and the army gave encouragement to the hide hunters. "[They] have done . . . more to settle the vexed Indian question than the entire regular army," General Sheridan told a joint session of the Texas legislature. "They are destroying the Indians' commissary. . . . For the sake of a lasting peace, let them kill, skin and sell until the buffaloes are exterminated."

This hand-colored woodcut shows passengers shooting buffalo from a Kansas Pacific Railroad train crossing the central plains. Wrote Theodore Davis, an artist who traveled through the West: "It would seem to be hardly possible to imagine a more novel sight than a small band of buffalo loping along within a few hundred feet of a railroad train in rapid motion, while the passengers are engaged in shooting, from every available window, with rifles, carbines, and revolvers. An American scene, certainly."

The slaughter of the huge buffalo herds destroyed the economic and cultural base of the Plains Indian nations. Without the buffalo, the Plains tribes had no choice but to submit to the U.S. Army, on which they became dependent for food and supplies.

Once a market for their hides developed after the Civil War, buffalo were shot down by professional hunters at an unbelievable rate. Between 1872 and 1874, more than four million were killed and their carcasses left to rot on the plains. By the late 1880s, only a few thousand remained. This illustration of hide hunters at work graced the December 12, 1874, cover of Harper's Weekly *magazine.*

OPPOSITE: *The Kiowa chief Lone Wolf, photographed during a visit to Washington, D.C., in 1872. The killing of his son turned him against the Americans, and he led his people in the Red River War of 1874–75. After his band was defeated at Palo Duro Canyon, he surrendered at Fort Sill and was sent to prison in Florida. Later released, he died of malaria in his homeland in 1879.*

As the hide hunters continued their mass killings and the buffalo all but disappeared from Kansas, the desperation and anger of the Indians increased. In the summer of 1874, in a determined effort to force the white hunters from the plains south of Kansas before the last of the herds vanished, Satanta, Lone Wolf, and Quanah Parker, the leader of the Kwahadi Comanches, led an allied force of seven hundred Kiowas, Kiowa-Apaches, Comanches, Cheyennes, and Arapahos in an attack on the hide hunters' base near Adobe Walls in the Texas Panhandle, the site of the crumbling ruins of an old adobe trading post.

The Indians launched assault after assault against the settlement's buildings, but they were no match for the defending hunters with their powerful buffalo guns. Each time, the Indians were driven off with losses. Finally, on the third day, after a hunter using a Sharps rifle with a telescopic sight knocked a warrior off his horse at a distance later measured at nearly a mile, the Indians gave up the fight and withdrew. Venting their frustration and fury elsewhere, they dispersed into smaller groups, ranging across large parts of the southern plains and killing whites in isolated attacks from Colorado to Texas. In response to their violence, the government announced that all Indians who did not enroll on their reservations by August 3 would be attacked as hostiles. Soon afterward, five columns of infantry and cavalry took the field against the holdouts.

It was the beginning of the end. Hemmed in by the ever-tightening bonds of ranches, farms, settlements, railroad lines, wagon roads, telegraph lines, and other marks of the white man's possession of what only recently had been buffalo range, the free bands were being strangled to death, with almost no place left for escape and few buffalo left for their survival. Some bands, in defeat, finally went onto the hated reservations. Lone Wolf's Kiowas, together with some of the Comanches and Cheyennes,

Quanah Parker led the Kwahadi band of Comanches against the United States in the Red River War. Outgunned and starving, his people were the last to give up, surrendering in the spring of 1875. After relocating from Texas to the Indian Territory, Parker—whose mother, Cynthia Ann Parker, had been a white captive of the Comanches—became a successful cattle rancher and supported the development of a religion later known as the Native American Church, which combined elements of Christianity and traditional Indian religions.

headed for their old secluded camping grounds in the Palo Duro Canyon, a formidable gash in the flat tableland of Texas's Staked Plain. Rugged and beautiful, the canyon was almost unknown to whites. Nevertheless, near the end of September 1874, one of the army columns found it, descending into its depths by a steep trail and surprising the Indian camps that were spread for two miles along the canyon's floor.

The Indians put up a brief resistance, then fled. Instead of pursuing them, the soldiers were content to destroy and burn the Indians' abandoned camps and everything in them—food, clothing, saddles, and personal possessions. Then they killed the Indians' horses and mules, some fourteen hundred animals, and departed from the canyon, leaving the Indians destitute and facing the approaching winter with no choice but to make their way as best they could to the reservations and surrender. Which is what they finally did.

One by one, the bands came in and settled down on the reservation. Satanta, who had been at the Adobe Walls fight, was arrested in November for violating his parole and sent back to prison at Huntsville, Texas. Four years later, in October 1878, it was announced that he had committed suicide by leaping out of a window of the prison hospital. Why he had done so was never answered satisfactorily. The Kiowas were never allowed to investigate, and those who knew the stout-hearted warrior were convinced that he was murdered.

Determined to break the southern Plains tribes forever, the army rounded up ten thousand of their horses and had them shot. By that time, they were no longer needed for buffalo hunting, because the buffalo were close to extinction. In the twelve years following 1874, the buffalo population of thirty million was reduced to fewer than one thousand. A bond of spiritual understanding between Native Americans and the buffalo, going back thousands of years, had been ripped apart. To a Kiowa woman named Old Lady Horse, it meant the disappearance of the people's way of life:

The Kiowas were camped on the north side of Mount Scott, those of them who were still free to camp. One young woman got up very early in the morning. The dawn mist was still rising from Medicine Creek, and as she looked across the water, peering through the haze, she saw . . . the last buffalo herd appear like a spirit dream.

Straight to Mount Scott the leader of the herd walked. Behind him came the cows and their calves, and the few young males who had survived. As the woman watched, the face of the mountain opened.

Inside Mount Scott the world was green and fresh, as it had been when she was a small girl. The rivers ran clear, not red. The wild plums were in blossom, chasing the red buds up the inside slopes. Into this world of beauty the buffalo walked, never to be seen again.

To non-Indian Americans, the railroad symbolized progress and the advance of civilization. As this 1867 painting by Theodor Kaufmann, titled Westward the Star of Empire, *suggests, the Plains Indians whose hunting grounds the iron horse invaded understood its threat to their survival.*

CHAPTER 8

THE END OF

FREEDOM

The Embattled Northern Plains

While the southern Plains tribes were fighting for their lands, those farther north were engaged in a similar struggle. In August 1862, some of the eastern, or Santee, Sioux tribes in Minnesota—mistreated beyond endurance by government cheats, thieving white traders, missionaries, and hordes of settlers who collectively robbed them of their lands and brought them to starvation—killed more than 350 whites in a desperate attempt to reclaim their country. Large American armies, diverted from Civil War battlefields, crushed the Indian forces and drove the Santees out of their ancestral Minnesota homeland and onto the plains of what are now North and South Dakota. Little Crow, a leading Santee chief and former friend of the Americans who reluctantly agreed to the demands of his people that he lead their struggle against the whites, was killed, and 38 Indians were hanged publicly in a mass execution in Mankato.

The Santees, woodland hunters, farmers, and gatherers of wild rice on Minnesota's lakes, were one of three major divisions of the populous Sioux tribes. Another division, composed of the Yankton and Yanktonai nations, lived on the tall-grass prairies of the eastern half of the present-day Dakotas. Beyond them were the Teton, or western, Sioux—known also as Lakotas—who dwelled generally on the semiarid plains of the western half of the Dakotas and in parts of present-day Nebraska, Kansas, Wyoming, and Montana. To the whites, in fact and legend, the mounted buffalo-hunting Yanktons, Yankto-

nais, and Lakotas—the last made up of seven autonomous tribes: Oglalas, Sicangus (Brulés), Hunkpapas, Miniconjous, Itazipchos (Sans Arcs), Oohenonpas (Two Boilings, or Two Kettles), and Sihasapas (Blackfeet)—became the archetypical Plains Indians.

Some of the dispersed Santees, fleeing from the American troops, sought sanctuary among the buffalo-hunting bands of Yanktonai in the eastern part of today's North Dakota. Others crossed for safety into the prairie provinces of Canada, where they have remained to this day. In the summers of both 1863 and 1864, the boastful, but somewhat deflated, Union general John Pope, "exiled" to fight the Indians in Minnesota after having led the North's Army of Virginia to disaster against the Confederates at the Second Battle of Bull Run, dispatched large expeditionary forces into the Dakotas, searching for the refugee Santees. With extreme recklessness and cruelty, the armies, diverted from the white men's Civil War, fell on peaceful camps of Yanktonais, Hunkpapas, and other western Sioux, killing scores of Indians who had had nothing to do with the conflict in Minnesota, burning their villages and

Karl Bodmer painted this view of a Sioux camp at Fort Pierre in the region of present-day South Dakota during his trip up the Missouri River with Prince Maximilian of Wied-Neuwied in 1833–34. Nearby, a tightly wrapped corpse lies on a funeral scaffold, out of reach of scavenging animals. Later, after it had decomposed in the dry air of the plains, it would be buried in the ground.

food supplies, making prisoners of Sioux women and children, and accomplishing nothing save arousing distrust, resentments, and hostility among the buffalo-hunting Plains Sioux, who wanted only to be left alone and allowed to live and hunt in peace.

At the same time, Chivington's massacre of the Cheyennes and Arapahos in Black Kettle's camp at Sand Creek in Colorado in 1864 persuaded the Oglala and Sicangu

Sioux bands, who were allies of the Cheyennes and Arapahos, that the time had arrived for the Plains tribes to let the aggressive Americans know that the Indians could, and would, retaliate for the slaughter of their people and would resist attempts to drive them off their lands. When the Cheyenne Dog Soldiers and other Cheyenne and Arapaho groups, determined to avenge Sand Creek, sent war pipes to their Sioux friends, the latter agreed to respond to the whites' provocations. In January and February 1865 allied war parties of Sioux, Cheyennes, and Arapahos raided along the Platte River and both its branches, setting fire to stage stations and ranches; ripping down miles of telegraph wire; burning the town of Julesburg; halting stages, supply trains, and mails; and cutting off Denver, Salt Lake City, and San Francisco from overland communication from the East.

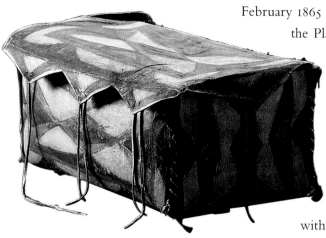

A Sioux parfleche box of stiffened and painted hide, used for storing and carrying possessions.

The Indian strikes created havoc among the white settlements lining the South Platte River route to Denver. "At night the whole valley was lighted up with the flames of burning ranches and stage stations," recalled George Bent, who was riding with one of the Cheyenne bands. Scores of ranchers, stage-station managers, freighters, telegraphers, and other whites were killed before the tribes agreed to end their attacks.

In mid-February, the Indians finally left Colorado and trailed north toward the White River country of South Dakota. There, the huge group—some six thousand men, women, and children—separated. The Southern Cheyennes and Arapahos followed the Oglala band under its chiefs, Red Cloud and Man Afraid of His Horse, to join the Miniconjous and other Lakotas at their favorite hunting grounds in the Powder River country between the Black Hills and the Bighorn Mountains in present-day Wyoming and Montana. The Sicangus, led by Sinte Gleshka (Spotted Tail), went to Fort Laramie, intending to offer peace to the soldiers and then return to the buffalo ranges of western Kansas and eastern Colorado, which they preferred to the Pow-

Charles Russell's Attack on the Wagon Train *depicts a scene that became commonplace along the trails of the central plains in 1865 when Indians sought revenge for Chivington's treacherous attack on Cheyennes and Arapahos at Sand Creek.*

der River country. At the fort, the commander had Sinte Gleshka and his people detained under guard as prisoners, then ordered them transferred to Fort Kearny, farther east, along with a thousand Sioux who camped permanently around the post and were considered a nuisance by the garrison officers. Soon after

leaving Fort Laramie, the Indians broke free from their army captors. Making their way west across the plains, Sinte Gleshka and the Sicangus again joined the other bands in the Powder River country.

In 1865, determined to defeat the Plains tribes and bring them under army control once and for all, the frustrated Pope prepared another summer campaign against them. Included in his plans was a two-pronged invasion of their Powder River hunting grounds to defeat the western Sioux and their allies, secure the western roads, and open new ones, especially the Bozeman Trail, a shortcut route promoted by John M. Bozeman and another white man that ran from a little west of Fort Laramie on the Oregon Trail to the busy mining regions in western Montana. Because the route cut directly through the Powder River buffalo range, threatening the principal hunting grounds and source of food of the Oglalas and other Lakotas, they tried to bar its use, and few whites risked taking it.

Among Plains Indians, horses became extremely important, and favorite war or buffalo-running horses were usually treated with praise and respect. This dramatic wooden effigy, carved by a Sioux, honored his mount that had been killed in battle.

An Indian war party in the foothills of the northern Rockies, shown in a chromolith illustration of the early 1870s by John Mix Stanley.

VICTOR RUNNELS/OGLALA

"The results of the contact with the white people that came were disastrous in that they destroyed our total economy, that was an economy that was built over hundreds of years of learning how to live off the land, how to gather the foods and the medicines they needed, and the reliance on the buffalo for food and clothing. So when the white man came in and killed all the buffalo herds, pushed us into smaller areas, it was a destruction of our total economy. We've never recovered from that since."

During a period of renewed conflict between army detachments and allied Indian groups along the Platte River that lasted from March through July 1865, Pope's new offensive began. Neither of the army's two invading prongs achieved its aims. One bogged down in Dakota Territory and never reached the Powder River country. The other, composed of three columns, floundered around in circles through what to the troops was poorly mapped country, its members suffering from hunger and thirst, losing scores of their weakened horses, enduring violent storms, fighting inconclusive engagements with elusive Indians, and threatening mutiny. Finally, the expensive operation was aborted. In time, the Americans viewed it as having been worse than a failure because it intensified the determination of the western Sioux nations to defend their lands.

The army's debacle, meanwhile, played into the hands of the growing peace forces in the East. The government's emphasis shifted to trying to win by peaceful negotiations and treaties what it had not been able to win by war. And yet neither policy for gaining control of the Plains tribes—the carrot or the stick—prevailed completely. Government agents made efforts to meet peaceably with the different tribes and persuade them to go onto reservations. Along the Missouri River, white commissioners and army officers got the leaders of a few small Sioux bands to make their X's on treaties, in which they agreed to move onto reservations in the Dakotas. The treaties were hardly worth the paper they were written on. The signers were not authorized to speak for the members of the powerful buffalo-hunting bands farther west who were determined to fight for their lands and freedom. Refusing to participate in treaty meetings, those bands presented a problem to the whites who advocated the "carrot" approach, or, as their opponents put it, a policy of "conquering the Indians with kindness."

Still, the government in Washington felt that something had to be done. In the wake of the Civil War, thousands of settlers, many making use of the new Homestead Act, were moving out on the plains, establishing homes and new settlements, and raising demands for Indian-owned lands. River traffic up the Missouri and wagon trails across the northern plains from Minnesota to the Montana mines, bringing whites into the hunting grounds of the Hunkpapas and other northern Sioux, were already stirring those tribes to threats of resistance, and the builders of the first transcontinental railroad were planning to appropriate the expansive Platte Valley buffalo ranges, the hunting grounds of some of the Sicangus, Oglalas, and their allies, for their tracks.

In their dilemma, both the army and the peace advocates, using different approaches to attain the same end—getting the tribes under lock and key on reservations—went simultaneously at the Indians, and both used every method they could

Fort Laramie, a large military post in Wyoming, was the scene of many important treaty councils between Sioux leaders and government negotiators. Here is the way it looked in 1868.

think of, including deception, to achieve their goals. In the East, the editor of the *Army and Navy Journal* observed the ambivalent situation and commented reproachfully: "We go to [the Indians] Janus-faced. One of our hands holds the rifle and the other the peace-pipe, and we blaze away with both instruments at the same time. The chief consequence is a great *smoke*—and there it ends."

Red Cloud's War

In 1866, the government decided, one way or the other, to open the Bozeman Trail for use that summer. First, the army, in anticipation of heavy traffic to the Montana mines, directed Colonel Henry B. Carrington and a battalion of seven hundred officers and men of the 18th Infantry to proceed to the Powder River country and establish a chain of forts to cow the Indians. At the same time, a government commission journeyed to Fort Laramie, hoping with gifts and other inducements to persuade the Sioux peaceably to allow whites to use the road through their buffalo country without interference.

Sinte Gleshka (Spotted Tail), at left, and Swift Bear, both Sicangu, or Brulé, Lakotas. Sinte Gleshka, who was born in 1833, was a respected leader of his people who eventually advocated peace with the United States. After negotiating their surrender following the Battle of the Little Bighorn, however, he lost influence among the Lakotas.

Summoned by runners, Oglalas, Sicangus, and a smattering of Cheyennes and Arapahos were waiting at the fort with their leaders when the commissioners arrived. Among them, the whites were heartened to see the Sicangu chiefs Sinte Gleshka and Swift Bear and the principal Oglala headmen Red Cloud and Man Afraid of His Horse. All of them were among the most influential and powerful Sioux chiefs and had been leading participants in the raids in Colorado. The Indians had not been told what the white men wanted to talk about—only that they had made peace with other tribes, giving them lavish gifts and payments for doing so, and were now offering the same opportunity to the bands in the Powder River country. The hunting had

been poor, many of the Indian families were hungry and destitute, and with the exception of groups like those of the young Oglala war leader Crazy Horse, the Miniconjous, and Sitting Bull's Hunkpapas, who wanted nothing to do with the Americans, most of the bands had come expectantly to the fort to meet with the negotiators.

When the conference opened on June 5, the commissioners told the Indians that all they wanted was peaceful relations and the right to make and use certain roads through their country "as may be deemed necessary for the public service and for the emigrants to mining districts of the West." Although the Indians recognized that the whites were talking about the Bozeman Trail, they seemed to have realized already that that was probably the principal reason for the meeting, and they did not appear perturbed. Nevertheless, the commissioners, fearful that the chiefs would walk out of the conference, continued with their cautious "forked-tongue" approach, making ridiculous promises—which the Indians knew that the commissioners knew were unenforceable—that travelers on the Bozeman Trail would be confined strictly to the roadway and would not be allowed "to molest or disturb the game in the country through which they passed."

To the Indians, the subject—and the payments involved—appeared worthy of consideration, and they asked for a postponement of the conference until they could get more of their people to Fort Laramie. On June 13, the meeting reconvened, but was immediately broken up by the arrival at the fort of Colonel Carrington and his troops, who were on their way to the Powder River country. When Carrington revealed that he was under orders to establish a chain of forts to protect the Bozeman Trail, the Indians were furious—and none more so than Red Cloud.

About forty-five years old, the Oglala war chief was an imposing man, with long black hair parted in the middle and falling to his shoulders. His many exploits against the Pawnees, Crows, and other enemies of the Sioux had made him widely known and respected as a warrior. But he was also an ambitious and wily politi-

Red Cloud, the famed Oglala Lakota chief, with his pipe. Under his leadership, the Lakotas in 1868 forced the U.S. Army to evacuate the forts in the Sioux hunting grounds of present-day Wyoming's Powder River country. After an agency bearing his name was established in what is now South Dakota, Red Cloud became a mediator between his people and the American government. His attempts to compromise pleased neither side, however, and his influence waned. He died in 1909, aged eighty-seven.

We go to [the Indians] Janus-faced. One of our hands holds the rifle and the other the peace-pipe.

—EDITOR, *ARMY AND NAVY JOURNAL*

cian and, though not a civil chief, had attained a position of influence among the Oglalas equal to, if not greater than, that of their nominal head chief, Man Afraid of His Horse.

Recognizing the commissioners' deceit, Red Cloud spoke to the white men accusingly:

Great Father sends us presents and wants new road. But white chief goes with soldiers to steal road before Indian says yes or no!

Then, as translated to the commissioners by an interpreter, he addressed the assembled Indians:

The white men have crowded the Indians back year by year until we are forced to live in a small country north of the Platte, and now our last hunting ground, the home of the People, is to be taken from us. Our women and children will starve, but for my part I prefer to die fighting rather than by starvation.

Red Cloud stormed out and led his Oglalas back north, determined to guard his lands. Only Sinte Gleshka, a few Cheyennes, and some minor Sioux chiefs, who had no interest in, or authority over, the Powder River country, signed the treaty, each one receiving the promise of an extraordinarily high annuity of seventy thousand dollars a year for twenty years in return for their agreement not to interfere with travelers on the Bozeman Trail. Unable apparently to be candid with anyone, the chief government negotiator wired the Commissioner of Indian Affairs in Washington: "Satisfactory treaty concluded with the Sioux and Cheyennes. Large representations. Most cordial feeling prevails."

That summer, Carrington established three forts along the Bozeman Trail, using the middle one, Fort Phil Kearny, on the pine-covered hills south of present-day Sheridan, Wyoming, as his headquarters. Crazy Horse and other warriors harassed the builders and, when the summer Sun Dances were finished, stepped up attacks along the trail, striking at wagon trains, emigrant parties, and messengers going to or from Montana, and raiding the forts themselves to drive off stock and kill members of the garrisons who had strayed outside the stockades. By October, the warriors had made

Painting hides was an ancient art among the Plains Indians. Here, Ute paintings on a deer hide depict Sun Dancers in their lodge (top) and, below them, the Bear Dance, which marked the end of winter, reflected in the bear's waking from hibernation.

Not all the names of the ledger-book artists have come down to us. These two happy recollections of life on the plains are unsigned, although both were made by a Cheyenne in prison at Fort Marion, Florida. The drawing above shows a Cheyenne visit to a Sioux camp.

the road as perilous as it had ever been and had placed Carrington's lonely forts in a state of siege.

In December, when the Indians' fall hunt had ended, Red Cloud was ready to begin his war in earnest and drive the soldiers out of the country. More than a thousand lodges drew together in a camp near Fort Phil Kearny. A first attempt to lure soldiers into an ambush among the hills failed when the troops refused to pursue a group of Sioux decoys. Cooped up impatiently inside the besieged fort, Carrington's officers grew restless and wanted to conduct offensive operations against the Indians. "With eighty men I could ride through the whole Sioux nation," boasted Captain William J. Fetterman, who had arrived with a cavalry unit in November to reinforce Carrington. Arrogant and contemptuous of the Indians, Fetterman got his chance on December 21. Sent out, by coincidence, with precisely eighty men to rescue a party of the fort's woodcutters whom the Sioux had trapped, Fetterman led his men impulsively into an ambush. Hundreds of Sioux overwhelmed them, killing Fetterman and all eighty of his men.

Plains Indians met for many purposes— dances, hunts, war councils. The artist of the ledger drawing to the right remembers such a meeting—this time to hunt.

Lakota chiefs (from left) Red Bear, Pecks His Drum, and Man Afraid of His Horse pose with unidentified whites at Fort Laramie after signing the Treaty of 1868, in which the government agreed to evacuate its forts along the Bozeman Trail and withdraw from the Powder River country.

The defeat shocked the government and strengthened the hand of the peace advocates. But the army was not ready to give up. "We must act with vindictive earnestness against the Sioux," General Sherman demanded, "even to their extermination, men, women, and children." It was an empty threat. Although the wintry weather forced the Indians to break off the siege and move to warmer campsites, they renewed their attacks in 1867, battling a haying detail and its escort at Fort C. F. Smith, Carrington's northernmost post, and, under Red Cloud's personal leadership, fighting a protracted engagement at Fort Phil Kearny with a party of woodcutters and troops, who defended themselves from within wheelless wagon boxes that they had formed in a circle.

Under pressure from the eastern peace forces, the government finally agreed that trying to open the Bozeman Trail was no longer worth the expense and the fighting and gave up. As long as Red Cloud kept the troops engaged simply defending and supplying themselves, travelers could get no protection, and the route continued to be too dangerous for them to use. Soon—the government also satisfied itself—the Bozeman Trail would no longer be needed anyway, since the transcontinental railroad would be completed, opening safer and shorter routes to the Montana mining districts from rail points farther west.

In 1868, the army announced to the tribes that it would evacuate the forts, and a commission that included General Sherman invited Red Cloud and the chiefs of his allied bands to meet again at Fort Laramie to sign a peace treaty. Red Cloud and many of the leading chiefs refused to come until the troops actually left the forts, but those, including Sinte Gleshka, who met with the commission made their marks on the treaty papers that were given to them. It seemed to be a complete victory for the bands that had fought for their lands. In July and August, the troops finally marched out of the Powder River country and left the hated forts to the war bands, who quickly burned them. Finally, Red Cloud, the leader of the coalition that had defeated the Americans, received permission from a council of the Oglalas to speak to the whites with the authority of a peace chief and came to Fort Laramie, accompanied by a hundred and twenty-five war chiefs and headmen of the Oglalas, Hunkpapas, Sicangus, Sihasapas, and Sans Arcs, and signed the treaty. His war had ended.

Years of Turmoil

Red Cloud's days as a war chief were over. But as the most powerful and influential leader among the Lakota tribes, he had little peace in his relations with the American government. He and other chiefs who signed the treaty understood that it promised to leave the Indians alone in their own country, to keep troops and other whites out of their hunting grounds, and to let them reopen trade for arms, powder, and lead necessary for their hunts, at posts along the Platte River, where they had traded peacefully for many years prior to the troubles that began with Chivington's massacre of the Cheyennes.

Soon, however, as the army began to implement orders from Washington, it became apparent to Red Cloud and the other chiefs that the government had an additional agenda of its own that it had not revealed or made clear to the Indians. For one thing, the government intended to establish all of present-day South Dakota west of the Missouri River as a reservation and, forcing all the western Sioux onto it, make them report to an agency at Fort Randall on the Missouri River at the reservation's southeastern tip, far from their buffalo ranges. Second, while the Indians could continue hunting in the Powder River country, the arrangement had been forced on the government, which considered it a temporary expedient. The land between the Black Hills and the Big Horn Mountains, so vigorously defended by Red Cloud's forces and now not included in the proposed reservation but referred to confusingly as "unceded land," might sooner or later have to be given up

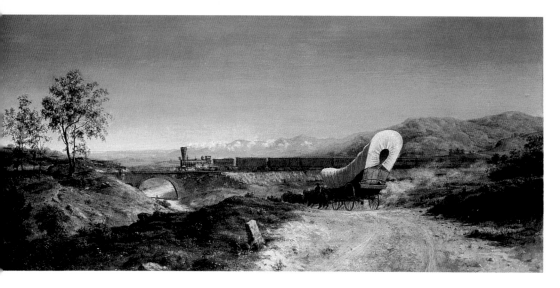

Settlers from the East poured across the plains in the 1860s, disturbing the hunting lands and sacred sites of the Sioux and other Indians. On the Road shows a covered wagon heading west after the railroads were built.

to Montana, Wyoming, and South Dakota whites, who were already clamoring for the right to hunt gold in the Big Horns and take up claims in watered areas of the plains.

Finally, the government, pushed by the railroad builders, who were trying to rush construction of the Union Pacific along the Platte River and finance its work by selling its grant lands in the Platte Valley to settlers, planned to force all Indians out of that valley, driving the Sioux north onto the new reservation in South Dakota, where they could not interfere with the construction of the railroad. Trading at the posts along the Platte would be prohibited.

As the bands that had fought for the Powder River country became aware of the government's intentions, many of them, including the followers of the rising young war leader Crazy Horse, grew suspicious of Red Cloud, who had signed the treaty that seemed to provide for a reservation and a far-off agency. Insisting that the treaty of peace had said nothing about a reservation or a ban against use of the Platte Valley, Red Cloud demanded to be taken to Washington to straighten things out. Because of his resistance to the troops in the Powder River country, he had become to white Americans the most famous Indian in the country, celebrated particularly by peace advocates, humanitarians, and reformers in the East. With their support, he won approval for his trip from President Grant, who thought it would also be wise to use his visit as an opportunity to impress him with the might and power of the white man's population centers—an old device used to awe recalcitrant chiefs into submission.

In 1870, Red Cloud and an Indian delegation traveled to Washington. This time, the white man's plan did not succeed. Conducting themselves with pride and dignity, Red Cloud and his fellow chiefs had little interest in seeing the sights or being put off by entertainment. After a polite but cool visit with President Grant, they got down

Red Cloud journeyed to Washington to discuss with President Ulysses S. Grant the provisions of the 1868 peace treaty he had signed, which were being interpreted quite differently after the fact. Here, he is with the delegation that accompanied him. From left to right: Red Dog, Little Wound, John Bridgeman (the interpreter), Red Cloud, American Horse, and Red Shirt.

to business with the secretary of the interior, who told them that they would have to take their people to the agencies on the new reservation. When Red Cloud refused angrily, the full text of the treaty was read to the chiefs. So much in it was apparently new to them that Red Cloud became furious and called it full of lies. "This is the first time I have heard of such a treaty," he declared. "I never heard of it and do not mean to follow it." When offered a copy of the treaty to take with him, he pushed it away, repeating, "It is all lies."

Newspaper reporters covering the meeting conveyed Red Cloud's charges to their readers, adding their own editorial reactions. Wrote *The New York Times*:

> We might search in vain through a month's file of the Congressional *Globe* for a speech so interesting as that delivered by Red Cloud at the Indian Council yesterday. . . .
>
> The clear conception which this unlettered savage possesses of what he claims as his rights, and what he is disposed to resent in his wrong, shows very plainly the necessity for treating with the leaders of the aboriginal "nations" on some straightforward and intelligible principle.
>
> The attempt to cajole and bamboozle [the Indians] as if they were deficient in intelligence, ought to be abandoned, no less than the policy of hunting them down like wild beasts.

Added the New York *Herald:*

> Palaver has very little effect on the Indian character . . . faithlessness on our part in the matter of treaties, and gross swindling of the Indians . . . are at the bottom of all this Indian trouble.

Enraged by the deceit and so shamed that some of the chiefs thought of committing suicide, the delegation demanded that they be returned to their homes immediately. Instead, the government sent them to New York, where it was hoped they would be further impressed by the strength and splendor of the white man's civilization. Again, Red Cloud had no interest in tourism but, at the invitation of reformers who believed that the government and the army were responsible for the Indian troubles in the West, delivered a stirring address at Cooper Institute, charging the whites with a long list of lies and broken promises. "We want to keep peace," he told the large, sympathetic audience. "Will you help us?" Then he went on to explain the current betrayal:

Angered by the American government's treatment of the Lakotas, Red Cloud, celebrated for his triumph over the army in 1868, addresses a sympathetic, standing-room-only audience at the Cooper Institute in New York City. This illustration of the meeting, with other Lakotas who accompanied him to the East sitting in the front rows, appeared in Harper's Weekly, July 2, 1870.

In 1868 men came out and brought papers. We could not read them, and they did not tell us what was in them. We thought the treaty was to remove the forts, and that we should then cease from fighting. . . .

When I reached Washington, the Great Father [President Grant] explained to me what the treaty was, and showed me that the interpreters had deceived me. All I want is right and just.

I wish to know why Commissioners are sent out to us who do nothing but rob us and get the riches of this world away from us.

His speech caused a sensation, and the ensuing appeals in the East for justice to his people forced the government to make some compromises. Red Cloud was given permission to visit trading posts near Fort Laramie in the North Platte Valley, and in 1871, despite angry protests from the anti-Indian white population in the West, a special agency for Red Cloud and his band was established thirty-two miles east of Fort Laramie, on the North Platte River. At the same time, Sinte Gleshka and the Sicangus received their own agency on the White River in northwestern Nebraska.

Meanwhile, many of the Sioux bands had grown wary of Red Cloud, finding fault with his ambition and imperious leadership and accusing him of having sold out to the whites for their gifts and favor. About two-thirds of the Oglalas followed him to his new agency. The others, determined to remain free and no longer trusting him to lead them in defense of their lands, stayed in the Powder River hunting grounds or moved north onto the Montana buffalo ranges, meeting Sitting Bull's Hunkpapa Sioux and other northern Teton bands and looking up to the brave and uncompromising leadership of the Oglala warrior Crazy Horse, who had turned against Red Cloud. In 1872, those who had lost faith in Red Cloud felt they were proved right. In behalf of the govern-

The attempt to cajole and bamboozle [the Indians] as if they were deficient in intelligence, ought to be abandoned, no less than the policy of hunting them down like wild beasts.

—THE NEW YORK TIMES

HIEF SITTING BULL
SIOUX —

Tatanka Yotanka (Sitting Bull), Hunkpapa Lakota war and spiritual leader, did not agree to the conditions of the Fort Laramie treaty of 1868 and would not abide by its provisions. Morally strong and uncompromising, he made himself highly and threateningly visible to whites, who targeted him as the most defiant and influential of all the "hostile" Sioux chiefs.

ment, Red Cloud sent a message to Sitting Bull and the other chiefs of the bands in the North that made clear his capitulation to the whites:

> Friends, I carried on the war against the whites with you until I went to see my Great Father [the President] two years ago. My Great Father spoke good to me. I remembered his words and came home. . . . I asked for many things for my people, he gave me those things. . . . I shall not go to war any more with the whites. I shall do as my Great Father says and make my people listen. . . . You must carry on the war your selves. I am done.

The next year, despite Red Cloud's protests, the government went back on its promise to him and moved his agency farther north, away from the railroad route and the growing numbers of whites in the Platte Valley and closer to Sinte Gleshka's agency in northwestern Nebraska. Many of the antiwhite bands in the North began an annual routine of trailing into the agencies to live on government rations during the winter and leaving in the summer to hunt where they pleased. In effect, the government had split the powerful Teton Sioux. To the whites, the followers of Red Cloud and Sinte Gleshka who stayed at the agencies were "friendlies"; the rest—the freedom-loving bands—were "hostiles."

"A Good Day to Die!"

In 1874, George Armstrong Custer, who six years before had slaughtered Black Kettle's Southern Cheyennes on the Washita River, brought all the western Sioux face-to-face with another crisis. Ignoring the Treaty of 1868, which guaranteed to the Sioux the western half of present-day South Dakota as a reservation for their perpetual and exclusive use, General Sheridan sent Custer and a large reconnaissance expedition into the Black Hills, in the heart of the reservation, to locate a site for a new fort.

The intrusion was a violation of the treaty, which read, "No white person or persons, shall be permitted to settle upon or occupy any portion of the [territory], or without the consent of the Indians . . . to pass through the same." To the Sioux, the sacred Paha Sapa, or Black Hills, were the spiritual center of their world, where their people withdrew from the hot plains to fast and pray, to cry for a vision, establish communion with the supernatural world, and, at the springs and among the cool, pine-covered hills, renew their strength and spiritual well-being.

Compounding the affront to the Indians, Custer turned the illegal invasion into a gold-seeking expedition. When he found gold and trumpeted the news to the world, the results were predictable. Thousands of miners, entrepreneurs, and adventurers overran the Black Hills and the sacred sites of the Sioux, throwing up mining camps and towns, cutting down the woods, polluting the streams, and resisting successfully the army's halfhearted attempts to eject them. United in their outrage, the Sioux threatened war against the invaders, who, in turn, raised an outcry for the removal of the Sioux from what, in fact, was still the Indians' country.

The government's solution, overlooking the sacred nature of the Black Hills and regarding them as just another piece of real estate, was to try to buy them from the Indians. Red Cloud and a number of agency chiefs were summoned to Washington and, although bullied and threatened, insisted that all of the Sioux would have to be consulted. In September 1875, a special government commission finally met at the Red Cloud agency with some twenty thousand Sioux, most of them from the agencies, but others representing the different "hostile" bands in the north.

PATRICIA LOCKE/HUNKPAPA OF THE STANDING ROCK NATION/ WHITE EARTH CHIPPEWA
"The Black Hills have great significance to the Lakota and Dakota people. It is said that the prayer of the white man, the Lord's Prayer, has meaning because the Black Hills is on Earth as it is in heaven. It mirrors the constellations."

After the Civil War, gold was discovered in the Black Hills, which soon became overrun with miners, abrogating the treaties signed by Red Cloud and the U.S. government. In this contemporary photograph, miners are camped along a river in the Black Hills.

ISAAC DOG EAGLE/HUNKPAPA LAKOTA

"Sitting Bull went along the Grand River, where he decided to live. And while he lived there, the government wanted him to have horses. I think one of the things that they wanted to do was make them into farmers. So they gave him teams, horses, plows, they gave him chickens, what a farmer would need. Built a house, he even built a barn, of all things. You probably don't know that, but he had a barn and so he was living there peacefully."

I wish to know why Commissioners are sent out to us who do nothing but rob us and get the riches of this world away from us. —RED CLOUD

One after another, tribal spokesmen condemned the government. Typical were the remarks of a Lower Yanktonai chief, Wanigi Ska (White Ghost):

You have driven away our game and our means of livelihood out of the country, until now we have nothing left that is valuable except the hills that you ask us to give up. . . . The earth is full of minerals of all kinds, and on the earth the ground is covered with forests of heavy pine, and when we give these up to the Great Father we know that we give up the last thing that is valuable either to us or the white people.

Tatanka Yotanka, or Sitting Bull, a great warrior and also a spiritual leader with strong powers, was not there, but Hunkpapas conveyed his warning:

We want no white men here. The Black Hills belong to me. If the whites try to take them, I will fight.

Red Cloud, trying to reassert his authority to speak for all, demanded six hundred million dollars for the Black Hills. The commissioners offered six million dollars, and the council broke up without accomplishing anything. In November, at the instigation of President Grant, the government ordered all the "hostile" bands to come into the Sioux agencies by January 31 or be driven in by troops. The belief was that once the militant Indians had been brought under control at the agencies, they could be induced to sell the Black Hills on the government's terms. But January 31 came and went, and the "hostile" hunting bands in the north either would not or could not come in on such short notice in the dead of the Great Plains winter. In February 1876, as the United States prepared to celebrate the centennial of its own freedom, General Sheridan set plans in motion for a three-pronged spring campaign to force the free bands to come into the agencies.

But the Sioux nations would not be bullied. As the weather warmed, hundreds of warriors left the agencies and swelled the ranks of the fighting bands in the north. On June 17, at Montana's Rosebud River, a thousand Sioux warriors, led by Crazy Horse, stopped the first prong of thirteen hundred troops, commanded by General George Crook and accompanied by Crow and Shoshoni scouts, and forced their withdrawal to a base camp in the south.

From the Rosebud, Crazy Horse's force crossed to the valley of the Little Bighorn River, known to the Indians as the Greasy Grass, and joined an enormous village of seven to ten thousand Lakotas, Yanktonais, Santees, Northern Arapahos,

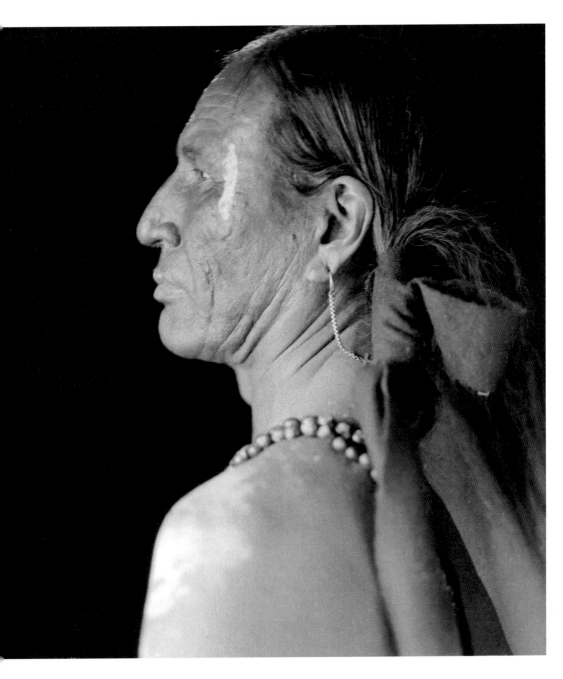

The Northern Cheyenne warrior Wooden Leg later wrote vividly of his experiences fighting Custer at the Battle of the Little Bighorn.

and Northern Cheyennes, whose camp circles stretched for almost three miles along the river. Farther north, the other two prongs of the army's campaign—one coming from the west in Montana, the other from the Missouri River in the east—met and turned south, hoping to trap the "hostile" bands. Advancing ahead of the main body, the 7th Cavalry, led by Custer—the man who had massacred Black Kettle's Cheyennes and had thought nothing of starting a gold rush into the Sioux's sacred country—sighted and prepared to attack the huge camp on the Little Bighorn.

Feeling secure in their own country, the Sioux and their allies had taken no precautions to guard against a surprise attack, and it was not until the dust of the approaching cavalrymen rose from the ridges east of the river that they were aware of the danger. Wooden Leg, a young Northern Cheyenne warrior, recalled the scene among the Cheyenne tipis, the northernmost in the line of camps:

> Women were screaming and men were letting out war cries. Through it all we could hear old men calling, "Soldiers are here! Young men, go out and fight them."

On the hills above the river, Custer divided his command. Some of the soldiers crossed the Little Bighorn south of the camps, turned north, and opened the battle by charging toward the Hunkpapa village, the southernmost of the Indian camps. As the soldiers came toward them, Sitting Bull rallied his men to protect the women and

Sitting Bull's Hunkpapa Sioux encampment on the Little Bighorn River is seen in this re-created version. With a total population of seven to ten thousand, the camp circles stretched for almost three miles along the stream, making the gathering one of the largest assemblies of Plains Indians in history.

children. Runs-the-Enemy, a Cut Head Yanktonai Sioux with the Hunkpapas, remembered hearing him:

> Sitting Bull . . . said . . . "A bird, when it is on its nest, spreads its wings to cover the nest and eggs and protect them. . . . We are here to protect our wives and children, and we must not let the soldiers get them." He was on a buckskin horse, and he rode from one end of the line to the other, calling out: "Make a brave fight!"

Chief Gall led the Hunkpapa warriors out of camp to fight off the soldiers. Later, he told whites who asked him what he had done:

> If you . . . had a country which was very valuable, which had always belonged to your people . . . and men of another race came to take it away by force, what would your people do? Would they fight?

Gall's fierce frontal attack hurled the soldiers back. In panic, they recrossed the river and scrambled up the bluffs, with the Hunkpapas after them. Meanwhile, other soldiers, led by Custer, marched north on the hills across the river from the Indians' camps, then came down near the Cheyenne camp to try to cross the river. Wooden Leg spoke of the confusion among his people:

> Women were hurriedly making up little packs for flight. Some were going off northward or across the river without any packs. Children were hunting for their mothers. Mothers were anxiously trying to find their children. . . . The air was so full of dust I could not see where to go. . . . Many hundreds of Indians on horseback were dashing to and fro in front of a body of soldiers. The soldiers were on the level valley ground and were shooting with rifles. Not many bullets were being sent back at them, but thousands of arrows were falling among them.

Chief Gall, leader of the Hunkpapa warriors at the Little Bighorn, first turned back Reno's attack on the Hunkpapa village, then helped destroy the companies with Custer. Raised as an orphan by Sitting Bull, he is seen here in one of many photographs taken of him by David F. Barry.

Two Moons, the leader of the Northern Cheyenne camp, heard the shooting from where he was swimming in the Little Bighorn below his village:

> I looked up the Little Horn towards Sitting Bull's camp. I saw a great dust rising. It looked like a whirlwind. . . . Chief Gall was there fighting, Crazy Horse also. . . . I saw flags come up over the hill to the east. . . . Then the soldiers rose all at once, all on horses. . . . Then the Sioux rode up the ridge on all sides, riding very fast. The Cheyennes went up the left way. Then the shooting was quick, quick. . . .

In the camps, the Indian women, children, and old people could hear the sounds of battle among the hills and coulees across the river, but in the smoke and dust they could not see which side was winning.

Led by Gall, the Hunkpapas broke off the fight on top of the bluffs where they had chased the first troops that had attacked them and, turning north, fell on the soldiers with Custer. At the same time, other Indians plunged across the river and attacked Custer's men from the west. Among them were the Cheyennes under Two Moons. "We circled all round [them]— swirling like water round a stone," he said later.

Meanwhile, in the Oglala camp, Crazy Horse mounted his horse and called for his Oglala warriors to follow him. "Come on, Lakotas! It's a good day to die," he yelled. Crossing the river, they flanked Custer's men on the north and east, tightening the Indian circle around the soldiers. Black Elk, a thirteen-year-old Oglala, watched the fighting from the village. "A big dust [was]

We want no white men here. The Black Hills belong to me. If the whites try to take them, I will fight.

—SITTING BULL

Chief Two Moons, seen in the long trailing headdress of eagle feathers that marked his many exploits, led the Cheyennes at the Little Bighorn.

Although no photograph was ever taken of the Oglala hero Crazy Horse, this painting by the Lakota Sioux artist Amos Bad Heart Bull shows him on a white horse charging in among Custer's fleeing troopers at the Battle of the Little Bighorn.

This highly dramatic lithograph, titled Custer's Last Charge, *was one of many imaginary depictions that appeared soon after the American defeat.*

whirling on the hill, and then the horses began coming out of it with empty saddles," he said.

The fight against the men with Custer was over in less than half an hour. "The shots quit coming from the soldiers," Wooden Leg recalled. "Warriors who had crept close to them began to call out that all of the white men were dead. All of the Indians then jumped up and rushed forward. . . . The air was full of dust and smoke."

Sitting Bull's nephew, White Bull, was one of several who thought he had killed Custer:

On the hill top, I met my [uncle]. . . . He had been around Fort Abraham Lincoln and knew [Custer] by sight. When he came to the tall soldier lying on his back . . . [he] pointed him out and said, "Long Hair thought he was the greatest man in the world. Now he lies there."

Throughout the rest of the day and that night, the Indians besieged the first troops who had attacked the Hunkpapa camp and whom they had chased back across the river and up the bluffs. On the following day, Sitting Bull's scouts sighted a second army coming up the valley of the Little Bighorn. Firing the grass as a smoke screen, the Indian forces broke camp and headed toward the Big Horn Mountains. News of the battle reached the outside world on July 4, 1876, casting a pall over the nation's celebration of its hundredth anniversary of independence. The next morning's newspapers, ignoring all evidence, called the Indians' battle victory a "massacre." Outraged by the blow

to their national pride, the American public cried out for the immediate punishment of the tribes, and revenge-hungry soldiers in the West struck back at any Indians they could find. One group that felt their fury was the Cheyenne band of Iron Teeth:

> When the snow had fallen deep, a great band of soldiers came. They rode right into our camp and shot women and children, as well as men. Crows, Pawnees, Shoshonis, some Arapahos and other Indians were with them. We who could do so ran away. . . . As our family were going out of camp, my husband and our older son kept behind and fought off the soldiers. . . . I saw [my husband] fall. . . . I wanted to go back to him, but my two sons made me go on. . . . From the hill-tops we Cheyennes looked back and saw all of our lodges and every-thing in them being burned into nothing but smoke and ashes. . . . When spring came, all of the Cheyennes surrendered to soldiers. . . .

Sitting Bull's camp broke up, and many Indians went to the agencies, where military rule was quickly imposed on them and their horses and weapons confiscated. In September, government commissioners met with the agency Sioux and their chiefs, including Red Cloud, and, threatening to cut off their rations, forced them to sign

away not only the Black Hills but all the unceded hunting grounds to the west, including the Powder River country and the Big Horn Mountains.

Throughout the fall and winter, armies, dedicated to revenge for the Little Bighorn defeat, pursued the "hostile" bands through the Black Hills and across the cold northern plains. Again and again, military units fell on the Indians' camps, capturing food, blankets, and supplies and gradually forcing individual groups to surrender and go to the agencies. Those who got away from the troops suffered intensely from hunger, blizzards, and the freezing weather.

Finally, in May 1877, Crazy Horse led some of the last of the free Sioux—almost nine hundred members of his own band of Oglalas, still defiant and unwhipped, but starving and tired from fighting and running—into the Red Cloud agency to surrender. Thousands of Oglalas,

Long after the Battle of the Little Bighorn, its site was enfolded in the Crow Indian reservation. This tranquil view of a Crow encampment on the Little Bighorn was taken in the twentieth century by Edward Curtis.

already at the agency, lined the route to witness their arrival. It was a proud procession, two miles in length, with the almost-legendary Crazy Horse and his war chiefs riding abreast in the lead, the warriors behind them in feathers and paint, carrying rifles, shields, and lances, and the whole village with its travois trailing after them in the rear. They moved in silence, but as they neared the watching soldiers at the agency's Fort Robinson, they began to sing their war songs. "By God!" one officer remarked. "This is a triumphal march, not a surrender!"

The next day, farther north, Sitting Bull, whose Hunkpapas had been dodging punitive army columns for months, led several hundred of his people across the border to safety in Canada, joining other refugees who had preceded him. Permitted to

THE END OF FREEDOM

remain under the watchful eye of the red-coated North-West Mounted Police, Sitting Bull and his followers were exiles from their own country and, separated from the other western Sioux, were alone in the world. Still, American agents, working through Canadian officials, tried to lure him back, and the chief's responses, like the following, pricking the conscience of humanitarians, appeared in the press and kept the world aware of his presence:

> When I was a boy the [Lakotas] owned the world; the sun rose and set on their land. . . . Where are the warriors today? Who slew them? Where are our lands? Who owns them? . . . What law have I broken? Is it wrong for me to love my own? Is it wicked for me because my skin is red? Because I am a [Lakota]; because I was born where my father lived; because I would die for my people and my country?

At the Red Cloud agency, meanwhile, the army considered Crazy Horse a dangerous Indian and, setting a close watch over him, believed every rumor and report that circulated about him. By the fall of 1877, the United States was at war with another Indian nation farther west—Chief Joseph's Nez Perces. An officer asked Crazy Horse if he would agree to lead Oglala scouts to help the army fight the Nez Perces. Objecting at first, Crazy Horse finally agreed, saying he would fight until not a Nez Perce was left. The interpreter, however, translated his reply to say that he would fight until not a white man was left. Infuriated, the army decided to send Crazy Horse to a prison in the Dry Tortugas off the Florida coast.

On September 5, 1877, believing that he was being taken to a meeting with General Crook, Crazy Horse was led into a guardroom. Seeing that he was being imprisoned, he resisted. As Indian guards tried to wrestle him down, the officer of the day went at him with his sword, yelling, "Kill the son of a bitch!" A soldier lunged with his bayonet, thrusting it deep into Crazy Horse's body. The young chief sagged, looking up at his captors. "Let me go, my friends," he pleaded. "You have hurt me enough."

Crazy Horse died that night, aged thirty-five, uttering his last words to his father: "Tell the people it is no use to depend on me any more now."

His people buried him in a secret place near Chankpe Opi Wakpala—the creek called Wounded Knee. His image was never captured by photographers or artists, but his spirit of resistance and pride lived on among the Sioux who were still to go on fighting for their country and their freedom.

Chief Joseph

The spectacular mountains, canyons, and grasslands of the interior plateau country where present-day Idaho, Washington, and Oregon meet was the home of the Nee Me Poo (the Real People), given the name Nez Perces by early French-Canadian fur trappers who thought they saw some of them wearing ornamental dentalium shells through the pierced septums of their noses. The Nez Perces had always been friends of the Americans. In 1805, they had helped save the Lewis and Clark Expedition, whose members might otherwise have starved in the Idaho mountains. Later, they had befriended fur traders, had sought missionaries for themselves (and many had become Christians), and had assisted American armies in wars against other Indian nations in the Northwest.

The Nez Perces were a democratic people, made up of many villages, each led by a headman. Sometimes villages were united in bands that looked up to a single civil leader and to councils whose members were respected for wisdom or special abilities, but there was no overall tribal political leader or organization. Each village or band grouping of villages was independent and ruled itself. The people lived largely on salmon, and the villages were located generally at or near good fishing stations along the rivers. In addition, the people followed a seasonal round, hunting deer, elk, bears, mountain sheep, and other game and gathering many kinds of roots and wild foods. After acquiring horses in the early eighteenth century, the Nez

OPPOSITE: *This lithograph of an 1853 meeting with a hunting party of Nez Perce Indians in a forest in western Montana is from a painting by John Mix Stanley to accompany the report of a government exploring party led by I. I. Stevens to find a route for a transcontinental railroad.*

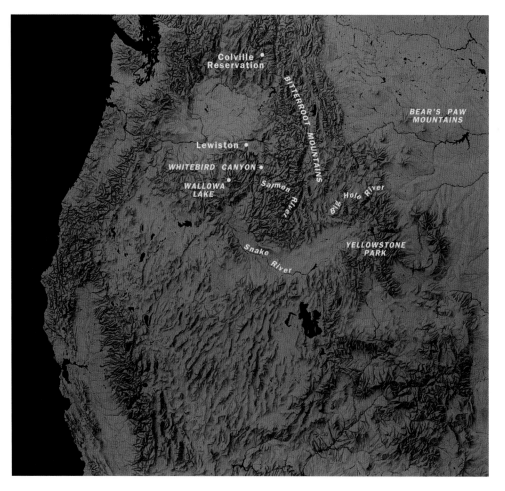

Perces became excellent horsemen, and some bands rode regularly to the east, crossing the mountains to the plains, where they joined Flat-heads, Crows, and other tribes in hunting buffalo. On these journeys, they adopted many elements of the Plains culture and added hide-covered tipis, travois, and other hallmarks of the Plains tribes to their own fishing-oriented culture.

In 1860, a party of prospectors stole onto the Nez Perce reservation, which the government in a treaty with the tribe five years earlier had promised to protect as Indian-owned country. The prospectors' discovery of gold brought a rush of thousands of miners who, defying the treaty, overran many parts of the reservation, establishing permanent white men's towns like the present-day Lewiston, Idaho, on the Indians' lands. For the first time, serious friction developed between the whites and the Nez Perces.

Under pressure from the miners to remove the Indians from the mineral centers, government commissioners in 1863 brought together all the Nez Perce bands and demanded that they cede nearly six million acres of their lands and accept a new, smaller reservation approximately a tenth the size of the old one. The new reservation would encompass the currently owned territories of some of the bands, including that of Chief Lawyer, a compliant friend of the Americans, but would exclude that of others who would have to give up their ancestral homelands and move onto the tiny, crowded reservation. Among the latter was the Wellamotkin band of the remote Wallowa country of northeastern Oregon, headed by Tuekakas, a gentle, elderly chief, who in 1839 had been one of the first two Nez Perces converted to Christianity and had received the name Joseph from the missionaries.

Tuekakas and several other chiefs who would have to give up their lands re-

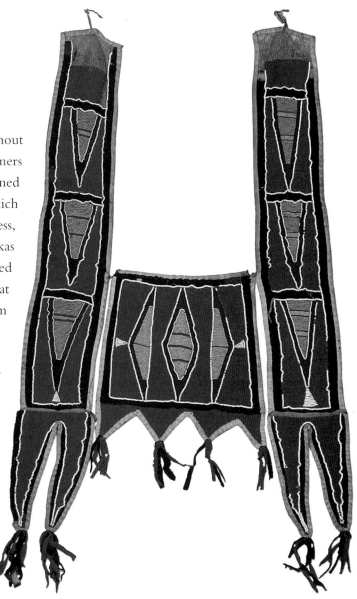

fused to accept the treaty and led their bands back home without signing it. As soon as they had gone, the government commissioners browbeat and bribed Lawyer and the other chiefs who had remained into signing the treaty in the name of the entire nation, which according to tribal custom they had no right to do. Nevertheless, the commissioners by trickery felt they had committed Tuekakas and the other holdout chiefs to the terms of the treaty and reported proudly to the Commissioner of Indian Affairs in Washington that they had managed to secure all the land they had demanded from the Nez Perces "at a cost not exceeding eight cents per acre."

When Tuekakas learned of the fraudulent action of the commissioners, he became angry and, maintaining that Lawyer had had no right to act for the Wallowa band, declared he would never give up his lands. At the same time, he threw away his Bible and returned to the religion of his own people. Although the government assumed that the Wallowa country of Oregon was now open to survey and white settlement, prospectors found no gold there, and for several years, largely because the area was canyon locked and difficult to access for families with wagons and livestock, no attempt was made to settle.

In 1871, however, the first settlers entered the Wallowa Valley, followed in succeeding years by many more. In 1871 also, Tuekakas, now blind and feeling death approaching, summoned his son, thirty-one-year-old Hin-mah-too-yah-lat-kekht (Thunder Traveling to Loftier Mountain Heights), who was known to the whites as Young Joseph, and, in words recounted later by Young Joseph, spoke to him of their Wallowa homeland:

Nez Perce horses were frequently decorated with beautifully beaded headstalls, collars, and other finery. The colorful piece opposite was attached to the bridle and worn on the horse's forehead. The handsome collar above probably developed from the functional martingale, the part of the bridle used to keep a horse from rearing or throwing back its head.

> My son, my body is returning to my mother earth, and my spirit is going very soon to see the Great Spirit Chief. When I am gone, think of your country. You are the chief of these people. They look to you to guide them. Always remember that your father never sold his country. You must stop your ears whenever you are asked to sign a treaty selling your home.
>
> A few years more, and white men will be all around you. They have their eyes on this land. My son, never forget my dying words. This country holds your father's body. Never sell the bones of your father and your mother.

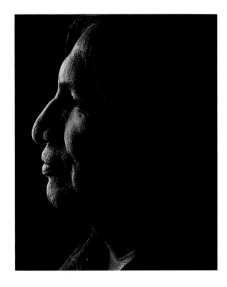

To which Young Joseph—soon to be known to the white man's world as Chief Joseph—added:

I buried him in that beautiful valley of the winding waters. I love that land more than all the rest of the world. A man who would not love his father's grave is worse than a wild animal.

As white settlers continued to enter the valley, creating homesteads, ranches, and towns for themselves, Young Joseph took over the leadership of the Wellamotkin band and for six years stood firmly against attempts to force the Nez Perces to leave the area and go onto the small new reservation in Idaho. Numerous councils were held between the Indians and civil and military officials, and at different times investigators concluded that the treaty of 1863 was defective and the government had not secured legal title to Joseph's lands. Convinced that an error had been made, the government in 1873 decided that the Indians still owned the area and, ordering the whites to move, turned most of the Wallowa country into a protected reservation for Joseph's band. As a result of the uproar that followed among the settlers and Oregon politicians, however, the government reversed itself almost immediately and decided the Nez Perces must leave.

The Bull's Head, a Nez Perce friend of American Rocky Mountain fur trappers and missionaries, was also known as Kentuck because of his frequent singing of a popular song of the times, "The Hunters of Kentucky." Later, with other northwestern Indians, he rode with Frémont during the conquest of California.

Still, there were delays and more councils, in which Joseph revealed himself not only as a skillful negotiator but also a warm and humane individual. Although he continued to explain that his people still owned the Wallowa country, he understood the dilemma of the whites who had believed that the government had purchased it legally and opened it for settlement. Hoping for a peaceful solution, he made many friends among the white settlers and won the sympathy of General Oliver O. Howard, the military commander whom the government had sent with troops to prevent hostilities and to try to solve the impasse.

In 1877, Howard concluded that the only solution politically practical to the government was to force all the Nez Perces, including Joseph and his people, who were still living in their own countries to sell their lands and move immediately onto the reservation. At a council, called at Lapwai on the reservation to deliver the ultimatum to the "nontreaty" bands—those who had not signed the 1863 treaty and were still off the reservation—tempers flared quickly. After urging the Nez Perces to resist, Toohoolhoolzote, an elderly leader of the traditional Indians' Dreamer religion and the headman of one of the bands, was ordered by Howard not to speak. Toohoolhoolzote rose in anger:

> Who are you that you ask us to talk and then tell me I shall not? . . . Are you the [Creator]? Did you make the world? . . . Did you make the rivers to run? . . . Did you make the grass to grow? Did you make all these things that you talk to us as though we were boys?

Howard lost his temper and placed Toohoolhoolzote in the guardhouse. To avoid what seemed to be an inevitable war that he felt the Indians could not win, Joseph finally agreed reluctantly to relinquish his homeland and bring his people onto the reservation. Returning to the Wallowa Valley, he led his band of approximately 250 Nez Perces, with all the livestock and possessions they could collect, sadly out of their country and across the Snake and Salmon rivers to an Idaho place of rendezvous where they had planned one last gathering in freedom with the other nontreaty bands. While the Indians socialized and rested before going onto the reservation, a young member of Chief White Bird's Salmon River band whose father had been murdered by a white man decided to seek revenge. Some friends, who also nursed grievances against the whites, joined him, and they rode away from camp and killed four settlers. Although the Indians were not members of Joseph's band, he later explained their rash actions:

You might as well expect the rivers to run backward as that any man who was born free should be contented penned up and denied liberty to go where he pleases.

—CHIEF JOSEPH

I know that my young men did a great wrong, but I ask, who was the first to blame? They had been insulted a thousand times; their fathers and brothers had been killed; their mothers and wives had been disgraced; they had been driven to madness by whisky sold to them by white men; they had been told by General Howard that all their horses and cattle . . . were to fall into the hands of white men; and, added to all this, they were homeless and desperate. I would have given my own life if I could have undone the killing of white men by my people.

Knowing that General Howard would now send troops after them, the bands withdrew to Whitebird Canyon. Although he had opposed war and had done everything to avoid it, Joseph threw in his lot with the other nontreaty groups and, joining them at the canyon, turned over his young men to the leadership of his brother, Ollokot, the band's war leader.

Guided by civilian scouts, Howard's troops soon appeared at the head of the canyon. Hoping to council peacefully and explain the impulsive actions of the few young men who had killed the whites, the Nez Perces sent out riders under a white flag. Ignoring the truce team, the troops opened fire, commencing a battle in which the Nez Perces, at almost no cost to themselves, wiped out a third of the soldiers and sent the rest fleeing for their lives.

Thus, exactly a year after the Sioux defeat of Custer, began what General Sherman would describe later as "one of the most extraordinary Indian wars of which there is any record." Outwitting and outmaneuvering one military force after another led by veteran Civil War officers who were sent out to overtake or intercept them, the united nontreaty Nez Perce bands of approximately 750 people, including women, children, and sick and old people, with all their baggage and a large horse herd, conducted an unprecedented fourteen-hundred-mile retreat, attempting to find safety from the troops. Circling through the mountains, canyons, and plateau prairies of Idaho, crossing the high ridges of the Bitterroot Mountains into Montana and Wyoming, colliding with frightened tourists in the newly created Yellowstone Park, eluding entrapment by a series of armies east of the park, and becoming surrounded finally on the cold plains of northern Montana, the Nez Perce warriors had to fight to protect their people almost all the way. Altogether, in three and a half months of flight, they battled two thousand American regular troops and volunteers of different military units, together with their Indian auxiliaries of many tribes, in a total of eighteen engagements, including four major battles and more than four fiercely fought skirmishes. At least 120 of their people, including 65 men and 55 women and children, lost their lives, and they killed approximately 180 whites and wounded 150.

"The Indians throughout displayed a courage and skill that elicited universal praise," observed General Sherman after the war. "They abstained from scalping; let captive women go free; did not commit indiscriminate murder of peaceful families, which is usual, and fought with almost scientific skill, using advance and rear guards, skirmish lines, and field fortifications." Throughout the retreat, the whites thought erroneously that Chief Joseph was leading the Indians, and newspaper reporters with the troops salved the generals' frustration by creating the myth that they were up against a "Red Napoleon," a true Indian military genius. Actually, the military genius was that of the people themselves, born of desperation. Decisions were made by councils of the war and civil leaders of all the bands, and until a disastrous surprise attack by the army that took the lives of many of the Nez Perces in the Big Hole country of Montana, the councils generally accepted the advice of Chief Looking Glass. After that, they looked to guidance and leadership from a half-breed Nez Perce Frenchman known as Lean Elk, or Poker Joe, who knew the geography of Montana. In battle, the war chiefs of each band led their followers. Joseph, as a civil chief, participated in councils, but in times of danger took care of the safety of the women, children, and old people.

At first, the bands thought they could find safety if they could get out of Idaho and reach Montana. When troops attacked them in Montana's Big Hole, killing so many of their people, they learned differently. Next, they believed that if they could reach

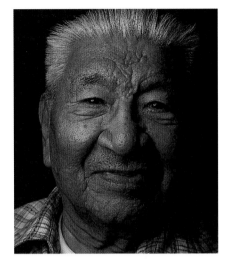

JOE REDTHUNDER/NEZ PERCE
"In early days, Chief Joseph had nothing against anybody. That's why he accepted those settlers to come into Wallowa Valley. Now just think what kinda people those settlers were. Wanting him out of there after he accepted them, see? Don't make sense. Now they're trying to control that Wallowa Valley. I think we have rights there. Still have."

Hohots Moxmox (Yellow Grizzly), an elder of the Palouse nation, some of whom fought against the Americans with their Nez Perce relatives in the 1877 war.

The Battle of the Big Hole in western Montana, where at dawn on August 9, 1877, pursuing army regulars aided by volunteers surprised a sleeping Nez Perce camp. Although the Indians turned the tables on the soldiers and managed to escape, casualties were high on both sides. This is an engraving of a painting made from a sketch by Granville Stuart, a pioneer Montana rancher who visited the site in the Big Hole Valley soon after the battle.

the Yellowstone country of their friends, the Crows, they could find sanctuary. They got there, but the Crows were no longer friends. Signed up by the Americans, Crow scouts and horse thieves attacked the column of Nez Perces, whose warriors had to drive them off, day after day, until they were out of the Crow country. Then the weary, dispirited Nez Perces decided to hurry to Canada and seek safety across the border in the camp of the self-exiled Sitting Bull.

Less than forty miles short of the Canadian border, near northern Montana's Bear's Paw Mountains, another army under Colonel Nelson A. Miles, which had been summoned by telegraph, surprised the Nez Perces on the open plains and, running off their remaining horses, surrounded the people in pits dug into the walls of coulees. During a five-day siege, Ollokot, Looking Glass, Lean Elk, Toohoolhoolzote, and many others were killed. Finally, with the women and children suffering terribly from hunger and the cold, Joseph surrendered on October 5, 1877. His eloquent surrender speech, delivered to General Howard and Colonel Miles, is among the most quoted of all Indian oratory:

> Tell General Howard I know his heart. What he told me before, I have it in my heart. I am tired of fighting. Our chiefs are killed. Looking Glass is dead. Toohoolhoolzote is dead. The old men are all dead. It is the young men who say, "Yes" or "No." He who led the young men [Ollokot] is dead. It is cold, and we have no blankets. The little children are freezing to death. My people, some of them, have run away to the hills, and have no blankets, no food. No one knows where they are—perhaps freezing to death. I want to have time to look for my children, and see how many of them I can find. Maybe I shall find them among the dead. Hear me, my chiefs! I am tired. My heart is sick and sad. From where the sun now stands I will fight no more forever.

That night, believing that the army would hang or severely punish those who surrendered, White Bird and others managed to escape in the dark through the army's lines and made their way successfully across the Canadian border to Sitting Bull's camp, where they finally found safety. Joseph claimed, however, that Colonel Miles

I buried [my father] in that beautiful valley of the winding waters. I love that land more than all the rest of the world.

—CHIEF JOSEPH

promised him that the Nez Perces would be returned to their own country in the Northwest. Neither occurred. After Joseph's surrender, the United States shipped the band south to a malarial bottomland near Fort Leavenworth in eastern Kansas, then to a hot, disease-ridden reservation in the Indian Territory. In both places, many of the Nez Perces who had survived the war died of sickness.

In exile, Joseph pleaded tirelessly in behalf of his people, attracting the support of influential reformers and humanitarians in the East and Midwest, who tried to help the Nez Perces gain permission to return to the cool, mountainous Northwest. In 1879, with their aid, Joseph was allowed to travel to Washington to plead his case in person to President Hayes and other government officials. On January 14, Joseph, celebrated as the Red Napoleon, spoke through an interpreter to a large gathering of cabinet members, congressmen, and diplomats in the capital. His stirring words were different from what the hushed audience had expected to hear from an Indian:

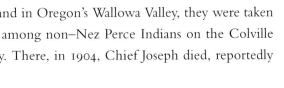

The aging Chief Joseph, photographed at his home in exile on the Colville reservation in Washington Territory. He died there on September 21, 1904, at the age of sixty-four of a broken heart, the Colville agency physician reported.

> There has been too much talking by men who had no right to talk. Too many misrepresentations have been made, too many misunderstandings have come up between the white men about the Indians. If the white man wants to live in peace with the Indian he can live in peace. There need be no trouble.
>
> Treat all men alike. Give them all the same law. Give them all an even chance to live and grow. All men were made by the same Great Spirit Chief. They are all brothers. . . .
>
> You might as well expect the rivers to run backward as that any man who was born free should be contented penned up and denied liberty to go where he pleases. . . .
>
> Let me be a free man—free to travel, free to stop, free to work, free to trade, where I choose, free to choose my own teachers, free to follow the religion of my fathers, free to think and talk and act for myself—and I will obey every law, or submit to the penalty.

In 1885, after eight long years and a massive campaign by the eastern humanitarians, Joseph and the other exiles were allowed to return to the Northwest. But Idaho's settlers and politicians still considered the 150 surviving Nez Perces "dangerous troublemakers," "criminals," and "murderers," and even threatened Chief Joseph with death. Unable to join the other Nez Perces on the Idaho reservation, or return to their own homeland in Oregon's Wallowa Valley, they were taken under military escort and dumped among non–Nez Perce Indians on the Colville reservation in Washington Territory. There, in 1904, Chief Joseph died, reportedly "of a broken heart"—and there, still in exile almost a century later, the descendants of his band continue to live, close to where he lies buried.

The Apaches of the Southwest

> Why is it that the Apaches wait to die—that they carry their lives on their finger nails? They roam over the hills and plains and want the heavens to fall on them. The Apaches were once a great nation; they are now but few, and because of this they want to die and so carry their lives on their finger nails.
>
> COCHISE, 1866, TO GENERAL GORDON GRANGER

OPPOSITE: *A young Chiricahua Apache demonstrates a one-string fiddle, probably inspired by Spanish musical instruments and made from a hollowed section of an agave plant.*

Far to the south of the Nez Perce country, the rugged mountains and deserts of present-day west Texas, parts of New Mexico and Arizona, and a strip of northern Mexico along its border with the United States were the home of the Apache Indians, whose name was derived from a Zuñi word meaning "enemy." Comprising six different tribes, each composed of autonomous bands—which, in turn, were made up of small, local groups of related families who often acted on their own under their own headmen—the Apaches had spread across the region after a long migration from the northwestern part of the continent that occurred sometime between the eleventh and sixteenth centuries.

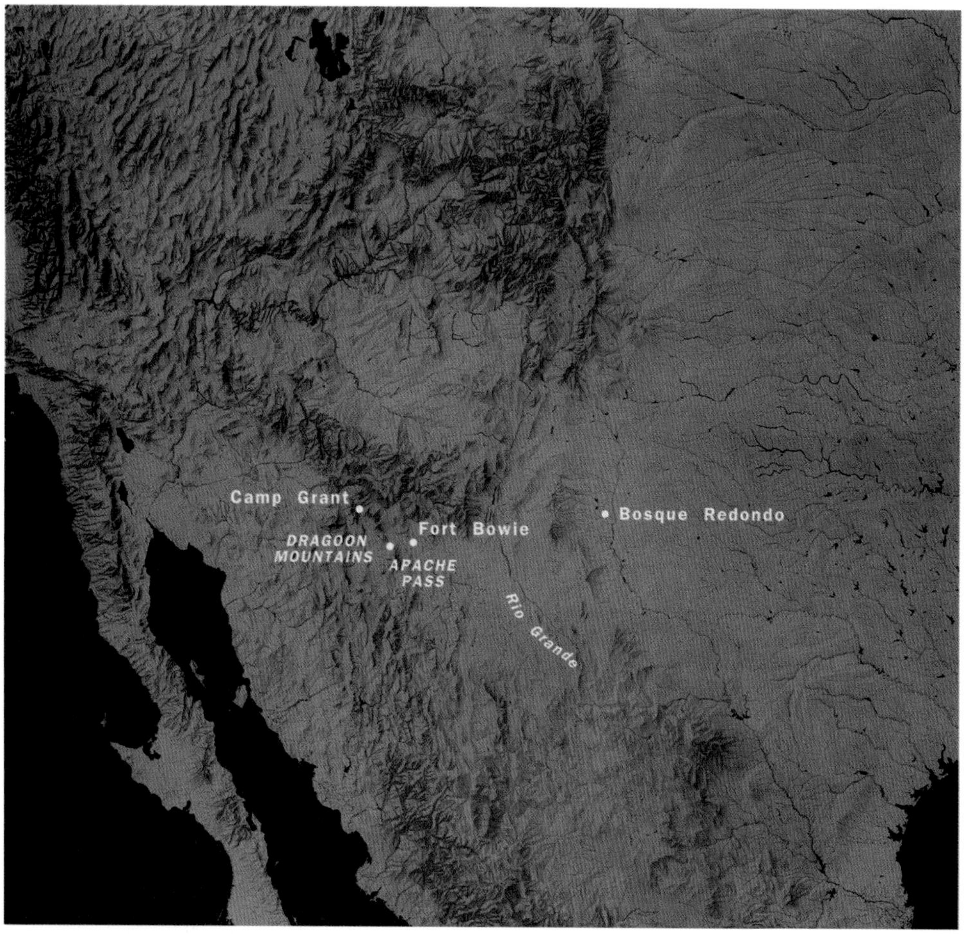

Alternately raiding and trading with the Puebloan and other nations who were already in the Southwest, some of the Apache groups adopted farming, but most followed seminomadic existences within their respective territories,

Camp Grant
DRAGOON MOUNTAINS
Fort Bowie
APACHE PASS
Bosque Redondo
Rio Grande

hunting deer, antelope, and other small game, gathering such wild foods as mesquite beans, juniper berries, acorns, agave leaves, and mescal heads, and maintaining home settlements or principal camps of circular thatched wickiups of cottonwood, willow, or mesquite poles, bound with yucca fiber and covered with brush and bear grass.

For generations prior to the American acquisition of the Southwest from Mexico in 1848, the Apaches were the victims of Spanish and Mexican slave catchers, and, in defense and retaliation, they waged unrelenting guerrilla warfare against the whites. Extraordinarily brave, resilient, and grimly cruel to their foes, they often traveled long distances to pounce on ranches and settlements for plunder and on livestock herds for food. In turn, their enemies raided them mercilessly for their scalps, which fetched bounties in Mexico, and for more captives, whom they could sell as slaves. When the Americans took over in the Southwest, the Apaches were at first friendly to them, but increasing threats to their lands and vicious and reckless provocations against them by miners, ranchers, U.S. troops, and outlaws turned them into enemies and brought on angry reprisals.

By the end of the 1850s, the Americans had replaced the Mexi-

cans, and, before them, the Spaniards, as the Apaches' principal enemy. With the outbreak of the Civil War, federal troops, needed in the East, were withdrawn from the Apaches' country; American forts in the region were evacuated and burned; and the overland stage line that ran through Confederate Texas and the Apaches' lands to California was moved farther north into securely held Union territory. Thinking that their resolute defense of their country had forced the soldiers and the mail coaches to leave, some of the Apache bands stepped up their killings, robbings, and burnings of settlers and travelers, hoping to drive all outsiders from their territories.

In June 1862, they clashed with Colonel James H. Carleton, the Union officer who two years later, as a general, would be responsible for Kit Carson's attack on the Navajos and for the surrendered Indians' Long Walk to exile on the Bosque Redondo reservation. Leading a column of federal volunteers from southern California to help confront Confederates on the Rio Grande, Carleton paused in Tucson and sent three couriers ahead to inform the Union troops in New Mexico that reinforcements were on the way. At Apache Pass, a rocky defile east of Tucson, Apaches ambushed the riders and killed two of them, chasing the third for forty miles before he got away. The Indians were members of a local band of Chiricahua Apaches, who called themselves Chookanéns and followed the leadership of a charismatic headman named Cochise.

To the Americans, Cochise had originally been one of the least hostile of the Apache leaders. He had allowed the overland stages to run through his peoples' territory, had supplied firewood to the stage station in Apache Pass, and had tolerated the use of the vital spring in the pass by passengers and the stage company's personnel and livestock. Early in 1861, however, a year and a half before the killing of Carleton's couriers, an army detachment, led by Lieutenant George N. Bascom, an inexperienced officer, had turned Cochise into an unforgiving enemy of the Americans by seizing him during a council in the erroneous belief that he had taken part in a raid on a ranch and had stolen livestock and kidnapped a boy. Cochise, whose people had had nothing to do with the affair, drew a knife, slashed his way out of a tent where the soldiers were holding him, and escaped in a volley of gunfire that wounded him in the leg. The troops managed to seize other Indians who had been waiting for Cochise and hanged six of them, including Cochise's brother and two of his nephews.

Cochise was enraged. "At last," he later told white men, "your soldiers did me a very great wrong, and I and my people went to war with them. . . ."

Now, in 1862, the Chiricahuas were not finished with Carleton. A week after they killed his two couriers, they murdered three troopers who had wandered away from a reconnaissance unit that Carleton had sent out to scout the road. And a few weeks after that, they ambushed Carleton's large advance wagon train in Apache Pass, killing several soldiers in a two-day battle among the rocks that lined the pass. The troops' howitzers, causing heavy casualties, finally forced the Apaches to withdraw.

Among the wounded was Cochise's father-in-law, Mangas Coloradas, a towering giant of a man and the head chief of the eastern band of Chiricahuas, known also as Mimbreño Apaches. Mangas had come with his warriors from their home in New Mexico's Mimbres Valley to help Cochise's people fight the new American army in their country. After the battle, the Mimbreños carried their wounded chief across the border to a doctor in the Mexican town of Janos, warning him that if he let Mangas die, the town would also die. The Mimbreño leader recovered, and Janos was spared a fiery death.

Mangas's reprieve from death would last less than a year. Establishing Fort Bowie to secure the route and protect the spring at Apache Pass, Carleton continued his march through the Apaches' country to the Rio Grande, where he found that the Confederate forces had retreated back to Texas. Placed in command of the federal troops in New Mexico, with no Southern army to fight, he commenced an all-out war against the different Apache tribes, issuing stern instructions to his officers: "There is to be no council held with the Indians nor any talks. The men are to be slain whenever and wherever they can be found. The women and children may be taken as prisoners. . . ."

This Apache Gan mask was worn by Crown Dancers who represented Mountain Spirits, or Gans, in important ceremonies. The hood that covered the dancer's head was made of painted buckskin or cloth and was surmounted by painted wooden uprights, or horns.

MELFERD YUZOS/MESCALERO APACHE

"A true Apache? Oh, the true Apache sees wealth as your family, that's wealth, your loved ones that are still alive, not what you have but who you have. That's what's wealth. We don't look for material things. I mean I'm glad to have the clothes I have, the jewelry I have, but I'd be happy as long as my family, my relatives are still living."

In January 1863, stirred by reports of the mineral wealth in the country of Mangas Coloradas's Mimbreño band, Carleton sent a force of his California volunteers under General Joseph R. West, a brutal, Indian-hating, peacetime newspaper publisher, to take care of Mangas and his followers. Lured from his camp for a talk under a white flag, the formidable chief, in his midsixties and well over six feet tall, was surrounded and taken at gunpoint. According to one of the California soldiers, West implied to the guards that they would have a free hand with the chief that night, telling them, "I want him dead or alive tomorrow morning, do you understand, I want him dead."

A gold miner in the camp watched the guards kill Mangas Coloradas during the night, first torturing him by burning his legs and feet with bayonets heated in their campfire, and then shooting him dead when his pain became unbearable and he tried to pull away. In the morning, the soldiers, claiming that the Apache chief had tried to escape, threw his body in a shallow ditch. Later, they cut off the head and boiled it in a big black kettle to remove the skin and flesh. Sent east, where scientists determined that it had a larger brain capacity than that of Daniel Webster, the skull eventually ended up in a cabinet in the Smithsonian Institution in Washington. To the Apaches, the decapitating of the body was much worse than death, for the body would have to go through eternity in its mutilated condition.

Although West, following Mangas's death, tried to exterminate the Mimbreños, even inviting one group to a feast to cement a peace and then opening fire and slaughtering them as they ate, he failed. Apaches retaliated, their terrorizing raids against the whites increased, and in the wars that followed during the next two decades as the gov-

Cochise's stronghold in the rugged Dragoon Mountains of southeastern Arizona. For ten years after a treacherous attempt to seize him, he and his fellow Chiricahuas conducted hit-and-run attacks on white travelers and settlements from this almost impregnable base.

ernment and the army tried to end Apache resistance and confine the people to reservations, new Indian leaders emerged and became legendary: Cochise, Eskiminzin, Juh, Victorio, Nana, Chato, Nachez, Loco, Chihuahua, Geronimo, and others.

The Apaches' resistance frustrated the growing number of whites in the Southwest and increased their fury against the Indians. In 1871, a mob of killers, dispatched by the citizens of Tucson, fell on an unarmed settlement of Eskiminzin's Apaches living peacefully under the eyes of the military commander at Camp Grant in Arizona and, in an orgy reminiscent of that at Sand Creek seven years earlier, massacred, raped, and mutilated the bodies of 144 helpless Indians, mostly women and children. A jury trial later found no one guilty of the atrocity. Weeks later, Eskiminzin, who had not been in the settlement when the mob attacked it, emerged from hiding to talk to a government investigator:

> If it had not been for the massacre, there would have been a great many more people here now; but after that massacre who could have stood it? . . . The people of Tucson and San Xavier must be crazy. They acted as though they had neither heads nor hearts . . . they must have a thirst for our blood. . . . Those Tucson people write for the papers and tell their own story. The Apaches have no one to tell their story.

Taza, Cochise's older son, became chief of the Chiricahua Apaches on his father's death in 1874. Under his leadership, the Chiricahuas agreed to move from their home area at Apache Pass to the newly established agency at San Carlos. Many refused to move, but Taza did not live to see the determined resistance that followed. He died of pneumonia in 1876 while on a diplomatic mission to Washington, D.C., and the leadership of the Chiricahuas passed to his brother, Naiche.

Meanwhile, in the rocky Dragoon Mountains of southeastern Arizona, Cochise maintained a hidden stronghold that commanded a sweeping view of the valley leading eastward to Apache Pass, from which the presence of the army's Fort Bowie had

After the deaths of his father, Cochise, and older brother, Taza, the tall, handsome Naiche, seen here in an 1884 photograph taken on the hated San Carlos reservation, became the hereditary leader of the Chiricahuas. With Geronimo, he led the resistance against government efforts to force the Chiricahuas to live at San Carlos. In 1886, he finally surrendered with Geronimo and was imprisoned at Fort Marion in Florida until 1894, when the Chiricahuas were relocated to the Indian Territory. In 1913, he was allowed to return to his Arizona homeland, where he died eight years later.

driven him. Cavalry under General George Crook combed the Dragoons, but Cochise's Chiricahuas held them at bay with guerrilla warfare and then eluded their pursuit in the rugged country.

In 1872, Tom Jeffords, a former stage driver and prospector, who had become a friend of Cochise and was known to the Indians as Taglito (the Red Beard), was permitted to bring General O. O. Howard—the officer who would later fight Chief Joseph—to Cochise's stronghold for peace talks. Fatally ill, Cochise won from Howard a promise that his people would be allowed to return to Apache Pass and live in peace on their own land. Before laying down his arms, he demanded of Howard a guarantee that he would be true to his word. Detesting the white men's lies to which he and other Apaches had so often been subjected, the Chiricahua chief warned the general:

I do not think you will keep the peace. . . . [Y]ou tell me we can stay in our mountains and our valleys. That is all we wish; we do not want to fight and kill whites, and we do not want the whites to fight and kill us. We want nothing but to live in peace. But I do not believe you will allow us to remain on the lands we love.

I warn you, if you try to move us again, war will start once more; it will be a war without end, a war in which every Apache will fight until he is dead. Prove to me that I am wrong; prove to me that this time I can trust you.

Taz-ayz-Slath, one of Geronimo's wives, with their child.

Howard agreed to Cochise's conditions, but, as the Apache chief foresaw, the general's promise would die with Cochise and the Indians would never be able to reclaim the region of Apache Pass. At the Chiricahua leader's death in 1874, his son Taza assumed the chieftainship of the tribe. But it was a medicine man of the Bedonkohe Apaches who would become the real force behind the continued Chiricahua resistance.

"Who Can Capture the Wind?"

About forty-four years old in 1874, Goyathley (One Who Yawns), whom the whites knew as Geronimo, had years before joined the bands of Mangas Coloradas and then of Cochise to fight the Americans. Now regarded as a Chiricahua and a war leader with strong spiritual powers, he had suffered at the hands of enemies of the

Apaches: twenty-five years earlier, his mother, wife, and three children had been murdered by Mexican troops. "I did not pray nor did I resolve to do anything in particular for I had no purpose left," he recalled in his old age. Nevertheless, the episode had given him compassion for the safety and well-being of his people, and a determination to protect them.

In the spring of 1877, the government ordered the removal of all Apaches to the San Carlos reservation in southeastern Arizona Terri-

Geronimo, photographed in 1887 by Ben Wittick. Aged about fifty-seven, the masterful leader of the last small resisting band of Chiricahua Apaches had become the most famous and feared American Indian.

OVERLEAF: *Naiche, the son of Cochise and the hereditary leader of the Chiricahuas, stands in the center of the front row of this group of Apaches who were led in their resistance by Geronimo.*

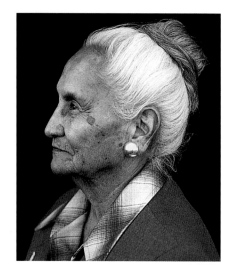

**MILDRED CLEGHORN/
FORT SILL APACHE**

"I'm almost sure we're the only tribe
that served that many years in prison.
I myself was born a prisoner of war, in
1910. We were freed in 1913, but we
had to stay here longer at Fort Sill in
order to get our allotments. . . . I grew
up here in Oklahoma, and never saw
my homeland at all, until 1986, a
hundred years later. Going, and looking
at those mountains, and having heard
about how they roamed up in the
Rocky Mountains and hid behind the
boulders and went into caves, and
having the opportunity of going into a
cave and looking up at the ceiling and
seeing the paintings that my people
put up there — that's too much. I can't
help but get emotional, because I can
just imagine how my grandmothers
and my grandfathers would have felt
if they had come back like I did. I saw
those places for them. I was able to
return, and see what they had left."

tory. Daklugie, the son of the Nednhi Apache leader Juh and a nephew of Geronimo,
described its harsh, barren land:

> The Creator did not make San Carlos. It is older than He . . . He just
> left it as a sample of the way they did jobs before He came along. . . .
> Take stones and ashes and thorns and, with some scorpions and rat-
> tlesnakes thrown in, dump the outfit on stones, heat the stones red-hot,
> set the United States Army after the Apaches, and you have San Carlos.

Although many Apaches relocated to the reservation, half of the Chiricahuas refused to do so and, according to Daklugie's narrative, followed Juh and Geronimo
into the mountains of northern Mexico:

> [Juh] told them that he could offer them nothing but hardship and
> death. . . . As he saw it they must choose between death from heat,
> starvation, and degradation at San Carlos and a wild, free life in Mex-
> ico—short, perhaps, but free. . . . Let them remember that if they
> took this step they would be hunted like wild animals by the troops of
> both the United States and Mexico. . . . All of us knew that we were
> doomed, but some preferred death to slavery and imprisonment.

For nearly a decade, the Apache resistance struggled on. By 1886, Juh was dead, and Geronimo, seventeen fighting men, and their families were being hunted from both sides of the border by five thousand American troops, thousands of civilian militia, five hundred Apache scouts, and three thousand Mexican volunteers. Daklugie continued:

> At that time [Geronimo] . . . had also Lozen . . . known as the Woman Warrior. Geronimo was handicapped by the presence, too, of women and children who must be defended and fed. Nobody ever captured Geronimo. I know. I was with him. Anyway, who can capture the wind?

On September 3, 1886, Geronimo surrendered to General Nelson Miles. He did so on Miles's promise that members of his band would be held as prisoners of war for two years, then be released and allowed to live in peace on the reservation. Nine years earlier, Miles had taken Chief Joseph's surrender in Montana, promising the Nez Perce chief untruthfully that his people would be returned to their country in the Northwest. Now Miles again promised more than he could deliver.

Although President Cleveland was applauded by whites in the Southwest when he recommended that Geronimo be hanged, the Apache leader and several hundred of his people, including Indians who had already been settled peacefully on the San Carlos reservation, were shipped to humid dungeons at Fort Marion in Florida, where more than a hundred of them died. There, too, all the Apache children were wrenched from their families and sent to the Carlisle Indian School in Pennsylvania, where sickness claimed the lives of more than thirty of them. Eventually, the Apaches in Florida were transferred to the Mount Vernon Barracks on Alabama's Mobile River. For twenty-three years, Geronimo was held by the government as a prisoner of war, exiled from his native land. Daklugie was proud of him:

> [A]bove all living men I respected Geronimo. He was the embodiment of the Apache spirit, of the fighting Chiricahua. . . . As long as Geronimo lived, he regretted having surrendered. He often said he wished he had died fighting in Mexico.

Transferred again, this time to Fort Sill, Oklahoma, Geronimo died and was buried there in 1909, still a prisoner in a foreign land.

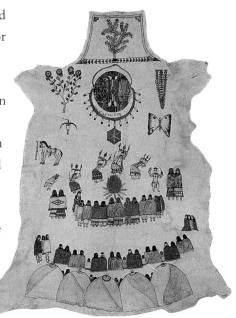

This depiction of Apache Crown Dancers participating in a girl's puberty rite was painted on a doeskin by Naiche in the 1890s.

OPPOSITE: *Apache prisoners, guarded by troops, pause on their way by train first to Fort Sam Houston in Texas and then to Fort Marion in Florida. Geronimo is third from the right in the front row, and Naiche sits just to his right. When Geronimo and his people surrendered to General Nelson Miles, they were told that they would be prisoners for two years. Twenty-three years later, when Geronimo died, he was still a prisoner of war.*

The Attack on Indian Culture

Our old chiefs are fast dying away, and our old Indian customs soon will pass out of sight, and the coming generations will not know anything about us. . . .
TWO MOONS, NORTHERN CHEYENNE

Twelve years of allotting reservation lands to individual Indians and opening surplus land to white settlers reduced Lakota tribal holdings on the Pine Ridge reservation in South Dakota from more than 2.5 million acres in 1904 to fewer than 150,000 in 1916. Here, Oglala Chief American Horse, a veteran of the Fetterman fight in Red Cloud's War for the Bozeman Trail in the 1860s, receives his allotment from government agents at Pine Ridge.

By the mid-1870s, reservations had become virtual prisons, ruled like empires by authoritarian agents who were given almost total power over the Indians. Shut inside the reservations, where outside eyes could not see them, the Indian peoples were subjected to unspeakable abuses. Housing monies were stolen, food rations were inadequate or spoiled, people were left to die without medical treatment or medicines, others were forcibly separated from their families to be punished without trial for real or trumped-up offenses, and individual Indians were frequently murdered.

The Indians were at the mercy of a system of corrupt government officials and private suppliers and speculators, known collectively as the Indian Ring, who, taking advantage of public indifference, cheated the powerless tribes. Trapped on the reservations, without freedom and the ability to provide for themselves in time-tested fashion or make their complaints known, the Indian families lived in poverty and misery. Eventually, eastern reformers became aware of the corruption of the Indian Ring, but despite their determination to destroy it, they believed that the only lasting solution was change—not of the Indian Service dictators and thieves, but of the Indians themselves. The Indians' traditions, beliefs, and ways of life were jumped on and condemned as backward, immoral, and wrong. If the Indians were to be helped and saved, the reformers believed, their tribal cultures and "Indianness" first had to be destroyed and

A southern plains woman, photographed in the Indian Territory near the turn of the century by the anthropologist James Mooney

forgotten. The Indian peoples would have to be remade—forced to assimilate into the mainstream culture of the country and become like all other Americans.

So began a period of deliberate deculturation. In 1887, an unseemly alliance of eastern reformers and western land-grabbers pushed through Congress the Dawes General Allotment Act, which broke up communal tribal reservation lands into small plots that were then assigned to individual Indians. The reformers' motive was to destroy the group-oriented institutions of tribes and chiefs by turning the Indians into independent, landowning farmers. Whatever land was left over after all allotments had been made could be sold to whites—which was the western land-grabbers' motive. Their foresight was correct. In 1887, the Indian nations in the United States still owned 138 million acres. By 1934, when the Allotment Act ended, 90 million of them had become white owned, and a large part of the remainder was leased out to whites.

Traditional Indian leaders across the country, recognizing the Allotment Act as an attack not only on Indian lands, but against tribal sovereignty and culture, tried to protest, but there were few who listened to them. "This is only another trick of the whites," declared Hollow Horn Bear, a prominent Sicangu Sioux chief. But Indian opposition such as his was ignored by government policy makers like President Benjamin Harrison's Commissioner of Indian Affairs, Thomas Jefferson Morgan, who in 1889 expressed his "strongly-cherished convictions" of what had to be done:

When I was a boy the [Lakotas] owned the world; the sun rose and set on their land. —SITTING BULL

> The logic of events demands the absorption of the Indians into our national life, not as Indians, but as American citizens. . . .
>
> The Indians must conform to "the white man's ways," peaceably if they will, forcibly if they must. They must . . . conform their mode of living substantially to our civilization. This civilization may not be the best possible, but it is the best the Indians can get. They can not escape it, and must either conform to it or be crushed by it. . . .
>
> The tribal relations should be broken up, socialism destroyed, and the family and the autonomy of the individual substituted.

In the field, the implementation of the Allotment Act was marked by wholesale fraud, trickery, and theft. Corrupt agents certified small children, dogs, and horses as allottees, then sold their allotments to whites. Indian orphans were shuffled off to white families, who adopted them to obtain title to their allotments. Meanwhile, the government adopted measures to strip the Indians of their Indianness and destroy their cultures. Their religions, rituals, and sacred ceremonies like the Sun Dance were banned. Medicine men and shamans who tried to continue their activities and counsel or cure Indians got into difficulties with the Christian missionaries on the reservations, and many of them were hustled into jail or exiled to the Indian Territory, far from their people. At the same time, old traditions, social dances and songs, games, the telling of Indian myths, legends, and folktales by grandparents, even the speaking of tribal languages, were frowned upon and usually forbidden.

Special attention was given to the education of the young Indians, who were frequently taken forcibly from objecting parents and sent to faraway, off-reservation boarding schools, where they were kept for years on end. Recognizing the importance of the role of the white men's schools in assuring that the next generation of Indians would not be "savages," Commissioner Morgan prescribed a procedure for taking the children away from their families:

> I would . . . use the Indian police if necessary. I would withhold from [the Indian adults] rations and supplies . . . and when every other means was exhausted . . . I would send a troop of United States soldiers, not to seize them, but simply to be present as an expression of the power of the government. Then I would say to these people, "Put your children in school"; and they would do it.

Morgan, on the same occasion, told of one of his own experiences:

> At San Carlos are the Apaches, who are regarded as the most vicious of the Indians with whom we have to deal. . . . These people decline to send their children to school; but I have within the last twelve months taken from that reservation about two hundred [children]. They are to-day well fed and properly clothed, are happy and contented, and making good progress. Did I do right?

ABOVE: *A kindergarten class at the Indian School in Riverside, California.*

ABOVE LEFT: *A biting cartoon of 1890 attacks corrupt government Indian agents. While the greedy agent is weighed down with the money bags of profits and wealth, the Indian, for whom the money was appropriated, is left only with starvation rations.*

In 1879, Captain Richard H. Pratt, who had been in charge of exiled Indian prisoners at Fort Marion, Florida, founded a school for Indians in buildings converted from a military post at Carlisle in southern Pennsylvania, where for eighty years cavalry officers had trained to fight Indians. Pratt had no trouble defining his goal in dealing with a young Indian who would be shipped to his boarding school from a reservation: "Kill the Indian in him and save the man." Instructing its students in vocational trades, as well as academic subjects, and thus intending to prepare the Indians for a life in the white man's world, Pratt's Carlisle Indian School, which lasted until 1918, inspired other Indian boarding schools that were established across the country.

Although the authorities in those schools could measure external changes in their Indian students, no measure recorded their torment. At Carlisle and the other schools, Indian children were stripped of all outward appearances that linked them to their Indian past. Their Indian clothing was taken away from them, their long hair was cut, and they were dressed in uniforms and Victorian garb. Under the frightening lash of "loud, shrill voices" commanding them to obey, to cease speaking their tribal languages, and to model themselves on white society, the children were dazed. Buffeted by distorted images of their own people as "evil," "heathenish," and "savage," most lost self-esteem and turned against, or came to doubt, their own identity. The school memories of Sun Elk, a Taos Pueblo Indian, were typical:

Late nineteenth-century government policy makers considered the conversion of Indians to Christianity of paramount importance if they were to be "Americanized" and set on the road to "civilization." During the Grant administration, the government even called on the various Christian denominations to appoint agents and teachers to take over the management of the reservations, giving them authority to convert the Indians. Shown here is a Methodist missionary with Kiowa children in the Indian Territory.

Indian students at government boarding schools spent much of their time learning vocational skills. Girls were taught to sew, iron, and do the laundry, while boys learned carpentry, blacksmithing, and, in the "Broom Brigade," the white man's ideas of orderliness. This picture was taken at the Indian School in Riverside, California.

We all wore white man's clothes and ate white man's food and went to white man's churches and spoke white man's talk. And so after a while we also began to say Indians were bad. We laughed at our own people and their blankets and cooking pots and sacred societies and dances.

Denied any knowledge of the true history, contributions, or achievements of Indians or the members and patriot leaders of her own nation—an obvious omission in the curricula of all the Indian schools—Mertha Bercier, a Chippewa student, told of emotional turmoil, loneliness, and alienation from her people:

Did I want to be an Indian? After looking at the pictures of the Indians on the warpath—fighting, scalping women and children, and Oh! such ugly faces. No! Indians are mean people—I'm glad I'm not an Indian, I thought. Each day stretched into another endless day, each night for tears to fall. "Tomorrow," my sister said. Tomorrow never came. And so the days passed by, and the changes slowly came to settle within me. . . . Gone were the vivid pictures of my parents, sisters and brothers. Only a blurred vision of what use[d] to be. Desperately, I tried to cling to the faded past which was slowly being erased from my mind.

Some youths resisted. After the events in the following account, Lone Wolf, a Blackfoot student from the northern plains, attacked his teacher with his fists. Transferred to another school, he was jailed for defending a fellow student against another disciplinarian teacher:

If we thought that the days were bad, the nights were much worse. This was the time when real loneliness set in. . . . Many boys ran away . . . but most of them were caught and brought back by the police. We were told never to talk Indian and if we were caught, we got a strapping with a leather belt.

I remember one evening when we were all lined up in a room and one of the boys said something in Indian to another boy. The man in charge . . . caught him by the shirt, and threw him across the room. Later we found out that his collar-bone was broken.

The boy's father, an old warrior, came to the school. He told the instructor that among his people, children were never punished by striking them. That was no way to teach children; kind words and good examples were much better. . . . Before the instructor could stop the old warrior he took his boy and left. The family then beat it to Canada and never came back.

An "after" picture of an Indian girl named Yellow Moon, taken six months after her arrival at the Carlisle boarding school.

MARCELLA LA BEAU/CHEYENNE RIVER SIOUX

"My experience at the boarding school was not being able to speak my own language. We were forbidden to speak Lakota, and those who did had their mouths washed out with soap and were punished. Fortunately, I knew both languages, the Lakota and the English, so I never had that done to me. And we had uniforms, blue uniforms which we wore and we were taught to march like they do in the military. I think it's very important to be able to speak your own language because there is a sensitivity that is lost when you translate into English. And also the humor, you lose a lot of the humor. And that's very important to me."

The boarding-school reduction of individual nations into a generalized melting pot reduced many Indians to nothing at all. Without self-esteem and a sense of their identity, thousands of Indian-school graduates, still alienated from, or rebuffed by, the white man's society and feeling insecure as Indians, fell between two worlds, failing as a "white," and no longer feeling comfortable on a reservation. Few of the people there had changed. Most had held firmly to their traditions, and returning graduates found they had no place in their old world. Poignantly, Sun Elk, the student from Taos Pueblo, recalled the tragic ending of his own schooling experience:

It was a warm summer evening when I got off the train at Taos station. The first Indian I met, I asked him to run out to the pueblo and tell my family I was home. The Indian couldn't speak English, and I had forgotten all my Pueblo language. . . . Next morning the governor of the pueblo and the two war chiefs . . . came into my father's house. They did not talk to me; they did not even look at me. . . . The chiefs said to my father, "Your son who calls himself Rafael has lived with the white men. He has been far away. . . . He has not . . . learned the things that Indian boys should learn. He has no hair. . . . He cannot even speak our language.

"He is not one of us."

ABOVE RIGHT: *A young Sioux boy about 1908.*

RIGHT: *European fine arts were also taught, as in this drawing class at the Phoenix Indian School.*

Traditional Plains Indian toys — beaded balls, lifelike dolls, and a miniature cradleboard.

BELOW: *"When the Sun died," said the Northern Paiute holy man Wovoka, "I went up to heaven and saw God and all the people who had died a long time ago. God told me to come back and tell my people they must be good and love one another, and not fight, or steal, or lie. He gave me this dance to give my people." Many years after he had founded what whites called the Ghost Dance religion, Wovoka was photographed making a motion picture near the Paiutes' Walker River reservation in Nevada.*

The Last Trail: To Chankpe Opi Wakpala

In 1888, to many of the conquered, despairing tribes in the West there came a sudden message of hope of a new life and of liberation from the bondage of their reservations. From Nevada, a new peaceful religion, preached by Wovoka, a Paiute man from the desert—with powerful medicine and messages from the supernatural world—spread like wildfire to the Lakota Sioux and other Plains tribes.

Performing special dances and songs and offering special prayers, all taught by Wovoka, his followers sought desperately to bring back the world they had lost, the vanished herds of buffalo and the times when their ancestors were alive and the Indian nations were free. Many danced all night and all day for a glimpse of the past. Some wore special shirts, which they believed would ward off the bullets of soldiers, who called the new religion the Ghost Dance and watched its growth with fear and hostility. Going into the Badlands and other places where they could avoid the whites, the Indians continued to dance. A young Lakota Sioux described their ecstasy:

> They danced without rest, on and on. . . . Occasionally someone thoroughly exhausted and dizzy fell unconscious into the center and lay there "dead." . . . After a while, many lay about in that condition. They were now "dead" and seeing their dear ones. . . . The visions . . . ended the same way, like a chorus describing a great encampment of all the Dakotas who had ever died, where . . . there was no sorrow but only joy, where relatives thronged out with happy laughter. . . .

Shirts worn by Ghost Dancers were usually covered with symbolic paintings. The stars on this Arapaho shirt symbolized the coming of a happy new age for the Indians, while the magpies and crows reflected the belief that the dancer would be flown from harm during the transition to the new day. Many dancers also believed that the shirt itself would protect them from the white men's bullets.

A photograph of the Ghost Dance, which was applied to a postcard and sold as a souvenir of the West.

The people went on and on and could not stop, day or night, hoping . . . to get a vision of their own dead. . . . And so I suppose the authorities did think they were crazy—but they weren't. They were only terribly unhappy.

Even old Red Cloud, who had counseled accommodation with the American government and now lived at the Oglalas' Pine Ridge agency in present-day South Dakota, understood and sympathized with the dancers:

The people were desperate from starvation—they had no hope. . . . We felt that we were mocked in our misery. We had no newspapers, and no one to speak for us. . . . We were faint with hunger and maddened by despair. We held our dying children, and felt their little bodies tremble as their souls went out and left only a dead weight in our hands. . . . Some [were] talking of the [Messiah]. . . . The people did not know; they did not care. They snatched at the hope. . . . The white men were frightened, and called for soldiers. We had begged for life, and the white men thought we wanted theirs.

As the Ghost Dance spread among the bands, the whites on the frontier panicked, assuming that the Indians were dancing a war dance and preparing for a huge, concerted uprising. Dedicated to the education and assimilation of the tribes, the government decided to halt the dances, but felt first that it would have to isolate the Indian leaders.

Sitting Bull, the Hunkpapa chief, did not join in the religious revival, but his commanding presence among the Sioux posed a continuing threat to the government's authority. After the defeat of Custer, he had been the last Lakota leader to surrender, finally ending his Canadian exile and giving himself up to the Americans at Fort Buford in present-day North Dakota in July 1881. After a period of imprisonment at Fort Randall, he was transferred to permanent residency among the Hunkpapas at the Standing Rock agency on the Sioux reservation.

Regarded as the man who had defeated Custer, he was celebrated by whites as the most famous living Indian, and for a while he toured with Buffalo Bill's Wild West Show, wryly reenacting his victory at the Little Bighorn and insulting white audiences in his own tongue, forcing nervous translators to think fast and conceal what he had said. When he returned to Standing Rock, he used his fame to agitate on behalf of his people, becoming a thorn in the side of the agent, who detested him and tried, unsuccessfully, to assert his authority over him.

Finally, the agent sent Sioux Indian police in the hire of the government to arrest Sitting Bull for allegedly supporting the Ghost Dancers at Standing Rock. Awakened from sleep at dawn on December 15, 1890, Sitting Bull was murdered by the police when other Sioux in his camp tried to help him. During the melee, Sitting Bull's circus horse—a gift from Buffalo Bill—began performing, sitting on its hind legs and pawing the air.

Some six hundred Oglala Sioux women wait patiently in line on ration day at the Pine Ridge agency in South Dakota to receive rations of flour, bacon, cornmeal, coffee, and sugar. Intended to help the Plains Indians make the transition from hunting to farming, the rations were cut by about 20 percent in 1890, a year that also saw a serious crop failure. Many Indians died of starvation, and the widespread suffering, together with the Lakotas' desire to regain freedom and control of their destiny, contributed to the popularity of the Ghost Dance.

After the murder of Sitting Bull, Chief Sitanka, or Big Foot, pictured here, led his band of Miniconjou Sioux on a wintry flight from the Cheyenne River reservation to the Pine Ridge reservation, where they thought they would find protection in Red Cloud's camp from hostile American soldiers. Near Wounded Knee Creek, the 7th Cavalry intercepted their path with tragic consequences.

The great chief's death portended further trouble. Ghost Dancers fled in terror, some attaching themselves to Big Foot's band of Miniconjou Lakotas on Cheyenne River. Although the band still contained many devout Ghost Dancers, Big Foot, a mild-mannered, peace-loving chief, and a number of his followers had recently stopped dancing and turned away from the religion, a fact unknown to the army. Troops now closed in on Big Foot's people, sending them in fearful flight for 150 miles across the wintry plains and Badlands to what they hoped would be safety with the Oglalas of powerful Chief Red Cloud at the Pine Ridge agency. Dying from pneumonia, which worsened during the journey, Big Foot was carried along in an open wagon. Short of their goal, the cold, hungry, and tired refugees were intercepted by the 7th Cavalry—Custer's old command—and taken to Chankpe Opi Wakpala (Wounded Knee Creek) on the Pine Ridge reservation.

There, on the morning of December 29, 1890, they were encircled by the troops and ordered to give up all their weapons. "It was understood that just as soon as all the guns were stacked in the center we were to continue on to Pine Ridge agency," recalled White Lance, one of the Miniconjous. Mrs. Louis Mousseau, the Sioux wife of a man half Indian, half white, who owned a log trading post at Wounded Knee, remembered later that "The white men were so thick here like a whole pile of maggots. . . . They took everything away from us that had a sharp point, any metal that had a sharp point. . . ."

On a hill overlooking the surrounded Indians, the troops set up a battery of four Hotchkiss guns, ready to fire on Big Foot's people. Down below, at a little distance from the circle of soldiers, was a newspaper correspondent, Thomas H. Tibbles of the Omaha *World-Herald,* who had ridden to Wounded Knee with the 7th Cavalry. "Suddenly," he wrote, "I heard a single shot from the direction of the troops—then three or four—a few more—and immediately a volley. At once came a general rattle of rifle firing. Then the Hotchkiss guns."

The single shot that Tibbles heard was an accidental one, coming from the rifle of a deaf Indian, who had not heard the soldiers' order to surrender their weapons and had raised his above his head, resisting efforts to take it from him. The shot panicked the troops, and in a fraction of a second, the soldiers and the Indians were shooting at each other. Screaming with fright, many of the Sioux burst through the army's lines, running for the protection of coulees. The soldiers chased them, shooting at everything that moved. Within the original circle, Big Foot, dozens of his people, as well as soldiers, lay dead, many of the latter felled by their own cross fire.

A Miniconjou woman, later known as Mrs. Rough Feather, was in the middle of the firing. "An awful noise was heard and I was paralyzed for a time," she remembered. "Then my head cleared and I saw nearly all the people on the ground bleeding. . . . My father, my mother, my grandmother, my older brother and my younger brother were all killed. My son, who was two years old, was shot in the mouth that later caused his death."

American Horse, an Oglala chief, described the deaths of the surrounded Indians and the Miniconjous' attempts to flee from the soldiers:

> There was a woman with an infant in her arms who was killed as she almost touched the flag of truce. . . . A mother was shot down with her infant; the child not knowing that its mother was dead was still nursing. . . . The women as they were fleeing with their babies were killed together, shot right through . . . and after most all of them had been killed a cry was made that all those who were not killed or wounded should come forth and they would be safe. Little boys . . . came out of their places of refuge, and as soon as they came in sight a number of soldiers surrounded them and butchered them there.

"Though the active attack lasted perhaps twenty minutes," correspondent Tibbles wrote, "the firing continued for an hour or two, wherever a soldier saw a sign of life. Indian women and children fled into the ravine to the south, and some of them on up out of it across the prairie, but soldiers followed them and shot them down mercilessly."

At sunset, the weather turned bitterly cold. After dark, cavalrymen arrived at the agency with a long train of army wagons bearing dead and wounded soldiers and Indians from Wounded Knee. The injured soldiers and Indian warriors were taken into the troops' quarters for medical attention, but forty-nine wounded Sioux women and children were left lying in a few open wagons in the freezing cold. Eventually, they were carried into the agency church, where they lay in silence on the floor beneath a pulpit decorated with a Christmas banner reading PEACE ON EARTH, GOOD WILL TO MEN.

"Nothing I have seen in my whole . . . life ever affected or depressed or haunted me like the scenes I saw that night in that church," Tibbles continued. "One unwounded old woman . . . held a baby on her lap. . . . I handed a cup of water to the old woman, telling her to give it to the child, who grabbed it as if parched with thirst. As she swallowed it hurriedly, I saw it gush right out again, a bloodstained stream, through a hole in her neck.

FLORENCE ARPAN/HOHWOJU AND TWO KETTLE BANDS
"I went to a meeting at Wounded Knee in November when there was snow all over the ground. And as we were traveling, and we were on our way to the burial site, I could not help but think back, how my people wandered, were wandering trying to find shelter for themselves out in the cold. And they camped along Wounded Knee Creek, where they were massacred. When we were there to that meeting, I was standing there at the burial site. And there was a feeling there. There was a feeling that those that were there in the grave were trying to tell me something and it brought tears to my eyes."

"Heartsick, I went to . . . find the surgeon. . . . For a moment he stood there near the door, looking over the mass of suffering and dying women and children. . . . The silence they kept was so complete that it was oppressive. . . . Then to my amazement I saw that the surgeon, who I knew had served in the Civil War, attending the wounded . . . from the Wilderness to Appomattox, begin to grow pale. . . . 'This is the first time I've seen a lot of women and children shot to pieces,' he [said]. 'I can't stand it.' . . .

"Out at Wounded Knee, because a storm set in, followed by a blizzard, the bodies of the slain Indians lay untouched for three days, frozen stiff where they had fallen. Finally they were buried in a large trench dug on the battlefield itself. On that third day Colonel Colby . . . saw the blanket of a corpse move. . . . Under the blanket, snuggled up to its dead mother . . . he found a little suckling baby girl."

The massacre of the Sioux at Wounded Knee, two years short of the four hundredth anniversary of the landing of Columbus in the Western Hemisphere, was a final exclamation mark to the long story of the white man's conquest of what is now the United States. The promises of Wovoka's religion did not long survive what happened at Wounded Knee. For the invaders, the American West was won. The attack on culture—and the resistance against it—would continue. For the Indians, the words of the Oglala holy man Black Elk, who was present at Pine Ridge in 1890, have moved humanity through the years:

I did not know then how much was ended. When I look back now from this high hill of my old age, I can still see the butchered women and children lying heaped and scattered all along the crooked gulch as plain as when I saw them with eyes still young. And I can see that something else died there in the bloody mud, and was buried in the blizzard. A people's dream died there. It was a beautiful dream. . . .

The nation's hoop is broken and scattered. There is no center any longer, and the sacred tree is dead.

The last decade of the nineteenth century and the first decade of the twentieth marked the low point for the Indian nations of North America. In Mexico and Central America, the descendants of the Aztec, Mayan, and other great pre-Columbian civilizations lay suppressed and mostly silent under foreign-dominated, imperialist dictatorships. In Canada, the Indian nations, broken into relatively small groups by the Dominion government to "diminish the offensive strength of the Indian tribes should they ever become restless," were scattered on more than fifteen hundred different reserves, living for the most part in poverty and neglect "out of sight and out of mind" of the non-Indian population. And in the United States, the Indian population was down from its pre-Columbian total of many millions to fewer than 250,000, and the traditional Indian, subjected to every pressure of coerced assimilation, had taken on the popular image of a "vanishing American."

MARIO GONZALEZ/OGLALA SIOUX

"We have lived under the white man's greed, the white man's deception, and we have suffered because of it. Our cultures have been assaulted, our lands have been stolen, but we're still here as a people. And we're fighting the same battles that have been fought for the last three hundred years, they're unresolved. And it's up to us to resolve them in a fair and honorable manner. Destiny is not a matter of fate, it's a matter of choice. And we have some choice of continuing to survive here on this planet as Indian people. That's our goal, and we're gonna accomplish that. We're gonna be here for many, many years to come as an Indian nation. . . ."

This 1891 photograph, titled Gathering Up the Dead, *was taken after the battle of Wounded Knee as bodies were removed from the field where they fell.*

OPPOSITE: *Piegan tipis like these, painted in the traditions of the tribe's forefathers and here photographed by Edward Curtis, can still be seen on the northern plains, standing like hallmarks of the future, as well as the past, of the American Indian nations.*

Since then, enormous changes have occurred. Population trends have reversed dramatically, and in the United States, for example, the Indians in 1990, a century after Wounded Knee, reached a total of approximately two million. Poverty, high unemployment, ill health, substandard housing, discrimination, racial and religious bigotry, homelessness, inadequate educational opportunities, stealing of land and natural resources, and other problems still afflict Indian nations everywhere. At the same time, after revitalized struggles during the twentieth century, many nations successfully defeated the white men's policies of forced assimilation and, reasserting pride in their histories, traditional cultures, and achievements as Indian peoples, took long steps forward on the road to restored self-determination, self-government, and sovereignty.

At the time of the five hundredth anniversary of Columbus's landing, tribal leaders of the United States gathered in ceremony in front of the Capitol in Washington, D.C. They gave speeches not about the shattered dreams of the past nor the broken hoop of the present, but about new dreams, a mended hoop, and the possibilities of the next five centuries for spiritually strong and determined peoples who, in the face of every travail and oppression, survived. That, in essence, was the story of the 500 Nations. They ended with the following words:

> We stand young warriors
> in the circle
> At dawn all storm clouds disappear
> The future brings all hope and glory,
> Ghost dancers rise
> Five-hundred years.

But that is another story. . . .

ACKNOWLEDGMENTS

This book adheres closely to an eight-hour CBS television film series titled *500 Nations,* narrating the history of the Indian nations of North America and produced by Kevin Costner, Jack Leustig, and Jim Wilson. Inevitably, it has borrowed extensively from the writings and research of those who contributed to the films, especially Jack Leustig, Roberta Grossman, John Pohl, Lee Miller, and W. T. Morgan, and from the picture research of Nazila Heyadat, Debra Spidell, and Corinne Szabo, and I am grateful to them for their generous role in the making of this book.

In addition, I want to thank the following: Jack Leustig, as well as Kevin Costner and Jim Wilson, for inviting me to write this volume to accompany their television series; Derek Milne and his colleagues at Pathways Productions for research assistance; Lynne Whiteford at Tig Productions; my editors, Ann Close and Ashbel Green, and Ann Kraybill at Knopf; Eric Baker and Kai Zimmerman, who designed the book; Peter Andersen, its art director; Susan Chun, the production manager; Sally Willcox of Creative Artists Agency, who brought me together with Tig Productions; Julian Bach, my agent; and my wife, Betsy, whose love, patience, and support, as usual, went into every page of this work.

Alvin M. Josephy, Jr.

Santa Barbara Studios, a special effects company, used state-of-the-art hardware and software technology to create the computer graphics imagery seen in *500 Nations.* This imagery included re-creations of the great cities of the Mayan, Cahokian, and Anasazi peoples, allowing us to travel through buildings, across plazas, and high above temples.

Visual Effects Supervisor, John Grower. Effects Producer, Bruce Jones. Animation Director, Eric Guaglione. Production Designer, Peter Lloyd.

NOTES

Chapter 1: A Continent Awakes

11 "My strength, my blood": Francis Garrecht, "An Indian Chief," *Washington Historical Quarterly* 19 (1928): 165–80.
    "When Earth was still": Glenebah Martinez, from a Taos folktale.

18 "The Crow country is": Washington Irving, *The Rocky Mountains, or Scenes, Incidents and Adventures in the Far West, digested from the Journal of Captain B.L.E. Bonneville, of the Army of the United States, and Illustrated from Various Other Sources,* vol. 1 (Philadelphia: Carey, Lea, & Blanchard, 1837), 212–14.

19 "The Great Father of Life": 36th U.S. Congress, House of Representatives, 1st sess.; as quoted in Virginia Armstrong, ed., *I Have Spoken* (Swallow Press), 77.

44 "Whenever the statesmen": *The Great Law of Peace of the People of the Longhouse (The Iroquois League of the Six Nations)* (Akwesasne: White Roots of Peace).

48 "In all your . . . acts": Ibid.; also quoted in Arthur Parker, "The Constitution of the Five Nations," *New York Museum Bulletin* 184 (1916): 7–158.

49 "Under the shade of this": Ibid.

50 "With endless patience": Ibid.

Chapter 2: Empires of the Sun

71 "They eventually went": From the Florentine Codex, bk. 10, 195; as quoted in Nigel Davies, *The Toltects* (Norman: University of Oklahoma Press, 1977), 50.

81 "Behold, a new sun": From the Florentine Codex, bk. 1, trans. Arthur J. O. Anderson and Charles E. Dibble (Santa Fe: The School of American Research, 1970).

83 "Now we have found the land": *Historia de las Indias de Nueva Espana y Islas de Tierra Firme* (unpublished manuscript, Madrid, 1581), trans. Catherine Goode.

87 "The might of our arms": Ibid.

94 "Proudly stands the city": Ronald Wright, *Stolen Continents* (Boston: Houghton Mifflin, 1992).

96 "They were very white": Father Bernardino de Sahagun, *The War of Conquest: How it Was Waged Here in Mexico,* trans. Arthur J. O. Anderson and Charles E. Dibble (Salt Lake City: University of Utah Press, 1978), 17.

98 "Then there arose from": Ibid., 23.

99 "When we saw so many": *El Castillo* (1916), trans. Garcia and Mauddey.

100 "The iron of their lances": Sahagun, 23.
    "Your Highnesses": Hernán Cortés, *Letters from Mexico,* trans. Anthony Pagden (New Haven: Yale University Press, 1986), 107–8.

102 "They [the Spaniards] charged": Sahagun, 43–4.
    "Great was the Stench": Adrian Recinos and Delia Goetz, *The Annals of the Cakchiquels: Title of the Lords of Totonicapan* (Norman: University of Oklahoma Press, 1953). Copyright © 1953 by the University of Oklahoma Press.

103 "That night at midnight": Sahagun, 53.

105 "The canal was filled": Ibid., 54, 62.
    "Once again the temples": Ibid., 63–4.

108 "Fighting continued, both sides": Ibid., 79, 86.
    "The battle just quietly": Ibid., 87, 89.

110 "Proudly stands the city": Wright, 15.

Chapter 3: Clash of Cultures

114 "[The Spaniards] made bets": Quoted in Kirkpatrick Sale, *Columbus: Conquest of Paradise* (New York: Knopf, 1990), 157.

115 "They believed very firmly": William Brandon, *American Heritage Book of the Indians* (New York:

American Heritage Press, 1993), 79-80. Reprinted by permission of American Heritage Magazine, a division of Forbes, Inc., © Forbes, Inc., 1993.

116 "These people are very unskilled": Ibid.

120 "I believe that they would": Oliver Dunn and James E. Kelley, Jr., *The Diario of Christopher Columbus's First Voyage to America, 1492–1493.* Copyright © 1989 by Oliver Dunn and James E. Kelley, Jr. Published by the University of Oklahoma Press, Norman.

121 "Note here . . . the natural": "The Life and Writings of Bartholomé de Las Casas," *Documents and Narrative Concerning the Discovery and Conquest of Latin America,* trans. Henry Raup Wagner and Helen Rand Parish (Albuquerque: University of New Mexico Press, 1967); as quoted in Wilford, 179-80.

122 "It is right that this": Dunn and Kelley.
"Columbus was pleased": Wagner and Parish, as quoted in Wilford.

123 "They are fit to be ordered": Dunn and Kelley.
"to capture" and "paying us the share": William D. Phillips and Carla R. Phillips, *The Worlds of Christopher Columbus* (New York: Cambridge University Press, 1992), 185.
"I took a most beautiful Carib": Ibid., 198.

125 "from the massacres": Sale, 159.
"anguish of mind": Ibid., 154.
"impossible and intolerable": Ibid., 155.
"Many went to the woods": Girolamo Benzoni, *Historia del Mundo Nuevo* (Venice, 1565); as quoted in *History of the New World* (London: Hakluyt Society, 1857), 77-8.

128 "as though he were the dung" Bartholomé de Las Casas, *Historia de las Indias,* bk. 3, chaps. 125-27, trans. Francis Augustus McNutt (New York: Putnam, 1909).

129 "Christians . . . are bad men": Las Casas.
"If we Christians had acted as": Wagner and Parish, as quoted in Wilford, 177.

139 "[Menéndez] has two hearts": Andres Gonzales de Barcia, *Barcia's Chronological History of Florida,* trans. Anthony Kerrigan (Gainesville: University of Florida Press, 1951), 139.

140 "We ask and require you": *Requerimiento.*

141 "conquer, pacify, and people": Garcilaso de la Vega, trans., and John Grier Varner and Jeannette Johnson, eds., *The Florida of the Inca* (Austin: University of Texas Press, 1951). Copyright © 1951. By permission of the University of Texas Press.

143 "I am king in my land": Ibid.

144 "sons of the devil": Ibid., 134-5.

146 "It was very fortunate": Ibid., 167.

147 "in the formal language": Ibid., 303.

150 "Who are these thieves": Ibid., 359.

151 "The Mobile fought with a desire to die": Ibid., 369.
"like a wooden statue": Ibid.

152 "[I am] not accustomed": Ibid.

153 "[Our] town had once": Charles Hudson et al., "The Tristan de Luna Expedition: 1559-1561," in *First Encounters: Spanish Explorations in the Caribbean and U.S., 1492–1570* (Gainesville: University of Florida Press), 128.

Chapter 4: European Expansion

160 "house doors studded": Alvin Josephy, *The Patriot Chiefs* (New York: Viking Penguin, 1958). Copyright © 1958, 1961, 1989 by Alvin M. Josephy, Jr. Used by permission of Viking Penguin, a division of Penguin Books USA Inc.

161 "has not told the truth": Ibid., 75.

163 "took his afternoon nap": Casteñada, *Coronado Expedition: Fourteenth Annual Report of the Smithsonian Institution, 1892–1893,* pt. 1 (Washington, D.C.: Bureau of Ethnology, 1896), 492-3.

165 "Your main purpose": Josephy, 130.

166 "once, twice and thrice": Ibid., 65.

168 "The village was very strong": Casteñada, 491.

"to the wonder and terror": Gaspar Perez de Villagra, *The History of New Mexico* (Los Angeles: The Quivera Society, 1933), 166-7.

174 "There is fear": Knud Rasmussen, *Across Arctic America: The Narrative of the Fifth Thule Expedition* (New York: Putnam, 1927).

180 "the brutish and uncivil people": Richard Collinson, *The Three Voyages of Martin Frobisher* (London: Hakluyt Society, 1867); also quoted in David Quinn, *The Roanoke Voyages.*

187 "very handsome and goodly": Thomas Harriot, as quoted in Quinn, *The Roanoke Voyages,* vol. 1, 101.

"there came downe": Ibid.

"buckes . . . hares, fishe": Ibid.

190 "[W]ithin a few days": Ibid., 378.

198 "such plenty of their fruits": Captain John Smith, *The General Historie of Virginia, New-England and the Summer Isles* (London, 1624), 44.

201 "a suit of red clothes": Helen Rountree, *Pocahontas' People: The Paladin Indians of Virginia Through Four Centuries* (Norman: University of Oklahoma Press, 1990), 40.

204 "Count the stars": Samuel Drake, *Biography and History of the Indians of North America* (Boston: B. B. Mussey & Co., 1848), 355.

211 "There is neither man": Alexander Young, *Chronicles of the Pilgrim Fathers of the Colony of Plymouth from 1602–1625* (Boston: Little & Brown, 1894), 182-3.

"a very lust man": Ibid.

215 "like the lightning on the edge of clouds": Samuel Goodrich, *Lives of Celebrated Indians* (Boston: Bradbury, Soden & Co., 1843), 200.

216 "terribly Barbikew'd": Cotton Mather, as quoted in Josephy, 55, 216.

"I like it well": Drake, 234.

217 "My heart breaks": Goodrich, 205.

"During the bloody": William Apess, *Eulogy on King Philip* (Boston, 1836), 48-9.

Chapter 5: The Cauldron of War

220 "ran up to the[ir] middle": Shaftesbury Papers, ed. Langdon Cheves (South Carolina Historical Society, 1897), 165-6; as quoted in Chapman Milling, *The Red Carolinians* (Columbia: University of South Carolina Press, 1969), 206-7.

"stroaked": Ibid., 207.

221 "brought deare": Ibid., 207.

"[Seeing] that the ships": John Lawson, *A New Voyage to Carolina* (London, 1709), 11-12.

222 "of the best sort": Ibid., 11-12.

223 "Nothing affront them more": John Lawson, *History of Carolina* (London, 1718), 10-13.

227 "You gave birth": Bernard de Voto, *The Course of Empire* (Boston: Houghton Mifflin, 1952), 93.

231 "[Before], they killed": Nicholas Denys, *The Description and Natural History of the Coasts of North America (Acadia), 1672,* trans. and ed. William F. Ganong (Toronto: The Champlain Society Publications, 1908), 426.

233 "They come like Foxes": Edna Kenton, ed., *Jesuit Relations* (New York: Vanguard Press, 1954), 303.

239 "a free and certain passage": Louis B. Wright, *The American Heritage History of the Thirteen Colonies* (New York: American Heritage Press, 1967), 253. Reprinted by permission of American Heritage Magazine, a division of Forbes, Inc., © Forbes, Inc., 1993.

241 "I am not afraid": Ibid.

242 "Without Indians to oppose": John Brown, *Old Frontiers* (Kingsport, Tenn.: Southern Publishers, 1938), 53. Courtesy Ayer Company Publishers, Inc., P.O. Box 958, Salem, NH 03079.

249 "We had the pleasure": Quoted in Milling, 301-2.

251 "thrown us behind [their] back": Wright, 258.

"It would be a strange thing": Carl Van Doren, *Benjamin Franklin* (New York: Viking Press, 1938), 209.

253 "If they are to fight": Alvin Josephy, *The Patriot Chiefs* (New York: Viking Penguin, 1958), 200.

254   "wretched" people. "The only true": Howard Peckham, *Pontiac and the Indian Uprising* (Princeton: Princeton University Press, 1947); as quoted in Josephy, 97.
      "I do not see why": Josephy, 106.

256   "Those cruel men": Leonard Labaree, ed., *The Papers of Benjamin Franklin*, vol. 2 (New Haven: Yale University Press, 1967), 47, 52-3.

257   "Could it not be contrived": Francis Parkman, *The Conspiracy of Pontiac and the Indian War After the Conquest of Canada,* vol. 2 (Boston: Little, Brown, 1898), 173.
      "You will do well": Ibid.

258   "not as a generous enemy": Josephy, 123.

260   "We never sold you": George Morgan, "Cornstalk to Congress, Pittsburgh, November 7, 1776," George Morgan's *Journal,* 73; as quoted in Gregory Schaff, *Wampum Belts and Peace Trees.* Manuscript in the collection of Gregory Schaff. Courtesy of Gregory Schaff.
      "do not conceive that": Reuben G. Thwaites, *Documentary History of Dunmore's War, 1774* (Madison: Wisconsin Historical Society, 1905), 371.

261   "I appeal to any white": Thomas Jefferson, *Notes on the State of Virginia* (Boston: Lilly & Wait, 1832), 66.

262   "Brother, I have spoken": George Morgan, "Coitcheleh to Morgan, Pittsburgh, October 30, 1776," George Morgan's *Journal,* 72; as quoted in Gregory Schaff, *Wampum Belts and Peace Trees.* Manuscript in the collection of Gregory Schaff. Courtesy of Gregory Schaff.

263   "In my opinion": George Washington to Continental Congress, New York, April 19, 1776; in *Papers of the Continental Congress* 1: 291-6.

264   "I apprehend it may occasion": George Morgan, "Morgan to the Commissioners for Indian Affairs, June 3, 1776," George Morgan's *Journal,* 18-19; as quoted in Gregory Schaff, *Wampum Belts and Peace Trees.* Manuscript in the collection of Gregory Schaff. Courtesy of Gregory Schaff.

266   "We have lost out of": Speech of the Oneida chiefs, January 19, 1777; in *Papers of the Continental Congress* 3: 55-7.
      "Times are altered": Indian Council, March 1778. From the Philip Schuyler Papers, Rare Books and Manuscripts Division, New York Public Library, Astor, Lenox and Tilden Foundations.
      "Brant came forward": Unpublished manuscript, Draper Collection, Wisconsin Historical Society; as quoted in Thomas Abler, ed., *Chainbreaker: The Revolutionary War Memoirs of Governor Blacksnake* (Lincoln: University of Nebraska Press, 1989), 74.

267   "War is war": Ibid., 75.
      "When I was young": C. Hale Sipe, *The Indian Chiefs of Pennsylvania* (Butler: Ziegler Printing Co., 1927), 436.
      "My son, the [Creator]": Ruben Gold Thwaites and Louise Phelps Kellog, eds., *Frontier Defense on the Upper Ohio, 1777–1778* (Madison: Wisconsin Historical Society, 1912), 126, 149, 160, 188-9.

269   "The Indians live much better": *The Sullivan-Clinton Campaign in 1779: Chronology and Selected Documents* (Albany: The University of the State of New York, 1929).

Chapter 6: Loss of the East

275   "When we passed through": John Brown, *Old Frontiers* (Kingsport, Tenn.: Southern Publishers, 1938), 142.

278   "Instead of conforming": Anthony F. C. Wallace, *Death and Rebirth of the Seneca* (New York: Knopf, 1970), 197.

280   "The Chippewas and all": Ibid., 152.

283   "Brother, we have scarcely": Thomas E. Sanders and Walter W. Peek, *Literature of the American Indian* (New York: Macmillan, 1976). Copyright © 1976 by Macmillan College Publishing Company, Inc. Reprinted with permission.

284   "I will soon go": Arthur C. Parker, "The Code of Handsome Lake, the Seneca Prophet," *New York Museum Bulletin* 163 (1913): 79-80.

286   "induce them to relinquish": Bill Gilbert, *God Gave Us This Country* (New York: Atheneum, 1989), 117.

291   "should be made to smart": Ibid., 136.

292   "For God's sakes retreat": Ibid., 138.

      "I expected little from it": Ibid., 143.

294   "The savages": Ibid., 160.

296   "The sentiments of the": Ibid., 166.

297   "peace was unattainable": Ibid., 169.

      "We did not effect peace": Ibid.

306   "Who is this pretended": Logan Esarey, ed., *Messages and Letters of William Henry Harrison,* vol. 1 (Indianapolis: Indiana Historical Commission, 1922), 182-4.

311   "I am a Shawnee": Samuel G. Drake, *The Book of the Indians of North America,* bk. 5 (Boston: Antiquarian Bookstore, 1833), 121; as quoted in Frederick W. Turner III, *The Portable North American Reader* (New York: Penguin, 1974), 245-6.

      "The implicit obedience": Harrison to the Secretary of War, August 7, 1811; in Logan, 548-51.

312   "affords a most": Ibid.

      "fell in avalanches": J. F. H. Claiborne, *The Life and Times of General Sam Dale: The Mississippi Partisan* (New York: Harper Bros., 1860), 51-6.

313   "Where today are the": Horatio Cushman, *History of the Choctaw, Chickasaw, and Natchez Indians* (Greenville: Headlight Printing House, 1899), 248-51.

316   "Listen, Father!": Logan, vol. 2, 541-3.

      "Father, tell your men" Draper Collection, Tecumseh Papers, Wisconsin Historical Society, citation no. 1YY162.

325   "wandering around": Angie Debo, *History of the Indians of the United States* (Norman: University of Oklahoma Press, 1970).

      "the greatest question": Anthony F. C. Wallace, *The Long Bitter Trail* (New York: Hill & Wang, 1993), 67.

326   "build a fire": John Ehle, *Trail of Tears: Rise and Fall of the Cherokee Nation* (Garden City, N.Y.: Doubleday, 1988), 220.

327   "We are men": Letter to Lieutenant Sprague, December 1836, Office of Indian Affairs, National Archives.

327   "domestic dependent nations": Chief Justice John Marshall, Cherokee Nation v. Georgia (March 5, 1831).

328   "The whole intercourse between": Chief Justice John Marshall, Worcester v. Georgia (1832).

329   "I know I take my life": *Cartersville Courant* (Cartersville, Ga.), March 26, 1885.

Chapter 7: Struggle for the West

336   "any religion which can": William Brandon, *American Heritage Book of the Indians* (New York: American Heritage Press, 1993), 283.

342   "[B]elieve me": Maynard Geiger, *Indians of Mission Santa Barbara in Paganism and Christianity* (Santa Barbara: Old Mission Santa Barbara Press, 1986), frontis.

343   "I and two of my relatives": Manuel C. Roja, "Testimonio de Janitil," from *Apuntes Historicos de la Bajo California,* University of California, Berkeley, Bancroft Library, manuscript no. 295. As quoted in Jack Forbes, *The Indian in America's Past.* Material from *The Indian in America's Past* by Jack Forbes is used with the permission of Simon & Schuster, Inc. Copyright © 1964 by Jack Forbes. Copyright renewed 1992 by Jack Forbes.

      "The treatment shown": H. H. Bancroft, *History of California,* vol. 1 (San Francisco, 1884); as quoted in Roy Gilmore and Gladys Gilmore, *Readings in California History* (New York: Crowell, 1966), 51.

345   "When all the Mission": John P. Harrington, *Breath of the Sun: Life in Early California as Told by a Chumash Indian, Fernando Librado to John P. Harrington* (Banning, Calif.: Malki Museum Press, 1979), 91. Courtesy of Malki Museum Press, Malki Museum, Inc.

346   "I am very old": Adam Johnson, Letter to the Commissioner of Indian Affairs, September 15, 1850, Office of Indian Affairs, National Archives.

347   "About twenty old people": "Stone & Kelsey 'Massacre' on the Shores of Clear Lake in 1849, the Indian viewpoint," *California Historical Society Quarterly* 11, no. 3 (September 1932). Courtesy California Historical Society.

347 "All the men": Ibid.

348 "The majority of": Johnson.

"Indiscriminate Massacre": *Northern Californian* (Union, Calif.), February 1860.

349 "Good Haul of Diggers": *Humbolt Times* (Calif.), January and April 1863.

"Upon my last visit": Harrington, 134.

"I once went over": Ibid., 33.

350 "From Fort Defiance": Clifford Earl Trafzer, *The Kit Carson Campaign: The Last Great Navajo War* (Norman: University of Oklahoma Press, 1982). Copyright © 1982 by the University of Oklahoma Press.

351 "Your army has horses": Virginia Hoffman, *Navajo Biographies,* vol. 1, (Chinle, Ariz.: Navajo Curriculum Center, 1974), 90.

"The water there is mine": Ibid., 91.

"We will stop this suffering": Ibid., 77.

353 "Another shot was heard": Trafzer, 159.

354 "Two girls who went": Ibid., 157.

355 "It was horrible the way": Ruth Roessel, *Navajo Stories of the Long Walk Period* (Tsaile, Ariz.: Navajo Community College Press, 1973), 103.

"[D]aughter got tired": Trafzer, 193.

"grand experiment to make": Gerald Thompson, *The Army and the Navajo* (Tucson: University of Arizona Press, 1976), 28.

"The surest way to kill": Eve Ball, *Indeh: An Apache Odyssey* (Norman: University of Oklahoma Press, 1988). Copyright © 1988 by the University of Oklahoma Press.

356 "My friend, we have": Hoffman, 137.

"I found the Bosque: Thompson, 151-2.

"When the Diné were first created": Hoffman, 110.

357 "If we are taken back": Ibid., 110-16.

"We told the drivers . . .": 49th U.S. Congress, House of Representatives, 1st sess., H. Doc. 263, 15.

359 "My grandmother told me": Thomas Daly Marquis, ed., *Cheyenne and Sioux: The Reminiscences of Four Indians and a White Soldier* (Stockton, Calif.: Pacific Center for Western Historical Studies, University of the Pacific, 1973), 4-5.

362 "My horse fights with me": Frank Linderman, *Plenty Coups: Chief of the Crows* (New York: HarperCollins, 1962), 100. Used by permission of HarperCollins Publishers.

363 "When you grow up": George Bird Grinell, *Pawnee Hero Stories and Folk Tales* (New York: Forest & Stream Publications, 1889), 45-7.

364 "We soon reached": Linderman, 144.

365 "All we ask is that": "Sand Creek Massacre," Report of the Secretary of War, 39th U.S. Congress, Senate, 2nd sess., S. Doc. 26, 213.

366 "So now [Black Kettle]": George E. Hyde, *Life of George Bent: Written from His Letters* (Norman: University of Oklahoma Press, 1968), 146-7.

"The Cheyennes will have": Chivington dispatch of May 31, 1864; in *The War of Rebellion* (Washington, D.C.: Government Printing Office, 1890-1900).

367 "I heard shouts and": Hyde, 151-5.

"Most of us who were hiding": Ibid., 155-8.

368 "That night will never": Ibid., 155-8.

"I once thought that I was": Stan Hoig, *Peace Chiefs of the Cheyennes* (Norman: University of Oklahoma Press, 1980), 112. Copyright © 1980 by the University of Oklahoma Press.

370 "This party going to": Hyde, 315.

"Black Kettle mounted a horse": Ibid., 316-17.

"Although wrongs have been": Hoig.

371 "You said that you": Ten Bears speech, Medicine Lodge Creek Treaty Meeting, October 20, 1867, Office of Indian Affairs, National Archives, 104.

372 "I love the land": Ibid.

"This is our country": Francis Stanley, *Satanta and the Kiowas* (Borger: Jim Hess Printers, 1968), 208.

373   "The white people are": Lawrie Tatum, *Our Red Brothers and the Peace of President Ulysses S. Grant* (Philadelphia, 1899), 116-17; as quoted in Mildred Mayhall, *The Kiowas* (Norman: University of Oklahoma Press, 1962), 270.

374   "Tell them that I am dead": James Mooney, "Calendar History of the Kiowa Indians," *17th Annual Report of the Bureau of American Ethnology* (Washington, D.C.: Smithsonian Institution, 1898), 329. "influences irresistibly evil": Robert Utley, *The Indian Frontier of the American West 1846–1890* (Albuquerque: University of New Mexico Press, 1984), 148.

374   "I believe in making a tour": Ralph Andrist, *The Long Death* (New York: Macmillan, 1964), 177.

375   "[They] have done": Wayne Gard, *The Great Buffalo Hunt* (New York: Knopf, 1959), 215.

379   "The Kiowas were camped": Alice Marriott and Carol Rachlin, *American Indian Mythology* (New York: Crowell, 1968), 139.

Chapter 8: The End of Freedom

384   "At night the whole valley": George E. Hyde, *Life of George Bent: Written from His Letters* (Norman: University of Oklahoma Press, 1968), 181.

387   "We go to [the Indians]": Robert G. Athearn, *William Tecumseh Sherman and the Settlement of the West* (Norman: University of Oklahoma Press, 1956), 219.

388   "as may be deemed": James Olson, *Red Cloud and the Sioux Problem* (Lincoln: University of Nebraska Press, 1965), 34. "to molest or disturb": Ibid.

389   "Great Father sends": Francis Carrington, *Army Life in the Plains* (Pruett, 1910). "The white men": Francis Carrington, *My Army Life and the Ft. Phil Kearny Massacre* (1911), 291-2. "Satisfactory treaty": Wire to Commissioner of Indian Affairs from chief government negotiator, Office of Indian Affairs, National Archives.

390   "With eighty men": Olson, 50.

391   "We must act": 40th U.S. Congress, Senate 1st sess., S. Doc. 13, 27.

394   "This is the first time": Olson, 107-8. "We might search": *New York Times,* June 8, 1870; as quoted in Olson, 106. "Palaver has very": New York *Herald,* June 9, 1870. "We want to keep": *New York Times,* July 17, 1870.

395   "In 1868": Ibid.

396   "Friends, I carried": Olson, 152-3.

398   "You have driven": Sioux Tribe of Indians v. the U.S. (1937). "We want no white man": Dee Brown, *Bury My Heart at Wounded Knee* (New York: Holt, 1970), 273. Copyright © 1970 by Dee Brown. Reprinted by permission of Henry Holt & Co., Inc., and by permission of Sterling Lord Literistic, Inc.

399   "Women were screaming": Thomas Marquis, ed., *Wooden Leg: A Warrior Who Fought Custer* (Lincoln: University of Nebraska Press, 1962), 217.

400   "Sitting Bull . . . said": Joseph Dixon, *The Vanishing Race* (New York: Doubleday, Page, 1913), 174-5. "If you . . . had a country": *Annual Report* (Washington, D.C.: U.S. Commissioner of Indian Affairs, 1875). "Women were hurriedly": Marquis, 219-20.

401   "I looked up the": Garland Hamlin, "General Custer's Last Fight as Seen by Two Moon," *McClure's Magazine* 11, no. 5 (September 1898). "We circled all around [them]": Ibid. "A big dust": John Neihardt, *Black Elk Speaks* (Lincoln: University of Nebraska Press, 1932), 113.

402   "The shots quit coming": Marquis, 237. "On the hill top": Stanley Vestal, *Sitting Bull: Champion of the Sioux: A Biography* (Norman: University of Oklahoma Press, 1956), 172. Copyright © 1956 by the University of Oklahoma Press.

403   "When the snow": Marquis, 18.

406   "By God! This is a triumphal": Stephen E. Ambrose, *Crazy Horse and Custer: The Parallel Lives of Two American Warriors* (New York: Meridian Press, 1975), 462.

407   "When I was a boy": W. Fletcher Johnson, *The Red Record of the Sioux, Life of Sitting Bull and the History of the Indian War of 1890–91* (Edgewood Publishing Co., 1891), 201.
"Kill the son of a bitch!": Mari Sandoz, *Crazy Horse* (New York: McIntosh & Otis, 1942), 408. Copyright © 1942 by Mari Sandoz.
"Let me go, my friends": Ibid.
"Tell the people": Ibid., 413.

411   "at a cost not exceeding eight": Alvin Josephy, *The Nez Perce Indians and the Opening of the Northwest* (New Haven: Yale University Press, 1965), 419.
"My son, my body": "An Indian's View of Indian Affairs," *North American Review* 269 (April 1879); as quoted in Josephy, *Nez Perce*, 442-3.

412   "I buried him in": Ibid.

413   "Who are you": Ibid., 421.

414   "I know that my": Ibid., 424-5.
"one of the most extraordinary": Correspondence, Sherman to Townsend, Office of Indian Affairs, National Archives.

415   "The Indians": Ibid.

416   "Tell General Howard": 45th U.S. Congress, House of Representatives, 2nd sess.

417   "There has been too much": *North American Review,* 432.

418   "Why is it that": A. N. Ellis, "Reflections of an Interview with Cochise," *Kansas State Historical Society* 13 (1913-1914).

421   "At last your soldiers": Henry Stuart Turrill, "A Vanished Race of Aboriginal Founders," *New York Society of Founders and Patriots of America* (February 14, 1907).
"There is to be no council": Robert N. Scott, *The War of the Rebellion: A Compilation of the Official Records of the Union and Confederate Armies,* series 1, vol. 15 (Washington, D.C.: Government Printing Office, 1886), 580.

422   "I want him dead or alive": Daniel E. Conner, *Josephy Reddiford Walker and the Arizona Adventure,* ed. Donald J. Berthrong and Odessa Davenport (Norman: University of Oklahoma Press, 1956), 34-42.

423   "If it had not been": Brown, 192.

425   "I do not think": David Cooke, *Fighting Indians of America* (New York: Dodd, Mead, 1954), 40.
"I did not pray": Stephen Melvil Barrett, *Geronimo's Story of His Life* (New York: Duffield & Co., 1906), 43-5.

428   "The Creator did not make": Eve Ball, *In the Days of Victorio: Recollections of a Warm Springs Apache* (Tucson: University of Arizona Press, 1970), 50.
"[Juh] told them": Eve Ball, *Indeh: An Apache Odyssey* (Norman: University of Oklahoma, 1988), 34. Copyright © 1988 by the University of Oklahoma Press.

429   "At that time": Ibid., 110.
"[A]bove all living men": Ibid., 134.

430   "Our old chiefs": *McClure's Magazine* 11 (November 1898).

431   "This is only another trick": Angie Debo, *A History of the Indians of the United States* (Norman: University of Oklahoma Press, 1970), 301-2. Copyright © 1970 by the University of Oklahoma Press.
"The logic of events": Francis Pruscha, ed., *Americanizing the American Indians* (Lincoln: University of Nebraska Press, 1978), 75.

432   "I would . . . use the Indian police": Ibid., 255-6.
"At San Carlos": Ibid., 254.

433   "Kill the Indian": Ibid., 261.

434   "We all wore": Edwin R. Embree, *Indians of the Americas* (Boston: Houghton Mifflin, 1939). Copyright renewed 1967 by Kate C. Embree. Used by permission of Houghton Mifflin Co. All rights reserved.
"Did I want to be": Metha Parisien Bercier, *Tomorrow, My Sister Said, But Tomorrow Never Came.* Unpublished manuscript. Copyright © Metha Parisien Bercier, Belcourt, North Dakota.

435   "If we thought that": Paul Dyck, "Lone Wolf Returns . . . To That Long Ago Time," *Montana: The Magazine of Western History* 22, no. 1 (January 1972).

436   "It was a warm": Embree.

437   "They danced without": Ella Deloria, *Speaking of Indians* (New York: Friendship Press, 1944), 82-3.

438   "The people were desperate": Johnson, 201.

440   "It was understood": James McGregor, *The Wounded Knee Massacre From the Viewpoint of the Sioux* (Baltimore: Wirth Bros., 1940), 118. Currently published by Fenwyn Press, Inc., Rapid City, South Dakota.

      "The white men were so thick": Ibid., 113.

      "Suddenly I heard a single": Thomas Tibbles, *Buckskin and Blanket Days* (Garden City, N.Y.: Doubleday, 1957), 312.

441   "An awful noise": McGregor, 128.

      "There was a woman": James Mooney, "The Ghost Dance Religion," *14th Annual Report of the Bureau of American Ethnology* (Washington, D.C.: Government Printing Office, 1896), 885-6.

      "Though the active attack": Tibbles, 313, 321.

      "Nothing I have seen": Tibbles, 322-3.

442   "I did not know": Neihardt, 276.

443   "diminish the offensive": Alvin Josephy, *Indian Heritage of America* (Boston: Houghton Mifflin, 1991), 371. Reprinted by permission of The Julian Bach Literary Agency, Copyright © 1991.

444   "*We stand young warriors*": Poem by the National Congress of American Indians; as quoted in Bill Richardson, "A Perspective on American Indians," Los Angeles *Times,* April 9, 1993.

INDEX

ILLUSTRATION CREDITS

Abbreviations

AMNH	American Museum of Natural History
CGI	Computer-Generated Image
GM	Gilcrease Museum, Tulsa, Okla.
INAH	Instituto Nacional de Antropologia e Historia
NAA	National Anthropological Archives, Smithsonian Institution
NMAA	National Museum of American Art, Smithsonian Institution
NMAI	National Museum of the American Indian, Smithsonian Institution
NMNH	National Museum of Natural History, Smithsonian Institution
PPDLC	Prints and Photographs Division, Library of Congress
RBSCLC	Rare Book and Special Collections Division, Library of Congress

T: page top   B: page bottom   L: page left   R: page right

Chapter 1: A Continent Awakes

a: INAH. Photo by Michel Zabe. i: Morgan Library. ii: Courtesy Buffalo Bill Historical Center, © Dirk Bakker, photographer. iv–v: GM. vi–vii: Haffenreffer Library, Rare Books Collection, Brown University. viii–ix: National Gallery of Canada. 2-3: GM. 4: Photo by Don Doll. 5 and 6T: Photos by Matt Gunther, Pathways Productions. 6B–10: PPDLC. 11T: NAA. 11B: PPDLC. 12T: NAA. 12B: PPDLC. 13: NAA. 14-18: PPDLC. 19T: NMNH. 19B: Courtesy of Private Collection. Photo by Addison Doty. 20: Photo by Ed Castle, courtesy of Smithsonian Books. 21: NMAI. 22: Walters Art Gallery, Baltimore. 23: Courtesy of James M. Calder. 24: Denver Art Museum. 25T: Courtesy Kathy and Alan Linn. 25B: Photo by Enrico Ferorelli. 26: Rollout photo © Justin Kerr. 27: Dumbarton Oaks Research Library and Collections, Washington, D.C. 28T: Rollout photo © Justin Kerr. 28B: INAH. Photo by Jack Leustig. 30: RBSCLC. 31T: © Merle Greene Robertson. 31B: INAH. Photo by Jack Leustig. 32: INAH. Photo by Michel Zabe. 33T: Dumbarton Oaks Research Library and Collections, Washington, D.C. 33B and 34T: Merle Greene Robertson. © 1976. 34B: Rollout photo © Justin Kerr. 36T: GM. 36B and 37T: Ohio Historical Society, Columbus. Photos © Dirk Bakker. 37B: Alabama Museum of Natural History. 38-9: Richard A. Cooke III. 40: Ohio Historical Society, Columbus. 41T: St. Louis Science Center. Photo © Dirk Bakker. 41B: GM. 42-3: CGI, Pathways Productions. 44: RBSCLC. 45: CGI, Pathways Productions. 46: RBSCLC. 47: NMAI. 48: RBSCLC. 49: Courtesy of the New York State Museum. 50: Pathways Productions, photo by Patrice Meigneux. 51-3: National Archives Canada, Ottawa. 54: Photo by Maximilien Bruggmann-Yverdon, Switzerland. 55T: NMAI. 55B and 56: Photos by Maximilien Bruggmann-Yverdon, Switzerland. 57T: CGI, Pathways Productions. 57B: Photo by Maximilien Bruggmann-Yverdon, Switzerland. 58T: CGI, Pathways Productions. 59-60: Photos by William M. Ferguson. 61: Photo by Matt Gunther, Pathways Productions.

Chapter 2: Empires of the Sun

62-3: INAH. Photo by Alex Galindo. 64: Denver Art Museum. 65: INAH. Photo by Jack Leustig. 66T: CGI, Pathways Productions. 66B: INAH. Photo by Jack Leustig. 67-8: Denver Art Museum. 69T: Photo by Michel Zabe. 69B: Biblioteca Medicea Laurenziana. 70: Akademische Druck, U. Verlagsanstalt, Graz, Austria. 71: INAH. Photo by Jack Leustig. 72-73T: Photos by Michel Zabe. 73B, 74-5: Akademische Druck, U. Verlagsanstalt, Graz, Austria. 77: INAH. Photo by Alex Galindo. 78-9: Akademische Druck, U. Verlagsanstalt, Graz, Austria. 80: INAH. Photo by Alex Galindo. 82: Newberry Library, Chicago. 83. Photo by Michel Zabe. 84: Bibliothèque Nationale, Paris. 85: Wurttembergisches Landesmuseum, Stuttgart. 86-7: Bodleian Library Manuscript Archive, Oxford University. 88-9: Museo de America, Madrid. 90: Bodleian Library Manuscript Archive, Oxford University. 91: Original paint-ings of Tenochtitlán by Stuart Gentling and Scott Gentling. 92-4: INAH. Photos by Michel Zabe. 95: Biblioteca Nacional, Madrid. 96T: RBSCLC. 96B: Biblioteca Medicea Laurenziana. 97: Biblioteca Na-cional, Madrid. 98: Courtesy of Wayne Ruwet. 99T: Biblioteca Medicea Laurenziana. 99B–101: INAH. Photos by Alex Galindo. 102: Biblioteca Medicea Laurenziana. 102-3: AMNH. 103: INAH. Photo by Michel Zabe. 104: Biblioteca Nacional, Madrid. 105T: Biblioteca Medicea Laurenziana. 105B: Courtesy of Wayne Ruwet. 106: INAH. Photo by Alex Galindo. 108-9: Biblioteca Medicea Laurenziana. 110: INAH. Photos by Jack Leustig. 111: INAH. Photo by Michel Zabe.

Chapter 3: Clash of Cultures

112-13: RBSCLC. 114: Architect of the Capitol. 115B–116: RBSCLC. 117-19: Pierpont Morgan Library, New York. 120-1: RBSCLC. 122: Copyright British Museum. 123: GM. Photo by Matt Gun-ther. 124: RBSCLC. 126: John Carter Brown Library at Brown University. 128: RBSCLC. 131: John Carter Brown Library at Brown University. 133: National Cowboy Hall of Fame and Western Heritage Center, Oklahoma City. 134-7: NMNH. 140-7: RBSCLC. 149: GM. 150T: NMAI. 150B: Georgia De-partment of Natural Resources. © Dirk Bakker, photographer. 151-2: RBSCLC. 153: Newberry Library.

Chapter 4: European Expansion

154-5: Copyright British Museum. 156: The University Museum, The University of Pennsylva-nia. 157: Peabody Museum, Harvard University. 158 and 160: Courtesy Museum of New Mexico. Pho-tos by Ben Wittick. 161: RBSCLC. 162: Photo by Maximilien Bruggmann-Yverdon, Switzerland. 163: Pathways Productions. Photo by Matt Gunther. 165: Courtesy Museum of New Mexico. Photo by Ben Wittick. 166: Courtesy School of American Research Collections in the Museum of New Mexico. Photo by Ben Wittick. 168T: Pathways Productions. Photo by Matt Gunther. 168B: Field Museum of Natural History, Chicago. 169: Peabody Museum, Harvard University. Photo by Hillel Burger. 170: NAA. 173-6: RBSCLC. 177: NMNH. 178-9: Copyright British Museum. 180: RBSCLC. 183: RBSCLC. Photo by Walter Bigbee. 185: Copyright British Museum. 186: RBSCLC. Photo by Walter Bigbee. 187-93: Copyright British Museum. 194: Ashmolean Museum, Oxford University. 195: RBSCLC. Photo by Walter Bigbee. 196-7: The Association for the Preservation of Virginia Antiqui-ties. 198: RBSCLC. 199: Portrait File. Miriam and Ira D. Wallach Division of Art, Prints and Pho-tographs. The New York Public Library. Astor, Lenox and Tilden Foundations. 202: RBSCLC. Photo by Walter Bigbee. 203: Architect of the Capitol. 204: Virginia State Library and Archives. 205: Virginia Historical Society. 207T: CGI, Pathways Productions. 207B: NMAI. 208: Courtesy of The Haffenreffer Museum of Anthropology, Brown University. 209: The Granger Collection, New York. 210-11: RBSCLC. Photo by Walter Bigbee. 212L: Pathways Productions. Photo by Patrice Meigneux. 212R: Copyright J.L.G. Ferris, Archives of 76, Westlake, Ohio. 213: RBSCLC. Photo by Walter Bigbee. 214: Pathways Productions. Photo by Patrice Meigneux. 215-6: RBSCLC. Photo by Walter Bigbee.

Chapter 5: The Cauldron of War

218-19: State Historical Society of Wisconsin. 221: The Royal Library of Denmark. 222: Burger-bibliothek, Bern. 224: From the Collections of the South Carolina Historical Society. 225: NAA. 226: Greenville County Museum of Art, Gift of the Association, Inc. 228: RBSCLC. 229: Beinecke Rare Book and Manuscript Library, Yale University. 230T: RBSCLC. 230B: Peabody Museum, Harvard Uni-versity. Photo by Hillel Burger. 231: NMNH. 232T: Pathways Productions. Photo by Patrice Meigneux. 232B: Western Canada Pictorial Index, University of Winnipeg. 233: RBSCLC. 234: Peabody Museum, Harvard University. 235: RBSCLC. 236-7: Courtesy of the Pennsylvania Academy of Fine Arts, Philadelphia. Gift of Mrs. Sarah Harrison. 238-42: RBSCLC. 244-5: Onondaga Historical Association, Syracuse, N.Y. 247: GM. 248: Tennessee Department of Environment and Conservation. Doug Henry, artist. 249: CGI, Pathways Productions. 250: NAA. 251: North Wind Picture Archives. 252: National

Portrait Gallery, Smithsonian Institution. 253T: Library of Congress. 253B: RBSCLC. 254: Courtesy of the Detroit Historical Department, Historic Fort Wayne. Photo by Nemo Warr. 255: The Granger Collection, New York. 256: Pathways Productions. Photo by Matt Gunther. 257-8: RBSCLC. 259: North Wind Picture Archives. 260: Washington University Gallery of Art. 262T: Courtesy Winterthur Museum. 262B: Print Collection. Miriam and Ira D. Wallach Division of Art, Prints and Photographs. The New York Public Library. Astor, Lenox and Tilden Foundations. 263: National Gallery of Canada, Ottawa. 265: RBSCLC. 266-7: Denver Art Museum. 268: NMNH. 269: CGI, Pathways Productions. 270: RBSCLC. 272: Collection of the Montreal Museum of Fine Arts.

Chapter 6: Loss of the East

275-7: Tippecanoe County Historical Association, Lafayette, Ind. Gift of Mrs. Cable G. Ball. 278: Gansevoort-Lansing Collection. The New York Public Library. 279: North Wind Picture Archives. 280: RBSCLC. 281: NMAI. 282: RBSCLC. 284: RBSCLC. 285R: Pathways Productions. Photo by Patrice Meigneux. 286: Courtesy of the Royal Ontario Museum, Toronto. 287T: Photo courtesy of Newberry Library. 287B: RBSCLC. 288: RBSCLC. 290: Collection of the Montreal Museum of Fine Arts. 292: Field Museum of Natural History, Chicago. 293: Detroit Institute of Arts. 295: Field Museum of Natural History, Chicago. 296: NMAA/Art Resource, New York. Museum purchase and promised gift of George M. Stanley. 298-301: Ohio Historical Society. 302: Courtesy National Archives. 303: Ohio Historical Society. 304: Photo courtesy of the New York State Museum. 305: NMAA/Art Resource, New York. 306: Archives of Ontario. 307: Tippecanoe County Historical Association, Lafayette, Ind. Gift of Mrs. Cable G. Ball. 309: CGI, Pathways Productions. 310: RBSCLC. 313: The Warner Collection of the Gulf States Paper Collection, Tuscaloosa, Ala. 314: NMAA/Art Resource, New York. Gift of Mrs. Joseph Harrison, Jr. 315: Government of Canada, Fort Malden National Historic Site. 316T: PPDLC. 316B: NMAA/Art Resource, New York. 318T: Charles Allan Munn Collection, Fordham University Library, Bronx, N.Y. 318B: National Portrait Gallery, Smithsonian Institution. 319: NMAA/Art Resource, New York. Gift of Mrs. Joseph Harrison, Jr. 320-1: RBSCLC. 322T: PPDLC. 322B: Special Collections Division, Georgetown University Library. 323L: RBSCLC. 323R: Pathways Productions. Photo by Matt Gunther. 324: GM. 325T: NMAI. 325B: CGI, Pathways Productions. 326T: GM. 326B–327: Joslyn Art Museum, Omaha, Nebr. Gift of the Enron Art Foundation. 328L: Pathways Productions. Photo by Patrice Meigneux. 329T: Collection of the New-York Historical Society. 329B: GM. 330: NMAA/Art Resource, New York. 331: Pathways Productions. Photo by Patrice Meigneux. 332: Courtesy of the Archives and Manuscripts Division of the Oklahoma Historical Society. 333: Peabody Museum, Harvard University.

Chapter 7: Struggle for the West

334: GM. 337: Louis Choris. 338L: Thomas Burke Memorial, Washington State Museum. Photo by Eduardo Calderon. 338TR and 338MR: The University Museum, University of Pennsylvania. 338BR: Thomas Burke Memorial, Washington State Museum. 339L: Beineke Rare Book and Manuscript Library, Yale University. 339R: NMNH. 340: Courtesy of the Southwest Museum, Los Angeles. 341T: CGI, Pathways Productions. 341B: RBSCLC. 342: Santa Barbara Mission Archive-Library. 343: Pathways Productions. Photo by Patrice Meigneux. 344-5: RBSCLC. 346L: Pathways Productions. Photo by Patrice Meigneux. 346R: RBSCLC. 348: Courtesy of Phoebe A. Hearst Museum of Anthropology. 349: Santa Barbara Museum of Natural History. 351: Staatliche Museen zu Berlin-Preubischer Kulturbesitz, Museum fur Volkerkunde. Photo by Dietrich Graf. 352: Courtesy School of American Research Collections in the Museum of New Mexico. Photo by Ben Wittick. 353: The St. Louis Art Museum. 354: Courtesy Colorado Historical Society. 355-6: NMNH. 357: PPDLC. 359: RBSCLC. 360: GM. 361-2: NMAA/Art Resource, New York. 363: The Denver Art Museum. 364: The Morning Star Gallery, Santa Fe, N.M. 365: Courtesy of The Panhandle-Plains Historical Society, Canyon, Tex. 366: Courtesy Colorado Historical Society. 367: Pathways Productions. Photo by Matt Gunther. 368-9: Courtesy Colorado Historical Society. 370: PPDLC. 371T: NMAA/Art Resource, New York. 371B:

GM. 372: Oklahoma Historical Society. 373T: Courtesy of Panhandle-Plains Historical Museum, Canyon, Tex. 373B: GM. 375T: North Wind Picture Archives. 375B: Montana Historical Society. 376: PPDLC. 377: NAA. 378: Baylor University, Texas Collection. 379: From the Collections of the St. Louis Mercantile Library Association.

Chapter 8: The End of Freedom

380-382T: GM. 382B: Buffalo Bill Historical Center, Cody, Wyo. Chandler-Pohrt Collection. 383B: RBSCLC. 384T: The Denver Art Museum. 384B: GM. 385T: South Dakota State Historical Society, Pierre. 385B: PPDLC. 386: Pathways Productions. Photo by Matt Gunther. 387T: National Park Service, Fort Laramie National Historic Site. 387B–388: NAA. 389: Denver Art Museum. 390: Morning Star Gallery, Santa Fe, N.M. 391: NAA. 392: The Nelson-Atkins Museum of Art, Kansas City, Mo. 393: NAA. 395: PPDLC. 396 and 397L: NAA. 397R and 398: Pathways Productions. Photo by Matt Gunther. 399: Courtesy Department of Library Services, AMNH. Photo by J. K. Dixon. 400T: CGI, Pathways Productions. 400B: NAA. 401: Courtesy of Panhandle-Plains Historical Museum, Canyon, Tex. 402T: The Beinecke Rare Books and Manuscript Library, Yale University. 402B: PPDLC. 403: Buffalo Bill Historical Center, Cody, Wyo. 406: Archives and Rare Books Department, University of Cincinnati. 408: PPDLC. 409: NAA. 410-11: Courtesy of the National Park Service, Nez Perce National Historical Park. 412T: Pathways Productions. Photo by Patrice Meigneux. 412B: NAA. 414: NAA. 415T: Pathways Productions. Photo by Patrice Meigneux. 415B: NAA. 416-17: NAA. 419: Courtesy Museum of New Mexico. Photo by Ben Wittick. 420: NMAI. 421: Denver Art Museum. 422T: Pathways Productions. Photo by Matt Gunther. 422B: NAA. 423: Courtesy of the Arizona Historical Society, Tucson. 424: Courtesy School of American Research Collections in the Museum of New Mexico. Photo by Ben Wittick. 425T: NAA. 425B: Courtesy of the Arizona Historical Society, Tucson. 426-7: NAA. 428T: Pathways Productions. Photo by Matt Gunther. 428B: NAA 429: NAA. 430: Photo by Edward Truman, Denver Public Library, Western History Department. 431: NAA. 432: PPDLC. 433: Western History Collections, University of Oklahoma Library. 434TL: NAA. 434TR: NAA. 434B–435B: Western History Collections, University of Oklahoma Library. 435R: NAA. 436TL: Pathways Productions. Photo by Matt Gunther. 436TR: NAA. 436B: NAA. 437T: Denver Art Museum. 437B: NAA. 438T: NMAI. 438B: Minnesota Historical Society. 439: Nebraska State Historical Society. 440: NAA. 441: Pathways Productions. Photo by Matt Gunther. 442-3: Huntington Library, San Marino, Calif. 443R: Pathways Productions. Photo by Matt Gunther. 444: NAA. 445: PPDLC.

A NOTE ON THE TYPE

The text of this book was set in Bembo, a facsimile of a typeface cut by Francesco Griffo for Aldus Manutius, the celebrated Venetian printer, in 1495. The face was named for Pietro Cardinal Bembo, the author of the small treatise entitled *De Ætna* in which it first appeared. Through the research of Stanley Morison, it is now generally acknowledged that all old-face type designs up to the time of William Caslon can be traced to the Bembo cut.

The present-day version of Bembo was introduced by The Monotype Corporation of London in 1929. Sturdy, well balanced, and finely proportioned, Bembo is a face of rare beauty and great legibility in all of its sizes.

Composed, with color separations, by North Market Street Graphics, Lancaster, Pennsylvania

Printed and bound by Quebecor Printing, Kingsport, Tennessee

Designed by Eric Baker Design Associates, New York, New York